Far Distant Ships

The Royal Navy and the Blockade of Brest 1793-1815

Quintin Barry

Helion & Company Limited

Helion & Company Limited
26 Willow Road
Solihull
West Midlands
B91 1UE
England
Tel. 0121 705 3393
Fax 0121 711 4075
Email: info@helion.co.uk
Website: www.helion.co.uk
Twitter: @helionbooks
Visit our blog at http://blog.helion.co.uk/

Published by Helion & Company 2017
Designed and typeset by Mach 3 Solutions Ltd (www.mach3solutions.co.uk)
Cover designed by Paul Hewitt, Battlefield Design (www.battlefield-design.co.uk)
Printed by Gutenberg Press Limited, Tarxien, Malta

Text © Quintin Barry 2017
Illustrations open source unless otherwise credited.
Maps © David Beckford 2017
Cover: 'Lord Bridport's Action off Port l'Orient June 23rd 1795' after Thomas Whitcombe
(Open source)

ISBN 978-1-911512-14-1

British Library Cataloguing-in-Publication Data.
A catalogue record for this book is available from the British Library.

For details of other military history titles published by Helion & Company Limited, contact
the above address, or visit our website: http://www.helion.co.uk

We always welcome receiving book proposals from prospective authors.

Contents

List of Illustrations

List of Maps

The first three maps provide strategic context and are presented at the beginning of the book for ease of reference; the remaining four are intended to illustrate specific actions and are presented at the appropriate points in the text.

Acknowledgements

I should first acknowledge an enormous debt to the Navy Records Society. I have drawn on a considerable number of the publications of the Society in the writing of this book. Founded in 1893, it has produced over 160 scholarly collections of documents relating to the Royal Navy, and is particularly rich in sources relating to the French Revolutionary and Napoleonic Wars. Its editors have over the years combined to produce an astonishingly vivid account of the navy and the way in which it was managed. In particular, of course, the volumes edited by Roger Morriss and John Leyland relating to the blockade of Brest have been especially valuable.

I must also record my gratitude to Tim Readman, who read the book in draft and made a number of valuable suggestions; to Duncan Rogers, my publisher, who was as always extremely supportive; to my editor, Andrew Bamford, who has been immensely helpful in editing the text and also in relation to the illustrations; and last but by no means least to Jean Hawkes, who patiently and skilfully typed the book from my lamentable manuscript. My thanks also go to the staff of the Caird Library at the National Maritime Museum, and those at the National Archives, for their assistance.

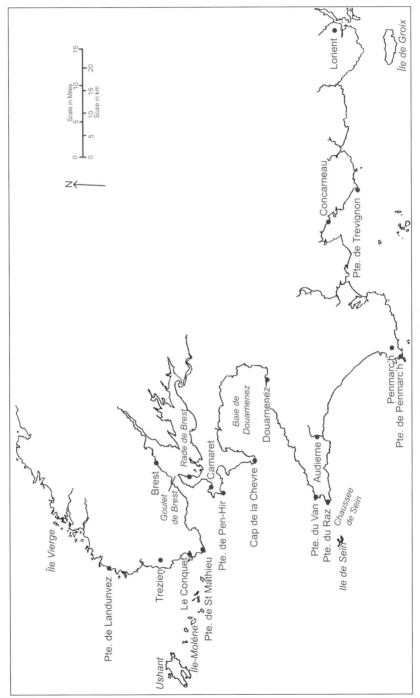

Map 1 Brest and Environs.

Île Vierge

Pte. de Landunvez

Ushant

Île-Molène

Pte. de St Mathieu

Le Conquet

Trezien

Brest

Goulet
de Brest

Rade de Brest

Camaret

Pte. de Pen-Hir

Cap de la Chevre

Baie de
Douarnenez

Douarnenez

Pte. du Van

Pte. du Raz

Audierne

Île de Sein

Chaussee
de Sein

Penmarch

Pte. de Penmarc'h

Pte. de Trevignon

Concarneau

Lorient

Île de Groix

N

Scale in Miles
0   5   10   15
Scale in km
0   5   10   15   20

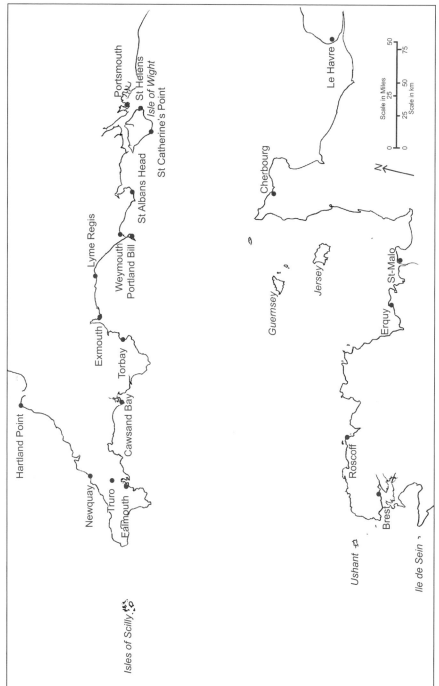

Map 2 The Channel Ports.

Hartland Point

Newquay

Truro

Falmouth

Isles of Scilly

Cawsand Bay

Torbay

Exmouth

Lyme Regis

Weymouth

Portland Bill

St Albans Head

St Catherine's Point

Isle of Wight

St Helens

Portsmouth

Le Havre

Cherbourg

Guernsey

Jersey

St-Malo

Erquy

Roscoff

Brest

Ushant

Ile de Sein

N

Scale in Miles
0   25   50

Scale in km
0   25   50   75

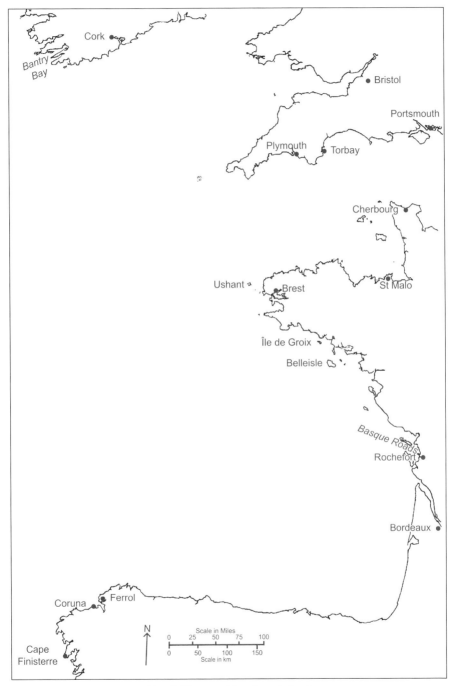

Map 3 Biscay and Southern Ireland.

1

The Outbreak of War

The British policy of maintaining a Western Squadron capable of keeping a close watch on the port of Brest, and strong enough to deal with the French fleet should it put to sea, had originated in the late seventeenth century. By then, during the reign of Louis XIV, Brest had been developed as the principal French naval base in northern waters. It was well chosen. It was ideally situated as a point from which an invasion of the British Isles might be launched, and from which a potentially crippling war against British trade could be carried on. Moreover, the geography of the place, and the navigational conditions which prevailed, made Brest a superb location for a major naval base.

During the Seven Years War Sir Edward Hawke had successfully maintained a close blockade of Brest, and this had been a central plank of British naval strategy. It ensured that the British fleet had the upper hand throughout the war, and led in due course to the crushing victory of Quiberon Bay. During the War of American Independence, however, a close blockade was not possible. With Britain facing the combined fleets of France and Spain, and with a large part of the fleet committed to North America and the West Indies, there were not sufficient ships available. This was certainly not the case when war against France broke out in 1793; there were plenty of ships to constitute a powerful Channel fleet. It was surprising, therefore, that a close blockade of Brest was not at once put in place.

An early proponent of the effectiveness of a close blockade was Admiral Vernon, who wrote in 1745:

> I have always looked upon squadrons in port as neither a defence for the kingdom, nor a security for our commerce, and that the surest means for the protection of both, was keeping a strong squadron in the soundings, which may answer both these purposes, as covering both Channels and Ireland, and at the same time secures our commerce.[1]

---

1   Bryan McL. Ranft (ed.), *The Vernon Papers* (London: Navy Records Society, 1958), pp.445-446.

He developed the point further, later that year, when concerned that the French would unite their squadrons from Brest, Rochefort and Ferrol; his fear was that posting a fleet in the Channel between the Lizard and the French coast would be ineffectual:

> That will leave all Ireland, the western coasts of this island, and even the Bristol Channel, and all our East and West Indian trade expected home, open to them to do what they please. Whereas a western squadron, formed as strong as we can make it … and got speedily out into Soundings might face their united force, cover both Great Britain and Ireland, and be in condition to pursue them wherever they went, and be at hand to secure the safe return of our homeward bound trade from the East and West Indies.[2]

Lord Anson took the same view, writing to Hawke ten years later:

> The best defence for our colonies, as well as our coasts, is to have a squadron always to the westward as may in all probability keep the French in port or give them battle with advantage if they come out.[3]

It was the wind that was the key determinant of blockading operations off Brest. A westerly wind made it difficult, if not impossible, for the Channel Fleet to get away from the English coast; but an easterly wind that enabled it to do so also enabled the French fleet to emerge from Brest. In 1759 Hawke had been forced back to Torbay by westerly gales; when on 14 November the wind changed easterly and he was able to return to his station, he found that it had also allowed the French to escape from Brest. As it turned out, notwithstanding appalling weather conditions, Hawke was able to catch and beat the French fleet at Quiberon Bay.

The strongest argument against the maintenance of a close blockade, however, was the heavy wear and tear on the ships exposed day after day to the ceaseless action of wind and sea, necessitating their frequent departure for one of the ports along the English coast where they could be repaired and refitted. After the end of the American War of Independence, during which no blockade of Brest was attempted, Lord Howe remarked that 'stationing a large fleet off the coast of France was a very improper and hazardous measure. The ships, particularly the large ones, were liable to receive great damage, the crews get sickly'.[4] He regarded a station off Brest as dangerous, and one that should only be taken in great emergency. This

---

2   Ranft, *Vernon Papers*, p.453.
3   Quoted Roger Morriss (ed.), *The Channel Fleet and the Blockade of Brest 1793-1801* (Aldershot: Navy Records Society, 2001), p.2.
4   Morriss (ed.), *Channel Fleet*, p.3.

view was widely held. Admiral Keppel argued that no large fleet could remain at sea for more than six months, and certainly not in winter: 'Indeed wisdom must direct the ships into port as soon as the bad weather months come on.' He added: 'Suppose the enemy should put to sea with their fleet – a thing much to be wished for by us. Let us act wiser, and keep ours in port; leave them to the mercy of long nights and hard gales.'[5]

It was upon Howe that the command of the Channel Fleet was conferred in 1793, although it was not until May 29 that he hoisted his flag in the *Queen Charlotte* at Portsmouth. It was a popular and more or less inevitable decision. Born in 1726, he had enjoyed an outstanding career. Commanding a ship of the line in 1755 under Boscawen, he took the French ship *Alcide* in an action which preceded the formal outbreak of the Seven Years War. As captain of the *Magnanime,* he led the British line at Quiberon Bay. By 1770, as a rear admiral, he was commanding the Mediterranean Fleet. When the American war broke out, he was for two years Commander in Chief in North America. In 1782 he became Commander in Chief of the Channel Fleet, and successfully relieved Gibraltar in October 1782. In January 1783 he became First Lord of the Admiralty under Shelburne, only to lose office when the ministry fell later in the year. Before the end of the year he was back in office again under Pitt, remaining as First Lord until 1788. In 1790, when the navy mobilised against Spain during the Nootka Sound crisis, he returned to the command of the Channel Fleet. He was the author of the *Signal Book for the Ships of War* which became the standard system of signalling until it was amalgamated into the first Admiralty Signal Book in 1799.[6] Although he was dour and unsmiling, he was idolised by the men of the Channel Fleet, to whom he was known as 'Black Dick' by reason of his dark complexion. Horace Walpole described him as 'undaunted as a rock and as silent.' One reason for his popularity was his consideration for the men under his command. Dr Thomas Trotter, the physician to the Channel Fleet, observed that 'with this good and great man, the health and comfort of his people were his first objects.'

Appointed to serve under Howe as second and third in command were Vice Admirals Thomas Graves and Sir Alexander Hood. The former had served successfully in North America during the American War of Independence, but it was the latter, who was in due course to succeed Howe as Commander in Chief, who was to play the more prominent part in the operations of the Channel Fleet. The younger brother of Samuel, Lord Hood, he was only nine months younger than Howe. He had served in the Channel Fleet under Howe in 1759, commanding a frigate. Two years later he made his name by recapturing the ship of the line *Warwick*, which had been taken by the French in 1756. In 1778, after commanding a 74 gun ship at

5   Quoted G.J. Marcus, *The Age of Nelson. The Royal Navy in the Age of Its Greatest Power and Glory, 1793-1815* (New York: Viking, 1971), p.30.
6   Morriss (ed.), *Channel Fleet*, p.16.

Admiral Richard Howe, 1st Earl Howe. (Anne S.K. Brown Collection)

the Battle of Ushant, he got into serious difficulties at the subsequent court martial of Admiral Keppel when he was alleged to have changed his log. He was a difficult colleague at the best of times, and Keppel did not forgive him for his part in his court martial, so his career was gravely jeopardised when Keppel became First Lord of the Admiralty. However, it was Howe who rescued Hood's career when he applied for him to replace Kempenfelt, lost when the *Royal George* capsized in August 1782. Hood thus returned to the Channel Fleet but, regrettably, showed no gratitude towards Howe, to whom he displayed a barely concealed hostility, possibly due to a dispute between them while Howe was First Lord. This had arisen when Hood, then Treasurer of the Navy, had objected when Howe as First Lord had demanded from him a sum of money due to Greenwich Hospital.

The instructions given by the Admiralty to Howe, on 3 July, reflected the view that a close blockade of Brest was neither necessary nor desirable, and made clear that the protection of British trade was for the moment to be his first concern:

> Whereas it is judged expedient that, as soon as the fifteen ships named in the margin, comprising part of the fleet put under your Lordship's command, and the necessary number of frigates, shall be in all respects in readiness for the sea, you should proceed with them to the westward. Your Lordship is hereby required and directed to use your utmost dispatch in getting them ready accordingly, and in proceeding at the first opportunity of wind and weather to sea, and you are to employ then either jointly or separately upon such stations as your Lordship shall judge most proper for protecting the trade of His Majesty's subjects coming into or going out of the Channel, and for taking or destroying the enemy's ships of war, privateers or trade going into or out of the Bay of Biscay, or navigation to or from any of the ports of west France.[7]

Howe was also warned that eight or nine French vessels had left Brest, perhaps to link up with possibly five others from Lorient and Rochefort, and he was directed to keep a strict watch on such ships and to prevent their return to Brest, or their junction with other ships from there; he was, if possible, to attack them separately. Subject to developments, he was, for his first cruise, to return to Torbay after a month. If he found it necessary to remain at sea, he was to report the situation and gather up the rest of his fleet from Spithead.

Howe could, of course, have interpreted the very free hand which he was given as allowing him to institute a close blockade of Brest, but he had no intention of doing so. For him, the first essential was to maintain his fleet in good order, and for this he was quite prepared to give up the strategic advantages which a close

7   Morriss (ed.), *Channel Fleet*, p.31.

blockade would provide, a judgment regarded by historian G.J. Marcus as incorrect. Marcus also notes another consequence of this mistaken policy:

> A fleet lying up for weeks, and even months, in some secure anchorage would never acquire the intimate knowledge of the enemy's coast or attain to anything like the same high level of seamanship which belonged to a squadron which was constantly on its blockading station.[8]

And, of course, the consequence was that the French could, and did, get in and out of Brest without Howe's knowledge, until it was too late for him to intercept them. Finally, although the bodily comfort of Howe's men might be enhanced by lengthy stays in Torbay, it did nothing to improve their morale.

The fleet which Howe, with his flag in the 100-gun *Queen Charlotte*, led down the Channel was part of a force which was overwhelmingly stronger than its immediate adversary. France, for the moment isolated, possessed 82 ships of the line, compared to the Royal Navy which had at the start of the war 145. What was more, during the years of peace, the British Admiralty had overseen a substantial programme of investment not only in ships but in the building up of reserves of stores and equipment. Although 87 per cent of the British battle fleet was originally out of commission in 1793, that proportion had dropped by 1797 to a mere 8 per cent. Inevitably, though, the wear and tear caused both by enemy action and by storm and tempest led to a steady increase in the number of vessels in dockyard hands. From 1798 onwards, between a fifth and a quarter of all ships of the line otherwise fit for sea were undergoing refits or repair.[9]

A more difficult task than fitting out and commissioning the ships was finding the men to man them. An enlistment bounty was extensively offered throughout the United Kingdom by local authorities. An example of this was the resolution of a Common Council of the City of London on 10 January 1793:

> That the sum of forty shillings for every able seaman, and twenty shillings for every ordinary seaman, over and above the Bounty granted by his Majesty, be given, during the pleasure of the Court, and not exceeding one month from the above date, of his Majesty's Navy.[10]

This did not by any means contribute nearly enough of the men needed. Once again, as in past wars, it was the Impress Service, more efficiently organised than previously, which found the men required. Even before the outbreak of war,

---

8   Marcus, *Age of Nelson*, p.30.
9   Marcus, *Age of Nelson*, p.5.
10 Nicholas Tracy (ed.), *The Naval Chronicle: The Contemporary Record of the Royal Navy at War* (London: Chatham, 1998), p.3.

impressment of seaman in the Port of London was successful in collecting large numbers of men, with immediate consequences for the merchant ships so ruthlessly stripped of their crews. The effect was reported in *The Times* in January 1794:

> Sailors are so scarce that upwards of sixty sail of merchants' ships bound to the West Indies and other places, are detained in the river, with their ladings on board; seven outward – bound East Indiamen are likewise detained at Gravesend for want of sailors to man them.[11]

The contrast between the preparedness of the British navy, thanks to the work done and investment made during the time of peace, and that of the French navy, was striking. As will be described in Chapter 3, the traditions of the old French royal navy had been effectively destroyed by the revolution. Although, therefore, most of the French admirals were career officers, with experience gained in former wars, albeit at a junior level, they were obliged to confront the fact that the weapon they wielded was, at best, by no means always to be relied on.

Howe's first operations with the Channel Fleet were something of an anti-climax. He sailed from Portsmouth on 14 July, but off the Scilly Isles the fleet was taken aback by a sudden squall; in the subsequent confusion the *Majestic* collided with the *Bellerophon,* which had to be towed into Plymouth, while on 23 July the rest of the fleet sailed into Torbay. Two days later Howe sailed again, and on 1 August was in sight of the French fleet, which he chased until obliged by stormy weather to return to Torbay. Thereafter, the Channel Fleet cruised a number of times in protection of various convoys.

Another operation, which also ended in anti-climax, arose from a curious breach of security on the part of the Admiralty, deriving from the practice of announcing the intended despatch of squadrons overseas. These announcements appeared in the London press, and from one such the French learned that a squadron under Sir John Jervis, with four ships of the line, and a convoy was to sail from Portsmouth to join Lord Hood at Toulon. A squadron of six of the newest and fastest French ships of the line, *Tigre, Jean Bart, Aquilon, Tourville, Impetueux* and *Révolution*, with the frigates *Insurgente* and *Sémillante*, the brig *Espiegle* and the schooner *Ballon,* under Commodore Vanstabel, was prepared to intercept Jervis. The latter, however, who was destined in fact not for Toulon but for Martinique, was delayed in getting away from St Helens, and did not sail until 26 November.

Vanstabel had put to sea on 13 November; on 19 November, believing that he had sighted a large merchant convoy, he bore down, before realising that he had in fact run into the Channel Fleet under Lord Howe. In heavy weather he made sail to get away from his vastly superior enemy. When the wind shifted, the frigate *Sémillante* was in danger of being cut off by the British frigate *Latona;* but

11   Quoted Marcus, *Age of Nelson*, p.23.

Vanstabel, seeing the danger, turned back in the *Tigre* with another 74 to rescue her, which he did successfully. The *Latona* bravely closed with the French flagship and inflicted some damage on her. During the night, Vanstabel bore away in a west south west direction. Next morning the *Bellerophon* found itself in touch with the French squadron, together with three frigates: the latter closed with the French squadron until it was clear that it was of superior strength, and then broke off the action.

Vanstabel's cruise was not, however, without result. On 30 November, he returned to Best, but not empty handed:

> On the very day, or, as some of the French accounts say, on the very hour on which he lost sight of the last ship of Lord Howe's fleet, he fell in with a British homeward bound convoy (believed from Newfoundland), and took from it 17 ships and brigs, all deeply laden.[12]

This fleeting contact occasioned some disappointment on the part of the British public, prompting the historian William James to offer some explanation of why this was misplaced:

> To suppose, however, that Lord Howe and his fleet had not, in both instances of his meeting the enemy, done all that was possible to bring on an engagement, betrayed a total unacquaintance with the subject. A fleet chasing in line of battle must not be expected to accomplish the best rate of sailing of the best sailer; for if one ship is inferior to the rest, the whole fleet must be detained, in order that the slowest ship should keep her station. The proverbial character of French ships renders it probable that the slowest sailer of the Brest fleet could have outsailed the swiftest sailer of Lord Howe's.[13]

The successful protection of convoys was unexciting work, but it was of crucial importance and it is no surprise that the protection of trade was first in the list of duties assigned by the Admiralty to the Channel Fleet. Vast convoys of merchant vessels would be assembled to make the outward passage through the Western Approaches or across the North Sea; likewise convoys homeward bound were organised to sail under escort by frigates, or smaller warships, and sometimes by ships of the line. Squadrons and individual warships leaving the United Kingdom would as a matter of course be assigned to convoy protection for the first part of their journey. The assembling of a convoy might include groups of merchantmen with different destinations; these would sail together for as long as their routes

---

12   William James, *The Naval History of Great Britain* (London: Richard Bentley, 1859), Vol.I, p.68.

13   James, *Naval History*, Vol.I, p.68.

would allow, before the convoy separated into its component parts. Most of the overseas trade was conducted securely in this way, while the coasting trade also from time to time sailed in convoy. Standing instructions were issued for the effective management of convoys, the first such being the King's Regulations and Admiralty Instructions of 1731.

It was not merely the huge convoys of merchantmen that required protection. The convoys of troop transports from England and Ireland outward bound for the Mediterranean and the West Indies were expressly identified in an order from the Admiralty to Howe of October 12. This required 'that the fleet under your Lordship's Command should keep the sea as long as circumstances may at this season of the year permit.'[14] He was to stay out as long as the state and condition of the fleet should render it advisable, and then return to Spithead, although he was given discretion to send ships into Plymouth as he thought fit. No question here arose of preventing any adventurous moves which the French fleet might attempt to make. It would be a convoy related operation that, in the following year, would bring about the first great fleet action of the war, although as it happened it would on this occasion be the Channel Fleet that was the predator and a French convoy the prey.

Meanwhile although the cruises of the Channel Fleet had not led to the anticipated fleet action, there had been a number of single ship actions between frigates and smaller vessels. One of the most notable of these was an engagement between the 36-gun frigate *Nymphe,* commanded by Captain Edward Pellew, and the French 36-gun frigate *Cléopatre* under Captain Jean Mullon. Sailing south from Start Point, Pellew was hoping to meet one of the two French frigates encountered by the frigate *Venus* on 27 May, one of which was in fact the *Cléopatre*. On June 18 Pellew sighted the *Cléopatre* at 4.00 and bore after her under full sail; seeing that the *Nymphe* was faster than his ship, Mullon slowed down to wait for her. At about 6.00, the ships were practically within hailing distance, but neither had opened fire. Mullon addressed his men from the gangway, evoking shouts of 'Vive la Republique'; Pellew, his hat in his hand, cried 'Long live King George.' The drums beat; at 6.15 Pellew put his hat on his head, a signal to open fire. The broadside exchanges which followed lasted some twenty minutes before a ball from the *Nymphe* hit the *Cléopatre's* wheel, brought down her mizzen, and fatally wounded Mullon. As a result of this the French frigate swung round to starboard and rammed the *Nymphe* amidships, her jib-boom finishing between the *Nymphe's* foremast and mainmast before it was carried away. The two vessels then came together head and stern; a boarding party from the *Nymphe* stormed on to the *Cléopatre*, and within a few minutes the ship was taken.[15]

14   Morriss (ed.), *Channel Fleet*, p.33.
15   James, *Naval History*, Vol.I, p.68; Taylor, Stephen, *Commander: The Life and Exploits of Britain's Greatest Frigate Captain* (London: Faber & Faber, 2012), p.71.

The news of Pellew's victory, the first of the war, quickly spread and he found himself a national hero. The King was especially pleased, and conferred a knighthood on him. Pellew, although an ardent monarchist, contemplated declining the honour as he could not afford to bear the expenses that would be associated with it; but the King, awarding a special pension of £150 to Pellew's wife to cover additional costs, insisted that he accept the title. Pellew, who had been born the son of the master of a Dover Packet, had come from modest origins; his victory ensured that he would be able in due course to have opportunities to make his family's fortune.

Pellew, a generous hearted man, corresponded with Mullon's widow, to whom he returned her husband's personal property, together with what financial assistance he could immediately afford.[16] Pellew was not unaware of the extent of his achievement; summarising the action, he wrote to his brother Samuel:

> We dished her up in fifty minutes, boarded and struck her colours. We have suffered much, but I was long determined to make a short affair of it. We conversed before we fired a shot, and then, God knows, hot enough it was, as you will see by the inclosed. I might have wrote for a month, had I entered on the description of every gallant action, but we were all in it, heart and soul.[17]

16   Taylor, *Commander*, p.72.
17   C. Northcote Parkinson, *Edward Pellew, Viscount Exmouth* (London: Methuen, 1934), p. 90.

2

The Admiralty

For the best part of three centuries the management of the Royal Navy had been headed by the Lord High Admiral or by a Board of Commissioners for executing his office. The last Lord High Admiral had held office at the start of the eighteenth century; since then a Board had been responsible, led by a First Lord. This post carried with it a seat in the Cabinet. It had been either held by a prominent politician or by a distinguished admiral, such as Lord Anson or Lord Howe. The members of the Board frequently had seats in the House of Commons, usually representing one of the so called 'Admiralty Boroughs' such as Portsmouth, Rochester or Sandwich.[1]

The Board usually consisted of seven members, the First Lord and three naval and three civil members. What were later to be known as Sea Lords were at the time of the French Revolutionary and Napoleonic Wars known as professional lords. It was not uncommon for one or more of them simultaneously to hold a seagoing appointment. A very large part of the work of administering the Navy fell to the Navy Board, a separate though subordinate organisation that was responsible for building or contracting for the building of ships, and repairing, manning, supplying and paying them off. The Navy Board was also charged with the management of the Royal Dockyards, auditing accounts and preparing the Navy Estimates. Its total establishment was of the order of 10,000 men.[2] It has been said of the division of responsibility between the Board of Admiralty and the Navy Board that the latter kept the King's ships at sea, but that it was the First Lord and the Cabinet that decided what should be done with them. There was not always, however, a particularly warm relationship between the two institutions.

In addition to the members of the Board of Admiralty, there were two Secretaries. The First Secretary exerted considerable political influence, dealing with a wide

1   Christopher Lloyd, *Mr Barrow of the Admiralty: A Life of Sir John Barrow 1764-1848* (London: Collins, 1970), p.75.
2   John E. Talbott, *The Pen and Ink Sailor: Charles Middleton and the King's Navy, 1778-1813* (London: Routledge, 1998), pp.28-29.

range of issues. He was responsible for the political aspects of naval affairs, and at times this post was held by a sitting Member of Parliament. The Second Secretary was responsible for the management of the Admiralty office, and supervising its voluminous correspondence with naval officers worldwide, as well as its relations with the Navy Board and the other boards subordinate to it. These were highly paid posts; the First Secretary was paid £4,000 a year and provided with an apartment in Admiralty House, while the Second Secretary received £2,000 a year (reduced to £1,500 in peacetime). These salaries compared favourably with those of the members of the Board of Admiralty, who were paid £1,000 a year, and of the First Lord who was paid £2,000 a year. The Secretaries were supported by a staff of six senior and twenty junior clerks.[3]

The power of the Board of Admiralty was supposed to be collective, but in practice the First Lord was usually able to exercise far more power and influence than his colleagues. The members of the Board were required to reach decisions in common; any binding decision of the Board was theoretically to be signed by three lords, as well as a Secretary. In practice, however, correspondence emanating from the Board and conveying its wishes was usually signed only by the First or Second Secretary, neither of whom was actually a member of the Board. It was to the Secretary that all letters to the Admiralty were required to be addressed.

The Navy Board, which was originally located at Seething Lane before its requirement for additional space led to its being transferred to Somerset House, consisted of the Principal Officers of the Navy, originally established in 1546 by Henry VIII. These were the Treasurer, the Comptroller, the Surveyor and the Clerk of the Ships, later called the Clerk of the Acts. There were also several Commissioners. The functions of the Navy Board were codified in 1662, in terms which Lord Barham's biographer has described as 'a model of ambiguity'.[4] The breadth of the Comptroller's responsibilities meant that he was the only member of the Board involved to a greater or lesser extent in the whole of the work of the Board; the instructions provided for him 'to lead his Fellow-Officers as well as to control their actions'. but decreed that they must not be precluded from advising him when it was necessary to do so.

The Commissioners had each a set of responsibilities for part of the activities of the Navy Board, together with their own staff, and they met together daily. It was the Surveyor who was in charge of designing, building and maintaining ships, the management of the dockyards and the distribution of supplies to the fleet. It might have been supposed that he would be the most influential member of the Navy Board, but it was the Comptroller who was in effect its chairman, and from whom came the lead on policy. The functions of the Treasurer were as the title suggests,

3   Lloyd, *Mr Barrow*, p.76.
4   Talbott, *Pen and Ink Sailor*, p.29.

while those of the Clerk of the Acts were principally concerned with the management of the Navy Office and its huge correspondence.

The First Lord, therefore, carried a large part of the burden of determining navy policy and in particular naval strategy. On occasion, of course, the Cabinet and even occasionally the King might intervene. George III was interested in naval matters, and the First Lord would, if he was wise, keep him informed on any questions that were likely to provoke expressions of Royal opinion. And, naturally, the Prime Minister and his ministerial colleagues would take a view on major questions of national security, but on the whole the Admiralty was left to manage its own affairs.

The Board met daily, usually between 11.00 am and 1.00 pm in the magnificent Admiralty Board Room. Attending all its meetings was the Reading Clerk, one Thomas Darch, whose task it was to read out letters to the Board. The Board Room was dominated by the famous wind indicator, of such crucial importance when the conduct of the blockade of Brest was under discussion, while over the superb fireplace there were charts on rollers which could be pulled down to illustrate questions on the agenda.

At the end of the War of American Independence, Lord Howe became First Lord, following his distinguished career at sea. As previously noted, he took office in January 1783, but his appointment was a stopgap measure: the Shelburne government was nearing its end, and it was believed essential that a senior admiral be appointed to supervise the winding down of the Navy into its peacetime establishment. As it turned out, Howe's term of office lasted only until April when, following the government's fall, the North-Fox coalition came to power, and Admiral Keppel became First Lord. The new government only survived until December, however, when William Pitt formed a government and Howe returned to the Admiralty as First Lord. Sir John Barrow, in his biography of the admiral, recorded the circumstances of his arrival:

> Thus was Lord Howe a second time brought into an office, for the duties of which he had little relish, and probably, for some of them, as little qualification; having frequently professed himself to be a very bad politician. It could, therefore, have been acceptable only, as connected with the naval service, to all and every part of which he was devotedly attached. The prominent situation in which the Noble Lord's career in the navy, and above all his moral worth and strict integrity as well as his professional character, had placed him in the public mind, pointed him out to the minister as one eminently suited to fill the office of First Lord of the Admiralty.[5]

---

5   Sir John Barrow, *The Life of Richard Earl Howe* (London: J. Murray, 1838), p.173.

Barrow, who occupied the post of Second Secretary for forty one years with only a short break between 1806 and 1807, was well placed to observe the functions of the First Lord of the Admiralty. He did not consider that the attributes of a successful post holder were required to be of the highest order: 'Good sense, honesty and impartiality, are the chief requisites to carry him smoothly and plausibly through the routine of business, provided a sufficient sum of money be granted in the Navy Estimates'.[6]

Almost as soon as he took office for the second time, however, Howe was faced with just the kind of problem suggested by Barrow. On coming to power Pitt found it necessary to seek very substantial public expenditure cuts, and the Navy was not exempt from these. This almost at once brought Howe into conflict with the Navy Board, through which most of the money for the Navy was spent. His suggestion was that as an economy measure the number of commissioners at the Navy Board might be reduced; Captains Edward Le Cras and Samuel Wallis had been appointed as additional commissioners during the American War, and Howe believed that they need not be retained. The Comptroller, Sir Charles Middleton, objected most strongly, writing a lengthy and argumentative letter to the First Lord advancing reasons to oppose the measure, and hinting that he might make it a resignation issue. Howe got his way, and Middleton nonetheless continued in office, but there was no love lost between the two men; 'A great difference of opinion, indeed an evident want of cordiality, and a stiffness of expression, appear in the whole of the correspondence between the First Lord and the Comptroller' was how Barrow put it, and they clashed over a large number of other issues.[7]

Middleton had been in post since 1778, and he did not at all enjoy not getting his own way. The most violent dispute between the two men concerned Middleton's desire for promotion when a number of captains junior to him were being considered for promotion to rear admiral. The problem was that by tradition the positions of Comptroller, and the other Commissioners at the Navy Board, were held by officers of the rank of captain so that if he was to get his promotion Middleton would have to give up his job. Howe, perhaps unconvincingly, told Middleton that if it was simply up to him he would allow the Comptroller to have flag rank, but opinion within the Navy made this impossible. Middleton, who enjoyed a good working relationship with the Prime Minister, appealed to him for support, and, in the event, received it, not least because Pitt was currently discontented with Howe. The issue provided an opportunity to make a change in the office of First Lord; Middleton got his promotion and in July 1788 Howe duly resigned.[8]

Pitt's relationship with Middleton was extremely important for the navy. The Prime Minister took a keen interest in naval affairs, and regularly dealt directly

6   Barrow, *Earl Howe*, p.173.
7   Barrow, *Earl Howe*, pp.178-179.
8   Talbott, *Pen and Ink Sailor*, p.129.

Admiral Charles
Middleton, later
Lord Barham.

with Middleton on the key issues which arose; he showed an immediate grasp of how they should be handled, as Sir Thomas Byam Martin, whose father succeeded Middleton as Comptroller, recalled:

> It was not likely that such a man would overlook the necessity of bringing the fleet into a state to maintain the high standing of the country in its naval character; and in this he set to work with his accustomed energy, neither sparing money nor means in the accomplishment of so vital a matter. It was no uncommon thing for Mr Pitt to visit the Navy Office to discuss naval matters with the Comptroller, and to see the returns made from the yards of the progress in building and repairing the ships of the line; he also desired to have a periodical statement from the Comptroller of the state of the fleet, wisely holding that officer responsible personally to him, without any regard to the Board.[9]

9   Sir Richard Vesey Hamilton (ed.), *Letters and Papers of Admiral of the Fleet Sir Thos. Byam Martin* (London: Navy Record Society, 1898-1903), Vol.III, p.381.

This relationship between the Prime Minister and an officer who was subordinate to him cannot have improved Howe's perception of either of them. In any case Howe and Middleton were both 'headstrong and obsessed with rank, position and their own self importance,' as David Syrett has pointed out.[10] Middleton was a skilful bureaucrat, the victor of many administrative battles; Howe, a successful fleet commander, was no administrator, and the outcome of a dispute between the two was probably inevitable. From the point of view of the Navy, this was just as well. Middleton, who was ultimately defeated in his long running attempt to reform the Navy Office, was largely responsible for the fact that Britain began the war in 1793 with a fleet that was in excellent shape. When he resigned in February 1790 over his failure to get even his watered-down proposals accepted, he left behind a draft note headed 'Reasons for resigning the office'. Written out by a clerk and referring to Middleton in the third person, the document set out in not unreasonable terms his claim on his country's gratitude:

> It is but fair in this place to add, that, at the time of Sir Charles Middleton's resignation the fleet is left in the best possible state; the number of serviceable ships, the greatest ever known in this country; the stores, appropriated to them, arranged in the most perfect order; the arsenals filled with every kind of proper stores, to the value of two millions sterling; three of the foreign yards completed since the peace ... The home yards are also in the greatest possible progress and even now ready for the most complete exertions. The use of copper has been established in all the branches to which it could be applied. In short, the remoter objects of the department are now in so fair a state, that nothing is wanting to perfect our naval economy, but the internal arrangements of the office itself respecting persons and their particular duties, in order to carry on business with life and dispatch.[11]

In 1793 it became apparent that he had made out his case.

With Howe gone, Pitt had to look around for a new First Lord. There appeared to be no senior admiral whose name suggested itself, and apparently on the recommendation of William Wilberforce, Pitt decided to appoint his elder brother John, Earl of Chatham. Pitt, who was 32 years of age, was evidently uncomfortable about such obvious nepotism, but it has been argued that he needed someone on whom he could rely, and Chatham, while lazy and unpunctual and rather too fond of the bottle, was not without ability. Furthermore, like his brother, he had a sound relationship with Middleton, on whom he could depend for advice. A professional

---

10   David Syrett, *Admiral Lord Howe* (Staplehurst: Spellmount, 2006), p.iii.
11   Sir John Knox Laughton, (ed.), *Letters and Papers of Charles, Lord Barham* (London: Navy Records Society, 1910), Vol.II, pp.349-350.

George, 2nd Earl Spencer, depicted some years after his tenure at the Admiralty.

soldier, Lord Chatham was not a very effective administrator; apparently, after he had left office, which he was to do in December 1794, many hundreds of unopened official letters were found in his house.[12]

Thus it was Chatham who was at the head of the Navy when war broke out in 1793, and he continued in office throughout that year and the following year. By then his brother had reached the conclusion that a change must be made at the Admiralty; he effected this by requiring Chatham and the 36 year old Earl Spencer, the Lord Privy Seal, to exchange offices. It was to prove an inspired decision.

Spencer had entered the House of Commons at the age of 22 and his ministerial career had begun when appointed a junior Lord of the Treasury. He was not long in the Commons, succeeding to the earldom in October 1783. When the group of Whigs led by the Duke of Portland split with Fox and went into coalition with Pitt's Tories in the summer of 1794, Spencer entered the Cabinet as Lord Privy Seal. He had already demonstrated considerable ability and force of character and almost immediately was sent on a mission to Vienna to persuade the Austrian government of the need to do something to support the unsatisfactory military situation in Holland. Austria, at that time engaged with Prussia and Russia in the

12   Morriss (ed.), *Channel Fleet*, p.6.

partition of Poland, was not very interested, and Spencer returned, with little to show for his efforts, in the autumn of 1794. By then the fleet action of the First of June had been fought, and the focus was now on Western France, where it was hoped that the Royalists might make headway against the forces of the Revolution. Since by now Pitt had been persuaded of the need to remove his brother from the Admiralty, it was in December 1794 that the job swap took place.

At the time Spencer came to the Admiralty the professional lords were Lord Hood, Sir Alan Gardner, Vice Admiral Philip Affleck and Vice Admiral Sir Charles Middleton. The latter had been serving as an unofficial confidential adviser since resigning as Comptroller, and joined the Board in May 1794. Hood had been serving as Commander-in-Chief in the Mediterranean, returning to England in December 1794 and stepping down from the Board in the following March.

At the outbreak of war the First Secretary was the long-serving Philip Stephens, who had been appointed Second Secretary during the Seven Years War, becoming First Secretary in 1763. After almost three and a half decades at the centre of Admiralty administration, serving in three major wars, Stephens retired from office, immediately becoming a civil member of the Board. He was succeeded by Evan Nepean. The Second Secretary was William Marsden. Nepean, a Cornishman, had began his career as a naval purser during the American War, before becoming a private secretary and then under secretary in a succession of departments.[13] Nepean sat in the House of Commons; Marsden, who was to succeed him as First Secretary, did not. Marsden's route to the Admiralty had taken him from the East India Company to become secretary to the Governor of Sumatra before returning to London and the private sector in 1785. He became Second Secretary in 1795.

One of Nepean's most sensitive duties at the Admiralty was the handling of intelligence. It was a function with which he had previously been concerned when serving as an Under Secretary at the Home Office, where part of the money appro-priated for secret service activities passed through his hands. As First Secretary it was recognised that he must be kept informed of even the most secret govern-ment information; in 1797, for instance, details of a particular operation were, the King decreed, to be kept from all but the Duke of York, Lord Spencer, the Prime Minister, and Evan Nepean. Nepean is recorded as having employed a number of informants, many of whom were British naval officers apparently not on the active list. One of these was Richard Oakes, who worked for the Admiralty before Nepean's appointment there, corresponding not only with Philip Stephens but also with the Prime Minister. The Admiralty's most important source of intelligence

---

13   C.I. Hamilton, *The Making of the Modern Admiralty: British Naval Policy-Making, 1805–1927* (Cambridge: Cambridge University Press, 2011), p.52.

about France was Captain Philippe d'Auvergne, who commanded first a frigate and then a squadron of smaller vessels based in the Channel Islands.[14]

All in all, the amount of work done at the Admiralty and the Navy Board, and all the subordinate institutions, was enormous. Given the huge delays from which all communication suffered, it is extraordinary that it was able to discharge so effectively the colossal burden of responsibility which it bore.

14 Steven E Maffeo, *Most Secret and Confidential: Intelligence in the Age of Nelson* (London: Chatham, 2003), pp.4-8.

3

Brest and the French Navy

The Revolution had inflicted serious damage on the French Navy. The naval ports had been particular centres of disruption, where the latent discontent among ships' crews broke out in violent indiscipline. One victim of this was the distinguished d'Albert de Rions, generally held to be France's most capable flag officer, renowned not only for his courage and professional skill, but also for his charitable and upright character. In 1789 he had been in command at Toulon; when endeavouring to deal with a disturbance on shore, he was attacked by a mob, injured, and thrown into prison. The National Assembly failed to support him, and he resigned. In the following year d'Albert was appointed to command the fleet at Brest. Again he encountered serious breaches of discipline, including a mutiny in one ship; again the Assembly failed to support him and, in disgust, he resigned his command and left the service. In this way France lost the services of her ablest naval commander.

Many of the officers of the navy were from the aristocracy, and a large number of these emigrated as the prolonged assault on the nobility continued. It was not only those from the Court aristocracy that thus voted with their feet; many of those from the lesser aristocracy also made their way abroad, leaving the navy desperately short of officers. It has been calculated that the wastage was such that by November 1791 the establishment at Brest was short of 30 captains and 160 lieutenants.[1]

It was partly as a result of this that in 1791 the Assembly established a completely different officer structure. The old officer corps was abolished as were the senior ranks of lieutenant général and chef d'escadre; in their place there were to be three admirals, nine vice admirals and eighteen rear admirals. There were to be 180 *capitaines de vaisseau*. The former distinction between nobles and professional seamen – the latter known as *officiers bleus* – was also abolished, so that officers might be appointed from the merchant marine. A historian of the French navy has observed:

---

1   E.H. Jenkins, *A History of the French Navy* (London: Macdonald and Jane's, 1973), p.205.

In view of the emigration it was fortunate for France that she had the latter to fall back upon, and a merchant skipper or reservist officer of eight years' sea time (including two in the navy) was eligible for posting as a captain.[2]

It was abundantly clear that those into whose hands had fallen the government of France had very little concept of the specialist skills required of competent naval officers, as further decrees demonstrated. In 1792 civil administrators were put in charge not only of ports but of the movement of ships within them. In January 1793 merchant skippers with five years' sea time were admitted to the junior ranks of the navy, and the bar was lowered again in further decrees during that year. Even more significant in its effect on battle efficiency was a decree of that year abolishing the corps of seaman gunners on the grounds that its existence created a kind of aristocracy among seamen; in the interests of equality, it was argued, any artilleryman should be able to serve aboard ship.

Perhaps the most disastrous of the politically inspired measures introduced by the Assembly was the decree of 'purification' of October 1793, making it possible for anyone to denounce a naval officer whose lack of devotion to the Revolution was suspect. Many officers were as a result dismissed from the service and a lot of them were imprisoned. This decree was largely the work of Jean-Bon St André, the member of the Committee of Public Safety with special responsibility for the navy. St André, born in Toulouse, had some knowledge of the merchant navy, which distinguished him from the other members of the committee, whose ignorance of maritime affairs was total. As a Jacobin, and as a former Protestant preacher, he particularly detested Catholic naval officers of the aristocracy.

By the time that war with Great Britain broke out, therefore, the French navy was in a poor state to oppose its traditional adversary. Without three quarters of the officer corps, promotion had been rapid; ships of the line were commanded by former sub lieutenants, and squadrons by former lieutenants. The organisation of the navy had effectively fallen apart, as Marcus graphically describes:

> Everywhere was carelessness, incompetence, disorder and neglect. The warships were dirty and ill-found. Victuals, sails, rigging, timber, and naval stores alike were lacking. […] The republican crews counted many sick and they were without proper clothing. Their pay was continually in arrears. A spirit of indiscipline developed into insubordination, and insubordination into something resembling anarchy.[3]

2   Jenkins, *French Navy*, p 206.
3   Marcus, *Age of Nelson*, p.21.

When war broke out the command of the fleet in Brest had passed to Vice Admiral Morard de Galles. He had served under Suffren, when he had shown that he was a competent officer, and he was loyal to France and to its navy. In March 1793 he had been required to take a force to sea to patrol the Channel, and succeeded in putting to sea with three ships of the line and four frigates. His cruise was a chaotic chapter of accidents; in his report he wrote that 'the spirit of the sailors is lost entirely; nothing can make them attend to their duties'.[4]

The disastrous events at Toulon, where the British Mediterranean Fleet under Lord Hood took possession of the place and, effectively, of the French fleet there, meant that something quickly had to be done to prevent a similar occurrence at Brest. Situated as it was in the west of France, where Royalist feeling was strongest, Brest was seen as potentially extremely vulnerable. It was upon Jean-Bon St André that the Committee of Public Safety laid the task of bringing order to the fleet and to the port.

He began as he meant to go on. 'Severity is the only means to make the conspirators tremble and to frighten the intriguers' was how he described his policy.[5] In practice, however, he was unable to apply this with the ferocity envisaged by the Committee of Public Safety, since he had sufficient grasp of reality to see how far he could go if there was to be anything left of the fleet. One of his first acts was to replace Morard de Galles. The latter had ventured out again with the fleet, but on sighting Howe with the Channel Fleet felt able to do no more than to escape to Quiberon Bay, where fortunately for him Howe made no attempt to follow. He had been given an impossible set of orders; to lie off Quiberon Bay to prevent any support for the Royalist rebels, to cover the coastal trade, and to bring in French convoys or attack those of the British.[6] He was refused leave to resign, and told to obey orders. In the event, the latter task proved impossible. Although he had been forbidden to return to Brest, his crews, suffering severely, finally insisted on this. Jean-Bon St André was therefore in no doubt that a change at the top of the fleet was essential.

His choice fell on Louis-Thomas Villaret-Joyeuse. This was perhaps surprising, since he was a nobleman who had, until recently, only reached the rank of lieutenant. He had, however, in 1790 distinguished himself in the process of bringing the rebellious colony of Saint Domingue to heel, as a result of which he was promoted to post captain and given command of a 74 gun ship of the line. On 16 November 1793, with the rank of rear admiral, he took command of the French fleet at Brest, for which a more ambitious strategy was now conceived. This was

---

4   Quoted Sam Willis, *The Glorious First of June: Fleet Battle in the Reign of Terror* (London: Quercus, 2011), p.15.
5   Willis, *Glorious First of June*, p.209.
6   Jenkins, *French Navy*, p.15.

nothing less than to prepare for an invasion of England, an objective that would call for a colossal effort.

First, however, discipline must be restored, and this was instilled by the imposition of a Code of Conduct that left no room for insubordination at any level. It was enforced by the ruthless employment of the guillotine for anyone convicted of inciting mutiny, or for any officer who failed to carry out orders. Many of the officers from the old navy were dismissed, with the exception of the *bleus* who were retained and given the chance of rapid promotion. These measures, E.H. Jenkins has written, 'brought the fleet to order, but not to efficiency.'[7]

St André was also active, however, in revitalising the work of the dockyards at Brest. 'The sounds of our axes, of our hammers, of our mallets, have reached London,' he wrote. There was a huge increase in activity, not only in the building of new ships and the repair of those existing, but in the reorganisation of the infrastructure of the port. Warships were properly equipped with all that was necessary for their crews to go to sea in the demanding waters of the Channel, the Bay of Biscay and the wider Atlantic.[8]

In Brest, the French navy had a port that was superbly located for operations against the British Isles, as well as southwards towards Spain. Brest was established as France's principal Atlantic base in the reign of Louis XIV, when the dockyard was set up by Colbert and the extensive fortifications built by Vauban. The dockyards were laid out on the banks of the river Penfeld, at the mouth of which was built a powerful castle. The most westerly point on the French coastline, its situation threatened British and Dutch trade routes both westwards to the New World, and south-westwards en route to the East. The growth in the size of warships meant that many of the smaller ports along the French coastline were unsuitable as a base for naval operations:

> What was needed was a roadstead in which a fleet could lie, and such a roadstead needed to provide reasonable shelter from gales, to be close to an actual harbour which could be a dockyard, and to be fortifiable in order to protect the fleet against an assault from seaward. For all this Brest was magnificently suitable.[9]

The city and dockyard of Brest lie on the north side of the roadstead, which is extremely spacious; it was estimated that as many as 500 warships could lie at anchor there in 8, 10, and 15 fathoms at low water. The entrance to the roadstead, known as Le Goulet, is narrow and easily defended. Two dangerous rocks, Les Fillettes and Le Mingan, make it difficult of entry, lying as they do almost in

7   Jenkins, *French Navy*, p.209.
8   Willis, *Glorious First of June*, pp.36-37.
9   Jenkins, *French Navy*, p.15.

mid-channel. On either side of the entrance, the coast is well fortified. Outside Le Goulet there are two anchorages, frequently used by warships. To the northward is Bertheaume Bay, sheltered from northerly, north-easterly and north-westerly winds; to the south is Camaret Bay, sheltered from winds blowing from the south, east-south-east and south-west.

Brest had other advantages that made blockade a difficult and dangerous undertaking, being surrounded by submerged rocks and skerries. Two promontories of small islands and reefs stand out: to the north from the Pointe de St Mathieu all the way to the island of Ushant; that to the south is the Chaussée de Sein, known to the British as the Saints, reaching out into the Atlantic from the Pointe du Raz.

There are three passages from the sea into the anchorages and into Brest Harbour itself; the Passage du Four, between the French coast and Ushant; the Passage de l'Iroise, between Ushant and the Isle des Saints; and the Passage de Raz, between the Isle des Saints and the Bec du Raz. Of these, the first and the third are the most dangerous; the Iroise, of considerable width, is the centre or west passage, and is that off which the British warships most usually cruised.

William James considered that 'it is scarcely possible, however, to blockade the port of Brest, if the enemy inside is as vigilant as he ought to be,' and overall the French could hardly have had a more convenient base for their principal fleet.[10] Its one serious drawback was that when the wind was in the west, it was practically impossible for square rigged ships to get out. As a result, therefore, when the British Channel Fleet was at Torbay or Spithead and was itself penned in by westerly winds, its commander could at any rate feel secure in the knowledge that the French fleet was similarly held in.

The importance of Brest was reinforced by the fact that whereas along the English coast of the Channel there were a number of ports capable of housing a battle fleet, this was not the case along the French coast. Apart from Cherbourg, which could possibly have been made suitable, there was nothing heading eastwards before the Texel. Strategically, therefore, the French were at a considerable disadvantage if circumstances required them to operate along the south coast of England. Their fleet would have to sail round from Brest; if it then had to retreat it might well be in difficulty, since the prevailing west and south-westerly winds would hamper its return to base. Likewise, when the Dutch became allied to France, the Dutch fleet was at a disadvantage; in that case the British were able to maintain a close watch on the Dutch coast from Yarmouth, the Thames Estuary and the Downs.

---

10   James, *Naval History*, Vol.I, p.65.

4

Ships

When war with France began in 1793, the British Royal Navy possessed a total of 498 warships, either in commission, undergoing repairs or refits, or 'in ordinary'. The latter term denoted ships that were laid up in reserve. All those vessels carrying 20 guns or more were classified according to a rating system, most recently revised in the 1750s. These vessels were known as post ships, being commanded by a post captain. A ship was, strictly defined, a large three masted vessel, square-rigged on all three masts. Smaller vessels could be commanded by lieutenants, promoted to the rank of master and commander, who were known by the courtesy title of captain. But it was to be a post captain of which every officer dreamed, for only then was his foot on the ladder of seniority which was the principal determinant of further promotion.

The rating of a ship was determined by its size and armament but, confusingly, these measures were not clear cut. The largest ships were the ships of the line, or line of battleships. A ship of the line was one which was theoretically fit to lie in the line of battle. This was the tactical formation that was gradually evolved to take account of the steadily increasing power of the guns carried aboard warships. The bulk of these guns were disposed on gun decks in broadsides. Firing solid shot, their capacity to inflict damage upon an adversary could be immense. However, the sides of a warship were designed to stand up to considerable punishment. It was only from ahead or astern that a ship was immediately vulnerable; if raked across its bow or stern by an adversary it could suffer enormous damage from shots which could smash along the whole length of the ship.

The weakness of the stern, which made a ship of the line so vulnerable in this way, was even more pronounced than that of the bows, because it was lightly constructed and broken up by windows and galleries. It may well be a source of wonder that so unprotected a feature remained in the design, particularly of ships of the line, but a clue to the explanation for this may lie in the fate of a new design produced by Sir Robert Seppings after the end of the Napoleonic Wars. He devised a round stern, which was much stronger, and gave more scope for the mounting of guns firing aft; but it was very unpopular, because it reduced the comfort of the officers and was considered to be ugly.[1]

Thus was adopted the tactical principle that a battle fleet should deploy and fight in line ahead, and this was the formation employed throughout most of the seventeenth and eighteenth centuries. In this way the vulnerable bow and stern of each vessel in the line was protected by the ships ahead and astern. One effect of this tactical deployment, however, was that battles could prove indecisive. This frequently proved to be the case, not least due to the time which it often took for the opposing fleets to sort themselves into line and then draw close enough to engage the enemy. By the time the ships were in range, it sometimes occurred that not much of the day was left; once darkness fell on the open sea the risk of confusion, and the impossibility of communication, meant that the battle had to be broken off.

'Fighting Instructions,' which laid down the tactics to be adopted by a sailing fleet in battle, were first produced as early as the sixteenth century. A Spanish writer, Alonso de Chaves, explained the need for such guidance:

> For ships at sea are as war horses on land, since admitting they are not very nimble at turning at any pace, nevertheless a regular formation increases their power. Moreover, at sea, so long as there be no storm, there will be nothing to hinder the using of any of the orders with which we have dealt, and if there be a storm the same terror will strike the one side as the other; for the storm is enough for all to war with, and in fighting it they will have peace with one another.[2]

The earliest 'Fighting Instructions' which called for the adoption of a single line ahead were issued by the English 'Generals at Sea' on 29 March 1653, during the First Dutch War. Their issue by the generals followed the action off Portland on February 18, after which 'it must have been clear to everyone that they narrowly escaped defeat through a want of cohesion between their squadrons.'[3] In subsequent actions against the Dutch the English fleet appears to have got into line, and during the Battle of the Texel on 31 July of the same year the Dutch seem to have done so also.

The 'Fighting Instructions' of 1691, which continued the emphasis on the line of battle, continued largely in force until the end of the next century. Instead of their being completely revised from time to time to reflect changes that were being introduced, there were published 'Additional Fighting Instructions'. These were devised by individual admirals for the use of the fleets which they commanded,

1   Robert Gardiner (ed.), *The Line of Battle* (Annapolis: Naval Institute Press, 1992), p 23.
2   Julian S. Corbett (ed.), *Fighting Instructions 1530-1816* (London: Navy Records Society, 1905), pp.44-45.
3   Corbett (ed.), *Fighting Instructions*, p.94.

and took account of practical experiences that gave rise to new ideas as to how a fleet action should be conducted. Ultimately, however, the development of the standing orders in this way had reached, prior to the outbreak of war in 1793, the point at which a root and branch reform was called for:

> It was the indefatigable hand of Lord Howe that dealt them the long-needed blow, and when the change came it was sweeping. It was no mere substitution of a new set of Instructions, but a complete revolution of method. The basis of the new tactical code was no longer the Fighting Instructions but the Signal Book.[4]

The concept of the line of battle remained, although by now qualified in a number of important respects intended to increase the chance of decisive victory, especially in relation to the need for concentration.

The line of battle was necessarily composed of the largest and stoutest ships of the fleet, capable of enduring the kind of battering that was to be expected as the two lines of ships engaged each other. As the years had gone by, ships had steadily increased in size and in the power of their armament. As recently as the Seven Years War, which ended in 1763, the line of battle had included ships of 50 and 60 guns, although by then the 50 gun ship had been officially relegated from the line. Three decades later, even 64 gun ships were no longer officially considered capable of standing in the line of battle, although in practice they did. There were few 50 gun ships still in service by 1793, but those that were frequently found employment as squadron flagships on overseas stations.[5] The *Leopard,* made famous by the pen of Patrick O'Brian, was still serving with the Channel Fleet in 1793.

The rating system was not merely a classification of ships devised for its own sake. In addition to determining the rank of a ship's commander, it also defined the official complement of each vessel, and specified other matters such as pay and the quantity of stores to be provided. The rating system, originally introduced in the reign of Charles I, lasted over two hundred years. It was originally based on the number of men carried per ton; in 1677 Pepys changed it to the number of men needed per gun. This meant that the number and weight of her guns determined the size of a ship's crew. There is apparently a theory that at first the rate meant the rate of the captains pay. However, once the gun establishment had been defined it was no longer necessary to consider the number of men, but merely to rate the ships according to the number of guns.

A ship of the line was an immensely complex fighting machine, which called for great expertise not only on the part of its captain and officers, but also from the specialist warrant officers such as the master, bosun, gunner and carpenter;

4   Corbett (ed.), *Fighting Instructions*, p.233.
5   Rif Winfield, *The 50-Gun Ship* (London: Chatham, 1997), p.63.

and, of course, from the skilled and experienced seamen required to perform the intricate and demanding tasks of setting, taking in or reefing the large number of sails that drove the ship. The fundamental elements of the design of a ship of the line had changed only slowly by 1793. E.H.H. Archibald has observed that the *Sovereign of the Seas* of 1637 'was the prototype for every English capital ship to be built until 1860':

> The *Sovereign* would have looked a bit odd at Trafalgar, with her long beak, her partially open quarter-galleries and old fashioned rig; but she still would have carried a hundred truck-mounted muzzle-loaders on three decks, just like the other three deckers, and would have been a force to reckon with.[6]

In 1793 the British navy possessed five first rate ships of the line, each of which officially carried 100 guns (although as will be seen this was not necessarily an accurate figure). Of these, the oldest was the *Britannia*, built in 1762. Of the same vintage was the *Victory* built in 1764. The others were all completed in the decade before the war. The first rates were up to 2,500 tons burthen. There were seventeen second rates, all 98 gun ships apart from *Blenheim* and *Namur*, of 90 guns. The oldest of these was the *Namur*, built in 1756; six of them had been completed since the end of the American War and were up to 2,200 tons burthen.

There were four third rates carrying 80 guns or more. Two were three deckers: the aged *Cambridge*, 80, built in 1755 and the even older *Royal William*, originally built as the 100 gun *Prince* in 1670, rebuilt in 1692 and 1719, when her name was changed, and cut down to 84 guns in 1756; she served as the guard ship in Portsmouth harbour where she wore the Port Admiral's flag.[7] The others were two deckers, the *Gibraltar*, 80, captured from the Spanish, and the newly-built *Caesar*, 80. It was, however, the 74 gun ships that provided the fire power of the British fleet, and were the standard ships of the line. They had a burthen of around 1,750 tons. In 1793 there were 64 of these, of which the oldest was the ex-French *Courageux*, built in 1753. Twenty six of these vessels had been completed since the end of the American War. There were still 37 third rate ships of the line of between 60 and 64 guns; the oldest was the *Yarmouth* of 1748. They were still being built, however, in the decade before 1793; during this period six new 64 guns ships came into service.

Finally, there were the 19 fourth rates, carrying from 50 to 60 guns, that were still in service in 1793. These had an average burthen of 1,100 tons. During the Revolutionary War two of these, *Isis* and *Adamant*, were at the battle of

6   E.H.H. Archibald, *The Wooden Fighting Ship in the Royal Navy AD 897-1860* (Poole: Arco, 1968), p.24.
7   Angus Konstam, *The British Napoleonic Ship-of-the-Line* (Oxford: Osprey, 2001), p.37.

Camperdown in 1797; *Leander* fought at the Nile in the following year; and the *Glatton* and *Isis* were at Copenhagen in 1801.

Fifth rates were vessels carrying between 32 and 44 guns and sixth rates carried from 20-28 guns. Of these rates, those carrying 28 guns or more were the frigates, which played an enormous part in carrying out the duties of the fleet. They had been introduced rather gradually into the Royal Navy, and this was only when it began to be apparent in the War of the Austrian Succession in the 1740s that the large frigates being built by the French could out-sail, and in rough weather out-gun, the British 40 gun ships of the period. There were only four 36 gun frigates in the Royal Navy of the Seven Years War; by the end of the American War there were seventeen frigates of 36 guns and seven of 38 guns. By this time the French were arming their frigates with heavier guns, and soon started building 44 gun ships. The British followed suit, but only slowly until after the outbreak of the Revolutionary and Napoleonic Wars.[8]

At the start of the Revolutionary War, the British had a total of 88 frigates in commission, of which 66 were fifth rates of between 32 and 44 guns and 22 were sixth rates of 28 guns. There were also ten sixth rates of from 20 to 24 guns, classified as post ships.[9]

A number of ships of the line had been captured during the American War from the French, and had entered the Royal Navy and were still in service in 1793. Many more were taken during the Revolutionary and Napoleonic Wars, and much interest was naturally taken in comparing them to the British built ships. British designers were considerably influenced by their French counterparts. One British historian rejects the widely held view that overall the French ships were superior to the British:

> It is certainly true that the French designers were more scientific in their approach to hull design, and showed the way where English designers had perforce to follow. But though it might have been fashionable for some English naval officers to say that the best ships in the service were French prizes, certainly French officers could not have had the satisfaction to claim that the worst ships in their service were English prizes.[10]

The French ships were, however, less well built, and of inferior materials. One French ship, the 80 gun *Sans Pareil*, which was taken during the battle of June 1 1794, was in the following year carrying the flag of Lord Hugh Seymour, who as a Lord Commissioner of the Admiralty reported to Spencer on her performance at the action off the Ile de Groix on June 19 1794:

8   Archibald, *Wooden Fighting Ship*, p.48.
9   James Henderson, *The Frigates* (New York: Dodd Mead, 1971), p.169.
10   Archibald, *Wooden Fighting Ship*, pp.63-64.

You will, I am persuaded, be happy to know that the *Sans Pareil* was among the foremost of the eight or nine sail who were enabled to get into action and will not be less so to learn from me that she answers in every respect, excepting in light winds, when I have reason to be dissatisfied with her, as the *Queen Charlotte, Orion* and *Irresistible* passed her in the course of the chase on Monday night.[11]

Prior to 1793 a 74 gun ship would typically have been about 165 feet in length excluding the jib-boom and bowsprit and about 46 feet in the beam, with a draft of about 21-23 feet. A three decker would be about 20 feet longer, 5 feet wider and 3 feet deeper.[12] By 1793 it was evident that longer ships, for a given number of decks, were better sailers; the limit on their length, however, was that very long ships were vulnerable to 'hogging', or sagging at the ends.[13]

Reference has already been made to the massive construction of a ship of the line. Throughout most of the hull, covering the gun decks, there was a total thickness of about 20 inches of solid wood, increasing in places to over 2 feet, excluding internal framing.

The deck beams were joined to the frames with large brackets or knees; between adjacent decks, and between the orlop beams and the keel, were sturdy pillars. The whole formed a sort of gigantic wooden box with very thick sides and extensive internal bracing, immensely strong.[14] It is no wonder that it has been estimated that it took about 80 acres of oak trees to construct one 74 gun ship or that, by the end of the Napoleonic War, the question of timber supply was approaching crisis point.

The guns carried by a ship of the line fell into three classes, defined by the weight of the solid shot which they fired. 32-pounders, weighing 55 hundredweight, were located on the lowest gun deck, 18-pounders on the upper deck or in the case of the three deckers on the two highest gun decks, with 9-pounders (later 12-pounders) on the quarterdeck. The guns were cumbersome, hard to manage, and required a considerable crew. Along the gun deck the guns were spaced at about 11 foot centres, mounted on wheeled carriages about five feet wide.

These were the guns of which account was taken in the rating of warships, but they were not the only guns carried. In 1752 General Robert Melville invented a new type of gun, manufactured for the Royal Navy by the Scottish firm of Carron, from which it took its name of carronade. It was a short, light barrelled gun with a large bore, which threw a ball of 32 lbs or even 68 lbs with a low initial velocity. At short range this had a smashing effect that was more destructive than a ball

---

11 Morriss (ed.), *Channel Fleet*, p 85.
12 David Davies, *Fighting Ships: Ships of the Line 1793-1815* (London: Constable, 1996), pp.24-25.
13 Gardiner (ed.), *Line of Battle*, p.21.
14 Davies, *Fighting Ships*, p.30.

propelled at a higher velocity. Carronades were very much lighter and more manageable than the traditional guns; a 32-pounder carronade weighed only 17 hundredweight compared with 33 hundredweight for a 12-pounder gun. They had, however, a much shorter range – 1,140 yards compared with the 1,580 yards of the long gun:

> This limited range made them unsuitable as the sole armament, since there would be a risk of being outranged. In several actions this inferiority proved decisive, notably in that between the British *Phoebe* and the American *Essex* in the year 1814, when the last named ship was armed almost entirely with them and was beaten in consequence. But as secondary guns their range was held to be sufficient, and the great smashing effect of a 32-pounder carronade compared with that of a 12-pounder long gun at short decisive ranges kept them in favour through three great wars.[15]

By 1793 carronades, which had previously been mounted on carriages like the long guns, were now mounted on a ring cast beneath the rear of the barrel, and a ring-breech, fitted to house an elevating screw. Carronades were not counted in the ratings of warships; their number varied from ship to ship. They were carried in addition to the long guns and in some instances replaced some of the lighter guns. The Americans adopted carronades enthusiastically, the French less so, not least because their favoured tactic was to stand off and fire at an enemy ship's rigging.

The French navy began the war with not much more than half the number of ships of the line possessed by the Royal Navy. Reviewing the disparity and its effect on the chances of French success, E.H. Jenkins concluded that the disadvantage was not as great as the mere numbers would suggest:

> Her ships numbered roughly two thirds of those of Britain; but as Britain would have to detach many to protect her colonies and her merchant shipping, the numbers would not be so disparate. Moreover, though in sum British ships of the line outnumbered the French by three to two, in total weight of broadside they were superior by only one sixth.[16]

In spite of the state of decrepitude into which the French naval infrastructure had been allowed to fall, France did have in its fighting ships a potentially formidable fleet, as William James observed:

> At no previous period had France possessed so powerful a navy as was now ready to second her efforts to humble, if not overthrow, her great

---

15   Sir Reginald Custance, *The Ship of the Line in Battle* (London: William Blackwood, 1912), p.2.
16   Jenkins, *French Navy*, pp.206-207.

maritime rival. It amounted altogether to about 250 vessels, of which 82 were of the line; and of these, nearly three fourths were ready for sea or in a serviceable state.[17]

In addition 25 further ships of the line had been ordered, as well as 46 others, and work was proceeding to develop the productive capability of the nation's gun foundries.

At the start of the war, according to James, there were at Brest a dozen ships of the line immediately ready for sea, with another seven fitting out. There were another dozen said to be in good condition, and sixteen which were not. Elsewhere, at Rochefort and Toulon, nine ships of the line were ready for sea, eight were fitting out, and nine more were in good condition: nine were said to be in poor condition. Overall, those that were ready for sea or were fitting out included five ships carrying a hundred guns or more, and seven 80-gun ships. The rest were 74s. In addition, at this time the French could dispose of no less than 79 frigates, of which fifteen carried forty or more guns. The names of a large number of the ships had been changed to convey appropriately Revolutionary fervour.

What was certain was that the evolving design of the warship had produced a great advance in seaworthiness, and this in its turn considerably affected the strategic options available. In the middle of the seventeenth century, during the Dutch Wars, the fleets fought only in the summer in the southern end of the North Sea, and not more than 100 miles from their home bases:

> A century later, warships were expected to sail anywhere in the world, to keep the seas throughout the winter, and to maintain their workaday station off ports such as Brest in all but the most difficult conditions.[18]

Although fleet commanders like Howe and Bridport were reluctant to accept it, this improvement in the sea-keeping qualities of their ships meant that close blockade of the enemy port was a real option, while the individual hitting power of each of their ships had also considerably increased.

17   James, *Naval History*, Vol.I, p.156.
18   Gardiner (ed.), *Line of Battle*, p.10.

5

The Grain Convoy

By January 1794 the British government had become aware of the substantial build-up of French merchant shipping in American ports. It consisted of a large number of vessels carrying valuable cargoes from the West Indies, and an even larger number carrying cargoes of flour and grain purchased in the United States by the French government in an effort to deal with the severe shortages in France. British consular officials sent regular reports of the preparations for a huge convoy to sail to France, and its capture was regarded by the Admiralty as 'an object of the most urgent importance to the success of the present war'.[1] Its preservation was even more important to the French government, and preparations for its safe transit across the Atlantic were put in hand as early as 25-27 January.

The escort was to be under the command of the newly promoted Rear Admiral Pierre Jean Vanstabel. Born in 1744, his early seagoing career was spent in command of privateers in the Channel during the American War. In February 1793 he was promoted to captain and took command of the frigate *Thétis*, in which he conducted an extremely successful war on British trade in the Channel, capturing some forty merchantmen in a period of four months. Following this he commanded the squadron which clashed with Howe and the Channel Fleet in the encounter described in Chapter 1. Now, he was sent across the Atlantic with two fast sailing 74 gun ships, *Tigre* and *Jean Bart,* which were to serve as the nucleus of the convoy escort. He was later reinforced by two more 74s together with a number of frigates and corvettes and a brig.

The problem for the Admiralty was that there was no firm intelligence of when the convoy was likely to sail or the route it would take. That being so, it seems surprising that a British squadron was not sent across the Atlantic in the hope of catching the convoy as it set out. Consular reports, which of course took a long time to reach London, indicated that it was preparing for sea at the end of March. In the event, Vanstabel was ready to sail on April 15, but adverse winds held him

---

1   Admiralty to Howe, April 17 1794, quoted in Morriss (ed.), *Channel Fleet*, p.34.

up, and it was two days later before he could get away. There are conflicting estimates of the size of the convoy, being put as high as 156 ships by Sam Willis and 127 by Michael Duffy. There is no doubt that its cargo was extremely valuable, being said to be worth £1.5m. The convoy carried 67,000 barrels of flour, with bacon, salt beef and hides; 11,241 barrels of coffee, and 7,163 barrels of sugar, as well as cotton, cocoa, rice and indigo.[2]

To beef up the escort as the convoy neared its destination, the French sent to sea Rear Admiral Joseph-Marie Nielly with five ships of the line, two frigates and a corvette, to meet Vanstabel. Nielly was another very capable officer. Born in 1751, he had served at various times in the navy and in the merchant marine. Still only a lieutenant in 1793, he was promoted to captain in the following year, commanding the frigate *Résolue* with considerable success. In November 1793 he reached the rank of rear admiral. Continuous westerly winds held up his departure, and it was not until April 10 that he was able to sail.

The final element in the French defence of the convoy was the main Brest fleet under Villaret-Joyeuse. It would be reinforced by eight ships of the line which were lying in Cancale in preparation for a descent on Jersey, under Rear Admiral Cornic. But the sole object of the main fleet putting to sea was to thwart any intervention by the Channel Fleet, as the French navy minister wrote to Villaret-Joyeuse on 26 April:

> The intention of the Committee of Public Safety is for the fleet to get under way to join Nielly and Vanstabel with the Cancale division, if the enemy itself gets under way. But in that case the safety of the convoy will be its only objective, the only rule of conduct for the commander of the fleet.[3]

At this stage of the war there would be little to be gained by the French in an all-out battle with the Channel Fleet for its own sake. The plan for a descent in due course on some part of the British Isles remained at the top of the French agenda, and it was important to husband the fleet for initiatives of that kind. However, the safe arrival of the convoy was the first priority, as Villaret-Joyeuse's final orders of 16 May made clear:

> We must not compromise our naval forces when all supplementary means are not yet put into execution and when the smallest failure could halt our plan of campaign against England... It is not a naval victory we need at

2   Michael Duffy, 'The Man who missed the Grain Convoy' in Michael Duffy and Roger Morriss (eds.), *The Glorious First of June* (Exeter: Exeter Maritime Studies, 2001) p 117; Willis, *Glorious First of June*, p.112.

3   André Delaporte, 'The Prairial Battles: The French Viewpoint' in Duffy and Morriss (eds.), *Glorious First of June*, p.13.

the moment, but our convoy; it is not a battle but a proud and imposing posture which will ward off the enemy or make it to hove to. To delay our revenge is to make it more sure.[4]

With these orders Villaret-Joyeuse sailed on the same day. He later claimed that Robespierre had made clear to him that if the convoy did not arrive safely he would go to the guillotine.

   With only limited intelligence available about the course or destination of the convoy, the Admiralty framed orders for Howe. He was to have a number of stated objectives. First, he was to protect the huge outbound East India convoy, not only down Channel, but also across the Bay of Biscay, detaching a squadron for the purpose. Secondly, he was to order the squadron escorting the East India convoy, having seen it safely past Cape Ortegal, to cruise from there to the latitude of Belleisle in order to intercept the French convoy. Beyond this, Howe had a general responsibility for the protection of trade,

> as well as of intercepting, and taking or destroying, the Ships of War, Privateers and Trade of the enemy bearing always in mind that a due regard to the Security of the Kingdoms of Great Britain and Ireland must ever form one of the most essential and constant Objects of your care and attention.[5]

What these instructions did not expressly suggest was that Howe should institute a blockade of Brest or use such frigates as he had to watch the approaches to any of the Biscay ports which Vanstabel might select as his landfall; Howe's discretion was very wide. He duly issued orders to Rear Admiral George Montagu to take command of the squadron which was to escort the East India convoy and then search for the French convoy. Montagu was the most junior of Howe's flag officers. He was born in 1750 into a well known naval family. He reached the rank of post captain in 1774 and had a successful career in the American War. The squadron which he was to command consisted of six ships of the line (*Hector, Arrogant, Theseus, Ganges, Bellona* and *Alexander*), and four frigates (*Pallas, Hebe, Venus* and *Circe*). He was to accompany the Channel Fleet in escorting the East India convoy down Channel, until the fleet reached Ushant. Thereafter he would shepherd the convoy across the Bay of Biscay to the latitude of Cape Finisterre, after which, with its sole escort the 74 gun *Suffolk*, it would continue on its way, while Montagu cruised from Cape Ortegal to the latitude of Belleisle to intercept Vanstabel's convoy. If, by May 15, he had neither found the French convoy nor acquired any firm intelligence of its

4   Delaporte, 'Prairial Battles' p.15.
5   Morriss (ed.), *Channel Fleet*, pp.34-35.

course and destination, he was to return to Torbay or Plymouth to resupply his ships and await further orders.[6]

When Howe sailed from St Helens on May 2, with Montagu and the East India convoy in company, neither he nor anyone else had any further reliable information about Vanstabel. By then of, course, the French admiral was deep into the Atlantic; a despatch had reached Brest from him to say that he expected to arrive there about May 4. Howe, before sailing, had revised Montagu's orders to provide for him to remain on his patrol line until May 20, and then return to the fleet rendezvous off Ushant. On May 4, Montagu and the East India convoy were detached to make their journey across the bay, and next day from his post at Ushant, Howe sent two frigates supported by two ships of the line to check that the French fleet was still there. Indeed it was; Sir Edward Thornborough of the frigate *Latona* reported that he had counted at least 22 ships of the line and a vast number of smaller vessels.

What happened next is a matter of some disagreement between historians of the ensuing battle. The majority view, led by William James, is that Howe deliberately left his station off Ushant; James put it thus:

> The British admiral, well aware that, if the French came out, it would be to afford protection to the convoy then hourly expected from America, steered straight for the latitude through which the latter would most probably pass. From the 5th to the 18th inclusive the fleet kept crossing the bay in various directions, without seeing an enemy sail.[7]

Clowes followed the account given by James very closely; so did Barrow, who recorded the fleet as cruising in foggy and blowing weather, keeping nearly in the parallel of Ushant.[8] Marcus merely observed that Howe stood to the westward;[9] Mahan says that Howe 'proceeded to cruise in the Bay of Biscay, moving backward and forward across the probable track of expected convoy'.[10] Warner offers a more positive account, claiming that Howe did not want to prevent the French coming out 'since he was as eager to defeat them as to capture the convoy. He therefore made no attempt to watch the port but advanced south westerly'.[11]

Most recent historians have followed the majority, Duffy observing that Howe 'departed to cruise the Bay of Biscay in accordance with his orders until 18 May'.[12]

---

6   Duffy, 'Grain Convoy', pp.103-104.
7   James, *Naval History*, Vol.I, p.140.
8   Barrow, *Earl Howe*, p.225.
9   Marcus, *Age of Nelson*, p.32.
10 A.T. Mahan, *The Influence of Sea Power upon the French Revolution and Empire* (London: Sampson Low, Marston and Co., 1893), Vol.I, p.126.
11 Oliver Warner, *The Glorious First of June* (London: Batsford, 1961), p.29.
12 Duffy, 'Grain Convoy', pp.106-107.

It is not apparent to which orders he is referring; the Admiralty instruction of 17 April made no such reference. Other contributors to *The Glorious First of June*, edited by Michael Duffy and Roger Morriss, take a similar view; the book contains a letter of Lieutenant Rowland Bevan, Second Lieutenant of the *Brunswick*, to a Mr T. Morgan, who wrote that after finding the French in port on 5 May, 'we them stood to the westward after our convoy'.[13]

All of this would seem conclusive, but it does not explain why Howe, leaving no one to watch Brest, and with no further useful intelligence, should then potter about the Bay of Biscay in the vague hope of Vanstabel running into his arms. An entirely different account of Howe's proceedings is provided by his most recent biographer, David Syrett:

> On 6 May the wind changed to the north-west and for several days continued to blow from the west and north-west. The Channel Fleet, to gain sea room, tacked to the northward. It was Howe's intention to return southward with the Channel Fleet and to take station off Ushant as soon as the wind and the weather would permit.[14]

Sam Willis, the most recent historian of the battle, would appear to agree with this:

> On 21 May, however, Howe was forced off station by prolonged westerly winds that threatened to drive his fleet onto the rocks protecting the approaches to Brest like sharpened stakes around a castle. Howe fled to the safety of the open sea leaving the way clear for Villaret who, now aware that the British main fleet was far out at sea, had no choice but to make sail.[15]

The confusion as to dates may arise from a passage by Christopher Ware in his 'The British Strategic Perspective' in *The Glorious First of June*, in which he wrote that 'on the 21 May the British fleet made some progress northward and stretched to the west; on the 22 May the wind drove them southward for which Howe has been much criticised'.[16]

One contemporary account would seem to support the view that it was a change in the wind rather than his choice that led to Howe's departure from Brest; Collingwood, in a letter to his father-in law on June 5, wrote: 'Unsettled weather, and the wind hanging to the north-eastward, set us to the southward, so that it

13   Duffy, 'Grain Convoy', p.93.
14   Syrett, *Lord Howe*, p.130.
15   Willis, *Glorious First of June*, p.121.
16   Duffy, 'Grain Convoy', p.33.

was fourteen days before we got off Brest again, and then found that the enemy's fleet was gone'.[17]

The proposition that Howe's departure from his station off Ushant was involuntary does seem to be quite persuasive, since the alternative explanation, that he ineffectually wandered about the Bay of Biscay, appears unlikely. At all events, by 19 May, having returned to his station off Brest, Howe was able to discover that Villaret-Joyeuse had indeed put to sea. In fact, it appears that the two fleets had unknowingly passed each other in a dense fog.[18]

That night Howe at last got some information about French movements. On May 15 while on his patrol line Montagu encountered and captured the 20 gun sloop *Maire-Guitton* which was on its way back to Brest with ten Channel Islands merchant vessels taken by Nielly's squadron from a Newfoundland convoy escorted by the frigate *Castor*, which was also taken. The examination of prisoners elicited the fact that Nielly, who was cruising between latitudes 45 and 48 North and two degrees east or west of the longitude of Tenerife (16 40 West), had still not met Vanstabel as recently as 12 May. This suggested that Vanstabel was still to the westward, but that Nielly would meet him before he reached Montagu's patrol line; the combined French force would then outnumber Montagu. Montagu sent off the frigate *Venus* to find Howe and report this news, while he moved his patrol line somewhat to the northward parallel to what he understood was Nielly's cruise line.

Now that he was aware that Villaret-Joyeuse was at sea, it seemed to Howe that there was a serious risk of Montagu running into all three of the French forces, and he sailed to the south west to support him. En route, however, he picked up further information when encountering a number of ships taken by the French fleet from a Dutch convoy, and received information that Villaret-Joyeuse was not far away to the west. he therefore altered course to follow, burning the recaptured prizes; he was not prepared to spare prize crews to take them back to port.

Montagu, meanwhile, remained on his patrol line several days longer than ordered in the hope of meeting Vanstabel; on 23 May one of his frigates gained information from another Dutch prize that Villaret-Joyeuse had sortied with 27 ships of the line and 8 frigates. In the light of this, it seemed to Montagu that a British concentration was essential, and he set off for the Ushant rendezvous. Before he got there, further recaptures told him that Howe had gone to the west, evidently in search of the French fleet. Turning over in his mind his next step, he concluded that, having missed Howe, he should comply with his fall back orders

---

17   Oliver Warner, *The Life and Letters of Vice Admiral Lord Collingwood* (Oxford: Oxford University Press, 1968), p.44.

18   Warner, *Glorious First of June*, p.29.

and return to Plymouth to replenish his ships. He arrived back on 31 May and reported to the Admiralty.[19]

While all this had been going on, Villaret-Joyeuse had been looking for Nielly. On 19 May he found the 74 gun *Patriote* which had become detached from Nielly's squadron, apparently due to poor seamanship. Since the *Patriote* soon afterwards collided with the corvette *Mutine* it seems likely that this was the case; perhaps, however, it was due to extensive sickness, since the *Patriote* repeatedly signalled Villaret-Joyeuse's flagship for supplies of medicine.[20]

By now, both main fleets were sailing westwards out into the Atlantic. Howe's course was taking him to the south of the course of the French. At noon on 24 May, the two fleets were closer than they realised; by that time Villaret-Joyeuse had come about and was slowly sailing eastwards. Next day Howe encountered, captured and burnt two French corvettes. Howe was not unaware of the feelings of his younger officers as they watched this spectacle, saying to them: 'It must be very unpleasant for you gentlemen to see your promotions burnt: but I shall shortly be able to make you amends for it'. He was still unwilling to deplete his ships' companies to provide prize crews. On 26 May Howe tacked, and steered north before, at about 9.00 am on the following day, he altered course to the eastward, so that he was virtually following the track of the French fleet.

The two fleets were now closing, and at about 6.00 am on 28 May the frigate *Phaeton* signalled that a strange fleet was in sight. Soon after this, Lieutenant Edward Codrington, Howe's flag lieutenant, who had gone to the masthead of the flagship *Queen Charlotte*, could see the fleet for himself about ten miles off. Villaret-Joyeuse, being to windward, had the advantage of the weather gauge. Howe, at 8.25 am, signalled to Rear Admiral Pasley, in the *Bellerophon*, to reconnoitre. Supported by the other three ships of Pasley's flying squadron, the *Bellerophon* inched ahead of the main fleet and towards what gradually became clear was the French fleet. At 11.13 Howe signalled: 'The people may have time to dine'. As the day wore on, the weather began to deteriorate, with gale force winds and rain sweeping across the two fleets. As the gap between them gradually closed, Howe hoisted signal number 29, 'To attack or harass the rear of the enemy... to bring on a general action,' and this was what Pasley proceeded to do. At approaching 2.00 that afternoon, Howe signalled for the fleet to 'take suitable stations for mutual support and engage the enemy as arriving up in succession'.[21]

While this was going on, Villaret-Joyeuse was endeavouring to get his fleet into line. Now that he was in contact with Howe's fleet, his first concern was to lead it away from what he presumed would be the track of the convoy, and once his ships were in some sort of a line he altered course to edge away from the British.

19 Duffy, 'Grain Convoy', pp.106-108.
20 Willis, *Glorious First of June*, p.131.
21 Warner, *Glorious First of June*, pp.168-171.

During the course of the afternoon, in the difficult weather conditions which now prevailed, Pasley and the leading British ships gradually got within range of the rearmost French ships. With the *Bellerophon* were the *Russell, Thunderer* and *Marlborough*, followed by the *Audacious* and *Leviathan*. At 2.30 the *Russell*, somewhat to windward of the rest, opened fire on the rear of the French line as it tacked; the French replied. While the rest of the Channel Fleet tacked, the *Russell, Thunderer* and *Marlborough*, with attendant frigates held on. Just after 5.00 pm the three decker *Révolutionnaire* dropped back to engage the British, and opened fire on the *Bellerophon*. Pasley wrote later:

> On that day, and for some days before, the *Bellerophon* was the worst-sailing ship of the flying squadron. Yet by embracing the moment for tacking after the enemy, she was enabled to bring them to action, with which she was engaged alone more than an hour and a half.[22]

During this engagement with the *Revolutionaire* the *Bellerophon* suffered considerable damage, and Howe ordered the *Russell, Audacious* and *Marlborough* to her assistance. But before they could all come up, however, Pasley was obliged to turn away, the *Bellerophon* having been badly damaged, her main mast likely to go over the side. By 8.00 pm the *Audacious,* at a range of 100 yards, was closely engaged with the French three decker, both giving and receiving considerable punishment in a contest that went on for nearly two hours. As darkness fell the two ships came close together:

> The *Audacious* and *Révolutionnaire* now became so closely engaged, and the latter so disabled in her masts and rigging, that it was with difficulty the former could prevent her huge opponent from falling on board of her. Towards 10.00 the *Révolutionnaire* having, besides the loss of her mizenmast, had her fore and main yards and maintopsail yard shot away, dropped across the hawse of the *Audacious*; but the latter quickly extricated herself, and the French ship, with her foretopsail full, but, owing to the sheets having been shot away, still flying, directed her course to leeward.[23]

Casualties aboard the *Audacious* were by no means as heavy as aboard the *Revlutionnaire*, which had suffered some 400 men killed and wounded; but the damage to the masts and rigging of the *Audacious* had been so serious that, as her log recorded, she had become 'entirely ungovernable,' and quite unable to make a prize of the *Révolutionnaire*.

---

22 Quoted David Cordingley, *Billy Ruffian* (London: Bloomsbury, 2008), pp.74-75.
23 James, Naval History, Vol.I, p.147.

Captain Albemarle Bertie, of the *Thunderer*, was uncertain whether the French three decker had struck her colours, and hailed William Parker, the captain of the *Audacious to* ask if this was so; Parker replied he did not know, so Bertie sailed up close to the *Révolutionnaire*. In reply to his hail, the French captain said he had struck, and Bertie went on his way.[24] Neither he, nor Captain Berkely of the *Marlborough* took possession of the Frenchman, however, while Parker was unaware that everyone else thought that he had accepted the surrender of the *Révolutionnaire*. As a result, the French vessel drifted helplessly until on 30 May she was rescued by the *Audacieux*, out of Nielly's squadron which had by then arrived, and towed back to Rochefort. The *Audacious*, meanwhile after enduring an attack from the French frigate *Bellone*, and from two of Nielly's ships of the line, but having effected some basic repairs, found that she could only run before the wind, so made her way back to Plymouth, arriving there on 3 June. On her way she passed the dismasted *Révolutionnaire* awaiting rescue.

During the night of 28/29 May, the two fleets sailed on parallel courses south-east by east, about three miles apart, in a south-south-west wind. The French remained to windward. Howe decided to make another attack on the rear of the French line, and at 6.00 am on 29 May ordered the ships of the Channel Fleet to tack in succession. Villaret-Joyeuse at once realised Howe's intention, and he ordered his ships to wear in succession and run down the lee side of his line in the opposite direction. There was some distant gunfire between the British van and the French rear, but by the time these manoeuvres had been carried out, the fleets were still steering parallel courses, but now closer together. Further broadsides were exchanged. Howe's intention was to try to get the weather gauge, and at 11.30 am he ordered the fleet to tack in succession, intending to break through the enemy's line. It then seemed to him premature, so he cancelled the order, only to repeat it at 1.15 pm. In his subsequent report of the battle Howe noted that the smoke and confusion made it unclear at first how far his intended manoeuvre had been carried out:

> It could not be for some time seen, through the fire from the two fleets in the van, to what extent that signal was complied with. But as the smoke at intervals dispersed, it was observed that the *Caesar*, the leading ship of the British van, after being about on the starboard tack, and come abreast of the *Queen Charlotte*, had not kept to the wind; and that the appointed movement would consequently be liable to fail of the purposed effect. The *Queen Charlotte* was therefore immediately tacked; and, followed by the *Bellerophon*, her second astern (and soon after joined by the *Leviathan*)

passed through in action between the fifth and sixth ships in the rear of the enemy's line.[25]

The *Queen Charlotte* had passed through the French line astern of the *Eole*; the *Bellerophon* in her turn went through ahead of the *Terrible*, while the *Leviathan* passed astern of that ship and immediately ahead of the *Tyrannicide*. This ship and the *Indomptable* were the last two ships in the French line and having already suffered serious damage were somewhat to leeward of the rest. Once through the line, *Queen Charlotte* concentrated her fire on the *Terrible*. The engagement continued at close quarters and in the confusion it was hard to see friend from foe. Captain Hope of the *Bellerophon* wrote: 'In passing we brought down a ship's topmasts and in the heat of the action it was English. We was all firing thro' one another'.[26]

The *Leviathan* had suffered particularly heavily, and, in spite of also having been seriously damaged, the *Queen Charlotte* came round to her assistance. Meanwhile as the rest of the British fleet came up, the detached *Tyrannicide* and *Indomptable* were subjected to a heavy fire. Seeing this, Villaret-Joyeuse turned his fleet to rescue them, as Collingwood, in the *Barfleur*, described in a letter to his father in law Sir Edward Blackett:

> The French made a good manoeuvre by which they covered the ships we bore hard on, and made a bold push at the *Queen* and the *Invincible,* two of ours that had suffered. Admiral Graves wore, and we after him, closing with the enemy's van, and turning them to leeward of the disabled *Queen*, so that she did not receive a shot from them. Foiled in this attempt, they bore away to repair their ships, three of which were quite like wrecks. It was then too late to do anything decisive, and the various movements we had made, had put us out of order.[27]

One British ship, the *Defence*, commanded by Captain James Gambier, attempted to tack but, failing, was obliged to wear, and nearly collided with another British ship, before being caught in stays and then remaining motionless under the fire of a French three decker. Midshipman Dillon described the scene on the *Defence's* quarter deck:

> Presently one of his shot struck the upper part of the Quarter Deck bulwark, on the larboard side, killed one man and wounded nine. One

25 Edward Hughes (ed.), *The Private Correspondence of Admiral Lord Collingwood* (London: Navy Record Society, 1957), p.47.
26 Cordingley, *Billy Ruffian*, p.77.
27 Warner, *Glorious First of June*, pp.168-171.

or two shots passed so close to the Captain that I thought he was hit. He clapped both hands upon his thighs with some emotion; then, recovering himself, he took out of his pocket a piece of biscuit, and began eating it as if nothing had happened. He had evidently been shook by the wind of the shot. He had on a cocked hat, and kept walking the deck, cheering up the seamen with the greatest coolness.[28]

Dillon recorded the surprise felt by those aboard the *Defence* that, having gained the windward gauge, Howe did not resume the attack on the evening of 29 May. Collingwood, as noted above, thought it far too late to achieve anything, and that was Howe's own view, as Edward Codrington recorded. What struck him about Howe's decision not to reengage was 'not his readiness to engage the enemy, but his cool determination in omitting to do so on the evening of 29th May, thereby running the risk of letting him escape in order to ensure the right conduct of the fleet'.[29]

Aboard the *Queen Charlotte*, one of the casualties was her second captain, Sir Andrew Snape Douglas, who was a victim of friendly fire. The *Gibraltar,* which had not broken through the French line, fired on the flagship from the other side of the French fleet, and Douglas was among those injured. After the battle Codrington, speaking to a Lieutenant Lloyd in the *Gibraltar*, demanded to know why that ship had engaged the *Queen Charlotte*. Lloyd told him that the *Gibraltar's* Captain Mackenzie was 'about the stupidest man possible,' and had entirely ignored the meaning of the flagship's signals.[30]

Determined to wait until the following day to renew the action, Howe began to get his ships into line, remaining to windward of the French so that he retained the initiative when Villaret-Joyeuse, having successfully protected his damaged ships, wore round and stood on the port tack, Howe followed suit, and both fleets set about effecting repairs to the damage sustained. Of the British fleet, only a few had suffered damage to their hull; the *Caesar* had had two 24-pounders explode, and was leaky from shot holes; the *Russell* was also taking water from shot holes; the *Queen's* hull was knocked about, but above the waterline; and the *Ramillies* had had one gun dismounted. All four of these had suffered damage to main sails and rigging, as had at least seven others; in some cases this was serious. Of the French fleet, no less than thirteen had been dismasted or had suffered heavy damage to sails, yards and rigging.

28   Michael Lewis, (ed.), *A Narrative of My Professional Adventures by Vice Admiral Sir William Dillon* (London: Navy Records Society, 1958), pp.124-125.
29   Quoted Warner, *Glorious First of June*, p.45.
30   Warner, *Glorious First of June*, p.50.

Total British casualties during the day's fighting amounted to 67 killed and 128 wounded.[31]

Thus far Villaret-Joyeuse had achieved his purpose. He had focused Howe's attention on his fleet rather than on Vanstabel's convoy, and his intention was to continue to follow the same policy. He had, of course, now lost the weather gauge, which meant that Howe could choose his moment to attack; but given that he was prepared to face this, rather than let Howe go off after the convoy, the loss of the weather gauge was not as serious as it might have been. In deciding not to renew the attack that night, Howe was able to assume that the French would still be prepared to accept battle in the following days; and although he may have considered that the reason for this was to keep him from the convoy, the French fleet seemed now his only concern. That night the two fleets remained only a few miles apart with the French bearing north west from the British; and that night, a thick fog came down. Next morning at about 9.00 am it cleared momentarily, and the two fleets could see each other. The French were on the starboard tack, but when contact was made hauled round to the port tack. Howe signalled for line ahead; the *Invincible* reported that she had sprung a mast, and he ordered that she leave the line and accept a tow from one of the frigates.[32] At 10.00 am Howe ordered that the fleet form two columns, the starboard of which was, by his next signal, to form on the *Queen Charlotte*; which led towards the enemy. At 10.30 am he asked all ships if they were in a condition to renew the action, and all save the *Caesar* confirmed that they were. He next ordered that the fleet tack in succession to port; and then the fog came down again, so thick that not only did he entirely lose sight of the French, but that for the rest of the day the British ships could scarcely even see those ahead or astern.

At some point Nielly, with three ships of the line, joined Villaret-Joyeuse (the *Patriote* and *Républicain* had arrived earlier); the *Indomptable* was sent back to Brest under escort of the *Mont Blanc*; and the French continued with their repair work, not without success. He was also reinforced by a further 74, the *Trente-et-un Mai* (Captain Honoré Ganteaume), which had not started with the rest of the squadron from Cancale. All this meant that Villaret-Joyeuse now had 26 ships of the line more or less fit for battle (the *Tyrannicide* was under tow). This, as it happened, was now the same number as Howe.

The fog did not lift again. Such contact as Howe could make with his fleet was by signals communicated through his frigates. By 7.43 pm all he could do was to order the fleet to close around the flagship. During the night he knew nothing of the whereabouts of his ships, and as dawn broke could see only two of them. He turned to the frigates to round up his battle fleet. By 9.00 am the *Latona* reported that the fleet bore east by south, on the opposite course to that of the *Queen*

31 James, *Naval History*, Vol.I, p.159.
32 James, *Naval History*, Vol.I, p.159.

Charlotte, and it was not until 1.00 pm that the frigate *Pegasus* was able to confirm that the fleet was now in company. At 1.45 the French were sighted again as the fog began rapidly to clear, and soon after 5.00.pm Howe ordered the fleet to engage the enemy, each ship directed to the corresponding vessel in the French line. It was soon evident to him, however, that it would be well into the evening before he could bring on a general action. He did not want to fight a night action, so just after 7.00 pm he hauled to the wind on the port tack, and resolved to wait for dawn. In order to keep *au fait* with what Villaret-Joyeuse was doing, he stationed the frigates *Phaeton* and *Latona* about a mile to leeward of the fleet. He certainly did not intend to lose the weather gauge. At the same time, he was not going to let the French get too far away, and the fleet was ordered to make sail accordingly.

6

The Glorious First of June

At dawn on Sunday, 1 June, the two fleets were some six miles apart, the French being on the starboard bow of the British, in line of battle on the port tack. The wind was now a moderate breeze from the south by west, and the sea was relatively calm. In the next few hours Howe adjusted the sailing order of his fleet. Pasley, with the five ships of the First Division of the van squadron, led the line; the *Caesar* was still the foremost ship. The Second Division of eight ships was headed by Graves, with his flag in the *Royal Sovereign*. The First Division of the centre squadron consisted of only the *Gibraltar* and the *Queen Charlotte*; the Second Division commanded by Rear Admiral Gardner, consisted of four ships. Finally, the rear squadron was led by the *Ramillies*, the lead ship of the First Division of four ships; Sir Alexander Hood, in the *Royal George*, was third in line. The Second Division of three ships was headed by the *Majestic*.

Midshipman Dillon, aboard the *Defence*, supposed that the devout Captain Gambier would on this day not have much time for prayers, 'as the work in hand would be of a very different nature'.

> Lord Howe drew up the fleet in capital order. He made several changes in the disposition of the ships, to render every part of his line equal. The *Defence* was the seventh ship in the van. When his Lordship had completed his arrangements for attacking the enemy, he made the signal for the different divisions, that is the van, centre and rear, to engage the opposite divisions of the French: then for each ship in the English line to pass through the enemy and attack his opponent to leeward. Next, the fleet was hove to, that the crews might have their breakfasts. This was going to work in a regular methodical manner. His Lordship knew that John Bull did not like fighting with an empty stomach; but it was a sorry meal, scarcely deserving the name.[1]

1   Lewis (ed.), *Sir William Dillon*, Vol.I, pp.127-128.

Prevailing Wind

British
French

Trajan (74)

Éole (74)

America (74)

Téméraire (74)

Terrible (110) [Bouvet]

Impétueux (74)

Mucius (74)

Tourville (74)

Gasparin (74)

Convention (74)

Caesar (80)

Trente-et-Un Mai (74)

[Pasley] Bellerophon (74)

Tyrannicide (74)

Leviathan (74)

Juste (80)

Russell (74)

Montagne (120) [Villaret-Joyeuse]

[Graves] Royal Sovereign (100)

Jacobin (80)

Marlborough (74)

Achille (74)

Defence (74)

Vengeur (74)

[Caldwell] Impregnable (98)

Patriote (74)

Tremendous (74)

Northumberland (74)

[Bowyer] Barfleur (98)

Entreprenant (74)

Invincible (74)

Jemmappes (74)

Culloden (74)

Neptune (74)

Gibraltar (80)

Pelletier (74)

[Howe] Queen Charlotte (100)

Républicain (110) [Nielly]

Brunswick (74)

Sans Pareil (80)

Valiant (74)

Scipion (74)

Orion (74)

[Gardner] Queen (98)

Ramillies (74)

Alfred (74)

Montagu (74)

[A. Hood] Royal George (100)

Majestic (74)

Glory (98)

Thunderer (74)

Map 4 The Glorious 1st of June, 1794.

The British fleet, after having paused for breakfast, sailed down towards the French making about five knots. These preparatory movements were being conducted at a very stately pace. Aboard the *Sans Pareil* Captain Thomas Troubridge, who had been captured with his frigate the *Castor,* responded to gibes about the apparent British hesitancy: 'Wait a little. English sailors never like to fight with empty stomachs; I see the signal flying for all hands to breakfast; after which take my word for it, they will pay you a visit'.[2]

Breakfast completed, at 7.30 Howe ordered General Signal No. 34; 'Having the wind of the enemy, the Admiral means to pass between the ships in the line for engaging them to leeward'. This would bring on a general mêlée, and it was Howe's belief that he would take a prize for every one of his own ships that was able to break through the French line. An hour later, he ordered General Signal No. 36: 'Each ship independently to steer for and engage her opponent in the enemy's line'. That done, he turned to his officers:

> And now, gentlemen, no more book, no more signals. I look to you to do the duty of the *Queen Charlotte* in engaging the French Admiral. I do not wish the ships to be bilge to bilge, but if you can lock the yard arms so much the better, the battle will be sooner decided.[3]

The van of the British fleet was slightly nearer the French line than the following ships as the two fleets came together. Howe may perhaps have thought that it would be the *Queen Charlotte,* as she bore down on the *Montagne,* that would be the first to break through, but it was in fact Gambier's *Defence*, which passed between the *Mucius* and the *Terrible,* respectively seventh and eighth in the French line. The first shots had been fired at 9.24 am, when the French van opened fire at long range, concentrating on the *Defence*, already closest to the French. Howe's resolution to make no more signals did not last long; he was soon signalling to the *Gibraltar, Culloden* and *Brunswick* to make more sail. He was even more concerned to see both the *Russell* (fourth in line) and the *Caesar* had their maintop sails aback to check their speed, even though neither was yet within range. It was the latter, in the van, that most occupied Howe's attention. Instead of attempting to pass through the French line, Molloy, her captain, had decided to engage to windward.

Howe had not wanted the *Caesar* to lead the line. He was seriously disapproving of Molloy's conduct during the earlier contacts with the French fleet, but had allowed himself to be persuaded by Sir Roger Curtis to let Molloy continue to head the van of the fleet. Seeing Molloy's failure even to attempt to break the French line

2   Barrow, *Earl Howe*, p.278.
3   Quoted Willis, *Glorious First of June*, pp.187-188.

he said, meaningly: 'Look, Curtis, there goes your friend! Who is mistaken now?'[4] In Molloy's defence, which was put forward at his subsequent court-martial, signal No. 34 was not absolutely binding, containing the following qualifying words:

> The different captains and commanders, not being able to effect the speci-fied intention in either case (the signal applying to the passage through a line to windward or to leeward), are at liberty to act as circumstances require.[5]

Molloy's belief was that to get under the stern of the leading enemy ship he would have had so much way on the *Caesar* that she would have shot ahead, and thus not be able to do much damage. When Pasley signalled him to comply with Howe's order, it was found that a shot had damaged the *Caesar's* rudder preventing her from wearing. In the meantime, under fire from several French ships, the *Caesar* had had seven of her guns disabled and another which burst, and had lost 14 men killed and 52 wounded. The *Bellerophon*, when bearing down on the enemy line, had been fired on by three French ships, and was quite seriously damaged; and at 10.50 am a shot struck Pasley, losing him his leg. Captain Hope was obliged to call upon the frigates for assistance, to which the *Latona* responded.

As the *Defence* neared the French line, Gambier tried to check her speed, first by taking in his main topgallant sail, and then by bracing back the mizzen topsail; but this spilled more wind into the maintop sail, and tended to accelerate the vessel. Twysden, the First Lieutenant, pointed this out; but Gambier, reluctant to give the impression that he was not complying with Howe's signal, refused to reduce sail, and the *Defence* went on. Dillon described how she approached the French line:

> Up went their Lower Deck ports, out came the guns, and the fire on us commenced from several of the enemy's van ships…We retained our fire till in the act of passing under the Frenchman's stern, then, throwing all our topsails aback, luffed up and poured in a most destructive broad-side. We heard most distinctly our shot striking the hull of the enemy. The carved work over his stern was shattered to pieces. Then, ranging up alongside of him within half pistol shot distance, our fire was kept up with the most determined spirit.[6]

As the action continued, however, the *Defence* lost both her mainmast and her mizzenmast, and she too was obliged to signal for assistance. By 1.00 pm the

4   William Clowes, *The Royal Navy: A History from the Earliest Times to 1900* (London: Sampson Low, Marston and Co., 1899), Vol.IV, p.228n.
5   James, *Naval History*, Vol.I, p.129.
6   Lewis (ed.), *Sir William Dillon*, Vol.I, p 129.

Defence, which had lost sixteen men killed and 34 wounded, was under tow from the frigate *Phaeton.*

Further down the line, the ships immediately ahead of the *Queen Charlotte* had not been so heavily engaged, although aboard the *Barfleur* Rear Admiral Bowyer was among those wounded; she lost a total of nine killed and 25 wounded. The flagship, meanwhile, had pressed on for the French line; Howe was keen, if he could, to be the first British ship to pass through. Coming under fire from the *Vengeur,* she did not respond, and was soon abreast of the *Achille,* the next ahead, which opened fire on her. The *Queen Charlotte* responded at 9.52 am, though Howe ordered that her fire be confined to the third and quarter decks. Hearing this, the officers on the lower gun decks thought that they were expected to join in. As the *Queen Charlotte* arrived on the *Montagne*'s quarter, she put up her helm to pass astern of the French flagship, when the following French ship intervened:

> The *Jacobin* was seen stretching ahead under the *Montagne*'s lee, as if afraid to encounter the broadside, which the *Charlotte,* in her passage through the line, would discharge into her bows. Passing close under the stern of the *Montagne,* so close that the fly of the French ensign, as it waved at her flagstaff, brushed the main and mizzen shrouds of the *Queen Charlotte,* the latter poured into the three decker a tremendous broadside.[7]

The *Jacobin,* running on, was almost abreast of the *Montagne,* which was where Howe had intended to be, and he did not think that there was sufficient room to squeeze between them. James Bowen, however, the flagship's master, was confident, saying 'My Lord, the *Queen Charlotte* will make room for herself'; and she did, engaging the *Montagne* broadside to broadside. As she broke through the line, however, she lost first her fore and then her main topmasts.

In the course of these manoeuvres the *Montagne* had suffered fearfully, her stern frame and starboard quarter having been badly shattered. She had sustained losses of more than 100 killed and nearly 200 wounded, but Villaret-Joyeuse, setting more sail, was able to range ahead of the *Queen Charlotte* to avoid further damage. The *Jacobin* also steered clear, leaving the British flagship to engage the *Juste* which had already been engaged by the *Invincible.* It seemed to Howe that the movements of the *Montagne* and the *Jacobin* might indicate that the French were trying to get away, and at 10.13 am he made the signal for a general chase. The *Queen Charlotte* remained in action against the *Juste*: the latter was also engaged with the *Invincible* on her windward side, and soon lost first her foremast and then her mainmast and mizzenmast as well. Although Howe was anxious to go forward to seek a fresh opponent, the *Queen Charlotte,* having already lost her main topmast,

7   James, *Naval History,* Vol.I, p.164.

The celebrated victory obtained by the British Fleet under the command of Earl Howe, over the French Fleet on the Glorious first of June 1794'. Contemporary engraving depicting Howe directing the action from the quarterdeck of the *Queen Charlotte*. (Anne S.K. Brown Collection)

could barely keep steerage way. Aboard the *Juste*, meanwhile, a spritsail had been hoisted in an attempt to get clear; wearing round, having been lost sight of in the smoke, she was able to deliver a broadside into the *Queen Charlotte*'s stern. Into the confused situation that had developed around the British flagship, the three decker *Républicain* now arrived; but just as she was about to deliver a broadside to the *Queen Charlotte*'s stern, she lost her main and mizzen masts.[8]

The flagship of Rear Admiral Gardner, the *Queen,* had been four ships astern of Howe's flagship. Her opponent should strictly have been the *Northumberland*, but this ship was drawing rapidly ahead, so the *Queen* concentrated her fire on the *Jemappes*, on which she inflicted considerable damage. In her turn, however, she also suffered severely; at about 11.00 am her mainmast went over the side, damaging her mizzenmast and, in its fall, carrying away part of the poop and the quarterdeck bulwark. Fifteen minutes later the mainmast of the *Jemappes* came down, followed by her foremast. Her crew would have surrendered; but her captain would have none of it, and the *Queen* was too much damaged to take possession of her. By 12.30 pm the *Queen*'s crew had more or less got her manageable, only to find, as the smoke cleared, a dozen French ships steering towards her.

These were headed by the *Montagne*, Villaret-Joyeuse having managed to collect them together. Neither the *Montagne* nor the next ship astern fired on the *Queen*; but all the rest did as they sailed past her, causing Howe to cry out to Sir Roger Curtis: 'Go down to the *Queen*, Sir; go down to the *Queen*'. The sight of the *Queen Charlotte*, and several ships behind her, heading towards the *Queen* was enough to discourage the French from pursuing their attack on her, and Villaret-Joyeuse now concentrated on seeing what he could do to assist his dismasted and damaged ships.

Some were beyond his aid. One of these was the *Vengeur,* which had been heavily engaged with the *Brunswick* since the latter had tried to force her way through the French line. The two ships became locked together when the three starboard anchors of the *Brunswick* became locked with the fore channels and fore shrouds of the *Vengeur*. The *Brunswick*'s master asked Captain Harvey if he should cut her clear; Harvey's reply was: 'No, we have got her and we will keep her'. A fierce engagement, at point blank range, ensued as the two ships swung out of line and, still locked together, and with their yards square, headed northward before the wind. Heavy casualties were sustained on both sides, one of whom was Harvey. At 11.00 am another ship bore down on the *Brunswick*'s part quarter, apparently with the intention of boarding her; this was the *Achille*, which had already lost her main and mizzen masts. Five or six rounds from the *Brunswick*'s after guns brought down the *Achille*'s foremast, and she struck her colours. There was nothing that

8   James, *Naval History*, Vol.I, p.167.

the *Brunswick* could do to take possession of her and, finding that no one else did, the *Achille* rehoisted her colours and, setting her spritsail, attempted to escape.[9]

Lieutenant Bevan described the *Brunswick*'s situation alongside the *Vengeur*, their guns running at times into each other's ports:

> We lay in this situation until one o'clock when she struck to us, our mizzen mast being gone, our other masts shot to pieces, not a boat that would swim. In this situation we were left to the mercy of the sea. On examining the ship we found we had lost 10 of our lower deck ports, 2 guns dismounted and the ship totally disabled. We had 40 men killed and 113 wounded. Our brave captain lost his right arm. I had the misfortune to be wounded in my left eye, my breast and both legs. The former wounds are much better, but my left leg still remains in a state of uncertainty whether I shall lose it or not.[10]

Bevan kept his leg; but sadly Captain Harvey, who had lost an arm, died of his wounds.

When the two ships finally separated, both were almost totally wrecked. The *Brunswick*, with what sail she could make, could do no more than head northward in the hope that she would not be fallen upon by any other French ship. On her way, she passed the dismasted *Jemappes*. The *Vengeur*, meanwhile, which had lost both her foremast and her mainmast, was rolling in the heavy swell, her ports in the water, and she was soon in a sinking condition. The *Culloden* and the *Alfred* made their way towards her to secure the prize; but it was soon clear that she would not survive, and the two ships and a cutter began to take off her crew. Over 500 were rescued, but many went down with the ship. The sinking of a ship of the line solely by gunfire in this way was an event unique in British and French naval history.[11] It was recorded that as she went down, members of her crew shouted 'Vive la nation! Vive la republique!' James, rather churlishly, believes that these were men 'who had flown to the spirit room for relief'. It was, however an incident of which the French government took full propaganda advantage. Among the survivors of the *Vengeur* were her captain, Jean-Francois Renaudin, and his twelve year old son; until they were reunited at Portsmouth, each thought the other had perished.[12] Meanwhile the *Achille*, endeavouring to escape with one small sail hoisted, was taken by the *Ramillies*.

Sir Alexander Hood, with the rear squadron, closed the French line somewhat later, but made at once to break the line in the *Royal George*. He opened fire at 9.38

---

9   James, *Naval History*, Vol.I, p.179.
10   Duffy and Morriss, *Glorious First of June*, p.94.
11   Willis, *Glorious First of June*, p.202.
12   James, *Naval History*, Vol.I, p.183.

am on both the *Sans Pareil* and the *Républicain* and soon, firing broadsides on both sides, passed between them. The rest of his squadron, including the *Ramillies* and the *Alfred*, sustained little or no damage, and neither did their scheduled opponents, the *Pelletier* and the *Entreprenant*. The *Montagne* had a brisk engagement with the *Neptune*, but neither was much damaged. Of the second division, the *Glory*, one of the slowest sailers in the fleet, was the only ship to break the French line. Engaging the *Scipion*, she brought down all three of her masts, at the expense of her own upper masts. She next drew alongside the *Sans Pareil*, who had just lost her foremast and mizzen mast to the fire of the *Royal George*, which had herself lost her foremast and main and mizzen topmasts. Neither the *Glory* nor the *Royal George* were in a state to take possession of any prizes.

Although the intensity of the battle had begun somewhat to slacken by noon, the fleets remained in contact. Villaret-Joyeuse, a realist, concentrated his efforts on rescuing those of his ships that he could assist, abandoning the others. Howe's fleet had effectively isolated seven French ships of the line; others were potentially there for the taking. The *Culloden* and *Thunderer* were in pursuit of two French ships when Howe signalled to them to rejoin the fleet. Schomberg, the captain of the *Culloden*, pointed out that the two ships had not been secured, and Howe reversed his order. The interruption had, however, enabled the French to cover them.

By 6.15 pm Villaret–Joyeuse, having saved four of his dismasted ships, two without any masts save their bowsprits, was out of sight to the northward; he left a frigate to monitor the further proceedings of the British fleet. Howe, meanwhile, concentrated his fleet and began to do what he could to ensure the survival of his own damaged ships and the six prizes he had taken. These were the *América*, *Impetueux, Juste, Achille, Northumberland* and *Sans Pareil,* all 74 gun ships except the *Juste* and the *Sans Pareil*, both of 80 guns. There was a huge amount to do. Of the British fleet, eleven ships had lost masts; these were principally topmasts and topgallant masts, but two ships, the *Marlborough* and the *Defence*, had lost all three masts, while the *Queen* had lost her mainmast as well as her mizzen topmast. All six of the prizes had lost all three lower masts. Of the damaged ships that Villaret-Joyeuse had been able to rescue, he brought home three that had lost all three masts (*Jemappes, Scipion* and *Mucius*), two that had lost mainmasts and mizzenmasts (*Terrible and Républicain*) and two that had lost topgallant masts and probably a topmast (*Trente-et-un Mai* and *Tyrannicide*).[13]

Casualties were high, but much greater on the French side. These were estimated at 3,000 killed and 7,000 wounded. The British losses amounted to 290 killed and 858 wounded. In addition to Captain Harvey, Captain John Hull of the *Queen* died of his wounds, Captain James Montagu of the *Montagu* was killed, and Vice Admiral Graves and Rear Admirals Bowyer and Pasley were among the wounded.

---

13   James, *Naval History*, Vol.I, p.168.

Among the captured French ships, the *Sans Pareil* suffered the heaviest casualties, estimated at 260 killed and 120 wounded.[14]

After five days of manoeuvring and three days of fighting Howe was physically exhausted. His frailty has been blamed by some critics for his failure to finish off the French fleet, allowing Villaret-Joyeuse to get away to safety with most of his battered ships. As it was, it was 3 June before Howe was able to make sail and it took his fleet ten days to sail back to Plymouth, where the news of his victory had already arrived. Villaret-Joyeuse and Nielly had reached Brest two days before this, having en route encountered Montagu's squadron, as described below. Vanstabel brought his convoy safely into Brest on 13 June; on 2 June he had picked up the *Montagnard,* damaged in the earlier fighting, and under tow from a frigate. In case the British had won the battle and were waiting for him off the mouth of the harbour, he came in through the dangerous Passage du Raz to the south, and joined Villaret-Joyeuse next day in Bertheaume Bay.

Meanwhile Montagu, in accordance with his orders, had returned to Plymouth, arriving on 31 May and at once reporting to the Admiralty. On 2 June the Admiralty sent him further orders, which reached him on the morning of 4 June. On the previous day the frigate *Pallas* had arrived in Plymouth, having spoken with the damaged *Audacious* as she made her way home after the action of 28 May, so Montagu now knew that Howe was in contact with the enemy. The *Audacious* dropped anchor in Plymouth Sound that evening, so Montagu was able to get full particulars of the situation out in the Atlantic. Montagu's new orders, which added further ships to his squadron, were explicit and urgent:

> It is of very great importance that you should return to sea as soon as possible with the said ships, and such of those hereafter mentioned as may be ready to accompany you. You are hereby required and directed to put to sea accordingly and proceed with the utmost expedition to his Lordship's rendezvous No. 5, and to continue thereon until further order, or until you receive any instructions from his Lordship, or such certain intelligence of his situation as may enable you to join him, which you are to endeavour to do. If, however, you should receive any well grounded information of the approach of the French convoy which may be daily expected from America and the course they are likely to steer, you will, then, make such a disposition of your squadron as you shall judge most likely to intercept the same.[15]

Interestingly, Chatham sent a private letter to Montagu to accompany these orders, emphasising the importance of Ushant; it offered the best chance of joining Howe,

14 James, *Naval History*, Vol.I, p.169.
15 Morriss (ed.), *Channel Fleet*, p.38.

and if there had been an action, of covering any damaged ships. It also enabled Montagu to watch Brest, to which either the French fleet or the convoy might be heading. As to the latter, his reinforcements would make him stronger than the combined forces of Vanstabel and Nielly, if the latter had joined the convoy.[16] Montagu sailed on 4 June; it is not clear whether new intelligence, sent down by the Admiralty on 3 June, reached him before he put to sea. This came from the owner of a merchant vessel, the *Kelly*, whose captain had sighted a large fleet of 150 sail standing to the south east in a position which suggested that they could not yet have reached France. The information was accompanied by further orders:

> In case on your arrival on the rendezvous No 5 (as directed by our instructions of yesterday's date) you should not have received, or receive, any orders from Earl Howe, or any further well grounded intelligence respecting the above mentioned convoy, you are, in that event, and on being joined by the *Colossus* and *Minotaur*, hereby required and directed immediately to stretch across the Bay with a view of intercepting the said convoy and, in case you should be well informed of its having passed, and there should be no probability of your over taking it, you are to return immediately to the rendezvous No 5.[17]

Montagu reached Ushant on 8 June. He had nine ships of the line and three frigates. Meeting a French squadron of eight ships of the line and four frigates he chased them into Brest, and took up a position west-north-west of Ushant, where his further reinforcements could safely join him. Next morning, Villaret-Joyeuse, returning from the battles with Howe, came in sight, with nineteen ships of the line, three frigates and two smaller vessels. Five of the ships of the line were under tow. Montagu, unable to weather the French with his force due to the poor sailers *Alexander* and *Ganges*, tacked to leeward; this left him between Villaret-Joyeuse and the squadron in Brest, so he edged away southward. He explained later that he intended to act against the French fleet if he got the chance, but 'they kept so closely connected and guarded with so much care their disabled ships that it was not in my power to take any step that was likely to contribute to His Majesty's Service'.[18] Villaret-Joyeuse made a half-hearted attempt to chase Montagu until about 5.00 pm, when he turned back towards Brest. Montagu sought for Howe to the North West, but not finding him assumed he had now entered the Channel. Accordingly, applying the letter of his orders, he returned to Plymouth. When he got back, he took sick leave, striking his flag. He was never employed at sea again, although St Vincent would have done so; apparently George III had effectively black listed

16   Duffy, 'Grain Convoy', p.108.
17   Morriss (ed.), *Channel Fleet*, pp.41-42.
18   Quoted Duffy, 'Grain Convoy', pp 110-111.

Montagu. In the end he accepted the post of Port Admiral at Portsmouth in 1803, serving there for five and a half years.

Howe, in his official reports of the battles, made a thorough mess of things. These reports were crucial in determining the rewards that might be given to those who had earned them. In his first despatch, dated 2 June, which was brought to the Admiralty by Sir Roger Curtis, he named and praised only Curtis, and his second captain Sir Andrew Snape Douglas. Next day he asked all his flag officers and captains for reports, so that he might 'transmit to the Board of Admiralty a just representation of their meritorious conduct'. The flag officers were also to report on the captains in their divisions. Based on these reports, Howe sent a second despatch on 6 June naming the officers 'who have such particular claim to my attention'. These were Graves, Hood, Bowyer, Gardner and Pasley, with thirteen captains and two lieutenants. Howe added, rather feebly, that his selections 'should not be construed to the disadvantage of other Commanders, who may have been equally deserving of the approbation of the Lords Commissioners of the Admiralty,' because he was not able to make 'a particular statement of their merits'. Among those omitted, and who resented their omission, were Rear Admiral Benjamin Caldwell, who endeavoured to correct the record, and Collingwood, who was so extremely angry that when, after the battle of Cape St Vincent in 1797 he was to be awarded a medal, he refused to accept it unless he was given one for the Glorious First of June (which, in the event he was). Graves and Hood were created barons of the Kingdom of Ireland (Hood taking the title of Lord Bridport); the other admirals and Curtis were made baronets, and there were promotions aplenty. When George III came aboard the *Queen Charlotte* on 26 June to present Howe with a diamond hilted sword worth 3,000 guineas, he announced that the named officers would receive gold chains and gold medals. He promised Howe the award of the Garter, but to the admiral's indignation Pitt diverted it to the Duke of Portland for political reasons and Howe had to wait three years before the King conferred the order on him.[19]

Collingwood did not mince his words when writing of the part played by Sir Roger Curtis in the framing of Howe's letters, and the resultant rewards bestowed on those named, writing to Sir Edward Blackett on 30 June:

> Lord Howe is less blamed for his letter than his Captain, who ever has been an artful, seeking creature, whose fawning insinuating manners creeps into the confidence of whoever he attacks, and whose rapacity wou'd grasp all honours and all profits that come within his view. The letter was an attempt upon the credulity of the world to make them believe the

19 Syrett, *Lord Howe*, p 142.

Queen Charlotte, with very little help, defeated the French fleet. It may be considered as a libel on the fleet.[20]

Collingwood had written admiringly of Howe's performance during the battle, remarking that 'he has outdone all opinion that could be formed. The proceedings of the 1st of June were like magic, and could only be effected by skill like his'. Subsequently, however, perhaps as a result of Howe's controversial letters, his opinion of the old admiral deteriorated. On September 1 he complained to Dr Alexander Carlyle of the failure to get the Channel Fleet to sea:

Lord Howe has been at St Helen's (a sort of advanced post) this ten days. Why he does not get to sea I do not know. Any body else at this time of year would find their way down the Channel, but he does everything with great parade... Any dull merchantmen can get down the Channel and yet this fleet of fast sailing ships cannot go because the wind will not admit of their sailing in certain forms. It would be reckoned nonsense in any but his Lordship.[21]

When Spencer became First Lord, Collingwood wrote approvingly of the way he was getting a grip on the management of the Navy; it was, he observed, very much approved:

You perceive that our ships are more at sea, and we have fuller possession of it, than when we moved in more parade. We are out of luck with our prize but I have no regrets on such subjects. I have no ambition to be rich.[22]

The work of the Channel Fleet continued. Because of Howe's concern for the damage that would thereby be inflicted on his ships, no close blockade of Brest was instituted. This did not accord with the views of Sir Charles Middleton, who in June drafted a memorandum covering deployment of practically the whole of the Royal Navy. His recommendations for the Channel Fleet were explicit:

From the decided superiority we have lately gained over the enemy's fleet, and supposing things to continue as they now are, I would propose 32 sail of the line and 12 frigates for this service, accompanied by one fire ship and six brigs or cutters, for the purpose of information. Of this force, I would propose 24 sail of the line and 8 frigates to cruise as constantly

20   Hughes (ed.), *Admiral Lord Collingwood*, p.50.
21   Hughes (ed.), *Admiral Lord Collingwood*, p.57-58.
22   Hughes (ed.), *Admiral Lord Collingwood*, p.69.

as possible off Brest, and 8 sail more and 4 frigates to refit at Plymouth, and rendezvous in summer, when complete, at Torbay, and be there kept in readiness to relieve those whose turn it may be to come into port. The three deckers to be confined, as much as circumstances may permit, to long days and summer cruising. With this force, the port of Brest may be generally blocked up and detachments made after every ship or squadron who may steal out from it or the other ports in the Bay. The squadrons so employed will stand –

3 ships of 100 guns	6 frigates of 38 and 36
5 ships of 90 guns	6 of 28 and 32
24 ships of 74 guns[23]	

In time this would become more or less the accepted wisdom of how to deal with Brest and the French fleet; but for the moment the opinion of Howe (which was also that of Hood, now his second in command) prevailed, and the plans for the operations during the rest of 1794 were drawn up accordingly. Howe was told on August 5 that a Portuguese squadron had arrived and would be put under his command. He was not enthusiastic, proposing to use them, in the event of a general engagement, as a detached squadron operating 'against the unoccupied ships of the enemy's rear or to attack any of their separated ships as circumstances render advisable'. As in the past, Howe's instructions gave him a wide discretion. He was to proceed to Ushant and then distribute his forces as he should judge most proper 'for the purpose of affording protection to the trade of His Majesty's subjects and Allies'.[24]

On 3 September Howe sailed from St Helens, arriving off Start Point the following evening. The weather deteriorated sharply, with thick fog and rain; at 4.00 am on 5 September the Channel Fleet ran into an East India convoy heading up Channel. As the convoy passed through the fleet, one East Indiaman, the *Royal Charlotte*, rammed the *Queen*, while another, the *Triton*, lost her masts when she ran into the frigate *Latona*. Several other ships were also damaged, and with an expectation of even worse weather, Howe anchored in Torbay, in order to repair his ships before sailing for Ushant. The French fleet was in Brest and for the next few days he remained off Ushant until he learned that two West Indian convoys had now arrived in the Channel. By then, with the wind in the west in storm force, Howe could not proceed into the Atlantic to a point where any enemy ships might be stationed to try and intercept the convoys; and on 20 September he returned to Torbay. Two Portuguese and four British ships of the line had suffered storm

---

23 Morriss (ed.), *Channel Fleet*, p.47.
24 Syrett, *Lord Howe*, p.142.

damage.[25] Howe's experiences with the Portuguese ships convinced him that it was not helpful for the Portuguese squadron to operate with the Channel Fleet, and it did not do so again.

The next cruise of the Channel Fleet, by now depleted by the detachment of seven ships to go to the West Indies, was delayed by bad weather, and it did not get away from Torbay until 21 October. The wind again intervened, changing to the northwest and driving him in storm force gales away from the French coast. Howe was back in Torbay by 31 October. He sailed back and forth to the west of the Scilly Isles for some time; he was out for the whole of November, until a south east wind drove him up Channel and he anchored at St Helens on 29 November.

These cruises had led to a good deal of damage being sustained by the Channel Fleet, a fact to which Howe and Hood could point in their rejection of a close blockade; but it seems that some at any rate of the damage was effectively self inflicted, as Midshipman Dillon noted:

> During the 15 months that I remained in the *Defence*, we lost, by being sprung or carried away, 18 topmasts. Our ships in those days were constantly losing these masts, and it became evident that there was something wrong in the fitting of them. In our ship we had reduced the number of backstays that support these masts, from a desire for neatness. So, as far as the *Defence* was concerned, we had in some measure brought the evil on ourselves.[26]

It was Lord Hugh Seymour who came up with the solution to the problem:

> He suggested the lengthening of the lower masthead, which would house the topmast better; and by lowering the crosstrees of the topmast head, the strain would not bear at the extremity. His plan was put in practice, and the consequence has been that a topmast is scarcely ever carried away, with proper care.[27]

While Howe was at sea with the Channel Fleet, the French had not been entirely idle. In November Nielly sortied from Brest with five 74s (*Marat, Tigre, Droits de l'Homme, Pelletier* and *Jean Bart*) three frigates (*Charente, Fraternité* and *Gentille*) and the corvette *Papillon*. His objective was to intercept the homeward bound Lisbon and Oporto convoy. On 6 November, having missed the convoy, he encountered two British 74s returning to England after having escorted the convoy to a safe latitude. These were the *Alexander* (Captain Richard Bligh)

25   Syrett, *Lord Howe*, p.143.
26   Lewis (ed.), *Sir William Dillon*, Vol.I, p.167.
27   Lewis (ed.), *Sir William Dillon*, Vol.I, p.167.

and the *Canada* (Captain Charles Hamilton), Bligh being the senior officer. The *Alexander* was, as has already been seen, a notoriously slow sailer. The two ships got to within half a mile of the French ships without being able to identify that it was an enemy squadron. At 7.30 am Nielly hoisted British colours, and the *Canada* and *Alexander* did the same; the French then displayed their own colours. It was only then that their identity became apparent. Nielly divided his forces; with two ships and two frigates he pursued the *Canada*, while the rest of his force went after the *Alexander*. Not surprisingly, those in pursuit of the *Alexander* soon came within range, and there was an exchange of gunfire between bow guns and stern chasers. Bligh ordered Hamilton to form ahead for mutual support; but Nielly forced the *Canada* away. Meanwhile the *Alexander* was in close action with the *Jean Bart*, and was getting the best of it until the other two ships closed on her. She fought on until just after 1.00 pm:

> She had her main yard, spanker boom and three topgallant masts shot away, her three lower masts shot through in many places, all the other masts and yards more or less wounded, nearly the whole of the standing and running rigging cut to pieces, her sails torn into ribands, her hull shattered, and on fire in several places and her hold nearly filled with water.[28]

By now Nielly and his other ships had abandoned the pursuit of the *Canada* and had turned to concentrate on the *Alexander*. Bligh saw that further resistance was impossible and struck his colours. The *Alexander*'s casualties amounted to 40 killed and wounded; but she had inflicted very much heavier casualties upon her opponents; these were estimated at a total of 450. During his captivity Bligh was promoted to rear admiral; and when, in the following year after he was exchanged, he was tried by court martial he was, naturally, honourably acquitted.

---

28   James, *Naval History*, Vol.I, p.204.

7

Cornwallis's Retreat

On taking up his post as First Lord on 19 December 1794, Spencer was at once faced with a problem that in various ways was to dog him throughout the early part of his period at the Admiralty. Two days earlier, anticipating his taking office, Howe had written to him to say that his 'increased deafness added to many constitutional infirmities' led him to repeat his request to be relieved from command of the Channel Fleet. This was not good news; replacing him would present serious difficulties, and on Christmas Day Spencer asked the old admiral to come to London from Bath for consultations, since his 'assistance cannot but be considered essentially necessary to the public service'. Howe at once agreed to come as soon as he could, though repeating his desire to be released. Spencer enlisted the services of George III, who agreed on January 6 to write to Howe on the matter, while adding a Royal hint as to how Spencer should proceed:

> I shall not fail to form my letter to prevent his retiring at present and I am certain I can put his continuance at the head of the Channel fleet [sic] in a light that will secure his taking the part which on many accounts I think highly necessary. As soon as I receive his answer I will communicate it to Earl Spencer that he may speak more positively to Lord Bridport, whose conduct will be highly absurd if he refuses to serve, and I confess, however I may think in general well of his nautical abilities, I do not look on them as superior to those of Vice Admiral Cornwallis.[1]

The King's letter did the trick; when Howe came to see him, he agreed to remain in command, although evasive about whether he would be prepared to go to sea in the winter. In his subsequent conversation with the King, he was, however, somewhat obscure about his intentions, as he usually was; the King remarked that he had so 'much reserve that at times envelopes his meaning that it is not at all times

1   Morriss (ed.), *Channel Fleet*, pp.50-53.

easy to bring him to the point.' At any rate, with Howe's acquiescence Bridport agreed to serve as second in command, so that, for the time being, was that.

Meanwhile Sir Sidney Smith in the *Diamond*, one of the frigates under the command of Rear Admiral Sir John Warren, had been looking into Brest. He passed a French ship of the line anchored between Ushant and Brest, which had evidently been damaged during the stormy weather then prevailing. On the morning of 4 January he was able to get into the harbour entrance by pretending to be a French vessel. A French frigate was lying at anchor there, as *The Naval Chronicle* reported:

> The ebb tide making down, before it was daylight, Sir Sidney Smith was obliged to keep under sail, to prevent his getting to leeward, or creating suspicion; and he continued to stand across the harbour, often within musket shot of the enemy. At daylight he stood close in; and, having satisfied himself that the French fleet were at sea, he bore away to rejoin Sir John Warren.[2]

On his way back he exchanged signals with the French ship of the line, from which he learned that she had been dismasted in a heavy gale and parted from the fleet three days before. His disguise had been sufficiently effective for none of the French vessels seen being aware of his true identity.

Public opinion was very agitated about the threat from the French fleet, as Bridport's brother Lord Hood wrote to him to explain. There was real anxiety, he thought, about the ability of the French to come and go as they pleased: 'I am afraid the Fleet will anchor at St Helens and if the arrival of more ships is waited for from Plymouth the French fleet will most probably be in port before ours is out. In that case the consequence will be dreadfully alarming'.[3] Not for the first time, Howe's slowness to act was causing jitters in the highest quarters: unnecessarily as it turned out, since the sortie of the French fleet from Brest, which, as noted by Sidney Smith, had begun on 31 December, had been aborted by bad weather in the course of which it suffered the loss of several vessels and a good deal of damage.

Howe had finally got the fleet away on 29 January, but adverse winds caused him to put into Torbay, from where he reported to Spencer. The latter suggested, not unreasonably, that it would be desirable to look into Brest: that, Howe pointed out, would only be possible if the wind was easterly or far northerly, and Spencer was quick to make clear that he was not teaching his grandmother to suck eggs. In any case, since it seemed that the French might have given up the idea of a sortie, it might be desirable for the fleet to return to Spithead.

Spencer was in receipt of regular reports from Lord Hugh Seymour, serving in the Channel Fleet while a member of the Board of Admiralty. It was in that

2   Tracy (ed.), *Naval Chronicle*, Vol.I, p.116.
3   Morriss (ed.), *Channel Fleet*, p.55.

capacity that he provided Spencer with a continuous commentary on the proceedings of the fleet and, especially, the state of feeling among the captains. In this way Spencer had an independent source of information as to what was actually going on. Seymour was emphatically of the opinion that the return to Spithead was correct; he did not think much of Torbay as a base:

> What I have lately seen of this place has confirmed the opinion I have long entertained of its being a very improper one for the rendezvous of large fleets at this season of the year, though it may occasionally serve as a temporary shelter to that employed in the Channel.[4]

The absence from the station off Brest of any part of the Channel Fleet enabled a squadron of six French ships of the line to depart for Toulon on 2 February. By the end of February Howe had had enough, and went on shore, leaving Bridport in charge during his absence. It was an arrangement with which the latter was becoming increasingly discontented, believing that he would do all the work and Howe, comfortably ashore, would take all the credit. For the moment however, there was not a lot going on in the Channel, though Warren, cruising with his frigates off Brest, was able to report that at least two French squadrons had been able to leave the port in recent weeks, and it was clearly desirable that the Channel Fleet should get to sea as soon as possible.

In the meantime however, Lord Hood had set the cat among the pigeons. He and his brother had never been shy of making their views known; on 28 April, as he was preparing to return to the Mediterranean, Hood wrote to the Admiralty to give his view of the situation there. This had been prompted by the arrival in Toulon of the six ships from Brest. Hood was extremely concerned at the disparity of force which now existed in the Mediterranean:

> As I am ever ready to put my name to any opinions I have given I owe it to myself to have it upon record, particularly as I am convinced the force under my command, when united in the Mediterranean, will be very equal to that of the enemy and the various services committed to my charge; but although I have not the shadow of prospect of being able to add lustre to the arms of his Majesty I entreat to have credit for doing my utmost that they are not disgraced. The force of the enemy at Toulon is at this time eighteen sail of the line and will probably be twenty by the end of May. The British fleet in the Mediterranean consists now but of fifteen sail of the line, inclusive of the *Berwick*, dismasted, upwards of one thousand four hundred seamen short of complement.[5]

---

4   Morriss (ed.), *Channel Fleet*, p.58.
5   Morriss (ed.), *Channel Fleet*, p.61.

Although still relatively new in office, Spencer was not going to stand for this sort of thing, and Hood was promptly relieved from his command. Hood apparently put it about that he was leaving his post of his own accord, because the government was not giving him the resources which he considered necessary. Seymour was concerned that 'much inconvenience' might result from public statements by Hood of this kind; on the other hand, he was pleased that an overbearing commander should be slapped down this way: 'I believe the Navy in general will be pleased at his being taught that there are bounds to the authority of all officers, which he appeared to have lost sight of.'[6] All the same, it had given Spencer a serious problem; although there were a lot of admirals, there were only a few with the authority to command a major fleet. His first thought was to appoint Jervis; but this was not immediately possible due to Jervis's close association with the Whig opposition, which would have made him unacceptable to the Cabinet. Spencer therefore decided to offer the Mediterranean command to Bridport who, however, declined indignantly to take his brother's place. Therefore Hotham, who had been Hood's second-in-command, was duly appointed.

Howe, continuing in command of the Channel Fleet, was ordered by the Admiralty on 6 June to put a force of 2,500 French Royalist troops ashore at Quiberon Bay. It was a key element of British strategy to take advantage of the Royalist sentiment that existed in the west of France, and to do everything possible to stimulate insurrection there. Howe did not feel up to the task himself, and forwarded the instructions at once to Bridport, telling him that 'the yet impaired state of his health did not allow him to take up the command'. and ordering him to put to sea as soon as he could. The orders emphasised the importance of blockading the enemy; the fleet was to be placed 'in such a situation as may under the circumstances of wind and weather be best calculated for preventing the departure of any of the enemy's ships from the port of Brest.'[7]

Spencer was soon becoming anxious about the fleet's failure to sail while the wind was fair, writing on 19 June to urge Bridport to put to sea, pointing out that even without waiting for the *Orion*, which was short of men, 'you will then have thirteen sail of the line, of which eight are three deckers, a force far superior to anything you can have to meet of the enemy.'[8] Seymour, with the fleet at Portsmouth, did his best to reassure the First Lord; Bridport, he told him, was doing his utmost to get out, although delayed by the need for the crews of *Irresistible* and *Prince* to be paid, and for the completion of a court martial. He thought that the fleet should be able to sail on 12 June:

6   Morriss (ed.), *Channel Fleet*, p.62.
7   Morriss (ed.), *Channel Fleet*, p.79.
8   Morriss (ed.), *Channel Fleet*, p.80.

I can only describe my eagerness to do so by recollecting and expressing how much depends upon our using the greatest dispatch into carrying your present plan into execution. I am happy to say that everything that I have witnessed or heard since my arrival here assures me that the conduct of the admirals under you gives the greatest satisfaction and diffuses the sort of spirit I ever wish to see pursued in the service I am so much attached to.[9]

The 'present plan' to which Seymour referred was the plan for the landing in Quiberon Bay. This expedition could not take place without the support of the Channel Fleet which did finally manage to put to sea on 12 June.

Before Bridport could put to sea, however, one squadron had already sailed from Spithead on 30 May, commanded by an admiral who was to prove one of the outstanding naval leaders of the Revolutionary and Napoleonic Wars. William Cornwallis, born in 1744, joined the Navy as a midshipman at the age of eleven, and before the end of the Seven Years War was serving as an acting lieutenant aboard the *Thunderer*, 74, when he was appointed to command the sloop *Wasp*. That appointment was cancelled in favour of the newly built sloop *Swift*, in which he served until 1765. He was then made post captain, commanding the frigates *Prince Edward* and then *Guadeloupe*, in which he served in North America and the West Indies. In 1775, in command of the 32 gun frigate *Pallas* he was back in the West Indies. After the outbreak of the American War, he commanded the *Isis*, 50, his first task being to escort a large convoy of transports to New York. His ship operated throughout 1777-1778 in support of the British army under his brother, Lord Cornwallis, He next commanded the ship of the line *Lion* at the Battle of Grenada, and then the *Canada* at the Battle of Les Saintes in 1782. During the peace that followed he was elected to Parliament, for the second time; he was not, however, an active member, and was no doubt relieved to be given command of the East India Squadron, with the rank of commodore, in 1788. His brother was now Governor-General in India, and his most serious problem was the ambition of Tippoo Sultan, with whom hostilities broke out in 1789. Peace was signed in 1792, but Cornwallis continued in command of the East India Squadron as a rear admiral, until relieved by Sir Peter Rainier in October 1793. He was back in England by April 1794; in July he was promoted vice admiral and given command of a squadron of the Channel Fleet. At first he flew his flag in the *Caesar*, but found her unsatisfactory, and asked that he be found another ship. He transferred to the *Prince* and then on 26 December to the new 100 gun ship *Royal Sovereign*. Cornwallis was a personal friend of Captain Molloy of the *Caesar*, and did not at all want to serve on the latter's court martial. He pleaded ill health; the court appears to have been sceptical, for it was only when the surgeon of the *Royal*

9   Morriss (ed.), *Channel Fleet*, p.81.

Admiral Sir William Cornwallis. (Anne S.K. Brown Collection)

Sovereign certified that Cornwallis was suffering from gout that he managed to evade a distasteful duty. Now, in 1795, he was to have an opportunity of demonstrating his considerable abilities.

Cornwallis's squadron consisted of five ships of the line (*Royal Sovereign*, *Triumph*, *Mars*, *Brunswick* and *Bellerophon*) two frigates (*Phaeton* and *Pallas*) and the brig *Kingfisher*. *Brunswick* and *Bellerophon* were notoriously slow sailers. Cornwallis had orders to cruise off Ushant, and on June 8 when off Penmarck Point he sighted a number of ships east by north. This was a squadron of three 74s and six or seven frigates, sent out from Brest by the French to bring in a very large convoy of coasters from Bordeaux, under Rear Admiral Vence. As soon as it was clear to Vence that he was in sight of a British force, he made for Belleisle as fast as he could. Cornwallis pursued, although his force became very strung out. By 2.00 pm the *Kingfisher*, *Phaeton* and *Triumph* were within range of Vence's rear, and opened fire. The leading French ships were already under the island, but at 4.00 Cornwallis was able to chase two French frigates, one with a ship under tow; this was cast off and abandoned, and taken as a prize, as were a few others of the convoy. Cornwallis then stood off, sending the *Kingfisher* into port with the prizes, while he continued to watch Vence's squadron.

In Brest, it was assumed wrongly that Vence had been blockaded – in fact, he could reach Lorient in perfect safety – and Villaret-Joyeuse was sent to sea. He had nine ships of the line, two 50 gun razees, seven frigates and four corvettes, and on 15 June met with Vence's squadron which was by now making its way to Brest. Next day, at 10.30 am the French sighted Cornwallis, sailing towards Belleisle with the wind west-north-west. The *Phaeton* signalled that the enemy was of superior force, but Cornwallis, thinking that it was merely Vence and the convoy, stood on towards the French. At 11.00am, however, he realised his mistake, and stood away under all sail in line ahead. Villaret-Joyeuse followed; at about 2.00 pm he split his fleet into two divisions, one tacking and standing to the north while the other continued southwards. Soon after this the wind veered round to the north, as Cornwallis described in his report of the action: 'In the afternoon the wind fell and came to the northward off the land, and of course brought those ships of the enemy which had tacked to windward, and the other ships laid up for us'.[10] By then the northern division of the French was some eight miles east by north of the British squadron and the other about ten miles south-east.

During the night the *Bellerophon* and the *Brunswick* had great difficulty in keeping their station, and both had to cut away their anchors and to throw overboard large quantities of gear and provisions to try to increase their speed. At daylight on 17 June it was seen that Villaret-Joyeuse, who was closing fast, had now formed his fleet in two divisions. The weather division, already abreast of Cornwallis's rear, consisted of three ships of the line and five frigates, and the lee

10   Quoted Marcus, *Age of Nelson*, p.40.

division of four ships of the line, five frigates, two brigs and two cutters. Villaret-Joyeuse could see clearly the opportunity presented to him, and meant to make the most of it.[11]

The British order of sailing was now *Brunswick, Bellerophon, Royal Sovereign, Triumph* and *Mars*; Cornwallis had ordered his two slowest sailers ahead, as they would be the most vulnerable if they lost a sail or a spar. In his report he explained that he intended keeping the *Bellerophon* in reserve, 'having reason at first to suppose that there would be full occasion for the utmost exertions of us all… I considered that ship a treasure in store, having heard of her former achievements.'[12] It was on the *Mars* upon which the French, opening fire at 9.00 am, at first concentrated. By noon all the British ships were in action, firing their stern and quarter guns as they bore. The British captains went to extraordinary lengths to maximise their fire: 'All five ships, however, sacrificed their stern frames and galleries more or less in order to keep up the heaviest possible stern fire; and the *Triumph* cut away a large part of her stern, except the timbers, so as to improvise the necessary ports'.[13]

By 1.30 pm the leading French ship, which had lost her main topgallant mast, turned away. The French lee division was by now inflicting considerable damage on the *Mars* (Sir Charles Cotton) throughout the afternoon and by about 5.00, seeing that she was beginning to fall back, Cornwallis ordered her to turn away from the French lee division, while in the *Royal Sovereign*, followed by the *Triumph*, he swung round to cover her, firing broadsides into the leading French ships. He was now able to reform his line and four French ships of the line, which had been hoping to take the *Mars*, now thought better of it. The French now confined their activity to firing at long range.

All this time the frigate *Phaeton* (Captain Robert Stopford), sailing several miles ahead of the British squadron, had been signalling as soon as it was light to an imaginary fleet over the horizon to windward. Stopford's performance was carefully calculated:

> Having got to the distance of some miles, the frigate made the signal for a strange sail west- north- west; soon afterwards, for four sail; and finally, the well known signal for a fleet, by letting fly the top gallant sheets, and firing two guns in quick succession. At 3.00 pm, being then very far ahead, the *Phaeton* made the private signal to the supposed fleet; and then, by the tabular signals, with which the French were well acquainted, she communicated to her own admiral that the fleet seen were friends and at 4.30, that they were ships of the line. The *Phaeton* then repeated the signal, as

11 Clowes, *Royal Navy*, Vol.IV, pp.256-257.
12 Quoted Cordingley, *Billy Ruffian*, p.99.
13 Clowes, *Royal Navy*, Vol.IV, p.258.

from the admiral to call in the strange fleet, by hoisting the Dutch ensign, and shortly afterwards shortened sail.[14]

This performance seems to have deceived Villaret-Joyeuse, and to have contributed to the decidedly diffident manner in which he conducted the action. At about 6.00 pm several sails were seen in the direction of the imaginary fleet, and Stopford wore round to re-join the squadron. Villaret-Joyeuse had seen enough; before the sun went down he went about, turning eastward, and Cornwallis was thus able to make his triumphant escape with five ships of the line from twelve.

British casualties were astonishingly light, considering the length of the action; the *Mars*, although having suffered severe damage to her masts and sails, had only twelve men wounded, with none killed. There were no other casualties in the squadron. *Mars* had been saved by Cornwallis's prompt action in turning back to cover her; modestly, the only reference to this that he made in his report was to remark of the enemy that 'in the evening they made show of a more serious attack upon the *Mars,* and obliged me to bear up for her support.' He thanked his squadron in generous terms:

> Vice Admiral Cornwallis returns his sincere thanks to the Captains, officers, seamen, and marines of the fleet under his orders, for their steady and gallant conduct in the presence of the French fleet yesterday; which firmness he has no doubt, deterred the enemy from making a more serious attack. It would give the Vice Admiral pleasure to put the whole of their exertions in effect by meeting a more equal force, when the country who received advantage, as it now does honour, from the spirit so truly manifested by its brave men.[15]

In his official report he repeated his praise for the men of his squadron, remarking that it had given him 'the greatest pleasure I ever received to see the spirit manifested in the men, who, instead of being cast down at seeing thirty sail of the enemy's ships attacking our little squadron, were in the highest sprits imaginable.'[16] It had been a remarkable action; although it was not a great victory, with no ships lost on either side, the *Naval Chronicle* was understandably euphoric, hailing it as an 'unparalleled achievement:'

> We have no hesitation in pronouncing (and think our opinion will be seconded by those who are best able to appreciate naval merit), that such a retreat as the one we have just described, reflects as much honour on the

14   James, *Naval History*, Vol.I, p.268.
15   Quoted Clowes, *Royal Navy*, Vol.IV, p.259.
16   Tracy (ed.), *Naval Chronicle*, Vol.II, p.122.

abilities of the man who conducted it, as would the achievement of the most splendid victory.[17]

At the Admiralty, Sir Charles Middleton wondered what Villaret-Joyeuse might have been up to; whatever it was, he thought that there was nothing to be done but to keep ships in readiness for sea. In a memorandum which he wrote for Spencer on 30 June, he gave high praise to Cornwallis for the brilliance of this retreat, and noted lessons for the future:

> I have read with much attention Vice Admiral Cornwallis's journal, and think his conduct so judicious in the management of his squadron that I should propose its being bound separate, and marked Vice Admiral Cornwallis's retreat. In less skilful hands that squadron must have been lost, and which points out the necessity of sending these squadrons under experienced flags, and the ships as far as can be of an equal rate of sailing.[18]

The Admiralty had been quick to recognise just how skilful Cornwallis had been, the First Secretary writing to him on 26 June:

> I have it in command from their Lordships to inform you that they very highly approve of your conduct, and that they feel the greatest satisfaction at the account you have given of the judicious and spirited behaviour of the officers and men serving under your command on that critical occasion.[19]

The public and private adulation heaped on Cornwallis was not, however, to save him from a painful and very unfortunate interruption to his career in the following year, when he seriously upset Spencer and the Board of Admiralty by what seemed to them to be a most serious breach of discipline. Cornwallis sailed on 29 February 1796 with his flag in the *Royal Sovereign*; she, however, was disabled when running into a severe gale, and Cornwallis returned aboard her to Spithead. He was then ordered to shift his flag to the 32 gun frigate *Astraea*, and proceed at once to the West Indies. It was felt that what he should have done was to send back the *Royal Sovereign*, having shifted his flag to another ship of the line of his squadron. Cornwallis considered the order to sail in the *Astraea* as a pointed mark of disapproval, and refused to undertake the voyage in a small frigate. He had not been well, and in any case it was inappropriate that he should be expected

17   Tracy (ed.), *Naval Chronicle*, Vol.II, p.123.
18   Julian S. Corbett (ed.), *Private Papers of George, Second Earl Spencer* (London: Navy Records Society, 1913), Vol.I, pp.219-220.
19   G. Cornwallis-West, *The Life and Letters of Admiral Cornwallis* (London: Robert Holden, 1927), p.271.

to hoist his flag in such a vessel. To the admiral's great surprise, however, Spencer was determined to take the matter further. He wrote to Cornwallis on 17 March to say that his refusal to sail in the *Astraea* indicated a determination to give up the West Indies appointment altogether:

> I am very sorry to be obliged to say that under the circumstances of your case such a determination puts it out of my power to continue you in employment without giving what I conceive would be a very dangerous example to the service, and entirely subverting every idea of the discipline so necessary to be maintained in it.[20]

Cornwallis was even more surprised next to learn that he was to be tried by court martial. He was very much annoyed to find that, having decided to try him, the Admiralty then were dragging their feet in convening the court martial. It was not until 4 April that it finally began, with Lord Howe presiding. The latter seems not to have had much sympathy with the Admiralty in the matter, and appears to have made up his mind in advance.[21] Cornwallis was represented by the brilliant lawyer Thomas Erskine, later to become Lord Chancellor. At the end of the hearing Cornwallis was acquitted; the court found that although he was to blame for not going on in one of his other ships, 'in consideration of the circumstances of the case, they do acquit him of any further censure on that account.' As to his refusal to sail in the *Astraea*, they found that the charge of disobedience was not proved, and acquitted him accordingly.

His biographer considers him 'lucky to get off as he did;' perhaps this is so, and perhaps Spencer felt he had no choice but to take a stand against disobedience at the highest level. At all events, he was probably sincere when he wrote to Cornwallis's brother to say that he had the satisfaction of having fulfilled his duty, and that it was a great relief to him in every point of view 'that nothing of a more disagreeable nature has arisen from it.'[22] Nevertheless, it was a regrettable fact that Cornwallis, though one of the ablest admirals in the service, received no further appointment during Spencer's tenure of office as First Lord. It was to be almost five years before he got another command, and that only after the fall of Pitt's government had swept Spencer out of the Admiralty. When the appointment came, however, it was to the command of the Channel Fleet: there was no man more suited to take up the task of blockading the French.

---

20   Corbett (ed.), *Spencer*, Vol.I, pp.219-220.
21   Cornwallis-West, *Admiral Cornwallis*, p.322.
22   Cornwallis-West, *Admiral Cornwallis*, p.340.

8

The Ile de Groix

After the action against Cornwallis and his squadron, Villaret-Joyeuse made his way back to Brest. Before he could reach port, however, a violent northerly gale which lasted for 27 hours scattered his fleet and drove him to shelter under Belleisle. There, he gradually reassembled his ships and having done so, put to sea, only to find, on the horizon, Bridport with the Channel Fleet, from which Warren, with his frigate squadron reinforced with three ships of the line to cover a convoy of 50 transports containing a Royalist army destined for the Vendée, had parted on 19 June. Bridport had then stood out from the coast in order to circumvent any interference from Brest, not knowing that Villaret-Joyeuse was already at sea. Warren, however, soon received a report from Captain Keats in the frigate *Galatea* that the French were at Belleisle, and sent at once to alert Bridport. Warren's report to Bridport was comprehensive:

> I had just lost sight of your Lordships' fleet about two hours after we made the Penmarks when I discovered a strange fleet to leeward in the SW. I immediately despatched two frigates to reconnoitre them. One of the headmost made several signals to our frigates, who were convinced of their being the enemy, consisting of 16 of the line, 7 frigates, 2 brigs and a cutter. They were close handed, standing to the NE and one of the headmost very near the *Arethusa*. An American ship we afterwards spoke to told us they had an action the day before with some ships which lasted two hours, when the others got off. He says they have been stationed off Belleisle and been out there three days. From the state of the weather and wind it is impossible they could get into Quiberon Bay or Rochefort and are consequently to windward.[1]

---

1   Morriss (ed.), *Channel Fleet*, p.83.

Next day Warren was already in sight of Bridport, from whom he had received an order to give up his three ships of the line, *Robust, Thunderer* and *Standard,* to reinforce the Channel Fleet.

Bridport, who before this had fourteen ships of the line, remained between Warren and the French fleet while Warren's three ships of the line endeavoured to join him; but it was not until the early hours of June 22 that Bridport finally sighted Villaret-Joyeuse. By then the Channel Fleet was some 42 miles off Belleisle. It soon became plain that Villaret-Joyeuse was not going to offer battle, and at

Admiral Alexander Hood, 1st Viscount Bridport.

6.30 am Bridport ordered four of his fastest-sailing ships to pursue the enemy fleet which was making for the land. These were the *Sans Pareil, Orion, Colossus,* and *Russell.* Fifteen minutes later, the breeze steadily dropping, he gave the same order to the rest of the fleet, which set all possible sail. By noon, however, the French fleet, bearing east-south-east, was still twelve miles off; the wind by now had faded almost to nothing, and had come round towards the south. Later, it picked up, and Bridport ordered at 7.00 pm that the vessels closest to the enemy should harass his rear. By 7.25 pm he was able to hoist a signal to the rest of the fleet to engage the enemy when within range, his ships to take station of mutual support. Although by sunset much ground had been made, at 10.30 the wind dropped away again, and it was not until 3.00 am on the following morning that it picked up, enabling the *Orion* and *Irresistible* to come up with the rearmost French ship, the *Alexandre,* by about 6.00 am, This ship, formerly the *Alexander,* had been taken by the French in 1794. She had always been a poor sailer when under British colours, and she was no better now. In an effort to save her, a French frigate had taken her in tow at about 5.00 am but when the *Orion* and *Irresistible* opened fire, the frigate abandoned her to her fate.[2]

Seymour, now flying his flag in the *Sans Pareil,* wrote to Spencer with his own account of the battle, describing the situation when the French fleet finally came within range:

> A breeze which sprung up at daylight yesterday, and which we got before the enemy, enabled us to get within gunshot of them at about six, when our advanced ships, about six or seven in number, began firing. The chase now grew very interesting, for the distance from the shore was so very small that it was doubtful whether it would be possible to stop any of the enemy before they reached Port Louis (within the Isle de Groix) for which they were pressing with every sail set. Fortunately they were so little satis-fied with the sailing of the *Alexander* that they directed a frigate to tow her, which threw her so much to leeward as to enable our ships to cut her off and, after having fought better than the others did, she fell into our hands.[3]

The French were sailing in close company, save for three stragglers, the other two being the *Tigre* and the *Formidable,* the latter being commanded by the future Admiral Linois. Close up with the *Irresistible* and the *Orion* came the *Queen Charlotte,* which opened fire on the *Formidable* at about 6.15 am, followed by Seymour's *Sans Pareil.* The captain of the *Queen Charlotte,* had been particularly assiduous in trying to bring his ship into action, as the *Naval Chronicle* reported:

2   Clowes, *Royal Navy,* Vol.IV, p.262.
3   Morriss (ed.), *Channel Fleet,* pp.84-85.

By watching every breath of wind that blew from the Heavens, and trimming incessantly to give it with the best advantage to the sails, Sir Andrew Douglas soon after the morning broke on the 23d, had the satisfaction to find himself within two miles of the enemy's rear. Undismayed by the fire which they soon poured upon the *Queen Charlotte*, and the slender prospect of an essential support, he appeared willing, if necessary, to sacrifice his ship for the public benefit. She was seen to approach the enemy with a silent intrepidity, that at least deserved a pointed notice; and with even royals and steering sails set, she dashed amid the thickest o the enemy.[4]

At about 6.30 the *Formidable* caught fire on her poop, and thereafter was in great difficulties, dropping further and farther behind under heavy fire; when her mizzen mast came down, she struck her colours. By then, in addition to those British ships previously mentioned, the *Colossus, Russell, London* and *Queen* had come up, and were engaging the *Peuple* (the flagship of Villaret-Joyeuse, formerly the *Montagne*), *Mucius, Wattignies, Nestor, Tigre* and *Redoutable* as well as the badly damaged *Alexandre*. The other four French ships of the line were out of range, as were the remaining British ships. The *Queen Charlotte* had by now suffered severely to her masts and sails, and was almost unmanageable, but was still able at 7.14 to fire a broadside into the *Alexandre*, which then struck. Meanwhile the *Tigre,* under fire from both *Queen* and *London*, also struck her colours.[5]

Bridport himself in the *Royal George* came up a few minutes before eight o'clock, passing the *Queen Charlotte* which was endeavouring to make good the damage sustained, but which at once tacked to support the flagship. However, at 8.15, Bridport signalled the *Colossus*, about a mile and a half away on the *Queen Charlotte*'s starboard bow, to break off the action, and five minutes later made the same signal to the *Sans Pareil*, about the same distance on the flagship's port bow. The *Royal George* was by now only half a mile from the Ile de Groix, so the fleet was getting into tight quarters. Bearing up, she fired her starboard broadside into the *Peuple*, which was now within range, and her port broadside into the *Tigre*, not aware that she had already struck.

Midshipman Dillon, aboard the *Prince George*, described the flagship's coming into action:

> In the meantime, up came the *Royal George*, Lord Bridport's ship. She had been a long way astern, and had been trying every possible means to join in the battle. All the enemy's ships but one were so close in with the land that the French batteries opened their fire upon us. However, Lord Bridport, by good management, contrived to get alongside of the

4   Tracy (ed.), *Naval Chronicle*, Vol.II, p.130.
5   Clowes, *Royal Navy*, Vol.IV, pp.262-263.

'Lord Bridport's Action off Port l'Orient June 23rd 1795'.

sternmost French ship, almost touching her, but did not fire until the *Royal George* completely covered the enemy. Then a broadside was poured into him with the most tremendous effect. As I saw what happened, I speak with certainty. The French ship was a two decker, *Le Tigre* of 74 guns. The weight of the *Royal George's* broadside was fired with such correct precision that, the shot all striking at the same time, it made the enemy heel over, and instantly haul down his colours.[6]

To Bridport it seemed unduly hazardous to attempt any more, and the *Royal George* wore round away from the land, followed by the rest of the fleet. Bridport ordered the *Prince*, *Barfleur* and *Prince George* to take the three prizes in tow and sailed off to the south west.

William James records the position as it stood then:

The weathermost French ships, when Lord Bridport discontinued the action, did not, it appears, point higher than the mouth of the river Quimperlay, and could therefore have been weathered by the *Royal George* and the other fresh ships that were coming up. Finding himself unexpectedly relieved, the French admiral kept his wind, and, after making several tacks, sheltered his fleet between Isle-Groix and the entrance to the Lorient.[7]

It was by no means certain to Villaret-Joyeuse what would be best next to do, so he called a council of his admirals on board the frigate *Proserpine* to discuss the matter, and in particular whether the fleet should anchor on the coast to resist the further attack which he expected from the British. He was firmly advised against this:

Rear Admirals Kerguelen and Bruix both assured Admiral Villaret that, if he adopted this measure the whole of his fleet would be lost; that the anchorage was very bad all along that coast; that his cables would be cut by the rocks; and that the British, having the weather gauge, would cannonade his ships when they pleased or probably send fire ships to destroy them.[8]

Their advice was to wait until the tide suited, and then enter the port of Lorient. This seemed sound to Villaret-Joyeuse, and by 8.00 pm he was safely anchored in harbour.

6   Lewis (ed.), *Sir William Dillon*, Vol.IV, p.193.
7   James, *Naval History*, Vol.I, p.274.
8   James, *Naval History*, Vol.I, p.276.

The British fleet had suffered little during the action. None had lost any spars, and the only ships to have sustained damage to masts and rigging were the *Queen Charlotte*, *Sans Pareil* and *Irresistible*. Total casualties were 31 killed and 113 wounded, the heaviest losses being in the *Queen Charlotte* and the *Colossus*. French casualties were very much heavier; a total of 670 were killed and wounded in the three prizes alone, of which nearly half were in the *Formidable*.[9]

Bridport had certainly won a victory, although even in his official letter written the day after the battle he found it necessary to explain why only three of the enemy had been taken:

> If the enemy had not been protected, and sheltered by the land, I have every reason to believe that a much greater number, if not all the line of battle ships, would have been taken or destroyed … Early on the morning of the twenty third, the headmost ships, the *Irresistible, Orion, Queen Charlotte, Russell, Colossus* and *Sans Pareil* were pretty well up with the enemy, and a little before six o'clock the action began, and near to some batteries, and in the face of a strong naval port; which will manifest to the public the zeal, intrepidity and skill of the Admirals, Captains and all other Officers, seamen and soldiers, employed on this service; and they are fully entitled to my warmest acknowledgements.[10]

Criticism of the failure to win a more comprehensive victory had already begun to be heard when the *Naval Chronicle* published an account of the battle, in which it offered a sharp rebuke to Bridport's critics, saying that 'this glorious victory is highly estimated by professional men':

> It certainly merits its due share of glory amid the victories of the present period, whose lustre can alone be abated by the injudicious comparisons of the ignorant, or those improper suggestions, which have in view to elevate a part above the rest.[11]

Always eager to accord praise, whether due or not, the *Naval Chronicle* also claimed, somewhat improbably, that Bridport had taken over the conning of the *Royal George*:

> So near the coast was the British fleet during the above action, that the pilot on board the *Royal George* absolutely refused to proceed; when the

9   Clowes, *Royal Navy*, Vol.IV, p.26.
10 Tracy (ed.), *Naval Chronicle*, Vol.II, p.128.
11 Tracy (ed.), *Naval Chronicle*, Vol.II, p.127.

gallant Lord Bridport, whose skill is alone equalled by his intrepidity, took charge of the ship himself. They who know the peculiar dangers of the French coast will best appreciate such an act of valour.[12]

Seymour, in his private report to the First Lord, seems to have been conscious of the possibility of criticism of the outcome; he was determined, however, to see the glass as half full:

> Had we been fortunate enough to have fallen in with this squadron two leagues further from the coast I have not a doubt but that the whole of it would have been taken but though we cannot prevent this idea from presenting itself to our minds I think it but fair to say that our success yesterday exceeded very much the expectations of the most sanguine person in our squadron, which you will readily conceive on recollecting how near to the enemy's shore our chase of twenty seven hours terminated and that one hour's more time would have placed the French beyond our grasp.[13]

Rear Admiral Gardner, whose flagship the *Queen* was barely up in time to engage the enemy, said much the same in a letter of congratulation which he wrote to Bridport on 24 June:

> I most sincerely congratulate you upon our success of yesterday and have only to lament that the French fleet were able to get so near to Port Louis before the van of our fleet were able to come up with them. Had they been only four or five miles farther from the Isle of Groix I have not the smallest doubt but that the whole of their line of battle ships would have been captured.[14]

Subsequent naval historians have not been so forgiving of Bridport for his caution in breaking off the action when he did. Mahan, for instance, was severe when he commented on the battle:

> Such was the extreme circumspection characterising the early naval operations of the British, until Jervis and Nelson enkindled their service with the relentless energy and spirit inspired by Bonaparte on land. Those to whom St Vincent and the Nile, Algeciras and Copenhagen, have become history, see with astonishment nine ships of capital importance permitted

---

12   Tracy (ed.), *Naval Chronicle*, Vol.II, pp.127-128.
13   Morriss (ed.), *Channel Fleet*, p.85.
14   Morriss (ed.), *Channel Fleet*, pp.86-87.

THE ILE DE GROIX 91

to escape thus easily from fourteen, forgetting the hold tradition has on the minds of men, and that it belongs to genius to open the way into which others then eagerly press. How the Admiralty viewed Bridport's action may be inferred from his retaining command of the fleet until April 1800. The ships that reached Lorient had to remain till the winter when they slipped back two or three at a time to Brest.[15]

One of the French admirals present at the action, Rear Admiral Kerguelen, who flew his flag in the frigate *Fraternité*, was in no doubt at all that the British had missed an opportunity: '*S'ils avait bien manoeuvré, ils auraient pu, ou prendre tous nos vaisseaux, ou les faire périr à la côte*'.[16] Clowes was extremely critical of Bridport's conduct of the action, finding him guilty of a 'strange and almost unaccountable forbearance'.

Perhaps, though, these judgements are unduly harsh. The complaints are not very different from those raised against Howe on 1 June 1794, when it was suggested that he let a number of damaged French ships get away. By the time that Bridport broke off the action, it was taking place in the restricted waters around the Ile de Groix, and he had still not got up more than half his fleet. At the same time, Villaret-Joyeuse's leading ships were by now far ahead. Bridport was certainly entitled to conclude that he should not take risks in those narrow waters. In any case, his principal object was to protect the expedition to Quiberon Bay, and his victory had ensured that Warren was able successfully to put ashore the troops and a large quantity of arms, ammunitions and stores. Unfortunately, it was militarily unsuccessful and the French Royalist troops were decisively defeated. The landing in October of 4,000 British troops having failed to restore the position, they were re-embarked in the face of strong French pressure.

Bridport did not attempt to blockade Lorient. Villaret-Joyeuse was short of supplies, and he was able to send the ships back to Brest three at a time, with the crews which ferried them there coming back to collect the next group.[17]

As a historian of the French navy has noted, the performance of the fleet at the Ile de Groix showed that things were badly wrong:

> In his reports, from the return from the foolish winter cruise onwards, Villaret had not minced his words. Gunners were lacking: 'our shots', he wrote, 'land in the water.' Above all, the officers were often incompetent

15   Mahan, *Sea Power*, Vol.I, p.178.
16   'If they had manoeuvred properly they would have been able either to take all our ships or to have driven them on shore'. Quoted Clowes, *Royal Navy*, Vol.IV, p.263.
17   Robert Gardner, (ed.), *Fleet Battle and Blockade* (London: Chatham, 1996), p.16.

and unsuitable. Nineteen out of twenty had merely sought their appointments, and thereafter intrigued for promotion, for the sake of the pay.[18]

Their selection had been, it was said, on the basis of their 'verbiage of patriotism', and they were insubordinate and ignorant. With such officers, no fleet could perform well.

18 Jenkins, *French Navy*, pp.220-221.

9

Closer Blockade

Meanwhile the awkward command arrangements of the Channel Fleet had prompted a good deal of correspondence. Howe, ashore in London, and still very conscious of his position as Commander-in-Chief, was annoyed to have heard nothing from Bridport after he had passed on the Admiralty's instructions to sail on 6 June. On 5 July he wrote to Bridport:

> I am to request you will furnish me with such returns of the state of the ships and account of your proceedings in conformity to the tenor of those instructions from time to time when you may be to forward similar advices for the information of the Board of Admiralty.[1]

He softened this request by adding his congratulations on Bridport's 'late defeat of the Brest squadron'; Bridport, however, was unlikely to be mollified by this. He was in correspondence at this time with Spencer, who had made the suggestion that Villaret-Joyeuse's ships in Lorient might be attacked with fire ships. He was scornful of this idea, of which he suspected Howe might have been the originator, writing sarcastically to the First Lord on 7 July:

> The ships driven into L'Orient and the road of Port Louis cannot in my opinion be attacked by fire ships or ships of force. Whoever has given your Lordship the idea of such a proposal, let the rank of those officers be ever so high, I must suffer with them. I think Lord Howe cannot be one of those officers because I know his Lordship's sentiments for declining to attack the fleet at anchor within the Isle of Groix when he fell in with the enemy's fleet the first cruise of this war. But should his Lordship have changed his opinion since that period and your Lordship should judge it expedient that the Earl should proceed to sea and resume the command of the fleet I shall be ready, as second officer, to support whatever plan

---

1   Morriss (ed.), *Channel Fleet*, p.89.

his Lordship shall judge for his Majesty's service to undertake or I shall most cheerfully resign my station in the fleet and beg your Lordship's permission tto return to England… The port of Brest should be narrowly watched, as well as all the other ports to the eastward in our Channel, not only for American ships but for such as shall attempt to get out of L'Orient and go through the Passage du Raz to Brest.[2]

Seymour was by now convinced of the necessity for instituting a close blockade, for which he believed it would be valuable for the Channel Fleet to be reinforced by Cornwallis and his squadron. This would ensure that there would be twenty ships of the line at sea, of which five could be placed close off Brest and the Penmarcks to interdict any of the ships there getting out. The rest of the fleet could effectively prevent any supplies reaching France through the Bay of Biscay, particularly from America. In his letter to Spencer of 8 July, in which he outlined this proposal, Seymour went on to deal with the question of the command:

Should you see this plan in the same point of view that I do, I have little reason to doubt your being able soon to carry it into execution and I think that Lord Howe's returning to his command, which we all in the squadron most anxiously hope he is enabled to do, would ensure the success I so particularly wish to attend this measure. The necessity of our ships returning to port is the only obstacle to it and that I should hope might be managed by relieving them regularly during the summer when we must have enough of command for the purpose. I presume that Lord Bridport gives himself some credit for not complaining of his want of strength to undergo the fatigues of his present employment from which I apprehend you will not have any difficulty in accommodating him by letting him remain onshore while Lord Howe is afloat. The service will not suffer from their being upon different elements for those do not in themselves differ more than the characters of the two officers under whose orders I am likely to act during his campaign.[3]

In this letter Seymour also warned Spencer privately that the relationship between Bridport and Warren was not good, adding that 'the communications between our chief and Sir John Warren will not be more regular than what necessity suggests'.

It can hardly have come as any surprise to Spencer to receive an opinion that Howe and Bridport were as like as chalk and cheese; but he was perfectly aware that getting Howe back to sea would not be easy. For the moment, he thought it wise to spell out to Bridport on 14 July the importance of imposing a close blockade:

2   Morriss (ed.), *Channel Fleet*, p.90.
3   Morriss (ed.), *Channel Fleet*, pp.92-93.

As it is now a principal object to keep up the command which by the action of the 23rd ultimo you have gained of the seas in that quarter, the plan adopted by Government is to keep by successive relief a squadron constantly cruising off the ports of Brest and Lorient and occasionally communicating with the officer commanding in Quiberon Bay. For this purpose I thought it most advisable to specify the ships which you should at present retain with you, equal I should hope and trust to anything which the debilitated naval force of the enemy can oppose to you, in order that by refitting with the utmost despatch these which you send home we may be enabled to escort the several divisions of troops that may be occasionally sent out to the coast of Brittany and relieve other ships of your squadron which may want refreshment or refitting at home.[4]

Spencer was at pains to make clear that Howe was not the author of the suggestion about the fire ships but, on the contrary, agreed with Bridport about the inadvisability of an attack on Port Louis.

Meanwhile Spencer had had a discussion with Howe about the latter's resumption of the active command of the Channel Fleet, which had, he thought, gone well. He was dismayed therefore on 24 July to get a letter from Howe asking to be relieved of the command. This he was not prepared to accept, since at their meeting it had seemed to him that Howe's health appeared to be perfectly restored; and, asking Howe to make no public statement, he once more turned to the King for help. George wrote to Howe assuming that this was only a temporary decision; he had, however, grasped the essence of the problem of the existing command structure:

I should think this circumstance, as Lord Bridport dislikes commanding under the orders of Earl Howe, gives good ground for Earl Spencer's offering the supreme command in the North Sea with an admiral's captain and that Sir John Jervis should command the detachment of the Channel Fleet on the coast of France under Earl Howe's orders.[5]

Spencer was dubious about this; sending Bridport to the North Sea would be convenient, but was not likely to be acceptable to that touchy and difficult individual, since he would probably see the transfer 'as entirely cutting him off from any chance of commanding the Channel Fleet in any event'. Instead, Spencer suggested that Bridport might be given a commission as 'Commander-in-Chief of a squadron to be employed on a particular service, which will give him all the emolument and rank to which he appears fairly entitled'. It would have the additional

4   Morriss (ed.), *Channel Fleet*, pp.95-96.
5   Morriss (ed.), *Channel Fleet*, p.99.

advantage that it would avoid any public suggestion that Howe had permanently retired from the Channel command.[6] On 29 July Bridport was sent the commission together with, quaintly, a fee of £5. 7. 6 for it: Spencer made it clear to Bridport that for the present he would receive his orders direct from the Admiralty; but the new arrangement 'must be understood not to prevent Lord Howe's return to the command of the Channel Fleet whenever His Majesty's service may require it and his Lordship's health may be sufficiently re-established to undertake that change'.[7] He added that it would be expedient that Bridport should continue his cruise for some time longer.

Seymour, when he heard of the arrangements which Spencer had made for the command of the Channel Fleet, thought that no better arrangement could have been made, and that Bridport 'should be as much satisfied with the compliment you have paid him as he is sure to be with the advantages and emoluments which he will derive from his new commission'.[8] In fact, Bridport had not been in the least satisfied. He wrote an angry letter on 9 August to Spencer, observing that his rank and long service were as well known before he sailed from Spithead as on 28 July, and that his situation vis-à-vis Howe had not changed since he sailed. Since Warren had been given a commission as a commodore with a captain under him, 'I do not think I am particularly honoured or that my commission comes to me so gratifying to my feelings'. As to the future command of the Channel Fleet, words failed him: 'It is not necessary for me to say one word on the subject of Lord Howe's return to the command of the Channel Fleet. When that event takes place I shall meet it with humble composure and proper resignation'. Turning to the suggestion that he should continue at sea, he pointed out that his cruise had already lasted eight weeks. The tasks he had to perform would still exist at the end of twelve weeks:

> Does your Lordship think that I can keep the sea that length of time without receiving the smallest supply for myself or the squadron or that the crews will not suffer much by the scurvy, which increases every day in the *Royal George* as well as in every other ship and it must ruin the fleet if not speedily allowed to return into port for refreshments?[9]

By now, Spencer had for the time being had enough of Lord Bridport. A formal letter from the Secretary of the Admiralty went to him to say that though the fleet should remain at sea, he was at liberty to return on shore if he wished, leaving the fleet in the hands of his second-in-command. Spencer wrote an icy personal

6   Morriss (ed.), *Channel Fleet*, p.100.
7   Morriss (ed.), *Channel Fleet*, p.103.
8   Seymour to Spencer, August 18 1795; Morriss (ed.), *Channel Fleet*, p.110.
9   Morriss (ed.), *Channel Fleet*, pp.107-108.

letter to him on 15 August to point out that he had repeatedly explained the policy relating to the Channel Fleet keeping the sea; as to the rest of Bridport's letter, he acknowledged it, saying that he would not fail to lay it before the King. He did so at once and the King's already poor opinion of Bridport was predictably accentuated, as he made clear in his very prompt response:

> I cannot see the private letter to the Earl Spencer from Lord Bridport but in a very different style than one should have supposed the granting him the very favour he seemed to look for must have dictated but it appears too plain that in his family self value is so predominant that all other objects are not sufficiently attended to and as much as I was desirous that Earl Howe's strength may be restored I cannot now but more eagerly wish it as the temper of the next in command is now so clearly seen.[10]

George's wish that Howe should return to active command was, however, unlikely to be gratified, and the unsatisfactory situation continued, with Bridport increasingly anxious about the condition of the fleet and in particular its crews.

All supplies were running low, especially water; but it was the onset of scurvy in particular that was the principal cause for concern. Bridport had sent Dr Trotter, the Physician of the Fleet, to visit every ship and make a report of the condition of each crew. His report on 16 August was alarming; overall there were 475 men on the sick list, many of these being serious cases of scurvy. In addition, there were men already suffering from the disease still on duty, and it was clear that scurvy was increasing rapidly. Dr Trotter warned that the situation could only get worse:

> Few precautions could have been practiced for the prevention of this disease, which is the common consequence of living for a length of time on salted provisions without recent vegetable matter. Even the mild summer weather seems to have had small share in retarding its approach. It is however to be the more dreaded as the season advances, and cold and rain set in. From the lemon juice supplied at the early part of the cruise, no deaths have happened; from the quantity just distributed we have also a right to expect that no immediate danger may be apprehended.[11]

It was clear to Dr Trotter that fresh meat and fresh vegetables must be distributed to the whole fleet; and that the sooner the fleet was back in port the more quickly would the problem of scurvy be eradicated. In the meantime he had some suggestions to make for improving the situation. It appears that the problem had to some extent been exacerbated by the need for economy; his proposals had, he pointed

---

10   Morriss (ed.), *Channel Fleet*, p.110.
11   Morriss (ed.), *Channel Fleet*, p.114.

out, had the effect that 'our sick are deriving much comfort without one farthing additional to Government'.

Bridport seems to have realised that he had overstepped the mark in his correspondence with Spencer. On 24 August he wrote officially to the Admiralty, rather than personally to the First Lord:

> I feel myself much obliged to their Lordships for their indulgence respecting my health by allowing me to return into port on that account. I desire you will inform their Lordships that it was never any intention to quit the squadron but to continue at sea as long as the *Royal George* was kept out on service.[12]

He could not, however, resist observing that if he was kept out at sea in any other ship 'it must be without a clean shirt to put upon my back or a morsel of fresh meat to place on my table but I am fully convinced their Lordships cannot propose such a measure'. If it would give their Lordships any satisfaction, he added, his health was better than it had been a month earlier.

By 24 August, a week after Dr Trotter's first report, the total number of those on the sick list, including those aboard the hospital ship *Charon*, had risen to 787, and Seymour followed up Bridport's warnings with a letter to the First Lord:

> I cannot help joining the Admiral in thinking it absolutely necessary that our ships should return into port as soon as possible. Those which sailed with Lord Bridport will soon complete their eleventh week without having received any refreshment, a term infinitely too long for any ships to keep the sea, particularly after such a winter as the last, the severity of which deprived the men belonging to the fleet of their normal supply of fresh meat, vegetables etc.[13]

Some relief had been hoped for from the arrival of Cornwallis with his squadron, but it soon became apparent that the situation in most of his ships was, if anything, even worse. Bridport noted on 26 August that the flagship now had no more than three weeks water remaining; he intended to stay out as long as he could, but the fleet must return to port very soon. Acknowledging his report, the Admiralty promised that he should have further instructions within a few hours. On 1 September the Admiralty notified Bridport that Rear Admiral Harvey had now sailed from St Helens to join the fleet, with *Queen Charlotte*, *Prince of Wales*, *Prince*, *Orion* and *Russell*; he would pick up the *Marlborough* at Plymouth on the way. Harvey would remain at sea off Brest with his original five ships plus *Brunswick*, *Bellerophon* and

12   Morriss (ed.), *Channel Fleet*, p.116.
13   Morriss (ed.), *Channel Fleet*, p.119.

Triumph, and three frigates. Bridport was then to return to port, with the rest of the fleet; one third of the ships were to go into Plymouth and the rest to Spithead.

When Harvey arrived, he brought with him Howe's letter to Bridport of 5 July, which sufficiently annoyed Bridport for him to write a disgracefully insolent reply on 15 September:

> The point for me at this time to answer is that I have not acknowledged the receipt of your Lordship's instructions of the 6th of June, forwarded to me by express before I left Spithead. I do not know that I can give your Lordship a more satisfactory answer to that part of your letter than by quoting the words of your Lordship's order – 'Being more over to send notice from time to time of your proceedings in pursuance of this appointment to Mr Secretary Nepean for the information of the Lords Commissioners of the Admiralty'. It is impossible for me to conceive that your Lordship put these words into the order to instruct me in my duty as they manifested to my weak understanding that your Lordship did not expect to be troubled with business in your retirement at Porter's Lodge for the recovery of the yet impaired state of your Lordship's health. But I find by your Lordship's letter that I am mistaken.[14]

He added that he had sent copies of the original orders and Howe's letter to Nepean, and that he was further to express his acknowledgments for the honour of Howe's congratulations on the defeat of the Brest fleet. Not surprisingly Howe regarded this letter as insulting: he told Curtis that he would never again serve with Bridport.[15] Clearly Spencer still had work to do to sort out the command arrangements for the Channel Fleet.

Bridport's return to Spithead on 19 September coincided with a note that day from the King to Spencer expressing approval of Warren's performance and anxiety about the situation in the Channel:

> I cannot help just writing a few lines to Earl Spencer expressive of my approbation of the conduct of Sir [John] Borlase Warren, who by the less proper one of Lord Bridport seems necessitated to return to Plymouth. If the French fleet in Quiberon Bay was nearly ready as Sir Borlase supposes it will be highly necessary to send out part of Lord Bridport's squadron with the greatest expedition to protect the East India ships, which must be hourly expected.[16]

---

14   Morriss (ed.), *Channel Fleet*, p.126.
15   Syrett, *Lord Howe*, p.148.
16   Morriss (ed.), *Channel Fleet*, p.128.

George's feelings about Bridport had not changed, nor were likely to do so.

One issue which particularly annoyed Bridport was the Admiralty's conclusion, expressed to him through Seymour, that not only Howe, but also Sir Roger Curtis, the Captain of the Fleet, was entitled to share in the prize money of the Channel Fleet for the ships taken on 23 June. In recording this to Bridport on October 8, Seymour emphasised that this was also the view of those captains in the fleet with whom he had discussed the matter.

This was followed by another effort by Spencer to grasp the nettle of the Channel command, and he wrote to Bridport to spell out the position for the future. Referring to the 'great inconvenience' resulting from the divided state of the command as it presently stood, he informed him on 20 October that the Board of Admiralty had decided:

> that all the ships which are meant in the present state of affairs to be employed in the Channel shall again be put under the orders of Lord Howe, through whom the several orders necessary to be given to them may pass to the senior officer who happens to be at Portsmouth at the time, with the exception of sailing orders which it is intended shall be issued from the Admiralty to the officer commanding whatever squadron is to sail on any service that many be required.[17]

The effect, Spencer explained, would be for the present to suspend Bridport's commission as Commander-in-Chief of a squadron.

Bridport, nettled by this, replied sarcastically to 'beg leave to return my best thanks for the attention your Lordship is pleased to show me'. He went on to remark that if his previous wishes and expectations had been complied with 'every difficulty which is now stated to exist in the issuing of orders would have been obviated':

> In which case I should, as well as the admirals under me, have reaped the full reward of our services instead of Lord Howe, Vice Admiral William Waldegrave and Sir Roger Curtis. Your Lordship will, I hope, excuse the stating of my feelings upon this subject.[18]

He concluded by unconvincingly expressing his pleasure that Lord Howe's health had been established, adding that he was ready to serve the King as long as his health and faculties would allow. When they did not, he would give no possible trouble, but would retire, 'as under such circumstances of bodily infirmities I will never receive the public money or take the reward of other men's labours'. Reading

17   Morriss (ed.), *Channel Fleet*, p.148.
18   Corbett (ed.), *Spencer*, Vol.I, p.136.

Bridport's aggressive correspondence, it is perhaps a little surprising that Spencer, and especially the King, tolerated him in a senior command at all. And yet, in the following year, his Irish peerage was raised to the status of a peerage of Great Britain, and he received the honorary rank of Vice Admiral of Great Britain and the United Kingdom. They recognised, perhaps, that in spite of his occasionally abrasive manner, he was after all a talented fleet commander.

For the moment, however, Bridport was not called upon to go to sea. Harvey remained with his squadron off Brest until the beginning of January 1796. He reported to Bridport on his arrival at Spithead that the squadron had remained very healthy during its long cruise, chiefly owing to the refreshments sent out and to taking shelter in Quiberon Bay during the fierce gales that had prevailed in October and November. The use of the anchorage there was of course valuable; but as Seymour pointed out to Spencer, it came at a cost. It would be necessary to keep as many ships there as the French could put to sea if it was to be secure, with all the consequences of supplying, docking and refitting the ships so employed.

Spencer's broadmindedness was shown again in March 1796, when the post of Governor of Greenwich Hospital became vacant. Chatham had apparently prom-ised it to Lord Hood, and Spencer wrote to the latter to honour the promise, subject to the King's approval. He added that his satisfaction in doing so 'would have been more complete on this occasion if it could have removed the impression made by the conduct your Lordship thought proper to adopt' in the previous year. He was, however, prepared to pass over this, even though his opinion was unchanged. Perhaps even more surprisingly, the King was prepared not to object, even though, as he observed, 'the last military transaction of Lord Hood greatly tarnished his former good conduct'.[19]

Spencer's generally tolerant attitude had not however prevented, towards the end of 1795, the loss of the most valuable member of the Board of Admiralty. A dispute with Middleton had arisen over the First Lord's decision to recall Sir John Laforey from the West Indies. Under pressure from the Secretary for War, Henry Dundas, who was Middleton's cousin, and in spite of Middleton's strong objec-tions, Spencer had finally agreed that Laforey should be replaced as commander-in-chief. Middleton refused to acquiesce in the decision, and this led to Spencer insisting that every member of the Board was required ultimately to concur in his wishes. He required Middleton to countersign the appropriate minute; Middleton, who was a friend of Laforey as well as having a high professional respect for him, refused to do so. When pressed effectively either to sign or to leave the Board, he was happy to make it a resignation issue, writing to Spencer on 26 October:

No consideration will induce me to concur in what I think an unjust measure, however recommended, because I know myself amenable to

19 Corbett (ed.), *Spencer*, Vol.I, p.148.

a much higher tribunal than any on earth. As your Lordship seems to insinuate a removal from office, I can only say that my seat is at your Lordship's service.[20]

He left the Board in the conviction that he had been perfectly right, observing in a subsequent letter to Spencer that he had no regrets in giving up his seat on the Board:

On the whole I shall certainly quit [it] with more pleasure than I had come into it. At the same time, my personal feelings would never have forced me to the step I have taken, if your Lordship's language had not rendered it indispensable.[21]

This was not, however, to be the last that the Admiralty saw of Sir Charles Middleton, and it was just as well for Great Britain that this was the case.

20 Corbett (ed.), *Spencer*, Vol.I, p.183.
21 Quoted Talbott, *Pen and Ink Sailor*, p.143.

10

Ireland

During the winter of 1795-1796 the French fleet in Brest had shown few signs of activity, and there were no indications from the intelligence reaching the Admiralty that any major operations were contemplated. For the moment, therefore, neither the ailing Commander-in-Chief nor his mulishly discontented subordinate, both of whom remained on shore, were called upon for active service. It was still considered necessary, however, for a close watch to be kept on Brest, and after Harvey's return this duty fell on Warren and Pellew and their squadrons of frigates, which gave rise to a number of actions against individual French ships and small squadrons. In addition, the forward policy of the Admiralty gave plenty of opportunities for the commanders of frigates and smaller vessels to distinguish themselves in minor operations off the French coast. Sidney Smith, in one of the many letters which he wrote to Spencer, summed up what he took that policy to be: 'My idea of the application of our naval force is to show that the frontier of Great Britain is high water mark in France. The uppermost seaweed belongs to us'.[1]

Sidney Smith, in his frigate *Diamond*, 38, was ceaselessly active against both French shipping and against shore establishments. A typical action took place on 2 September 1795, when he chased and drove on to the rocks of the Breton coast the French *Assemblée Nationale*, of 14 guns. Early in the following year he achieved a striking success when operating with two smaller vessels, the *Liberty,* 14, and the *Aristocrat.* On 18 March 1796 he launched a sudden assault on the Breton port of Erqui, in which lay the French corvette *Etourdie*, 16, with a number of smaller vessels. Smith sailed boldly into the harbour and landed a party of seamen and marines, which stormed three guns mounted in commanding positions overlooking the port. The *Etourdie*, together with four brigs, two sloops and a lugger were set on fire and destroyed. British casualties amounted to only 2 killed and 7 wounded in this operation.[2]

---

1   Morriss (ed.), *Channel Fleet*, p.96.
2   Clowes, *Royal Navy*, Vol.IV, p.495.

Although these minor operations very frequently resulted in a British success, this was not always the case, as Smith found out to his cost on 17 April. Learning that a French privateer, the *Vengeur*, was lying at anchor at Le Havre, he resolved to cut her out. He led a boat attack from the *Diamond* and successfully boarded the *Vengeur*. However, the latter's crew had, when the attack commenced, cut their cable, and the rising tide carried the *Vengeur* up river, two miles above Le Havre. Smith tried to escape in the *Diamond's* boats but this proved impossible, as there were now French vessels blocking the mouth of the river. Smith and his men were soon surrounded by small craft and obliged to surrender with the loss of 4 killed and 7 wounded. Smith and Midshipman Wright, who were as a result of his activities along the coast considered to be state prisoners, were taken to Paris to the Temple prison, from which, in May 1798, they succeeded in escaping.

Earlier, on 20 March, the usually reliable Warren had failed to distinguish himself in an action off the Pointe du Raz. He had with him, in addition to his own *Pomone*, 40, the frigates *Anson*, 44, *Artois*, 38, and *Galatea*, 32, when he encountered a large French convoy. This was escorted by the frigate *Proserpine*, 40, the 36 gun frigates *Unité*, *Coquille* and *Tamise*, and the corvette *Cigogne*, 20. The British squadron succeeded in taking several prizes from the convoy, before passing the French squadron on the opposite tack, exchanging fire, in the course of which the *Galatea* was severely damaged. The French steered for the Pointe de Raz and Brest, pursued by the British. However, although taking an armed store ship, Warren was unable to prevent their escape. In the account of the action contained in Clowes' *Royal Navy*, written by H.W. Wilson, the latter was scathing:

> The force of the British was superior in this affair, and it is not obvious why the French escaped so easily. Warren, the British senior officer, absurdly exaggerated the strength of his enemy in his report of the business. Of the convoy six ships in all were taken. The British loss was 2 killed and 6 wounded.[3]

Wilson's judgment, however, scarcely does justice to Warren, whose report refers only to the French men of war without numbering them; he went on to explain how the action came to an end:

> Perceiving them rallying round the Commodore close in shore and beginning to form again I made the signal for ours in close order to endeavour to break their line by cutting off the rear ships and directed the *Galatea* to lead course for that purpose. But the enemy bore away and made all sail possible from us and stood into the narrow part of the Raz de Fontenay among the rocks. I was, however, enabled to cut off their rear ship. Night

3   Clowes, *Royal Navy*, Vol.IV, p.495.

approaching and being unacquainted with the passage, I did not think it proper to continue the pursuit further at the risk of losing some of our ships in so difficult a pass.[4]

Pellew, meanwhile, was enjoying rather greater success with his squadron. On 12 April, while cruising off Brest, he sighted and chased the French frigate *Unité*, 36. Pellew's squadron consisted of five frigates, and one of them, *Révolutionnaire*, 36, closed the *Unité* after nightfall, and called on her to surrender. The French captain, Linois, refused, and a short but fierce action followed before he was obliged to strike his colours. The *Révolutionnaire*, herself captured previously from the French, was much larger and more heavily armed, and by the end of the action was supported by the *Concorde*, 36.

In the following week Pellew struck again, With his own *Indefatigable*, 44, and the two 36 gun frigates *Concorde* and *Amazon*, he fell in with the French frigate *Virginie*, 40, off the Lizard on 20 April. With the wind in the southeast, the *Virginie* could not make her escape to Brest; after a chase of fifteen hours, she was caught by the *Indefatigable*. Both ships sustained damage, but when the *Concorde* and *Amazon* arrived, the *Virginie* had no choice but to strike her colours.[5]

A week later, the British frigate *Niger* came upon an armed lugger, the *Ecureuil*, and drove her on to the Penmarck rocks. To make assurance doubly sure, Captain Foote of the *Niger* sent a party in his boats after cannonading the *Ecureuil*, which boarded the French vessel and burned her. It was actions such as these that made it so difficult for the French to rely on coastal traffic, both for trading purposes and to collect substantial forces in Brest for larger scale operations.

Warren continued to keep Brest under observation, sending in frigates to check on any activity on the part of the French fleet. Typical of the reports he received was one from Captain Richard Keats in the *Galatea* on 19 May:

> In execution of your order of the 17th to reconnoitre and ascertain the force of the enemy in Brest Water I arrived with the *Galatea* and *Valiant* lugger off the Parquet last night but finding when the weather cleared away as we entered the channel this morning between St Mathews Point and those rocks three frigates, two ships and a brig corvette at anchor in Bertheaume Road, some of which made preparations to get under sail I could not proceed much nearer the Goulet than St Mathews Point.[6]

He was able to see, however, that the French had eight ships of the line, five or six frigates and four or five corvettes apparently ready for sea.

4   Morriss (ed.), *Channel Fleet*, p.149.
5   Clowes, Royal Navy, Vol.IV, p.497.
6   Morriss (ed.), *Channel Fleet*, p.151.

Operations against French shipping in the Channel and the Bay of Biscay continued. In June the frigates *Santa Margarita*, 36, and *Unicorn*, 32, encountered and after a lengthy action captured the French *Tamise*, 40, and *Tribune*, 38; the former had been previously the British frigate *Thames*, under which name she was restored to the Royal Navy. On 11 June, the *Amazon*, 38, and other frigates of Pellew's squadron snapped up the French corvettes *Trois Couleurs*, 14, and *Betsy*, 18, off Brest; and on 22 June the *Apollo*, 38, and *Doris*, 36, captured the French corvette *Légère*. On 23 August, the redoubtable Keats, in the *Galatea* with the sloop *Sylph*, 18, drove the French frigate *Andromaque* on shore, and burned her.[7]

It was beginning to look as if the French were planning an operation. In addition to the number of ships apparently ready for sea in Brest Roads, d'Auvergne's informants were providing him with firm intelligence not only of the number of ships being assembled, but also of the troops marching to the port, even with details of the regiments concerned. What was not apparent, though, was the destination for which this force was intended. There were suggestions that they might be intended for India, or for Portugal, or to San Domingo to suppress the revolt there.[8] Other possible destinations were Gibraltar or Ireland, and it was the latter which d'Auvergne regarded as the most probable. All this suggested the need to strengthen the watch on Brest, and while the bulk of the Channel Fleet remained at Spithead, a squadron under Vice Admiral Sir Charles Thompson, in the *London*, 98, was stationed off Brest while another, under Rear Admiral Sir Roger Curtis in the *Formidable*, 98, cruised to the westward to cover Ireland.[9]

In August Vice Admiral Sir Alan Gardner took a squadron to Brest to replace that of Thompson. By mid September, after five weeks at sea, he was warning Spencer about the state of the water throughout the squadron. This, he reckoned, was 'so much reduced as to put it out of my power to pursue the enemy to any considerable distance to the westward should they escape us in the night'.[10] With the risk that the enemy in Brest might by reinforced by the squadron of Admiral de Richery, which had put to sea from Toulon, Gardner did not feel able to weaken his squadron by sending in two at a time to Cawsand Bay for refreshment. His letter illustrated, very clearly, the extent to which the blockade of Brest was decidedly porous. This was confirmed in the following month, when Spencer told Gardner that two ships of the line from Rochefort, and three more from Lorient, were said to be en route to Brest. Gardner was asked to look out for their having arrived in Brest, to which a large number of transports were also said to have sailed. The plain fact was that the French were finding it a reasonably straight forward matter

7   Clowes, *Royal Navy*, Vol.IV, pp.498-502.
8   Robert Balleine (ed.), *The Tragedy of Philippe d'Auvergne* (London: Phillimore, 1973), p.86.
9   Clowes, *Royal Navy*, Vol.IV, p.283.
10   Morriss (ed.), *Channel Fleet*, p.155.

to pass warships in and out of the port; it was more a matter of luck than judgment if any of these were encountered at sea.

Meanwhile Bridport, at home at Cricket Lodge, had been getting restless, and he sent a pointed reminder to Spencer on 24 October:

> As the *Royal George* is returning to Spithead I wish she might not again proceed to sea without my flag, but on this subject I will say no more, trusting that your Lordship will call on me when His Majesty's service shall require me to repair to my duty.[11]

In his reassuring reply, Spencer observed that if, as he believed, it would be necessary to collect ten or twelve ships of the line, he would feel 'great satisfaction' at seeing such a squadron under Bridport's orders. Prudently, however, he added that this was presently his idea but it must of course be subject to any change of circumstances.

Gardner's squadron off Brest had been replaced in due course by a squadron under Vice Admiral John Colpoys, who reported to Spencer on 7 December: 'The account this morning from Brest looks as if the enemy meant to take the sea air, which if they should, I hope it may be by daylight, for to be sure, blocking up a port with 14 hours night is trying to an admiral's nerves'.[12] Spencer had been chancing his arm in leaving only a squadron off Brest, given the size and the increasing state of readiness of the French fleet, and the time had now come for Bridport to take command of the Channel Fleet at Spithead and put to sea. Colpoys, still cruising off Brest on 11 December, still suspected that something was going on. For more than a month nothing of consequence had left Brest, which might indicate enhanced security to prevent any information leaking out. On 23 December Colpoys encountered a squadron of five ships of the line under Rear Admiral Villeneuve from Toulon, which was intended to reinforce the fleet in Brest, and drove it to take refuge in Lorient.

By then, however, the long planned French operation had begun. The original intention had been for Villaret-Joyeuse, with fifteen of the line from Brest, to carry a first wave of an invasion force to be landed in Ireland. The second wave, escorted by seven ships of the line under Rear Admiral de Richery from Lorient and Villeneuve's squadron from Toulon, was to follow. Meanwhile Villaret-Joyeuse, having landed the troops with him, was to sail with his eight fastest ships to the Indian Ocean, to link up there with Rear Admiral Sercey. The overall military commander of the expedition was General Lazare Hoche, who had successfully repelled the Royalist invasion at Quiberon Bay. Believing that Villaret-Joyeuse was more interested in the Indian part of the plan, he prevailed on Vice Admiral Truguet, the French Minister

11 Morriss (ed.), *Channel Fleet*, p.157.
12 Morriss (ed.), *Channel Fleet*, pp.159-160.

of Marine, for Vice Admiral Morard de Galles to supersede Villaret-Joyeuse.[13] On 8 December de Richery arrived at Brest, having been delayed by the necessity of putting into Rochefort to evade the squadron under Curtis. He seems, however, to have had no difficulty in slipping past Colpoys, who was sure that he had not missed anything. Of de Richery's ships only two were fit to take part in the expedition, but it was decided to wait no longer, and on 15 December the first part of the invasion fleet moved out and anchored outside the port.

Morard de Galles had a powerful force, with seventeen ships of the line, one razee, twelve frigates, six brigs and a powder vessel, together with seven transports. A total of 18,000 troops were aboard. Morard de Galles's flagship was the *Indomptable*, 80, but he and his subordinate admirals Nielly and Bouvet transferred their flags to frigates to make the journey to Ireland. He had intended to go out by the Passage du Raz, but after the whole fleet had been collected on 16 December he changed his mind, and as darkness fell ordered that the Passage d'Iroise be followed instead. Unluckily, however, his signal was taken in by only some of the fleet, so part took the Passage du Raz as originally intended. Aboard the frigate *Fraternité*, Morard de Galles endeavoured unsuccessfully by flares and the firing of guns to clear up the confusion, which made matters worse. By now Pellew was on the scene in the *Indefatigable* and the firing of his guns, and the distress signals from the *Séduisante*, 74, which had struck on the Grand Stevenet, added to the confusion.

Pellew who had four frigates, had sent the *Amazon* to England and the *Phoebe* to Colpoys to report de Richery's arrival. The *Phoebe* had returned to him, and was sent off again on 15 December to tell Colpoys that the French were coming out; next day Pellew sent off the *Révolutionnaire* to Colpoys with the latest information. Colpoys, however, did not get the news until 19 December having been driven by strong winds off his station; it was on the following day that he sighted Villeneuve's squadron, and chased it into Lorient. Having then been struck by a gale, Colpoys made his way back to Spithead, and took no further part in the operations. Meanwhile Pellew had sent off an armed lugger to Falmouth on 17 December with a report of the French fleet's movement; he stayed in touch with the enemy until that night, but then lost contact, and so made his way back to Falmouth.

Rear Admiral Bouvet, in the frigate *Immortalité*, had been in that part of the French fleet that cleared the Passage du Raz by the morning of 17 December. There was no sign of the rest of the fleet, so he opened his sealed orders; these required him to proceed to Mizen Head, in southern Ireland, and to cruise off it for five days. On the morning of 19 December he fell in with the bulk of the fleet; still missing, however, were Morard de Galles, who with Hoche was still aboard the *Fraternité*, the 74 gun ship *Nestor*, (of which the ubiquitous Linois was now captain) the frigates *Cocarde* and *Romaine*, three brigs and two transports. Bouvet

---

13   Clowes, *Royal Navy*, Vol.IV, p.297.

thus found himself in command of the expedition and, reaching Mizen Head on 21 December, ordered his fleet to anchor in Bantry Bay, its objective.

While all this was going on Bridport, at Spithead, was getting ready to sail. He went on board the *Royal George* on 20 December, where a messenger reached him with the news that the French were out and had evaded Colpoys. In reply, he reported that he hoped to be able to sail on 24 or 25 December. On 22 December, the Admiralty sent him his orders. He was to link up with Colpoys, who would join his fleet. If he could not find him, he was to show himself off Brest and then, in the absence of any clear intelligence of the whereabouts of the French fleet, he was to search for it off Ireland. If he could not locate it, he was to return to Brest, and take up his station there.[14] Two days later he received confirmatory orders, emphasising that he should not waste time looking for Colpoys, but in any case if he had news that the French had gone to Ireland he should go straight there.

Bridport intended to put to sea on 24 December, but was prevented by an easterly wind; he was further delayed during the process of assembling the fleet at St Helens by five of his ships being involved in collisions, grounding or accidents. Seymour aboard the *Sans Pareil* wrote to Spencer to report on those incidents:

> In the course of working down several accidents took place, which I much feared would reduce the force of the squadron but I now believe that when the wind moderates we shall move together. The *Prince,* having missed stays when she, with the *Sans Pareil*, was close over upon the Isle of Wight shore, came on board her and for some minutes the ships were locked in the most unpleasant way, the bowsprit of the former being placed just before our main mast.[15]

The *Atlas* grounded for three hours on a sandbank, and the *Formidable* and *Ville de Paris* collided, but without any serious injury. The wind, however, continued to be very unfavourable, and the fleet was only finally assembled at St Helens on 29 December.

In the event Bridport did not get away until 3 January, by which date a report had been received from Vice Admiral Kingsmill, commanding on the coast of Ireland, of Bouvet's arrival at Bantry Bay; he had subsequently sailed from there but his destination was unknown. Meanwhile Colpoys had returned to Spithead on 31 December, enabling two ships of his squadron to reinforce Bridport. This still left the Channel Fleet under strength, in the latter's opinion, which made it impossible for him to detach Rear Admiral Sir William Parker for convoy escort duties. Bridport had a total of 14 ships of the line, which was, he considered, less than he needed if he were to meet the entire French fleet.

14   Morriss (ed.), *Channel Fleet*, p.169.
15   Clowes, *Royal Navy*, Vol.IV, p.304.

This, however, was not to be. Bouvet, still aboard the *Immortalité*, had in the face of a stiff east wind, been lost to sight. Grouchy, the senior military commander, proposed to land troops on 24 December, but the weather again worsened, making this impossible, and on Christmas Day became so bad that the whole fleet was driven to sea. For three days it was impossible to re-enter Bantry Bay. When, on 29 December, the weather moderated Bouvet decided, as his provisions were running low, to abort the mission and return to Brest.[16]

Morard de Galles, in the *Fraternité*, had lost touch with the *Nestor* and the other separated units of the fleet. After being chased by a British frigate, it was not until 29 December that he was able to head for Bantry Bay. En route he met the *Révolution*, 74, which was taking aboard the crew of the razee *Scévola*, which was in a sinking condition. There were no other French ships to be seen so, over-crowded and short of provisions, Morard de Galles and Hoche reckoned that they, too, must return to France. They had a couple of scares en route, sighting two British frigates on 8 January, and being chased by the Channel Fleet two days later. They escaped in the thick weather, and on 14 January reached Rochefort.

There was to be one more spectacular encounter arising from the abortive mission to Bantry Bay. A number of ships which had failed to reach that place had sailed to the mouth of the Shannon, but found nothing useful to do there, and set off back to France. One of them was the 74 gun *Droits de l'Homme* (Captain La Crosse); after capturing the *Cumberland* letter of marque and then revisiting Bantry Bay to see if any of her consorts were still there, she left on 9 January for Brest. Nearing his destination on 13 January La Crosse ran into Pellew in the *Indefatigable* at 3.30 pm which, with the *Amazon*, was still watching Brest. The weather was bad, and the *Droits de l'Homme* lost her main topsail braces and then her fore and main topmasts. By the time the *Indefatigable* came up, at 5.30 pm, seven miles ahead of the *Amazon*, the French crew had cleared the wreckage, and a fierce engagement began. The French vessel, although of course of much greater force than her opponent, was hampered by the loss of her topmast, and, rolling heavily, could not open the gunports on her lower deck. At 6.45 the *Amazon* joined in the fight, La Crosse skilfully avoided being raked, and at 7.30 the two frigates shot ahead of the *Droits de l'Homme*, giving her the chance to continue running east-south-east. At 8.30 pm, however, the frigates were up with her, one on either bow. As the fight continued, the French ship had at 10.30 pm to cut away her mizzen mast; the *Indefatigable* and *Amazon* fired heavily into her on her quarters. At 4.20 am next morning, the engagement was brought to a sudden end when breakers were seen dead ahead. The *Indefatigable* hauled off to the southward but the *Amazon* was not so fortunate: attempting to wear to the northward but, due to the damage she had suffered, she could not haul off and ran aground, quickly becoming a wreck. Her crew apart from six men got safely ashore; all were made prisoners.

---

16 Clowes, *Royal Navy*, Vol.IV, p.301.

The *Indefatigable*, badly damaged, got safely clear, having suffered only nineteen wounded in the battle. The *Droits de l'Homme*, which had already sustained about 250 casualties, struck hard on a sandbank in Audierne Bay, her mainmast going by the board. For the next two days she lay there, pounded into ruins by the force of the sea. On 17 January two vessels managed to reach her, and took off the survivors; but it was estimated that more than 1,000 men had lost their lives.[17] A British infantry officer, Lieutenant Elias Pipon, who had been taken prisoner when the *Cumberland* was captured, together with two other infantry officers, two merchant captains, two women and forty eight seamen and soldiers, wrote a graphic account of the end of the *Droits de l'Homme*. Confined in the cable tier, the British prisoners were told to climb up, or they would be lost:

> Everyone rather flew than climbed up. Though scarcely able before to move, from sickness, I now found an energetic strength in all my frame, and soon gained the upper decks, but oh, what a sight! Dead, wounded, and living, intermingled in a state too shocking to describe; not a mast standing, a dreadful loom of the land, and breakers all around us. The *Indefatigable*, on the starboard quarter, appeared standing off in a most tremendous sea, from the Penmark Rocks, which threatened her with instant destruction. To the great humanity of her commander those few persons who survived the shipwreck, were indebted for their lives, for had another broadside been fired, the commanding situation of the *Indefatigable* must have swept off at least a thousand men. On the larboard side, was seen the *Amazon*, within two miles, just struck on the shore – our own fate drew near. The ship struck, and immediately sunk![18]

Pipon described the desperate attempts at rescue; he estimated that of all those on board only about 320 had survived.

Bridport's sweep, when he finally got to sea, yielded no results. He sailed to Ushant to try to pick up some news of the French; finding none, he sailed north west to Cape Clear. On 9 January he checked out Bantry Bay and, finding nothing there, he sailed for Ushant, chasing Morard de Galles in *Fraternité* on 10 January 10 to no avail. Arriving off Ushant, he remained on station for about a week, but saw nothing of the surviving French ships as they made their way back in Brest. The weather continued to be very bad, and at the end of the month Bridport sailed for Torbay, leaving at sea only one ship of the line and five frigates for convoy protection. He was subsequently ordered back to Spithead to refit, where he arrived on 3 February, nursing a powerful grievance.

17   Clowes, *Royal Navy*, Vol.IV, p.304.
18   Tracy (ed.), *Naval Chronicle*, Vol.II, p.169.

11

Bridport: Commander-in-Chief at Last

What had seriously annoyed Lord Bridport was an incident which Seymour described in a letter to Spencer from Torbay on 1 February. While Bridport with the Channel Fleet was searching for the French fleet, unaware that it had by then got back to Brest, a squadron of frigates, which it was soon established was British, appeared and made the private recognition signals. The squadron did not, however, respond to Bridport's signals ordering it to join him. Bridport sent the *Triumph* together with three frigates to catch up with the errant squadron but they failed to do so and lost them during the night. On this occasion Seymour had a good deal of sympathy with Bridport:

> I am yet ignorant what are the ships which acted in this most reprehen-
> sible and un-officer like manner but I take it for granted that our chief,
> who cannot fail to have been much hurt with it, will apply publicly for an
> enquiry in the conduct of the officer commanding them. I am sure that
> he should do so and that notice should be taken of so glaring a breach
> of discipline and a piece of disobedience which should be reprobated on
> every occasion and more especially under the particular circumstances of
> time and place when we fell in with this detachment of our fleet.[1]

Bridport must have had a shrewd suspicion that the offender was Warren, which would have served to sharpen his displeasure.

Indeed it was Warren, to whom Spencer wrote on 10 March to ask for an expla-
nation, having received Bridport's formal complaint. On 14 March Warren wrote to explain what had occurred. It is doubtful whether Bridport would have been satisfied; but it seems that the Admiralty must have been, for no action was taken. Warren wrote that being far to windward he had made the private signal to a ship to leeward, which was answered:

---

1   Morriss (ed.), *Channel Fleet*, pp.178-179.

I then tacked, conceiving that our services were not required by the Commander-in-Chief, and therefore proceeded with all despatch to fulfil the orders I had received from their Lordships; and the day being dark and hazy I did not observe any other signals addressed to us.[2]

He was, he said extremely sorry; and in future would make it his best object, when the fleet was in sight, 'to go down and receive the Commander-in-Chief's orders and to which I shall ever show the strictest attention'.

Spencer, meanwhile, had been endeavouring to please Bridport by giving his cousin, Alexander Hood, the command of the *Ville de Paris*, 110. He did not have much hope, however, that the gesture would be appreciated, and would not have been surprised to hear from Seymour on the subject:

> I have made Captain Hood sensible of your kind intentions towards him by appointing him to her, but I might work from this day to the end of my life in endeavouring to make Lord Bridport feel the compliment you meant to pay him through your attention to his nephew without making him acknowledge it.[3]

Spencer's very able frigate squadron commanders were, one way and another, giving him a certain amount of trouble. Pellew, who was always rather money-conscious, wrote to him rather cheekily on 10 March to ask to be given a cruise to give him a chance of some prize money. Spencer had, he said, presided over the navy for some two years:

> During this period I refer myself to your Lordship's judgment if I have not taken my full share of the fag of the service. In the present moment I see many of my juniors placed in situations to make prize money. I have never for the whole war been permitted to run loose for a cruise. I may add to it the promises of the former Admiralty of being placed in a situation where I might reasonably expect some emolument. It hath never happened to me to capture a merchant ship for the war, unless indeed a few empty chasse-marées may be called so and all I have made I have fought hard for. I have watched the port of Brest and performed a hazardous service at Quiberon. Give me then my Lordship the first time in my life the chance of getting a prize.[4]

2   Morriss (ed.), *Channel Fleet*, p.186.
3   Morriss (ed.), *Channel Fleet*, p.179.
4   Morriss (ed.), *Channel Fleet*, pp.184-185.

Spencer was sympathetic but unhelpful. The naval service, he told Pellew 'is and always must be a lottery as to profit'. His present station gave him plenty of opportunity for pursuit and capture, and had always been looked on as the most desirable in the Admiralty's appointment. Even if he could properly move Pellew elsewhere, he could not see where he could be sent to give him a better chance of prize money.

Warren, too, thought a cruise would be good, writing to Spencer on 24 March:

> I therefore trust and rely upon your Lordship's kindness on allowing me to own that it would essentially serve us if we were favoured with a cruise off the island of Madeira that we may be thrown into fortune's way. We could afterwards remain off Cape Ortegal or between that place and Ireland so as to cut the line of Rochefort and Bordeaux with great advantage to the service.[5]

What Warren really wanted was to get away from Bridport, as he candidly explained. He was 'advancing high upon the list' and it would be hard if, now that he had incurred Bridport's displeasure, that he should have to 'serve under him in a post that is liable to much misconstruction'. If he could not get his cruise, he would, he said, be glad to serve with Seymour in any station or with Jervis on the coast of Spain.

Getting away from Bridport was also high on Pellew's agenda; in this, Spencer was able to give him some reassurance:

> I think you will readily perceive that you are not intended to be constantly under the orders of the Channel Fleet Admiral; on the contrary from the sort of cruising which that fleet will be to carry on during the summer it will very probably be but seldom that you will meet unless you seek him for the purpose of giving intelligence.[6]

Meanwhile, Spencer had to continue managing Bridport. It seemed evident that a much closer watch must be maintained on Brest, since the French were still able to get in and out, and were sending out stronger forces, necessitating an increase in the strength of the blockading fleet. However, Bridport was not convinced that this was either possible or necessary. Strong easterly winds had blown the Channel Fleet off its station off Ushant; frigates on station in the mouth of the Goulet were equally vulnerable to such winds. Bridport was also dismissive of the value of much of the intelligence that was gathered:

5   Morriss (ed.), *Channel Fleet*, p.187.
6   Morriss (ed.), *Channel Fleet*, p.188.

There is no reliance on the appearance of ships at anchor. I mean such as are not apparently ready for sea. Neither is there any dependence to be placed on the reports of prisoners. They speak the language they are told.[7]

The value of a blockade that meant that the battle fleet had to retreat 200 miles to Spithead was, it seemed, very doubtful.

One suggestion for increasing its effectiveness came from both Pellew and Warren, and this was a proposal to base the blockading fleet on Douarnenez Bay, south of the entrance to Brest Roads. It was, Warren pointed out, as well sheltered and as large as Torbay; a fleet anchored there could get out on the same wind that would carry the French out of Brest, while frigates in an advanced position off the Black Rocks and the Toulinquet Rocks could give immediate warning by cutter of a sortie. In response, Spencer asked whether a fleet of any size could use the anchorage and be out of range of gunfire from the shore.[8] In answer to this question Warren referred to the conclusion of the late Lord Bristol:

He has given his decided opinion in behalf of such a measure and from every observation I could form in being twice all round it appears to possess great advantages capable of containing any number of men of war. There are differences in particular places but as it is larger than Torbay it is impossible for shells to range far enough to annoy shipping.[9]

It was as Captain Augustus Hervey that Lord Bristol had forwarded to Sir Edward Hawke a report from Captain Clements of a visit to Douarnenez Bay in October 1759, in which it was said that 'the whole bay seemed a very fair one and very good anchoring, with a westerly wind being landlocked at about two miles from the shore'.[10] Two months later, while still on blockade duty off the Black Rocks, Hervey wrote to Hawke that 'Douarnenez must be the resource if catched with any sudden gale westerly'.[11]

Spencer remained impressed with the possibilities of Douarnenez Bay, and on April 9 1798 he asked Bridport to give some thoughts to the suggestion:

I have heard from some officers that the Bay of Douarnenez would be a good station for the purpose of blocking Brest but being on the enemy's coast and so near one of their arsenals I should be a [little] apprehensive of the squadron anchored in that bay being a little liable to sudden attacks

7   Bridport to Spencer, March 30 1797; Morriss (ed.), *Channel Fleet*, p.188.
8   Morriss (ed.), *Channel Fleet*, p.175.
9   Morriss (ed.), *Channel Fleet*, p.176.
10   Ruddock Mackay (ed.), *The Hawke Papers* (Aldershot: Navy Records Society, 1990), p.263.
11   Mackay (ed.), *Hawke Papers*, p.312.

by fire ships or gun boats and perhaps also to annoyance from mortar batteries on shore.[12]

He also, in the same letter, floated the possibility of an anchorage in the Scilly Isles, which had been the subject of a written proposal which he forwarded to Bridport.

Bridport was thoroughly unimpressed with both these suggestions:

> I have fully considered the subject of the road of St Mary's Scilly, and the Bay of Douarnenez. When I was captain of a frigate I have frequently anchored her in Camaret Bay and have often reconnoitred Douarnenez Bay which I consider as unsafe to anchor the King's fleet in except in the pursuit of an enemy. What supplies can it receive when at anchor in that bay? And are the proposers of this plan sure that the watching the port of Brest is obtained by that anchorage?

Bridport was even more scathing about St Mary's roadstead in the Scilly Isles, pointing out that even the author of the paper sent to him conceded 'that in putting to sea with the wind westerly there is not room for line of battle ships to cast and they must slip their cables'. He wondered how and when the ships would get their anchors and cables again. He concluded magisterially: 'Upon the whole of this subject I cannot give my consent to hazarding the King's fleet in Douarnenez Bay or to risk the loss of it in detail on the rocks of Scilly'.[13] So that, for the moment, was that; but the idea of using Douarnenez Bay was to recur under a later commander.

Bridport was not to have much respite. Intelligence that the French were preparing a sortie from Brest meant that the Channel Fleet must put to sea again as soon as possible, and orders to this effect went to Bridport on 26 February. His mission was to sail as soon as possible and take up a station off Brest to prevent any ships of the enemy leaving the port, or to destroy them if they did come out. It was at this point far from certain that the French had not already sailed:

> If your Lordship should obtain certain information of the enemy's fleet being at sea, and of its actual situation, you are immediately to proceed in quest of it; but if you only gain intelligence that it has sailed without being able to learn its course, you are in such case to make the best of your way to Cape Clear, and then repair off the Lizard for further orders, transmitting to us as expeditiously as possible an account of your arrival and proceedings.[14]

12   Morriss (ed.), *Channel Fleet*, p.289.
13   Morriss (ed.), *Channel Fleet*, p.291.
14   Morriss (ed.), *Channel Fleet*, p.182.

If the French were still in Brest, he was to cruise off that port to prevent their putting to sea, at least while the wind was in the east; if it shifted westerly, he was to return to the Lizard and try to keep station there while awaiting further orders. Finally, if the wind changed again before such orders came, enabling the French to get out, he was to return at once to Brest. It was difficult for the Admiralty to plan for every contingency, when all depended on the weather; but this was the best that could be done.

Bridport was in no doubt that the French would come out, if they had not already done so, and might have 25 ships of the line to his 15; he hoped that this was not true, as he would much rather attack than defend against a superior fleet, 'both for myself and the country'. This was a sentiment which Spencer warmly endorsed. As it happened, the wind not only prevented any action, but even precluded an inspection of the port, a circumstance which illustrates clearly the very great difficulty faced by a blockading fleet. Bridport reported to Spencer from Spithead on 30 March:

> The squadron under my command arrived here this day as I have stated in my letter to Mr Nepean, by which your Lordship will see I was driven far to the westward of my station by the strong easterly wind; during which time the Brest ships might have put to sea if they had received orders and were in all respects prepared for sailing. It was my intention to have sent two ships to look into Brest on the 25th but it blew so strong that day I did not think it prudent to give orders for their proceeding. Your Lordship will perceive how impossible it is to keep frigates cruising in sight of the enemy's ships at Brest or even to preserve a station within a correct distance.[15]

It turned out that French preparations for a sortie were not as far advanced as supposed, and it was found sufficient to send out Sir Roger Curtis with nine ships of the line on 6 April to keep watch on Brest.

Spencer and Bridport were not entirely at one in the matter of maintaining the blockade. The First Lord wanted to see a 'stricter and more systematic' policy applied, and this, he told Bridport, required that all the officers of the Channel Fleet should be kept together as much as possible so that it might put to sea at the shortest notice. Bridport, because of the difficulties of a close blockade, took a more laid back view.

It was now that Lord Howe's continued ill health obliged him to give up the formal command of the Channel Fleet, and this time there was no question of talking him out of it. His resignation came on 8 April, and on 13 April Bridport was able at last to acknowledge receipt of his commission as Commander-in-Chief.

15 Morriss (ed.), *Channel Fleet*, p.188.

To Spencer he wrote: 'I hope that my heath will enable me to execute the duties of my station to the end of the war, though I must own I sometimes feel checks to that explanation'.[16] Before Bridport could put to sea in his new status, however, a major crisis erupted which was to threaten the very existence of his command.

16   Morriss (ed.), *Channel Fleet*, p.190.

12

Mutiny

Bridport had returned to Spithead with the Channel Fleet on 30 March. He had then gone on leave, returning to the fleet on 10 April. Two days later he received news which was utterly shocking. It came originally from Captain Patton, an officer in the Transport Office, who heard on the evening of 12 April that there were rumblings of discontent in the fleet which had culminated in the decision to lodge a formal petition of the seamen's grievances. He hastened to the Port Admiral, Sir Peter Parker, to tell him what he had heard, and then rowed out through the darkness to the *Royal George* to break the news to Bridport. It was plain to the Commander-in-Chief that the situation was potentially of the utmost gravity, and next morning he sent Captain Glynn to London with a brief note to Spencer:

> I am sorry to inform your Lordship that a circumstance reached me yesterday which gave me much concern. It has been stated to me that representations have been made by the crews of the Channel Fleet to Lord Howe and the Admiralty for an increase of pay. If this should be the case it would be very desirable for me to know what steps have been taken in consequence thereof. I am particularly anxious to receive such instructions as your Lordship and the Board may think expedient with as little delay as possible as I yesterday heard that some disagreeable combinations were forming among the ships at Spithead on this subject. Captain Glynn will deliver this with the utmost expedition to your Lordship. He is not acquainted with the contents.[1]

At this stage Bridport still had no idea of the advanced situation that had been reached; Patton had only mentioned that there had been petitions but knew little more. When Bridport got Spencer's reply of the following day he was flabbergasted. Spencer told him that Lord Howe had passed on to Lord Hugh Seymour

---

1   Morriss (ed.), *Channel Fleet*, p.196.

eleven letters each purporting to come from the crew of a ship of the line. Howe had suspected, because of the similarity of the wording, that they had come from one source. Howe had not acknowledged them, but gave them to Seymour for the information of the Board; the Board did absolutely nothing, as Spencer explained to Bridport:

> As it appeared impossible to do anything officially on the subject without running the risk of unpleasant consequences by a public agitation of so delicate a topic it was judged most advisable by the Board to take no notice of the circumstance, hoping that it might go no further.[2]

Spencer forwarded the eleven letters to Bridport; asked what information he had received; and advised him of the need for 'great circumspection'.

A more feeble instance of ostrich-like behaviour is difficult to imagine. Bridport, appalled, controlled his propensity for extravagant and sarcastic language in the separate replies he sent on 15 April to Spencer and to Nepean as First Secretary. Having seen the letters, which be returned to Nepean, he was now aware of the ships from which petitions had been sent to Howe, the first four of which, from the *Royal George, Formidable, Ramillies* and *Queen Charlotte* were dated 28 February, and were received by the old admiral while he was taking the waters at Bath during the first three days of March. When Howe had read them, he had written to Seymour to ask him to make some enquiries as to whether there had been any signs of discontent in the fleet, and the latter reported that there were none. Howe, therefore, took no action beyond giving the letters to Seymour when he went to London on 22 March.[3] There had been previous petitions received at the Admiralty but, amazingly, these had not been shown to the First Lord. When Spencer saw the letters, his reaction was a horrified anxiety at what the seamen's demands might cost. He had little excuse for being surprised; Captain Thomas Pakenham had written to him on 11 December of the previous year to warn him that it was widely felt that the seamen would press for a rise in pay following increases not only in the pay of soldiers, but also of naval officers. Foreshadowing his response in the following year to the petitions sent to Howe, Spencer pointed out in his reply to Pakenham 'the utter impossibility in the present state of the country of adopting the measure you mention of increasing the wages to seamen'. which would be 'an enormous increase to our disbursements'.[4]

The seamen's petitions to Howe were sent to the one man, above all, that they trusted and respected: to them, he was 'Black Dick, the sailor's friend,' and he had done a lot to deserve their affection; besides this, he had led them to victory in

2   Morriss (ed.), *Channel Fleet*, p.197.
3   G.E. Manwaring and Bonamy Dobrée, *The Floating Republic* (London: Harcourt Brace, 1937), p.33.
4   Corbett (ed.), *Spencer*, Vol.II, pp.105-109.

1794, and was venerated throughout the country as a national hero. He, it was felt, would take up the cudgels on their behalf. The petitions displayed a remarkable restraint:

> The leaders were determined to have right on their side all through; they would take no step which might be misinterpreted; they would take care not to huff the Admiralty, and would allow no mutinous act to spoil their chances. Their grammar might be questionable, their pompous dignity in writing to each other may seem comic, but they had clear, responsible minds and determined hearts.[5]

What is also remarkable is that the movement should have been so well organised, and kept so secret, when communication through the ships of the fleet was so difficult. Their restraint was so notable that Bridport was much affected by it, and it heavily conditioned his response to the situation. Mutiny, or the threat of it, amounting to the calamitous breakdown of discipline in a fighting organisation, imposes huge pressures on both the leaders and the led if it is not to end badly. At Spithead, the seamen had a firm determination not to exceed the bounds of reasonableness and in Bridport at any rate they had a leader who understood the realities of the situation. But the resolution of the crisis was not in his hands, and the early reactions of the Admiralty were not encouraging.

In the circumstances which had arisen, there were only three options available to the government – to do nothing, to crack down hard on the seamen, or to conciliate them with an acceptable settlement. It was immediately apparent to Bridport, as it had not been to Spencer and his colleagues, that only the third option was practicable. To do nothing would allow the situation to spiral out of control; to take repressive action would destroy the relationship with the seamen entirely. It was not Bridport's call, however, and it remained to be seen how far he could influence the Admiralty's handling of an extremely difficult problem.

The Admiralty's first official response was to endorse the Port Admiral's instruction to all captains to sleep on board their respective ships, and to order Bridport on 15 April to ensure that captains and officers should, upon discovering any disposition to mutiny, 'take immediately the most vigorous and efficient measures for checking its progress and securing the ring leaders'.[6] On the same day Bridport was ordered to be at short notice to put to sea and in the meantime to move Gardner's squadron of eight ships of the line to St Helens. Bridport, meanwhile, in sending back the eleven letters to Nepean, made his views clearly known:

5   Manwaring and Dobrée, *Floating Republic*, p.31.
6   Morriss (ed.), *Channel Fleet*, p.198.

> I have very much to lament that some answer had not been given to the various letters transmitted to Earl Howe and the Admiralty, which would in my humble opinion have prevented the disappointment and ill humour which at present prevails in the ships under my orders.[7]

In this, of course, he was perfectly right, as he was when he went on to point out the folly of attempting to put to sea before the matter was resolved, as 'it could not be put in execution without the appearance of serious consequences which the complexion of the fleet manifestly indicates'.

The answer which the Admiralty suggested was as fatuous as their previous reaction; it was that the seamen should be told that 'their application has been communicated to their Lordships and that the subject will have the serous consideration which its importance requires'. Again the Admiralty insisted that Gardner's squadron be moved to St Helens. Bridport continued to point out the absurdity of the Admiralty's position, writing on 16 April that he saw no means of checking the progress of the affair other than 'by complying in some measure with the prayers of the petitions'.[8] Bridport carried out the Admiralty's request to give the seamen the futile answer proposed, adding his hope that the crews would return to duty, 'as the service of the country requires their proceeding to sea'. This, of course, cut no ice at all with the seaman.

Reluctantly, Bridport flew the signal for Gardner's squadron to proceed to St Helens, very much aware that this might ignite serious trouble. All eyes were on Gardner's flagship, the *Royal Sovereign*, to see whether the crew would carry out the order. Nothing happened, in spite of all that the officers and especially Gardner could do; and it produced an impulsive response from the crew of the *Queen Charlotte*, who manned the yards and gave three cheers, echoed by all the other ships. It was the signal that the mutiny had finally begun.

Off his own bat, however, Bridport took a step which Manwaring and Dobreé describe as being one 'which perhaps only one man in a hundred would have been sensible enough to do,' ordering each captain to muster his men and ask them to state their grievances. Meanwhile be sent Rear Admiral Pole off to London on the evening of 16 April with his letter advising a substantive response to the petitions.[9] He also warned Vice Admiral Colpoys, his choleric subordinate, not to resist the visits of seamen to the *London* to arrange for a meeting of delegates from every ship to discuss the situation. These, as has been noted, were moderate in their requests, pointing out that the seamen's wages had been settled in the time of Charles II, since when the cost of living had doubled: the petitions humbly implored that the Lords Commissioners of the Admiralty would comply with their prayers 'and

7   Morriss (ed.), *Channel Fleet*, p.200.
8   Morriss (ed.), *Channel Fleet*, p.202.
9   Manwaring and Dobrée, *Floating Republic*, p.42.

grant such addition will be made in their pay as in their Lordships' wisdom they shall think meet'.

The lack of any meaningful response to these petitions now led the seamen to formalise their proceedings, and that evening two delegates from each of the sixteen ships of the line duly met in Howe's state cabin on the *Queen Charlotte* to consider what next should be done. What they decided was as remarkable in its orderliness as the moderation that had characterised their proceedings so far. They were still determined to keep the issues within the bounds of their original requests:

> They therefore drew up an exemplary set of rules, most of which ended with the warning that any man neglecting them would be rigorously dealt with – paradoxically unmutinous rules, as: 'The greatest attention to be paid to the orders of the officers. Any person failing in respect due to them, or neglecting their duty, shall be severely punished'.[10]

The next move lay with the Admiralty; the situation had reached crisis point.

It was Spencer who took the decisive step. Pole reached London at midnight on 16 April, and at once briefed Nepean and the First Lord. Spencer now showed himself the right man in the right place:

> Calm, gentle, dignified, distinguished by his grace, his learning and his humanity … if he was merely a representative Englishman of the governing class, with plenty of sound sense and a kindly nature, he made up for any lack of genius by the activity and enthusiasm with which he pursued his duties; he never left unanswered a letter from the meanest individual, and manifested his virtues by a rigorous punctuality.[11]

Next morning Spencer reported to Pitt, and told him that he meant at once to go to Portsmouth himself; and he wrote to the King to tell him what had happened, and what he meant to do about 'the very delicate subject of an increase in pay, which appears to have been brought forward and enforced in an unpleasant manner'.[12] At 5.00 pm Spencer set off with Lord Arden, Rear Admiral Young and William Marsden, arriving at Portsmouth at noon on 18 April. There, at the Fountain Inn, they met with Bridport and others to get an update on the situation, and then prepared a document containing a proposal to the delegates to be taken by Gardner, Colpoys and Pole to the assembly aboard the *Queen Charlotte*. The admirals returned with the information that an answer would be given at 10.00

10   Manwaring and Dobrée, *Floating Republic*, p.45.
11   Manwaring and Dobrée, *Floating Republic*, p.49.
12   Corbett (ed.), *Spencer*, Vol.II, p.110.

am on the following day. The delegates were thoroughly disappointed with the proposal, as they were entitled to be. It failed to address a number of the issues raised through Bridport, and offered only four shillings a month extra for able seamen, with less for ordinary seamen and landsmen.

Meanwhile, as the delegates deliberated, the fleet and the inhabitants of Portsmouth were treated to a spectacle which, in all the circumstances, was totally bizarre. The Prince of Württemberg, who was shortly to marry the Princess Royal, came to the city to receive its freedom, with much pageantry. Spencer and Bridport, with the Governor Sir William Pitt, took him round the fleet in the Commissioners' barge, and the seamen manned the yards to salute them. It was a performance which, on both sides of the dispute, demonstrated the most extraordinary tolerance.

In the event it took until the afternoon of 19 April for the delegates to compose their response, which was a rejection of the proposal, and a restatement of their demands for a shilling a day for able seaman with others in the usual proportions; for a 'pound' of food to really weigh sixteen ounces and not fourteen as the custom; for shore leave; for increase in the pay of marines while aboard ship; and for the pensions at Greenwich Hospital to be raised to £10. Until these demands were met, together with particular grievances from individual ships, and an Act of Indemnity passed, they were determined not to lift an anchor. The Board, having now enjoyed a comfortable dinner, were outraged and, for the moment, full of fight, and determined to take a hard line. Bridport, Gardner, Colpoys and Pole were summoned to a meeting next morning, together with all sixteen captains.

When they came, however, they quickly poured cold water on the Board's belligerence. Their very strong advice was that the seamen's demands should be met, and in the face of this Spencer and others had no choice but to give way. Even now, however, while conceding the pay increases, and the sixteen ounce pound, they insisted on a shilling a month less for landsman, and said nothing about food, or leave, or pensions, or individual grievances. They embodied their decision in a letter which was sent to every ship on 21 April. Pitt, meanwhile, in a note to Spencer of the previous night, emphasised that the cost of the pay increases was a sum 'comparatively of no consequence,' which was something that the Board should have realised from the outset.[13]

The ships' crews received the letter not unfavourably, but resolved to see what the delegates made of it. As time passed, Gardner, for one, became very restless, and he took the unwise decision to go and talk to the Assembly in person. Accompanied by Colpoys and Pole, he went out to the *Queen Charlotte* and began his exposition, which went down well enough at first, in spite of a suggestion that a rejection of the letter would bring down a heavy handed response. Before a suitable letter could be completed, however, the delegates from the *Royal George* and *Queen Charlotte*,

13 Corbett (ed.), *Spencer*, Vol.II, p.116.

who had been on shore, arrived to join the meeting. Their comments completely turned the tide; what was now insisted on was a Royal Pardon. At this, Gardner lost his temper completely, shouting at the delegates for 'a damned mutinous blackguard set' and seizing one and shaking him violently. He threatened to hang him and every fifth man in the fleet, and there was complete uproar until the three admirals were hustled off the ship.[14]

Gardner's ill judged intervention led to an incident aboard the *Royal George*, where two delegates resolved to call another meeting aboard, hoisting a red flag to signify this. The officers, taking this to be a mark of revolution, attempted to prevent the signal; Captain Domett, as a mark of his disgust, hauled down Bridport's flag, and the admiral vowed not to hoist it on the ship again. The delegates, assembled again, were alarmed by Gardner's furious outburst, and ordered the guns run out; the officers were generally confined although some of the most unpopular were sent on shore; and a circular went round the fleet stating flatly that their demands must be met, agreed in writing, supported by an Act of Parliament, and that a Royal Pardon be issued. Spencer meanwhile, having received Gardner's account of his visit to the *Queen Charlotte*, set off at midnight to organise the Royal Pardon.

The reason for so many hiccups in getting a settlement was, on both sides, fear. On the one hand the Admiralty feared to agree the demands in full because they might be seen to have given in too easily, while on the other they feared the irreparable damage that might be done to the Navy in time of war. The seamen, mistrusting the authorities, feared on the one hand that they might be swindled, and on the other feared the loss of unity among them, recognising that it was in that unity that their real strength lay. To the extent that they could be said to have leaders, it was their recognition of this, and of the need to avoid extremes, that would ultimately lead to success. It has been suggested that if one of the delegates was the leader, it was probably Valentine Joyce, one of the delegates from the *Royal George*, a twenty six year old quartermaster's mate, who kept his head throughout. Like many of the delegates, he had attained the rank of a respected and trust-worthy seaman.[15]

Thinking it over, the delegates thought it best to explain to Bridport just what had happened, and on 22 April wrote to him to say that nothing less than a full settle-ment of all their demands would be acceptable. The incident of the previous day had arisen 'from the endeavours of Admiral Gardner to sow division and mistrust in the fleet and in fact to separate our interests'. With Bridport the seamen had no quarrel:

> We trust however that your Lordship will consider the whole fleet as universally and zealously attached to your Lordship as their father and

14   Manwaring and Dobrée, *Floating Republic*, pp.56-57.
15   Manwaring and Dobrée, *Floating Republic*, pp.43-44.

their friend and in short as a noble man willing to assist and further our honest endeavours.[16]

Spencer, meanwhile, had met with the Cabinet on 22 April and obtained approval to a Royal Pardon. He drove off at 5.00 pm to Windsor to obtain the signed proclamation. He wrote at once to Bridport to confirm the arrangements for the announcement of the settlement and the granting of the pardon. Bridport, he suggested, might now hoist his flag again aboard the *Royal George*, since his presence there might be of material advantage, but he left this to the Commander- in-Chief's discretion. Next day an exhausted Bridport was able to write to Spencer to tell him that at about 6.00 pm 'the whole painful business was settled at Spithead'. During the day he had twice addressed the crew of the flagship while awaiting the final acceptance from the delegates aboard the *Queen Charlotte*.[17]

It seemed, therefore a time for congratulations all round. Writing to Spencer on 24 April, however, Bridport was aware that there were still some aftershocks to overcome. One was the removal of officers against whom there were particular complaints; another was the question of what to do about the *Queen Charlotte*, for he did not know the officer who would wish to command her. Meanwhile Gardner had gone to St Helens with six of his ships, while Colpoys remained at Spithead with the rest of the fleet. Bridport asked if he could himself come up to London for a short time. Spencer, however, told him next day that the expectation of an imminent attack on Ireland made it 'a matter of absolute necessity' for Bridport to put to sea with as many ships as possible. This could not happen immediately; a strong southwest gale was blowing at Spithead.

It was that gale, and the dilatory methods of the Privy Council, that undid all the efforts that had gone into producing the settlement. Instead of sending the Bill to Parliament at once, a committee was appointed formally to consider the proposals, which did not report until 3 May. The delay appeared to the fleet to be inexplicable, and as the ships continued to lie at anchor a mounting suspicion developed that after all the government was intending to play them false. From Plymouth came the news that the squadron of Sir Roger Curtis had mutinied in sympathy, and delegates from four of the ships there set off on 28 April, promising to return by the evening of 1 May. This they did, after an interview with Sir Peter Parker who was able to confirm that a settlement had been reached. This might have been seen as good reason to hasten the Parliamentary formalities, but it was not; and the continuing delay was compounded by Spencer's reluctance to give any information to the House of Lords when asked for a statement by the leader of the opposition there.

16 Morriss (ed.), *Channel Fleet*, p.212.
17 Morriss (ed.), *Channel Fleet*, pp.213-214.

On top of all this, the Admiralty regressed into the kind of mindless stupidity with which they had originally handled the matter, by issuing an order on 1 May to all captains to ensure that the arms and ammunition of the marines should 'be constantly in good order,' adding an injunction that officers were to be ready 'on the first appearance of mutiny to use the most vigorous means to suppress it, and bring the ringleaders to punishment'.[18] The captains, of course, knew that if the seamen got wind of this order it would have the most explosive consequences.

Rumours of the government's bad faith continued to circulate. Spencer's reticence in the House of Lords seemed altogether consistent with the possibility that either Parliament or the government intended to disavow the settlement. Aware of the mounting suspicions, Bridport did his best to reassure by reading out the copy of the Bill drafted by the Privy Council. This did not dispel the seamen's fears, and when news leaked out of the Admiralty's order of 1 May, the crew of the *Duke* burst into Captain Holloway's cabin to demand a sight of the order. He had, prudently, destroyed it; thus thwarted, the crew seized him and a message was sent to Bridport that if they did not get the order, Holloway would be hanged or subjected to a degrading punishment. Bridport could do nothing but produce a copy of the order, in order to save Holloway. This incendiary document quickly went round the fleet, and the delegates aboard the *Queen Charlotte* circulated a note restating a refusal to go to sea until all their demands had been met. Not surprisingly, the most pessimistic opinions about the situation received the widest currency.

Thus it was when, in the early morning of Sunday 7 May, the wind veered easterly, which would enable the fleet to put to sea, Bridport knew that it would be futile to hoist the signal to weigh anchor. Cheers resounded from every ship; by 11.00 am, as the delegates gathered once more on the *Queen Charlotte*, the situation had reverted to that of 16 April. The mutineers were in total control. Bridport reported in despair to Spencer, suggesting in a private letter that it might be better for him to strike his flag and go on shore; to the Admiralty he wrote to describe the present situation:

> The whole fleet is returned again into the highest pitch of mutiny and disobedience to every officer of the fleet. I have endeavoured to prevent this mischief by every argument in my power but without effect and I cannot command the fleet as all authority is taken from me. I intended to have made the signal for the fleet to weigh this morning as the wind was easterly but I am compelled to remain here unless the Vote of Supply in the House of Commons for the increases of the seamen's pay and provisions should arrive and give the crews of the fleet satisfaction. The boats are now rowing round the fleet in the same manner as they did this day

18 Manwaring and Dobrée, *Floating Republic*, pp.79-80.

fortnight. My mind is so deeply wounded by all these proceedings and I am so unwell that I can scarcely hold my pen to write these sentiments of despair.[19]

As the day wore on, the situation went from bad to worse and then to near catastrophe. The agent of this disaster was the not-very-bright Vice Admiral Colpoys, who had been stopped by Bridport on 16 April from attempting a violent resistance. This time, however, aboard the *London* lying at Spithead, he resolved to take matters into his own hands. After a meeting with the crew, in which neither side fully understood what the other was saying, Colpoys thought he had persuaded his men, and sent them below, so that he could prevent the boats from St Helens from coming aboard; some of the crew, however, remained on the forecastle. The hatchways were closed, and the armed officers and marines prepared to resist the arrival of the oncoming boats. These went first to the *Marlborough*, where the delegates ordered the crew to send ashore the officers against whom they had a grievance, and then to take the ship to St Helens. When they reached the *London*, the crew of that vessel tried to force their way back on deck, and the men on the forecastle moved threateningly towards the officers. Some of them began to shift a gun to point at the quarterdeck. The first lieutenant, Peter Boves, warned them that he would fire unless they desisted; one man did not, and Boves shot him. There was pandemonium; the rest of the crew forced their way on deck; in the confusion, firing began, three sailors being killed and a delegate wounded, while several marines and a midshipman were wounded. The marines deserted to the seamen and Colpoys, realising he was beaten, called his officers back.

The crew, however, had seized Boves and were about to hang him, when Joyce, not for the first time, made a decisive intervention. This was to save Boves and bring the situation under control:

> Valentine Joyce, hurling himself through the dense pack, flung his arms around his neck, and screamed out above the wild tumult, 'If you hang this young man you shall hang me, for I shall never quit him'. And one of the top men shouted out that Boves was 'a brave boy'.[20]

Joyce's intervention gave Colpoys the chance to shout that Boves had simply been obeying his orders, in accordance with the recent instructions from the Port Admiral. The seamen demanded to see these; while Colpoys went to his cabin to get them, taking as much time as he dared, Valentine Joyce and a delegate from the *Terrible* managed to calm the men. When Colpoys produced the order, calm was

19   Morriss (ed.), *Channel Fleet*, pp.223-224.
20   Manwaring and Dobrée, *Floating Republic*, p.90.

restored; but he, his flag captain Griffith and Boves were locked up in their cabins to be the subject of a court martial.

On the following day, most of the ships having sent on shore their unpopular officers, the vessels remaining at Spithead removed to St Helens. From these Bridport, having heard of the events aboard the *London*, wrote to the Admiralty sadly to report that the fleet was now in a more disorderly state than when he wrote on the previous day, and that many officers had been turned out of their ships. The point had been made that it was not that the seamen wished to have no

Vice Admiral Sir John Colpoys. (Anne S.K. Brown Collection)

officers, but simply to get rid of those that had made themselves obnoxious. The crew of the *Nymphe*, for instance, wrote to Bridport to say that they loved good order and discipline, and begged him to send them a captain and two lieutenants so that they should be ready to put to sea.[21] The delegates, contemplating the case of Lieutenant Boves, decided that he should be released; the fate of Colpoys and Griffith remained for the moment undecided.

In Parliament the opposition enjoyed themselves at the government's expense. There was no question of the resolution for the additional estimate of £372,000 not being passed, but before it was, Charles James Fox denounced the official handling of the crises:

> How could ministers expect blind confidence when they had so blatantly shown themselves worthy of none at all? – who had displayed, in fact, 'a degree of guilt or incapacity, or both, that has led us to the brink of destruction'.[22]

After the resolution was finally passed Pitt introduced a Bill to make it law; it then went to the Lords and finally, in double quick time, received the Royal Assent. The resolution had already been sent down to Portsmouth, and in spite of a high sea running one ship that could receive a copy was the *London*, where, after it was read, Colpoys and Griffith were released. They, with Boves, underwent a civil trial on 11 May, when a verdict of justifiable homicide was reached; so that was that – although in the event Colpoys was not again employed at sea.

But the mutiny was not yet over until a second Royal Pardon had been produced; the delegates not unnaturally were not prepared to suspend their mistrust of the government. At this point the suggestion was made that Howe should go down to meet the crews of every ship and thereby to bring everything to a final conclusion. Whose idea this was is uncertain; it may have been the King or the Prime Minister who put forward the suggestion, but it was at once seen as the very best way to reach out to the seamen, who had always seen Howe as their friend. Howe was not very well; he had just recovered from a severe attack of gout, but he at once agreed to go, and Lady Howe went with him.

This was a move about which Bridport was entitled to have very mixed feelings, in the light of his past relationship with Howe. Spencer of course, was well aware of this, and wrote to him on 10 May in an effort to sugar the pill:

> This instructions would have been directed to your Lordship as Commander-in- Chief of the Channel Fleet if it had not (in the most serious and mature deliberation we could give to the subject) been decided

21 Manwaring and Dobrée, *Floating Republic*, pp.96-97.
22 Manwaring and Dobrée, *Floating Republic*, p.101.

that the circumstance of your being their commanding officer on this occasion suggested many reasons against your being personally charged with the execution of this measure.[23]

A more persuasive reassurance came from Pitt, who wrote to Bridport on the same day:

It was thought best to make this a civil commission in order not to interfere with the military command of the Fleet, and at the same time to give the commission to a distinguished naval character, though not with any naval authority or functions… I am sure you will continue to contribute your exertions with the same zeal and public spirit which you have shown under such trying difficulties to bring this arduous work, if possible, to a happy termination'.[24]

Pitt had struck the right note. Bridport's response reflected great credit on him, as the historians of the mutiny justly recorded:

Bridport may not have been a brilliant sailor, but he was, as he showed all through the mutiny, a man of unruffled sense and great moral courage; that he was a man of unusual generosity as well is revealed in his reply. He swallowed the affront, put his pride in his pocket in the good cause, and wrote to Pitt the next day.[25]

To Pitt, therefore, he said that he was 'much honoured by your most obliging and affectionate letter'. He hoped that Howe's mission would restore regular order, and he would himself give every assistance in his power. He did not spare the Admiralty in his further comments:

I have had, my dear sir, a most anxious time and much to encounter with and if I had not kept quiet, calm and composed the consequences would have been more alarming. I have always considered peevish works and hasty orders detrimental and it has been my study not to allow the one or issue the other. I wish that rule had guided the conduct of those in higher situations as I think 'tis wiser to soothe than combat disturbed and agitated minds.[26]

23   Morriss (ed.), *Channel Fleet*, p.228.
24   Manwaring and Dobrée, *Floating Republic*, p.104.
25   Manwaring and Dobrée, *Floating Republic*, p.104.
26   Morriss (ed.), *Channel Fleet*, p.229.

It was characteristic of Bridport that he noted that the Act referred to the increase in pay being effective from 24 April; it should, he pointed out, run from 20 April when the promise was first made.

Howe wasted no time on arriving at Portsmouth on 11 May, going out at once to the *Royal George*, where he met Bridport before next talking to the crew of the flagship. He spent three hours aboard, before going on to the *Queen Charlotte* and then the *Duke*. Next day he resumed his tour of the fleet, going to every ship in turn. Conscious of the fact that the seamen had got all that they had asked for, he insisted that they acknowledge their wrongdoing; this, the delegates were perfectly ready to do, as he reported:

> I left the fleet today under agreement with the deputies that the seamen, at large, should request, in suitable terms of decency and contrition, my interposition to obtain the King's pardon for their transgressions. And, in order to qualify their *unalterable adherence* to the change of particular officers of different ships, I engaged to use my best endeavours to obtain their removal, upon receiving, in addition to the former dutiful application, a *special one* of the same nature from each of the ships concerned, praying that his Majesty would indulge them with the appointment of other officers to those ships.[27]

Next day, 13 May, the delegates arrived aboard the *Royal William*, which, as the guard ship and flagship of Admiral Sir Peter Parker, lay at anchor in Portsmouth Harbour, where Howe received them in the Admiral's cabin. The final issue had been the removal of the objectionable officers; Howe was in no doubt that he must give way over this question since, as he said, 'however ineligible the concession, it was become indispensably necessary'.[28] Accordingly, with agreement now reached, it was arranged that there should be a final meeting aboard the *Royal William* on the following day. That might have seemed to Howe the end of the day's activities, but during the afternoon Curtis's squadron of eight ships of the line sailed from Plymouth into Spithead, flying the red flags of mutiny, and the exhausted Howe was obliged to go out to the *Prince* and negotiate with the men of this squadron for their return to duty, upon the basis that they too might get rid of the officers against whom they had grievances. That done, Howe went back on shore.

Bridport, who was still in touch with Lord Chatham, the previous First Lord, had written to him to tell him of the events at Spithead, and had evidently floated the possibility that he might step down as Commander-in-Chief. Chatham was firm in his dismissal of this:

---

27 Barrow, *Earl Howe*, p.335.
28 Manwaring and Dobrée, *Floating Republic*, p.115.

With a view, however, to the public good I should consider any change in the command of the fleet as most unfortunate. With regard to your conduct in all this unhappy business I am happy in thinking there is but one opinion and I am sure that your continuing in your present situation, however painful to yourself, must ensure you the approbation of every well – wisher to his country.[29]

Bridport was no doubt pleased to receive this, since just at that moment he was feeling rather bruised as a result of the terms in which he had again, on 13 May, received a letter from the Admiralty pressing him to put to sea. He wrote back to say that he was as anxious as the Admiralty to do so, but in the present situation it was impossible, adding: 'I own I feel rather hurt on being so often pressed upon that object, which rather indicates neglect of my duty'.[30] He was entitled to feel put out by the oafish way in which, throughout the crisis, he had been told by the Admiralty to put to sea when it was not practicable to do so. Before their Lordships received his quite moderate protest, he got another letter on the same subject, while even Spencer, writing to congratulate him on the settlement of the dispute, included a hope that no further impediment would prevent him from putting to sea. On 14 May their Lordships came as close as they were ever likely to apologise, Nepean writing to assure Bridport that neither of his recent letters on the urgency of leaving St Helens was intended to imply any delay on his part. Later that day Spencer wrote to him on similar lines.

Thus the mutiny ended. On Sunday, which dawned in thick fog, the delegates arrived at the *Royal William* only to find that the long-awaited Royal Pardon had still not arrived, so it was arranged that there be a grand celebratory procession round the fleet on the following day. On shore, Valentine Joyce agreed with Howe for the time for the procession to start, and then the old Admiral invited him into the Governor's house to drink a glass of wine with him. Before dusk the pardon arrived; and next day the delegates rowed ashore, and, headed by their bands, marched up to the Governor's house for refreshments, before embarking aboard the boats for the procession. This was headed by a boat flying the Union Jack, and carrying the bandsmen; next came the Royal Barge, containing Lord Howe, followed by other boats with the official party. Arriving at the *Royal George*, Howe read out the Royal Pardon to thunderous cheers from the crew, who hauled down the red flag and replaced it with the Royal Standard. Howe repeated the process with the other ships, and those of Curtis's squadron, before returning on shore, completely worn out, at 6.00 pm, to be carried on the shoulders of the delegates

29 Morriss (ed.), *Channel Fleet*, p.222-223.
30 Morriss (ed.), *Channel Fleet*, p.232.

to the Governor's house. There, he entertained the delegates to dinner before they returned in the moonlight to St Helens.[31]

Just over one hundred officers went on shore and were not to return to their ships, leaving Bridport still offended by the attitude of the Admiralty and perplexed to know how he was to carry the fleet to sea, as he wrote to Spencer on 15 May:

> This is the condition of the ships under my orders and that I am immediately expected to carry to sea to meet the enemy who may be already sailed from Brest. I have written a second letter to Sir Peter Parker on the subject of the officers and I am told he has only five lieutenants to spare and I have only two to appoint that are qualified. I am too much hurried to write more and I feel too much hurt at the various circumstances that have taken place to make my letter acceptable to your Lordship. While I remain in command I will do my duty to the King and the public.[32]

As the mutiny drew to a close, the delegates had been visited by a deputation from the ships at the Nore which had also mutinied; now, with the celebrations of the peaceful conclusion at Spithead duly concluded, the deputation made its way back to the Nore, where a very different atmosphere prevailed which was to lead to a very different culmination. Bringing the mutiny at the Nore to an end would cause a great deal of heartache to all concerned, not least Lord Spencer, who went through agonies of spirit before its conclusion.

Most observers were profoundly grateful to Howe for the part that he played in ensuring that at Spithead there was a peaceful end to the crisis. Not, however, Edmund Burke, obsessed with the fear of revolution, who wrote to William Windhan:

> But among all the parts of this fatal measure the Mission of my Lord Howe has been by far the most mischievous. Had a great naval commander been sent down – *Gravem pietate et meritis virium quem* – to awe the seditious into obedience, it would have been the best thing that could have been thought of; but to send the first name in the Navy, and who had been but lately a Cabinet Minister and First Lord of the Admiralty, at upwards of 70 years of age, to hunt among mutineers for grievances, to take the law from Joyce, a seditious clubist of Belfast, and to remove by his orders some of the principal Officers of the Navy, puts an end to all hopes for ever. Such mischief need not to have been attended with so much degradation.[33]

31 Manwaring and Dobrée, *Floating Republic*, p.118-121
32 Morriss (ed.), *Channel Fleet*, pp.236-237.
33 Quoted Manwaring and Dobrée, *Floating Republic*, p.103; the Latin tag translates roughly as 'of great piety and service to the forces'.

As has often been pointed out, the mutiny at Spithead was essentially an industrial dispute, not a revolution; but in the context of the time there were many who, like Burke saw it as the start of a revolution and wished to see it dealt with accordingly.

The events at Spithead in the spring of 1797 have an almost surreal quality, in which nothing was quite as it seemed, and the behaviour of the adversaries appeared at times to be wholly inconsistent with the grim reality of what was actually happening. A large scale naval mutiny in the middle of a desperate war, involving the total breakdown of discipline, might have been expected to lead to a bloody conclusion. That it did not was to the credit of a number of key figures. First among these was perhaps Bridport, who had a far clearer understanding of the message which the seamen were trying to convey and the tone in which it was expressed than the Board of Admiralty on the one hand or his less thoughtful subordinates such as Gardner and Colpoys on the other. Howe, of course, did not spare himself in his crucial contribution to the final settlement. Next must come Valentine Joyce, and the other opinion formers among the delegates, who managed almost throughout to keep the mutineers in a state of reasonableness.

Joyce's subsequent career has been carefully researched by Len Barnett, who also conclusively put paid to the suggestions, readily accepted by Edmund Burke, that he came from Belfast and had been imprisoned for sedition. In fact, Joyce was born in Jersey in 1769 and brought up in Portsmouth before entering the navy; the first official record of this was in 1788 when he joined the 36 gun frigate *Perseverance*, in which he sailed to the East Indies. He joined the *Royal George* in October 1793, and was rated quartermaster's mate. Aboard this vessel he saw action at the Glorious First of June in 1794 and also at the Ile de Groix in the following year. After the settlement, he continued to serve in the *Royal George* until May 1798; thereafter he served as quartermaster aboard the bomb vessel *Vesuvius*, being rated as master's mate on 27 January 1799 and in the following month as midshipman. In November 1799 he was appointed to the 18 gun sloop *Brazen* on patrol in the English Channel: sadly, in the following January the vessel was lost when going on the rocks near Newhaven and Joyce was not one of those who survived. Thus ended the life of one who made a decided impact on history, and who might have enjoyed a distinguished naval career.[34]

Among others who made a significant contribution to a peaceful resolution, Spencer and Pitt kept the Cabinet and the Admiralty under control. It would have been so easy for hardliners to escalate the crisis, with disastrous results. Credit, too, must go to those officers who understood and sympathised with the seamen's demands and, of course, the seamen and particularly their delegates who followed the careful line of their leaders. But it had been a near run thing.

34   Len Barnett, 'Valentine Joyce – Naval Mutineer of 1797' at www.tribejoyce.com/valentine-joyce-naval-mutineer-of-1797/.

13

Frigates

1797 was to produce two thumping victories for the Royal Navy. On 14 February Admiral Sir John Jervis won a convincing victory over the Spanish at Cape St Vincent; and on 11 October Admiral Adam Duncan beat the Dutch at Camperdown. For the Channel Fleet, however, the twelve months that followed the settlement of the Spithead mutiny afforded no such dramatic events.

The Admiralty's orders to Bridport on 15 May had a familiar ring. Bridport was to proceed to Plymouth to pick up five 74s and a frigate:

> But if the said ships should have left Plymouth before you arrive there, your Lordship is to proceed off the Lizard where you may expect to fall in with them, and upon doing so take them under your command and proceed immediately with the whole of your force off Brest, for the purpose of watching the motions of the enemy at that place, and using your best endeavours to take or destroy any of their ships should they attempt to put to sea.[1]

If the French were gone from Brest, and he could not ascertain their course, Bridport was to sail for the coast of Ireland. The Admiralty was mindful of the problems of remaining on station; he was to take 'every precaution' in his power to avoid being driven so far to the westward as to enable the French to get out into the Channel. On 27 May the Admiralty notified Bridport that Pellew's frigate squadron had been ordered to join him; with this reinforcement, the Admiralty reckoned that Bridport, while on station off Brest, would be able 'to afford the necessary protection to the trade of His Majesty's subjects'.[2]

Bridport was thoroughly discontented by the lack of senior support, pointing out to Spencer that the only admiral with him was Sir Alan Gardner; he sent a list of the comparable complement of admirals of the Brest fleet, the Dutch fleet,

1   Morriss (ed.), *Channel Fleet*, p.245.
2   Morriss (ed.), *Channel Fleet*, p.246.

the British North Sea Fleet and above all, of the Channel Fleet under Howe, when the latter was supported by no less than seven admirals.[3] Spencer endeavoured to soothe him by telling him that he would shortly be joined by Vice Admiral Lord Keith and Rear Admiral Sir John Orde. Keith, when he hoisted his flag in the *Queen Charlotte*, demonstrated a remarkable lack of inhibition when he wrote to Spencer to suggest that his recent efforts to bring the naval mutinies at the Nore under control would justify his being given an English peerage (his present title being in the Irish peerage). Spencer was decidedly unimpressed; while Keith's performance had given the King and others 'a very favourable impression of your energy and activity on his service,' such an application as Keith had made would have greater prospect of success on some future occasion.[4]

Keith, who was born George Keith Elphinstone in 1746, entered the navy at the age of sixteen, passing for lieutenant in 1769. He was made post at the start of the American War and served principally in that theatre, taking a leading part in the siege and capture of Charlestown. As Captain of the *Warwick*, 50, he took the Dutch *Rotterdam*, 52, in English waters before returning to America. During this time he was elected to Parliament, making important political connections. In 1793 he was active under Lord Hood at Toulon, and supervised the evacuation of that place. Returning home, he became Knight of the Bath and was promoted to rear admiral; he became a supporter of William Pitt and Lord Spencer, relationships which stood him in good stead. After a short period with the Channel Fleet – he missed the Glorious First of June – he commanded the squadron which seized the Cape of Good Hope, and operated with success in the Indian Ocean. On his return he was awarded an Irish peerage, taking the title Lord Keith. He was highly regarded, not only by Pitt, but also by his fellow Scotsman Henry Dundas, the Secretary of War, and by the King.

The Admiralty was by now becoming concerned with the problems of supply as well as the inevitable wear and tear of the ships of the Channel Fleet while on station off Brest. It would be best, it was considered, for Bridport to send his ships of the line into Cawsand Bay two at a time for provisioning, rather than to return to Torbay with the whole fleet, which was Bridport's usual practice. He was there at the beginning of July, writing to the Admiralty to report that, as requested, he had reinforced Warren's squadron off Brest with three ships of the line and three frigates; he had also ordered Pellew to return to Falmouth. Latest reports from Brest suggested that the French were up to something. Captain Gore, of the frigate *Triton*, reported to Warren that they appeared to have nineteen ships of the line and seven frigates ready for sea in all respects apart from a shortage of seamen. That deficiency would be made good by no less than 40,000 troops expected at Brest, evidently with an expedition to Ireland in mind. There were, in addition,

---

3   Morriss (ed.), *Channel Fleet*, p.250.
4   Morriss (ed.), *Channel Fleet*, p.260.

four more ships of the line and seven frigates which were or soon would be available. The information was corroborated by a sailor from the frigate *Amazon* who had escaped from prison a week previously.[5]

By the end of July Bridport was off Brest again, but still complaining to Spencer of the shortage of frigates which was seriously hampering him. At the best of times, Bridport was always grumbling about the frigate shortage, not least because he did not at all approve of Warren and Pellew; he had previously told Spencer that he thought it strange that they had continued in command of frigates notwithstanding their seniority. Spencer was having none of this, tartly replying that the service on which they were employed 'was of a description which seemed to require their experience and ability to conduct it, which I should think would easily account to your Lordship for their being continued upon it'.[6] In fact Warren, extremely anxious to get away from Bridport, finally accepted the command of the *Canada*, 74, in September.

Pellew, however, was not to be lured away from his frigate squadron. Receiving the offer of a ship of the line from Bridport, he wrote an exceedingly polite and grossly insincere letter of refusal on 1 July:

> I am much flattered by the interest your Lordship takes in my welfare, and can not but feel very thankful for the suggestions Your kindness offers to my Consideration, which I am well aware originate in the best motives; but it has long been my determination, my Lord, to serve the war out in my present command.

He concluded his letter with some even more unconvincing sentiments:

> Whenever I shall serve in a ship of the Line, I have long cherish'd the ambition of being under your Lordship's Command; from motives both of great public respect and private Esteem.[7]

It is unlikely that Bridport paid much attention to hypocritical nonsense of this sort. Coming from a man whose real opinion of his Commander-in-Chief was that he was 'scarcely worth drowning, a more contemptible or more miserable animal does not exist,' Pellew's extravagant flattery tends to take the breath away.

Bridport's desire that both Warren and Pellew and their squadrons should be under his command, therefore, may well have been sharpened by the fact that in that case he would have an admiral's share of the prize money which they could earn. During the course of his career Pellew earned, it has been calculated, some

---

5   Morriss (ed.), *Channel Fleet*, p.258.
6   Morriss (ed.), *Channel Fleet*, p.254.
7   Parkinson, *Edward Pellew*, pp.197-198.

Sir Edward Pellew, depicted in later life by which time he was Admiral of the Blue and had been ennobled as Viscount Exmouth. (Anne S.K. Brown Collection)

£200,000 in prize money and freight money, a staggering sum at the rates then prevailing.[8] Notwithstanding his considerable record of success, Pellew had, as has been seen, still felt able to plead with Spencer for 'the indulgence of a cruise'. He was, it must be accepted, inordinately fond of increasing his considerable wealth. He was also capable of vast hypocrisy, writing to a friend in 1795: 'I never cared much about riches'. It should, though, be noted that Pellew's latest biographer takes a different view, arguing that his supposed personal greed was largely a myth and that it was mainly a case of fearing a return to his original poverty.[9]

The depth of the animosity between Bridport and Pellew was examined by C. Northcote Parkinson in his biography of the latter:

> Bridport's detestation for Pellew requires explanation. It was not personal, in that the two men had hardly met. Like most naval feuds it was a matter of prize money. As long as Warren, Pellew, Saumarez, and their like, were given separate commands in the Channel, very little profit came to the Commander-in-Chief. Frigates under Admiralty orders did not share profits with flag officers. Now, avarice was Bridport's particular weakness. His large fortune, based on what he acquired by marrying two heiresses in succession, would have been larger still but for Pellew. The continual presence of the Falmouth squadrons both literally and figuratively to windward of him was the Commander-in-Chief's perpetual grievance. But while Bridport's opinion of Pellew can be traced fairly directly to his avarice, it must not be thought that he was singular in this respect. His Captains were in hearty agreement with him on the subject. ... Bridport was not alone, nor entirely mistaken in regarding Pellew with suspicion. And if he erred, it was in good company.[10]

The legend of Bridport's avarice has followed him through history. It is at least possible, since few of those historians who have accused him in this way have produced anything much by way of evidence, that his general unpopularity may well have accounted for the additional charge of greed, and that this opinion was promoted by such as Pellew and Warren since the subject of prize money was at least as close to their hearts. As for Parkinson's snide hint that Bridport was a fortune hunter, it is worth recalling what one historian of the Hood family wrote about his first marriage:

---

8   Richard Hill, *The Prizes of War The Naval Prize System in the Napoleonic Wars 1793-1815*. (Stroud: Sutton, 1998), p.222.

9   Taylor, *Commander*, p.166.

10   Parkinson, *Edward Pellew*, p.196.

Captain Alexander insisted that his bride's handsome fortune be settled on herself; otherwise under the then Law it would have become his when they married. He was very fond of her and their friends, though amused, watched their continued happiness with sympathy.[11]

It is certainly true that Bridport took a strong position over the entitlement of Sir Roger Curtis, Howe's captain of the fleet, to share in prize money. The decision ultimately went against him, but this of itself is scarcely evidence of exceptional avarice. This allegation against Bridport was, perhaps, merely an instance of giving a dog a bad name.

Meanwhile the relationship between Bridport and Pellew continued to be very poor. On 24 July Bridport ordered him to join the fleet off Brest; to his fury Pellew, who had already spent twelve days in harbour at Falmouth, did not sail until 2 August. Bridport pointed out to Spencer that if the Admiralty had wanted Pellew to remain in Falmouth, there had been plenty of time to send an order to that effect; he ended his letter sarcastically observing: 'But I conclude when ships are put under my orders I am authorised to direct their proceedings to the best of my judgment for the services committed to my charge so long as they shall remain a part of my squadron'.[12]

Spencer displayed almost limitless tolerance towards those who addressed correspondence to him directly, whatever the subject. Pellew, like Sidney Smith, was a regular writer, but by 1797 even Spencer's patience was wearing thin. Pellew finally overreached himself over the question of the employment of his brother Captain Israel Pellew, who had been sent on shore at the behest of mutineers. Spencer had wearily promised 'to find a situation for Captain Pellew on board some other ship as soon as I can,' but this was not considered good enough. Pellew put pen to paper again, telling Spencer:

Not only my brother's future prospects in the navy are at stake but that my own cannot but be greatly influenced by the measures taken respecting him, in the steps I may be induced to pursue myself.[13]

The hint of a threat to resign cut no ice with Spencer and thereafter Pellew could no longer count on a sympathetic ear on the part of the First Lord.

This was illustrated by Spencer's response to a plea from Pellew to be employed elsewhere than in the Channel Fleet; if there were more frigates available, he would 'be very glad to employ the *Indefatigable* in pleasanter service,' but as it was, it was absolutely necessary that he remain under Bridport's orders. Pellew was furious.

11   Dorothy Hood, *The Admirals Hood* (London: Hutchinson, 1941), p.24.
12   Morriss (ed.), *Channel Fleet*, pp.262-263.
13   Parkinson, *Edward Pellew*, pp.192-193.

He wrote again to Spencer, referring to the 'jaundiced eye' with which his squadron was viewed. If Spencer was aware of this, he said, 'I am satisfied you would see how much we stand in need of your protection and I venture to hope the zeal with which we have served may flatter us with attaining so desirable an object'. To this, Spencer replied that he could not interfere with Bridport's arrangements, and if he could, he doubted whether it would do any good.[14]

As it happened, however, Pellew was released from his captivity for a while, being sent on 22 September to escort a convoy as far as Madeira. Whether this was a humiliating penance imposed on him by a malicious Commander-in-Chief, or a temporary liberation suggested by the First Lord to avert some irrevocable act of defiance on Pellew's part is unclear. At all events, returning from Madeira, Pellew was able to console himself by picking up two prizes – a French corvette off Tenerife, and a large French privateer operating out of Bayonne. In this prize money Bridport of course had a share; when he released Pellew next year to operate in the Channel, the latter was delighted to snap up a rich Dutch East Indianan in which, apparently, Bridport had no share.[15]

Spencer was doing his best to keep Bridport happy. On 8 September he was able to assure the Commander-in-Chief that with the addition of the frigate *Melampus* to the Channel Fleet he would have as many as fifteen frigates and two brigs under his orders, of which only three or four of the frigates were to be left at Plymouth. And, since Bridport greatly preferred Cawsand Bay to Falmouth as an anchorage for the frigates, he was to instruct his frigate commanders accordingly. Bridport should have been pleased with this, but perhaps his reaction was similar to that noted by Even Nepean on 11 September in connection with another matter on which he was reporting to the First Lord:

> I have only therefore, to add on the subject of your Lordship's note that the three commissions mentioned in it have been forwarded by this post to Lord Bridport, who ought to be pleased, though he is never likely to be so.[16]

As summer gave way to autumn it became less convenient to use Torbay as the base for the blockading fleet, and the Admiralty assented to the use of Cawsand Bay or Spithead. By 11 November the Admiralty judged it necessary to make new arrangements for the continuing blockade of Brest, and sent very specific orders to Bridport with regard to these. The original intention had been for Keith to assume command of the ships blockading Brest, and Bridport had issued the necessary

14   Morriss (ed.), *Channel Fleet*, p.266.
15   Taylor, *Commander*, p.141.
16   Morriss (ed.), *Channel Fleet*, p.269.

orders for this, before fresh instructions arrived from the Admiralty.[17] Two ships of the line, the *Leviathan* and *Cumberland,* were to go to Ireland; Keith was to go at once to Spithead with the *Queen Charlotte*, *Sans Pareil* and *Saturn*, and the rest of the fleet was to remain off Brest under Curtis. The Admiralty showed that it was intended to exercise a close control on the way in which Curtis was to operate; he was to station three ships of the line and a frigate to the north of the Passage du Four, and 'a proper number' of frigates off the Saints, while he was to cruise with the rest 'to the westward of Brest for the purpose of preventing the sailing of the enemy's frigates lying there'. The frigates off the Saints were to monitor the French fleet for any sign that the ships of the line were being made ready, and to report promptly if this was the case:

> The Rear Admiral is also to direct the senior officer of the ships stationed off the Saints in case he should receive intelligence that may be depended upon of the sailing of the enemy's frigates from Brest to lose not a moment's time in giving him, as well as the senior officer of the ships stationed to the northward of the Passage du Four, information thereof and if no certain account can be obtained of the destination of the enemy the Rear Admiral is to proceed immediately off Cork for intelligence and the ships stationed off the Passage du Four are to proceed off the Lizard for the like purpose.[18]

It was the threat to Ireland that particularly concerned the Admiralty, since all the available intelligence indicated that this would be the next French move. It was not, however, the only threat. D'Auvergne had reported as early as April 1797 that orders had been placed with ship builders all the way from Dunkirk to Brest for the construction of 600 flat gun boats; his spies had even obtained plans and specifications of these craft. At this stage he had no indication whatever of their probable destination. In May he had received even more alarming news from Brest:

> Vice Admiral Cheyla has arrived from Paris with considerable funds to accelerate preparations for an expedition. The orders are to arm with all possible celerity every vessel susceptible. There are 32 line of battle ships, ten frigates, and a score of corvettes here, susceptible of armament. Men are now working on these with the greatest activity. Commissaries of Provisions for the troops have arrived with instructions to prepare rations and quarters for 50,000 men.[19]

17 Christopher Lloyd (ed.), *The Keith Papers* (London: Navy Records Society, 1950), Vol.II, p.29.
18 Morriss (ed.), *Channel Fleet*, pp.271-272.
19 Balleine (ed.), *Philippe d'Auvergne*, p.90.

By October d'Auvergne was reporting that the troops in the west of France had been designated the Army of England, and that Bonaparte was to take command.

Bridport meanwhile, had made his way back to Spithead, worn out by his activities during the year; not unreasonably, he felt that he had earned a period of leave, writing to Spencer on 14 November:

> After having been at sea near twenty one weeks, and having never slept one night out of the *Royal George* since the 27th of April last nor had my foot upon the shore for more than ten hours since that time and under circumstances, as your Lordship knows, the most painful and afflicting to an anxious and feeling mind, I therefore hope your Lordship will not think me unreasonable in requesting some time of break from public business and soliciting a leave of absence for the recovery of my health by going for a short time to my house in the country and afterwards to Bath, as I conclude I shall not be wanted in Town upon any public occasion.[20]

Curtis was not long to remain on station off Brest. On 29 November he was ordered, as soon as the winds settled in the west, to return home, the three deckers to go to Spithead and the two deckers to Cawsand Bay. There, they were to refit and complete their stores and provisions and be ready to put to sea at the shortest notice. The frigates, however, were to remain on watch, sending frequent accounts to the Admiralty of what the French were doing in Brest.

Bridport's leave was, however disturbed by a flurry of correspondence about the activities of Captain Sir Harry Neale in the frigate *San Fiorenzo*, who appeared to have gone off on a frolic of his own. It appeared that he had acted in breach of Bridport's orders, and the Admiralty was 'displeased' at his conduct; Bridport, however, was able to save Neale from censure by writing that Neale had had his verbal permission to go further than stated in the written orders. The Admiralty was, however, not prepared to leave it at that. Bridport was firmly told that he should not permit his ships to cruise beyond the limits of the express orders 'without very certain information to occasion the same'.[21] Neale was a strong willed frigate captain, and like most of these was always ready to look out for the opportunities of being in action, especially if there was a chance of prize money. Bridport and he got on well, in contrast to the former's relationship with Pellew and Warren.

Bridport resented the implied criticism of the way in which he had dealt with Neale, and wrote an indignant letter on 5 January from Bath to defend his handling of the matter. He had, he said, but one principle for the government of his conduct, which was 'to serve the King with zeal and fidelity and the public with unshakeable attachment'. This said, he wondered, if Neale and another

---

20   Morriss (ed.), *Channel Fleet*, pp.272-273.
21   Morriss (ed.), *Channel Fleet*, pp.277-278.

captain, Cunningham, had while off station attacked and taken two French frigates, 'whether these two excellent officers would not have met with approbation from their Lordships instead of calling upon Sir Harry Neale for having disobeyed my orders and whether the verbal latitude I had given him would have merited the animadversions I have received'.[22]

It will be recalled that the possibility of using St Mary's Road in the Scilly Isles as a base for the Channel Fleet had been firmly rejected by Bridport. Its potential had not, however, been entirely abandoned by the Admiralty, and part of the winter of 1797-1798 was spent by Pellew in making a survey of the location, which he submitted in a report of 24 December. His report was favourable, and it apparently generated a good deal of discussion, although in the end nothing was done about it.[23]

In January 1798 Vice Admiral Sir Charles Thompson took command of the squadron to take up its station off Brest. His arrival to join the Channel Fleet had seriously upset Keith, who wrote to Bridport on 25 November that he was 'much astonished' when he arrived at Spithead to find Thompson in port. This had seriously put his nose out of joint, possibly over the question of seniority: since he had been told that he was to command a division of the Channel Fleet, he demanded an immediate explanation. He concluded: 'If it ends in my resignation I beg your Lordship to accept my sincere thanks for your attention so long as I had the honour to serve in the fleet under you'. Apparently he did not get a satisfactory explanation, since he went on leave for a year.[24] In February he seems to have proposed to Spencer that he be assigned to the Mediterranean fleet under St Vincent, but got a dusty answer, Spencer pointing out that his being out of service at that time was entirely his own act, and he could not rearrange the posting of St Vincent's flag officers to suit Keith. A few days later, Spencer wrote to Keith again:

> Whenever your Lordship shall think fit to make an offer of your service generally, without any stipulation or restrictions, if the dispositions and arrangements of the naval forces at the time shall be such as to admit of it I shall be very glad to avail myself of your offer, being well persuaded that the service allotted to you will be well executed.[25]

Spencer was by now well used to admirals getting above themselves.

Bridport's leave ended on 3 March, when he arrived at Portsmouth to hoist his flag. Next day he wrote a grumpy letter to Spencer to complain that, six frigates having been taken from him, he was left with only three. He was also offended by

22   Morriss (ed.), *Channel Fleet*, pp.278-279.
23   Parkinson, *Edward Pellew*, p.201.
24   Lloyd (ed.), *Keith Papers* Vol.II, p 30; Morriss (ed.), *Channel Fleet*, p 273.
25   Morriss (ed.), *Channel Fleet*, p.280.

orders from the Admiralty that he was not to send any of his ships to sea without directions so to do. Sulkily, he told Spencer that he would hold himself 'bound strictly to obey these directions as long as they shall remain in force'.[26] Spencer replied soothingly to point out that there were a substantial number of frigates cruising off Brest which could join him in an emergency. As to the order which had so offended Bridport, he explained that it was to keep his force together to meet any threatened attack on the English Coast. Bridport spelled out his own view of the matter on 21 March:

> Your Lordship will allow me to suggest what forcibly strikes me in the present state of things. Ireland seems to be the place the enemy mean to attack. It seems therefore highly proper that the naval commander in that station should not in this awful crisis be permitted to send one ship to move from the coast but to keep all cruising off every port to guard and protect it against invasion.[27]

In reply to this Spencer was able to confirm that the C-in-C in Ireland had been generally instructed in this sense.

The mounting concern of the Admiralty about the threat to Ireland led to the detachment from Bridport's command of the squadron under Curtis, which was to be placed under Kingsmill for the time being. Spencer explained the thinking behind this more in a letter to Bridport on 7 April:

> An urgent necessity has arisen from information which has been obtained from France to reinforce for a short time the squadron on the south and west coast of that kingdom [Ireland] and to do so it seemed requisite to put for that time the whole of the ships which we meant to station there under the Command of the Vice Admiral commanding on the station.[28]

Anticipating a roar of protest from Bridport, he was careful to add that Curtis and his squadron would return to the Channel Fleet after a fixed period.

It remained, however, essential that the watch on the French fleet should be such that it could not leave port without being followed. Spencer emphasised this in his letter to Bridport of 9 April:

> As the season advances and the equipments at Brest get forwarder it will become more and more desirable to take the most effectual means possible for watching the operations from that port and ensuring as far

26 Morriss (ed.), *Channel Fleet*, p.288.
27 Morriss (ed.), *Channel Fleet*, p.286.
28 Morriss (ed.), *Channel Fleet*, p.288.

as is practicable their not moving without being closely followed by our Channel fleet.[29]

In the circumstances this was hardly more than a statement of the extremely obvious.

Bridport left St Helens on 12 April to cruise off Brest; he had with him only ten ships of the line following the detachment of Curtis and his squadron, since Thompson was now cruising in the Bay of Biscay with twelve ships of the line and three frigates. On 21 April, while Bridport was standing across the Iroise passage on the port tack, the 74 gun ships *Mars* (Captain Alexander Hood) and *Ramillies* (Captain Henry Inman) spotted two ships to the eastward, and gave chase. At about 2 pm another larger vessel was seen to the east-south-east, and the British ships, now joined by the frigate *Jason*, turned to pursue her. She was the French 74 *Hercule*. None of the rest of the Channel Fleet was near enough to join in. At 6.20 the *Ramillies* lost her foretopmast, and dropped away. At about 8.30 pm, with the Bec du Raz about three miles to the north-east, Captain l'Héritier of the *Hercule*, unable to work up against the strong current, dropped anchor and prepared to receive the attack of the *Mars*. As he closed, Hood found the current would not permit him to take up a good position, and he too anchored, causing her to drop back. The respective anchors became locked together, and in this position a fierce engagement began, of which *Mars* got much the better. Badly damaged in her hull, and after the failure of two boarding attempts, the *Hercule* struck. Most of the damage sustained by the *Hercule* was along her starboard side, riddled in many places. William James described her resulting state:

> Several of the ports were unhinged; and in some instances, the spaces between the ports entirely laid open, The contrast between the two sides of the ship was, indeed, most remarkable; the larboard side, which had been very slightly injured, was of a bright yellow; while the starboard side, of what remained of it, was burnt as black as a cinder. The five aftermost starboard lower deck guns of the *Hercule* were dismounted, and several of the others much damaged.[30]

The French casualties were high, the killed and wounded amounting to about 200 of her crew of 680. The *Mars*, too, suffered considerably, losing a total of 30 killed and missing, and 60 wounded, out of her crew of 634. Among the killed was her captain, Bridport's cousin. The admiral wrote sadly to the Admiralty:

29   Morriss (ed.), *Channel Fleet*, p.289.
30   James, *Naval History*, Vol.II, p.122.

The death of Captn. Alexr. Hood of the Mars 74 guns, after engaging and capturing L'Hercule French 74', contemporary mezzotint. (Anne S.K. Brown Collection)

No praise of mine can add one ray of brilliancy to the distinguished valour of Captain Alexander Hood, who carried his ship nobly into battle and who died of the wounds he received in supporting the just cause of his country. It is impossible for me not to sincerely lament his loss as he was an honour to the service and universally beloved.[31]

Bridport, it is good to record, took up the question of a pension for Alexander Hood's widow and children, and continued to take a supportive interest in his nephew's family.

The *Hercule* was brought back to Plymouth, but her condition was so bad that it was only with the greatest difficulty that her prize crew was able to bring her safely into port. She was subsequently repaired, at a cost of £12,000, and bought into the Royal Navy under her original name; the decision to employ her was no doubt because she was a brand new ship, having only been launched at Lorient some ten months previously.[32]

The world-wide commitments required of the British navy were causing Spencer great anxiety. The attrition caused by the blockade of Brest was a serious concern; it was essential, he considered, to husband the ships as far as possible, especially if there was no convenient anchorage which would enable the fleet to watch Brest without wearing itself out by cruising. One way to reduce the wear and tear on the Channel Fleet was put forward by Bridport in conversation with Seymour, as the latter reported to Spencer on 15 May from Torbay:

He wishes much to have the power of placing two or three ships of the line off Brest when he quits that station. His idea is that these ships with the frigates would prevent the Bertheaume squadron or any other squadron of that kind from coming out, and if they should escape from thence, immediately on their quitting that ground they would drive from their stations all he frigates we have cruising to the southwest.[33]

Seymour thought this not a bad plan.

Another aspect of the cumulative damage at the hands of wind and weather was the vulnerability of that highly prized article, the frigate. Bridport, to be fair, was conscious of the considerable demands in various theatres for frigates; and he had been thinking about what was needed:

The Channel frigates should be strong and in perfect condition. What occasioned my desiring English built frigates arose from the consideration

31 Morriss (ed.), *Channel Fleet*, p.292.
32 James, *Naval History*, Vol.II, p.124.
33 Morriss (ed.), *Channel Fleet*, p.395.

of the boisterous seas they had to encounter and knowing that I have six French built frigates already with me and that I find them oftener and longer in post at a time than our own built frigates.[34]

It was not unreasonable, he suggested to Spencer, to insist that of his frigates no more than six should be French built. His opinion was noteworthy, coming as it did at a time when the English designers were heavily influenced by the design of captured French vessels.

34   Morriss (ed.), *Channel Fleet*, p.296.

14

Bompart

The size of the force necessary for watching or blockading the French fleet in Brest was the subject of continuous discussion between the Admiralty and the local commanders. Bridport, writing to Spencer on 17 May, suggested that if no more than ten or eleven ships were on station at any one time it did not need three admirals. Spencer replied that it was effectively impossible to lay down any specific requirement:

> It must so entirely depend on the circumstances of the moment that I do not see how it can be possible to fix upon any precise arrangement beforehand. All I can say in that matter therefore is that in the present state of our force it will be necessary to make such arrangements as shall be calculated for wearing out the ships as little as possible.[1]

This was obviously the only sensible way to approach the matter. There was no doubt that the Channel Fleet's range of responsibilities made it a very resource intensive operation. Sir Andrew Hamond, the Comptroller since 1794, had been looking into the question, and wrote to Spencer from the Navy Board on 13 April:

> I have been maturely considering the question whether a fleet abroad is more or less expensive than the same number of ships on the Channel service; and the more I examine the subject the stronger my opinion is, that a fleet of twenty sail-of- the -line with a proportion of frigates, once properly equipped and sent abroad, will cost much less in the space of three years than if they had remained at home. It is true, the part of the world they are sent to serve in will make some difference by increasing perhaps the difficulty of supplying them with stores and provisions; but as it is a well-known fact, that ships on foreign service make every article of their stores and furniture last considerably longer

1   Morriss (ed.), *Channel Fleet*, p.297.

than when they have frequent opportunities of being supplied from the King's dockyards, I should apprehend the balance of expense would be in favour of the fleet abroad; and the circumstance of the ships' companies not being paid wages when abroad makes a considerable saving on the interest of money.[2]

Hamond added that he was collecting further information for 1796 and 1797, but he did not make any suggestions as to how the cost of the Channel Fleet might be reduced. Given the serious and continuing threat to both the English and Irish coast, it is difficult to see what could have been done.

One man, at any rate, who did not consider the cost of the Channel Fleet as money well spent, was St Vincent, who wrote to Spencer from his station off Cadiz on 28 May in violently critical terms:

> The squadron your Lordship has sent me under the orders of Rear Admiral Sir Roger Curtis exhibits a lamentable specimen of the state of your fleet at home…unless your admirals and captains are compelled to sleep on board their ships and keep all their officers tightly to their duty when at Spithead, Plymouth Sound and Cawsand Bay your navy will be ruined past redemption. There is a dreadful licentiousness in the conversation of the officers which is very soon conveyed to the men and I attribute in a great degree the disgraces which have befallen your fleet at home to this decay of discipline.[3]

What was needed, St Vincent suggested, was an officer of 'vigour and disposition to lay the axe to the root of this evil,' who should be given the most unequivocal support.

The Admiralty, meanwhile, continued to be profoundly apprehensive of the likelihood of a descent upon Ireland and gave orders accordingly: Bridport, who had gone back to Cawsand Bay so that the crew of the *Royal George* might be paid, hurriedly returned to his station off Ushant; he arrived there on 30 May after a passage of only 21½ hours, which he was at pains to report. The Admiralty required him to take especial care to prevent five French ships seen under Pointe St Mathieu escaping from that anchorage; Bridport huffily replied that Brest was being as closely watched as was possible, and that the ships in question comprised the enemy's advanced squadron in Bertheaume Bay. He was anxious to impress on Spencer that it was at Torbay that could be found the good port to the westward about which the First Lord frequently pestered him and on 19 June he wrote:

2   Corbett (ed.), *Spencer*, Vol.II, pp.216-217.
3   Morriss (ed.), *Channel Fleet*, p.305.

For a great national object I know no place so proper as Torbay, where the whole navy of England may anchor as well as its trading ships, where water is plenty both at Brixham and Torquay. The country surrounding the bay full of riches in the fruits of the earth. Corn, apples, vegetables of the best sort and every other production for ample supplies.[4]

Scilly, on the other hand, he considered to be 'a vain and useless speculation' from which nothing was to be had but dangerous prospects.

The relationship between Bridport and the Admiralty had by now become, as Roger Morriss points out, 'personal and acrimonious'. It was the admiral's belief that he had been consistently badly treated; he wrote a lengthy protest to an Admiralty Commissioner on 2 July to complain of ships being taken from him and of others put under his orders. He rejected the suggestion that had evidently been made that he put 'a stronger and unfavourable construction on some things than they were meant to convey'. He needed nothing to stimulate him to the strict execution of his orders; the case of the five ships at Pointe St Mathieu had evidently especially annoyed him, and he was pleased to point out that he had already driven this squadron from its anchorage into Brest.[5] Bridport had by now been in effective command of the Channel Fleet for three years; it is remarkable that in spite of his many and varied disputes with the Admiralty, he was to continue in post for two further years.

The anxiety of the Admiralty about Ireland was entirely justified. Reliable intelligence from d'Auvergne in the Channel Islands left no doubt as to what the French intended; he reported on 30 July:

The *Hoche* of 74 guns, the *Fraternité, Bellone, Resolue, Embuscade, Loire* and *Immortalité* of 40 guns are lying in the road with foretopsails loose, destined to throw succours into Ireland. The 4 line of battle ships (*Mont Blanc, Révolution, Wattigny, Fougueux*) ordered for a second division have had their crews completed from ships in the harbour. Forty waggons with cases of arms, etc, arrived yesterday with 4 million of livres in specie.[6]

The French had by no means given up the idea of invasion, and their determination was strengthened in 1798 by news of the Wexford rising. The operation to land troops in support of the rebels was, however, seriously delayed, and it was not until August that it got under way. The plan was for two forces to set sail simultaneously, one from Brest and one from Rochefort. The Brest expedition was further held up by the need to pay both the sailors and the soldiers involved, and that from

4   Morriss (ed.), *Channel Fleet*, p.310.
5   Morriss (ed.), *Channel Fleet*, pp.311-312.
6   Morriss (ed.), *Channel Fleet*, p.321.

Rochefort sailed on its own, on 6 August. Under the command of Commodore Savary, it comprised four frigates, and carried 1,150 troops with 4 guns under the command of General Humbert. On 21 August the squadron reached the west coast of Ireland; contrary winds drove it towards the bay of Killala where on the evening of the following day the troops landed, with the guns, ammunition, and uniforms and equipment for 3,000 rebels.[7]

A brief clash with a detachment of Fencibles yielded a number of prisoners, with which Savary shortly afterwards sailed away, returning safely to Rochefort. Humbert was joined by several bands of United Irishmen and had several skirmishes with the mounting forces sent against him; including a successful engagement with 2,000 British troops at Castlebar. Finally, though, on 8 September, he surrendered at Ballinamuck to a superior force under Lieutenant General Lake, 843 of his men being taken prisoner.

The larger part of the French forces for the invasion, sailing from Brest, was carried by a squadron commanded by Commodore Bompart. He had the *Hoche*, 74, with nine frigates and a schooner. The troops, some 3,000 in number, were commanded by Generals Hardy and Ménage, and were accompanied by a large artillery train, some siege guns and a large quantity of military stores. Bompart did not find a favourable wind until 16 September, when he put to sea through the Passage du Raz. He was spotted next morning at daybreak by a force commanded by Captain Richard Keats in the frigate *Boadicea*, who had with him the frigate *Ethalion* (Captain Countess) and the brig-sloop *Sylph* (Captain White). Leaving the others to follow the enemy, Keats crowded on sail to the northward to report to Bridport.

Bompart, in an effort to convince his pursuers that he was bound for the West Indies, having first steered for Lorient, on 18 September altered course and steered south-west by south. By now his followers had been joined by the *Amelia*, 38, (Captain Hubert) and the *Anson*, 44, (Captain Durham). These remained in touch, at noon on 22 September being within eight or nine miles of the French squadron, which was now steering west-north-west. Countess, perfectly clear as to Bompart's destination, on the following day sent off the *Sylph* to keep Bridport informed. On 25 September a chance encounter with a large British convoy that included a number of East Indiamen gave Bompart a difficult command decision; whether to attack the convoy or to continue with the operation for which he had put to sea. He may have been deceived by the warlike appearance of the Indiamen, or he may have thought his frigates too scattered to take on the convoy escort, or he may have felt that he must stick to his orders. James reckoned that attacking the convoy would have been more beneficial than safely disembarking his troops, or even returning with them to Brest; at all events, however, Bompart let the convoy go.[8]

7   James, *Naval History*, Vol.III, p.138.
8   James, *Naval History*, Vol.II, p.141.

Next day, and again on 29 September, Bompart employed his frigates in abortive attempts to drive off the British frigates that still pursued him closely. Failing in this, he resolved to steer straight for his destination. Finally, on 4 October, he managed to lose his pursuers when the weather came on thick and began to blow very hard. The *Amelia* became separated from the others, linking up with Warren's squadron that was also in pursuit of Bompart's force. On 11 October at dawn, the *Ethalion* and *Anson* saw and chased two ships, one of which was the *Amelia* and the other one of the ships from Warren's squadron.

Warren had put to sea from Cawsand Bay on 23 September, after it was known that Bompart had sailed, and headed for Achill Head; it was assumed that the French would make for a landing point close to that at which Humbert had disembarked. On October 11 Warren's force consisted of three ships of the line (*Canada*, 74, *Foudroyant*, 80 and *Robust*, 74) and five frigates (*Magnanime* and *Anson* of 44 guns, *Ethalion* and *Amelia* of 38 guns and *Melampus* of 36 guns). Although Bompart had originally intended to land at Killala Bay, it was assumed that Humbert might have pushed northwards, so the destination was changed to Lough Swilly. As he headed in that direction, however, the *Immortalité* signalled the appearance of Warren's force, and Bompart bore away southwest, resolved to land his troops wherever he got the chance. Warren ordered a general chase, in the stiff north-north-westerly wind. During the night both sides suffered damage. The *Hoche* lost her main topmast and her fore and mizzen topgallant masts, and the *Résolue* sprang a serious leak, while the *Anson* lost her mizzen mast, and her main yard and main topsail yard.

By 5.30 am on the following day the two squadrons were again in sight of each other, the force of the wind having dropped. Warren's ships were in an arc which left Bompart only the southwest as a direction of escape. Sending *Résolue* inshore on account of her leak, accompanied by the *Biche*, Bompart formed his remaining force into line headed by the *Sémillante*. Instead of persisting with the general chase, Warren also formed line of battle, coming into range soon after 7.00 am. There followed a fierce engagement as the two squadrons closed; by 8.50 am the *Robust*, leading Warren's line, was in action against the *Hoche*.[9] Bompart's flagship put up a vigorous defence but after two hours was obliged to strike. Warren laconically recorded the outcome of the engagement:

> The frigates made sail from us; the signal to pursue the enemy was immediately made, and, in five hours afterwards, three of the frigates hauled down their colours also; but they, as well as the *Hoche*, were obstinately defended, all of them being heavy frigates, entirely new, full of troops and stores, and everything necessary for the establishment of their plans in Ireland.[10]

9   Clowes, *Royal Navy*, Vol.IV, p.347.
10   Quoted Marcus, *Age of Nelson*, p.52.

'Admiral Sir J.B. Warren, Bart. K.B. and the victory off Ireland'. (Anne S.K. Brown Collection)

The three frigates which struck during the action were *Embuscade, Coquille* and *Bellone. Résolue, Loire* and *Immortalité* also failed to return home, being taken in a series of frigate actions.

Clowes was critical of Warren's handling of his squadron, observing that 'it can hardly be said that Warren's conduct of this little action was particularly brilliant, or that his subsequent dispositions were particularly wise'.[11] The latter point was a reference to the fact that he ordered the *Robust*, which was seriously crippled, to tow the *Hoche* into Lough Swilly, and as a result nearly lost her.

In France, meanwhile, there was concern as to what had become both of Humbert's force and Bompart's expedition, and Savary was sent out again from Rochefort to find out what had happened. He was evidently a lucky commander: after reaching Ireland, and learning what had occurred, he made his way safely home, in spite of being chased by two ships of the line and a frigate. By the time Savary got back, however, the news of the disasters had preceded him, with the return of the frigate *Romaine* to Brest. D'Auvergne reported on 24 October the dismay with which the news was received in Brest:

> The arrival of the frigate *La Romaine* at Brest, extremely shattered in battle, solved all doubts as to the fate of the Irish expedition. It has thrown the port into great consternation. The immediate effect has been the desertion of all the sailors on shore, though every precaution was taken that details of the defeat should not be known.[12]

The destruction of Bompart's squadron was reported to Bridport by Captain Durham of the *Anson*; but to the irritation of the Commander-in-Chief he received no report from Warren. This, as the Admiralty explained to him, was because while operating off the coast of Ireland he was under the orders of Kingsmill, the local commander. For the moment, Bridport judged that there was not much more for him to do, so he went on leave; Gardner, in his absence, commanded the Channel Fleet, although the weather soon drove him into Torbay. From his beloved Cricket Lodge, Bridport remained in close touch with the fleet's operations, anxious as always about the lack of sufficient frigates. The return of the fleet to Torbay necessitated a large force of frigates to watch Brest and Bridport urged the Admiralty not only to make good two recent losses, but to support the squadron of frigates by one or two ships of the line. His letter to the Admiralty was, however, endorsed to the effect that 'their Lordships had no frigates to spare and did not judge it necessary to keep line of battle ships off Brest'.[13]

11   Clowes, *Royal Navy*, Vol.IV, p.349.
12   Quoted Balleine (ed.), *Philippe d'Auvergne*, p.93.
13   Morriss (ed.), *Channel Fleet*, p.339.

Bridport and Spencer ended the year with a testy exchange arising from the loss of the *Colossus*, wrecked at St Mary's in the Scilly Isles. This 74, which was bringing home Sir William Hamilton's collection of classical vases from Naples, was lost on 11 December, and Bridport, reminding Spencer of his views of the safety of that anchorage, could not resist saying, in effect, 'I told you so'. Put out by this, Spencer wrote to him on 27 December to say in answer to Bridport's snide comments about the opinion of experienced seamen about the place, that the person from whom he had the comments on St Mary's was Pellew, 'than whom I do not believe there are many more experienced or able seamen in His Majesty's service'. Bridport could not let this pass; he had an equally high opinion of Pellew, he said, 'but I am inclined to believe his local attachments bias his mind rather too much for correct judgement'.[14]

In January 1799 Bridport went to Bath to take the waters there, but he continued to exercise control over the Channel Fleet. Information from d'Auvergne suggested that a number of French convoys were expected to sail from Rochefort, and he sent off orders to Countess to take the frigates *Ethalion* and *Anson* to cruise off that part. He also wanted to send two more to cruise off Corunna, but the Admiralty firmly slapped down this proposal, telling him that he was not to do so without receiving instruction. His subsequent plan to send the *San Fiorenzo* and *Naiad* to cruise between the Penmarcks and Lorient was, however approved.

Meanwhile Warren was chafing at the fact that he still had to serve under Bridport's command, and he wrote to Spencer to complain:

> I cannot avoid trespassing upon that kindness you have expressed to me to state to your Lordship that being kept in the Channel fleet under circumstances peculiarly unpleasant I must consider as an unhandsome and very hard fate. I am well aware that Lord Bridport's favourite argument against detaching me from the fleet is there being five or six senior officers to me in it but these gentlemen (however superior their merits may be considered) have never yet been called into detached service, consequently they cannot feel that mortification that I must ever do at remaining off Brest after having for three years successively borne a broad pendant.[15]

Even Spencer, tolerant to a fault of the importunities of some of his officers, was not putting up with that:

> The situation in which you are at present placed was the unavoidable consequence of the nature of the naval war at the time and the circumstance of

---

14 Morriss (ed.), *Channel Fleet*, pp.338-340.
15 Morriss (ed.), *Channel Fleet*, p.344.

your being removed to a line of battle ship, which removal took place in consequence of a request of your own.[16]

One of the officers senior to Warren and who was rather more positive about his situation was Collingwood, who had recently come on shore, and who was reflecting philosophically on the lack of promotion in the navy, especially when compared with that in the army. He wrote to his uncle Dr Carlyle on 11 January, stating 'the general opinion in the Navy that if the country was happily restored to peace, there would not be any promotion until we were threatened with another war'.[17] His pessimism was soon proved to be ill founded; in the following month he was promoted to rear admiral. Overjoyed to be reunited with his wife and two daughters, he wrote to Dr Carlyle to observe that if the promotion meant that he would not have the opportunity to serve at sea, he had 'as many comforts, and sources of rational happiness, to resort to as any person:'

> But I shall never lose sight of the duty I owe to my country. I immediately on being made a Rear Admiral wrote to Lord Spencer to offer myself for service and to solicit an appointment on any station he might judge proper to employ me. If I find on my going to town there is a prospect of my succeeding, I shall not return to the North, but leave the beauties of Morpeth to take care of themselves, and my dear Sarah will then come to me.[18]

In the event he was to be on shore only until May, when he rejoined the Channel Fleet, hoisting his flag in the *Triumph*.

---

16 Morriss (ed.), *Channel Fleet*, p.345.
17 Hughes (ed.), *Admiral Lord Collingwood*, p.93.
18 Hughes (ed.), *Admiral Lord Collingwood*, p.95.

15

Bruix

Etienne Eustache Bruix was born in 1759 at Fort Dauphin, into a noble family. He joined the French navy at the age of nineteen, and at the commencement of the French Revolution held the rank of *lieutenant de vaisseau*. In spite of his origins he was promoted to captain in 1793 but in the following year, however, his noble birth caught up with him, and he was discharged from the navy. In 1795 he was recalled, serving under Villaret-Joyeuse and Morard de Galles, acting as chief of staff to the latter. He was promoted to rear admiral in May 1797, and in April 1798 was named as Minister of Marine. One of his first responsibilities was to complete the supervision of Napoleon Bonaparte's expedition to Egypt, a huge operation involving some 350 vessels sailing from Toulon and from other ports on the French and Italian coast. Bruix displayed energy and efficiency in supporting the drive and determination of Bonaparte, and the expedition sailed in May 1798, the fleet being commanded by Vice Admiral Brueys d'Aigalliers. It was to lead to a stunning defeat at the hands of Nelson in Aboukir Bay in August, which left Bonaparte and his army marooned in Egypt.

In 1799 plans were put in hand for an expedition to extricate the French army. By now a vice admiral, Bruix went to Brest to oversee the fitting out of the fleet to undertake this operation, of which he decided to take personal command. In order to assist the escape of the French fleet, an armed cutter, the *Rebecca*, was sent out with false despatches which it was intended should be captured. In fact, the vessel's condition was such that her captain was obliged to report to Bruix on 16 April that she was not in a state to carry out her part in the deception, and it was necessary to equip another vessel to take her place. Also to be named *Rebecca*, to conform with the documentation, she duly sailed and was taken by the lugger *Black Joke* on 27 April. The latter's commander, Lieutenant James Nicolson, at once sent the captured despatches to Bridport. These professed to instruct the *Rebecca* to proceed to Ireland in advance of an expedition of the French fleet; the delay in the sailing of the *Rebecca* meant that they were dated as early as 5 April and this, coupled with the fact that no attempt was made to throw the despatches overboard, soon gave rise to suspicions that they were a *ruse de guerre*.

Historians are divided as to the extent to which the decoy orders carried by the *Rebecca* influenced the decision making of the British Cabinet and the Admiralty. Piers Mackesy's opinion is that the politicians were entirely deceived; Spencer at Bath, the first minister to hear the news, regarded it as confirmation of his view that part of the Brest fleet was destined for Ireland, and Grenville, the Foreign Secretary, wrote to his brother Lord Buckingham: 'I have no doubt the intelligence is such as may be relied on'. Mackesy goes on, however, to contrast with this the naval opinion:

> In chorus the admirals pointed to the suspicious circumstances in which the French lugger had been taken; Kingsmill at Cobh, Lord Howe in his London home, Young at the Admiralty. The prize had sailed with orders of 5 April to proceed at once to Ireland, yet she was still hanging about off Ushant when she was taken on the 27th. She was supposed to bring the Irish vessels advanced notice that the French fleet was coming, but was taken after it had sailed. She was chased for four hours, yet the despatches which should have been sunk without trace were still in the cabin when she was overhauled.[1]

Marcus, always ready to blame Bridport, writes that 'such was the laxity and inefficiency of his blockade that the lugger which was sent to mislead the British with false dispatches had to cruise for several days before she discovered a frigate obliging enough to capture her'.[2]

In the meantime, Bruix had put to sea. Bridport had sailed from St Helens on 13 April with eight ships of the line, intending to join Berkeley who was already at sea with seven more. Illustrative of the hands on approach now adopted by the Admiralty, he was ordered to employ the frigate *Nymphe* in watching the port of Brest.[3] Similar instructions were sent in respect of the frigate *Amiable*. Bridport meanwhile had been making further reconnaissances of the port, sending Captain Sir James Saumarez in the *Caesar* to make a report of the advancing preparations of the French fleet. Saumarez reported that there were a total of 19 ships of the line apparently getting under sail, seven at anchor in Camaret Bay, five outside the roadstead and seven more with frigates in the road. Next day a further reconnaissance produced a report by Captain Campbell of the *Dragon* to the effect that there were now 12 ships of the line in the outer road, with five frigates or sloops, with four further ships of the line and five frigates or sloops, with six other sail, in the outer road. On 26 April Bridport was some twelve miles off Ushant, in fresh breezes and cloudy weather, having sent *Nymphe* (Captain Fraser) into Brest Bay

1   Piers Mackesy, *The Strategy of Overthrow 1798-1799* (London: Longman, 1974), p.100.
2   Marcus, *Age of Nelson*, p.144.
3   Morriss (ed.), *Channel Fleet*, p.360.

during the previous night. She soon ran into thick fog and was still unable to see anything on the morning of 26 April when she stood in to the Black Rocks at 5.00 am. At 8.30 she stood in again, visibility having improved, and at 9.00 sighted the French fleet, eleven ships of the line standing out preceded by a large frigate with others making sail. At 9.30 Captain Fraser signalled to the *Superb* and *Dragon* that the enemy were in sight on the larboard tack, and giving their bearing. At 12.30 the fog had again become so thick that Fraser lost sight of the French; the leading French frigate was seen to wear, and Fraser assumed that the rest of the fleet had returned to its anchorage. Meanwhile, however, Bridport had made a signal for a general chase. Given his understanding of the situation, this alarmed Fraser, as he later reported to Pole:

> Observing several of the ships of the line making a great deal of sail and fearing the consequences I made the signal of annul and which signal, I conclude, has made the Admiral suppose that I had not seen anything but there is no signal in the book that I could make to indicate that I had lost sight of the enemy and I did not think it proper to make the signal for the enemy being again at anchor until I was certain they were so, though it appeared to me that they had returned again as I ran down and must have crossed within sight of them had they run to the southward.[4]

Bridport had, at 12.15 signalled his fleet to prepare for battle and at 2.56 pm made the signal for a general chase, but on receiving the *Nymphe's* signal of annul ordered the chase to be discontinued. Once it was clear that the bird had flown, Bridport sent off reports to this effect. The sloop *Childers* went with despatches for St Vincent and Keith (in case Bruix had gone south) and the *Dolly* cutter to Plymouth. Since it was most likely that the French were in fact heading for Ireland, Bridport set off himself in the direction of Cape Clear. On receiving the news that the French were at sea, the Admiralty took the same view, writing to Bridport on 1 May:

> It is much to be lamented that Captain Fraser had not been able to keep sight of the enemy's squadron and to have given your Lordship more satis- factory information by which you might have been enabled to fall in with it before it had reached any considerable distance from Brest, or to have followed it to the point of its actual destination. Under the present state of uncertainty, however, their Lordships cannot but approve of the decision you have pursued of proceeding in the first instance off Cape Clear, where your Lordship will continue until you shall have gained some further

4   Morriss (ed.), *Channel Fleet*, p.367.

account of the enemy and where you will be joined by the *Polyphemus* from Cork.[5]

Bruix had sailed with 25 ships of the line, five frigates and a number of smaller vessels, a fleet which was described by one historian as 'one of the best manned and best found fleets that ever issued from a French harbour'.[6] Blame for his escape has been generally laid at Bridport's door. Observing that the Admiralty, with plenty of warning that the French were fitting out a squadron, had gravely miscalculated, Marcus wrote:

> Bridport, moreover, had wholly failed to learn from experience: as usual he was in no hurry to get to sea, and, when he finally did so, his plans miscarried ('a horrible bungling work,' was Collingwood's comment); back on his station, the few cruisers he had with him were improvidently dispersed – and this despite the Admiralty's warning.[7]

The quotation from Collingwood is perhaps somewhat selective. It comes in a letter of 12 June to his sister, as he explains what had happened:

> The look out frigate saw the French fleet come out – the weather was thick and hazy – the signals he made cou'd not be distinguished for some hours after. By the thickness of the weather, and their increased distance as they went on their voyage, Capt Percy lost sight of them and unaccountably taking it into his head (which I shou'd imagine is something like the weather) that they were all gone into port again, as if the French fleet wou'd come out merely to shew how well they cou'd go in again, he annulled all the signals he had made, as if the whole had been a miscomprehension of his, and their circumstance, which he had indicated by his signals, had not occurred.[8]

James observed that Bridport, by taking up a position off Ushant, 'had thus left open the principal passage in and out of Brest'.[9] This was probably due to Bridport's concern for his primary objective, the protection of Ireland; but it does seem surprising, given the number and state of readiness of the French ships, that he moved quite so far away from the entrance to Brest and the adjacent anchorages; the extract from Bridport's Journal, quoted by Morriss, gives no explanation for

5   Morriss (ed.), *Channel Fleet*, p.371.
6   Clowes, *Royal Navy*, Vol.IV, p.380.
7   Marcus, *Age of Nelson*, p.144.
8   Hughes (ed.), *Admiral Lord Collingwood*, p.99.
9   James, *Naval History*, Vol.II, p.285.

the decision.[10] Mahan is sharply critical, noting that, with the wind favouring an exit to the south, Bridport was some thirty miles from the Passage du Raz through which Bruix made his getaway. He goes on to blame Bridport for his conviction that Ireland would be the destination of the French, remarking that he, 'in spite of the reports from merchant vessels that had seen the French to the southward, and steering south, refused to believe that Ireland was safe'.[11] This is certainly unfair; Bridport, in taking up a position to cover Ireland, was effectively only carrying out standing orders, and by the time he knew anything about Bruix's whereabouts the French admiral was much too far away to be pursued effectively.

In this connection, however, the terms of the Admiralty's instructions to Bridport of 26 April must be borne in mind:

> Their Lordships will send you as many frigates as other necessary services will admit, which you will employ in watching the enemy's ships in Brest, particularly directing their commanders to be careful it does not escape unperceived to the southward for though the absolute necessity of protecting the coast of Ireland must make that the first object of your attention if the enemy should be able to put to sea without being seen by your cruisers, yet there is very great reason to believe that the expedition fitting out at Brest is intended against Portugal, the success of which undertaking it is most essentially necessary to prevent.[12]

By the time Bridport received this, of course, Bruix was well on his way. Significantly, on the same day, when forwarding the report of the reconnaissance by Saumarez, Bridport told the Admiralty that he thought the enemy would put to sea; 'and should they do it unobserved I shall lose no time in proceeding with the whole of my present force off of Cape Clear or other parts of the coast of Ireland as intelligence may direct me'.[13]

It is also not unreasonable to consider the serious difficulties which Bridport faced due to the lack of sufficient frigates to monitor Bruix's proceedings. Admiral Richmond, in his introduction to that section of *The Spencer Papers* dealing with these operations, put it this way:

> The one way of guarding against whatever the enemy might intend was to get and keep touch with him at the point of his departure, Brest. But the means he had of doing so were less than the nature of the services demanded. Frigates, which he had been told would be sent to him as other

---

10   Morriss (ed.), *Channel Fleet*, pp.365-366.
11   Mahan, *Sea Power*, Vol.I, p.306.
12   Morriss (ed.), *Channel Fleet*, pp.362-63.
13   Morriss (ed.), *Channel Fleet*, p.363.

services admitted, were not provided in time, or in sufficient numbers; but very specific instructions had been given him that the employment of those he had should be confined to the essential duties… Notwithstanding this strict and proper definition of the use to which the frigates were to be put, the number available never proved adequate. There are traces in some of the papers of earlier date in the eighteenth century of the expression of an accepted principle governing the observation of an enemy force – namely, that frigates should work in pairs. One of the ships on sighting an enemy should carry the information gathered – his strength, whereabouts, departure, course etc – to the flag and be able to act as circumstances required in bringing later information.[14]

In fairness to Bridport, his concerns about the insufficiency of frigates available to him had been raised countless times. As to responsibility for Bruix's escape he was perhaps unlucky rather than blameworthy.

Kingsmill, writing to Spencer on 12 May, had by now concluded that it was not probable that Bruix was in fact headed for Ireland, citing the length of time the French had been out without having been seen, as well as the unconvincing nature of the despatches taken aboard the *Rebecca*; he was able to reassure the First Lord that they were 'well prepared for their reception in every point'.[15]

By 14 May it seemed evident to Spencer and the Admiralty that Bruix had indeed gone south:

On that day instructions were went to St Vincent saying that no information had been received from which any probability appeared that the enemy was destined for Ireland, and therefore it was concluded that that he had gone to the southward; and it was highly probable that a large fleet of the united forces of France and Spain was intended for Cadiz or the Mediterranean, while a detachment might be intended for distant service.[16]

The instructions to St Vincent, who at this time was on shore in Gibraltar, leaving Keith commanding the blockading force at Cadiz, were necessarily complicated, covering a number of the possible scenarios for action on the part of Bruix and the action that St Vincent was in each case to take. Five ships of the line under Rear Admiral Whitshed had already been despatched from Cawsand Bay to reinforce St Vincent. The lack of any transports with Bruix made it seem unlikely that he

14   Corbett (ed.), *Spencer*, Vol.II, pp.47-48.
15   Corbett (ed.), *Spencer*, Vol.II, p.85.
16   Corbett (ed.), *Spencer*, Vol.II, p.51.

was going either to Ireland or to Portugal, unless he called at Rochefort to pick up troops from there, so the Mediterranean certainly appeared more probable.

As the days passed this appeared certainly to be the case, although a suggestion that Bruix might be heading for Ferrol, there to pick up troops, caused some concern, and led Pitt to urge Spencer (who was in Bath) via the Admiralty to reinforce Bridport. In fact Bruix had appeared off Cadiz in a north westerly gale on 4 May, where he met Keith with 15 ships of the line. Upon the latter showing a bold front, Bruix made off to the southwest, and St Vincent was able to report to Spencer on 10 May:

> Lord Keith has shown great manhood and ability before Cadiz, his position having been very critical, exposed to a hard gale of wind blowing directly on the shore, with an enemy of superior force to windward of him, and twenty two ships of the line in the Bay of Cadiz, ready to profit of any disaster which might have befallen him.[17]

Five ships of the line had been sent to reinforce Bridport, who was on 13 May directed to Bantry Bay to re-provision his fleet, after which he was to detach Gardner with 16 ships of the line to strengthen St Vincent. With the rest of the Channel Fleet he was to look for a Spanish squadron from Ferrol to prevent it joining with Bruix; it might be found in Rochefort, or in Ferrol. It was reported in the Paris press that the squadron was in Aix Roads, a fact that was confirmed by Captain Durham of the *Anson* on 4 June 4, and the question was now what should be done about it. Bridport regarded it as impracticable to destroy the Spanish vessels, adding:

> And the keeping it from putting to sea very uncertain unless a squadron shall be ordered out to anchor in Basque Road under the command of some officer of experience and, if bombs were sent with that officer, the squadron at anchor under the protection of Ile d'Aix might be disturbed and obliged to move up the Charente for shelter and security.[18]

Meanwhile d'Auvergne had been collecting further intelligence which strongly suggested that the French were building up a further squadron in Brest which, with the ships being fitted out, together with the Spanish ships from Rochefort, with another French ship from there and one from Lorient would amount to 13 ships of the line. This indicated the desirability of doing something about the Spanish squadron as soon as possible. Bridport himself had arrived back in Cawsand Bay, leaving Berkeley on station off Rochefort; the latter was thoroughly discontented,

17   Corbett (ed.), *Spencer*, Vol.II, p.81.
18   Morriss (ed.), *Channel Fleet*, pp.387-388.

as Bridport reported to Spencer. The First Lord was not happy to leave the operation to attack the Spanish ships to Berkeley, and ordered Bridport to take charge
of the operation; three bomb vessels were added to his command. Spencer was,
however, optimistic about the success of the venture, not least because he had been
told that ships of the size of the Spanish squadron could not anchor close enough
to the shore to be protected by the land batteries.[19] Bridport was put out by the
peremptory requirement that he return to sea at once; if there was no absolute
necessity for him to command off Rochefort, he requested 'some relaxation from
my public duty which I feel my health requires;' To this their Lordships assented,
and Pole was ordered to hoist his flag on board the *Royal George*, and to lead the
operation against the Spanish ships.[20]

By 3 July Pole was gloomily reporting the failure of the attack on the Spanish
ships; they proved to be beyond the range of the bomb vessels, while the latter were
under constant fire from the enemy. Moving them nearer would simply hasten
their own destruction, as the Spanish vessels could comfortably move further
in shore. Later that month, learning that Bruix might be returning to the north,
Pole left his station and in accordance with Admiralty orders made his way to
Torbay. Sufficient anxiety was felt about what the French actually intended for the
Admiralty to order Pole 'to arrange the ships in Torbay in the best manner you
may be able for resisting any attack which may be made upon them by the enemy's
fleet'. Bridport, at the same time, was ordered to Torbay to retake command of the
fleet.[21]

Bruix, meanwhile, had been causing fearful alarm in the Mediterranean, where
the size of his fleet was seen to threaten all aspects of the British position there. In
the event, however, his cruise produced no tangible results, although Mahan drew
important conclusions from it:

> To the student of naval war, its incidents are most instructive. It is scarcely
> too much to say that never was there a greater opportunity than that
> offered to the French fleet, had it been a valid force, by the scattered condi-
> tion of its enemies on this occasion; nor can failure deprive the incident
> of its durable significance, as illustrating the advantage, to the inferior
> navy, when the enemy, though superior, is by the nature of the contest
> compelled to disseminate his squadrons.[22]

Bruix, having achieved none of his possible objectives apart from the re-vict-
ualling of French forces in Genoa, sailed first to Toulon and then to Cartagena,

---

19   Morriss (ed.), *Channel Fleet*, p.391.
20   Morriss (ed.), *Channel Fleet*, p.393-394.
21   Morriss (ed.), *Channel Fleet*, p.399.
22   Mahan, *Sea Power*, Vol.II, p.305.

where on 22 June he joined the principal Spanish fleet from Cadiz, which had eluded Keith's blockading squadron. Early in July the Combined Fleet left the Mediterranean and arrived at Cadiz with forty ships of the line, leaving that port on 21 July to head northwards. On 30 July Keith, with 31 ships of the line, also passed through the Straits of Gibraltar, and set off in hot pursuit of Bruix. In the event, Bruix got back to Brest on 8 August, one day ahead of Keith, to the latter's intense frustration. With the ships already there as reported by d'Auvergne, the French had an immensely powerful fleet. Pellew, in the *Impetueux*, 74, sent in by Keith to reconnoitre, reported from 45-50 large ships: although some of these appeared ready for sea, the state of most suggested that no immediate operations were contemplated. He saw the flags of one Spanish admiral, one vice admiral and two rear admirals, and one French admiral, two vice admirals, a rear admiral and a commodore.

Aboard the *Triumph* in Torbay, Collingwood felt thoroughly unimpressed with the conduct of affairs of the British fleet in its reaction to Bruix's appearance in the Mediterranean, noting that having pursued the French fleet to Genoa, and with the enemy in sight, Keith 'bethought of Minorca's safety and bore away for its protection, and left the French to follow their schemes at their leisure'. He sardonically continued:

> Our whole operations were of this class and managed with the same degree of skill. It was obvious to every person that the French might have been come up with before they left Carthagena, and as obvious to most men that they never cou'd be come up with. Lord St Vincent's sagacity and penetration I am sure saw this man failing in every thing, without displeasure; he wou'd have ill brooked the laurels which presented themselves to us, being gathered by another hand under his nose as it were and perhaps he does not like him... The short story is that the whole business had been dreadfully marr'd, and the British navy suffered much in our own opinions, and no doubt will be sharply handled by our friends on shore.[23]

On 5 August, while his mind was occupied with concerns about the threat posed to the English and Irish coasts by the oncoming Combined Fleet, Spencer received the sad news of the death that morning of Lord Howe. It raised immediate questions of precedence and personality about which he at once consulted the Prime Minister, since Howe's death left vacant hugely prestigious and valuable offices of state. The first of these was Admiral of the Fleet, which passed automatically to the most senior admiral, who was Sir Peter Parker. The latter was Port Admiral at Portsmouth and he would be obliged to retire from that post, leaving the First

23   Hughes (ed.), *Admiral Lord Collingwood*, p.100.

Vice Admiral Cuthbert Collingwood, 1st Baron Collingwood. (Anne S.K. Brown Collection)

Lord the difficult task of finding a replacement. The next was the Generalship of Marines, which Spencer felt must go to the current holder of the Lieutenant Generalship, Admiral Barrington, since he thought it would not be right to appoint as General of Marines anyone junior to him. If that were done, the Lieutenant Generalship would be disposable, but he did not know to whom it should be given:

> If to Lord Bridport, it should be on condition of his resigning his office of Vice Admiral of England and Treasurer of Greenwich Hospital, or at least

one of them; and I confess at any other moment than just the present, I should have been disposed to make use of it as an inducement to him to retire from active service, for which I think his energy and other qualifications are nearly passed by; but if he were to retire it would be impossible to find at this moment another Admiral to command the Channel Fleet which we are collecting and he must therefore go to sea again to endeavour to counteract the operations of these combined fleets, which you will have learned have sailed from Cadiz and will not improbably be very shortly either in the Channel or upon the coast of Ireland.[24]

Pitt's reply was robust; for a long time Barrington had declined all chief commands, and he thought that the higher honours of the profession would be better bestowed on those who had continued in active service, 'and out of that description, I suppose, Lord Bridport, from standing, would have the best pretensions'. He thought that Bridport should give up at least one of his present sinecures; and, as to the command of the Channel Fleet, he could see no objection to his remaining in command on the understanding that he should retire when the emergency was over.[25] The honorary office held by Bridport of Vice Admiral of Great Britain, was held by him until his death in 1814; he had succeeded Howe in this in 1796 when the latter became Admiral of the Fleet.

This exchange did not of course reflect the greatest confidence on the part of the Prime Minister and First Lord either in the current holder of the most important active post in the Navy or indeed in the candidates who might be seen as immediately suitable to succeed him. Both St Vincent and Duncan were, apparently, seen for the moment as too unwell to be considered. Although Keith had gained in reputation as St Vincent's deputy, issues of seniority ruled him out, while there was no confidence in Gardner. Seniority, too, precluded the recall of Nelson to the command of the Channel Fleet. The only other possible candidate, floated very diffidently by Pitt, might have been Lord Hood, but the King would no doubt have had something to say about that. And there were no circumstances in which Spencer would consider appointing Cornwallis after their contretemps of 1796. Bridport, therefore, sublimely unaware of this correspondence about his future must, *faute de mieux*, continue in command.

24   Corbett (ed.), *Spencer*, Vol.III, pp.11-12.
25   Corbett (ed.), *Spencer*, Vol.III, p.14.

16

Bridport Strikes His Flag

Confronted by the potentially very serious threat from the whole of the Combined Fleet now concentrated in Brest, the Admiralty turned its attention to the possibility of a land attack on the port. It was a tempting prospect; a successful attack would destroy the enemy fleet at a single stroke. The first suggestion came from Henry Dundas, Secretary of State for War, well before Bruix re-entered Brest, when he wrote to Spencer on 19 July to speculate what the Combined Fleet would now do:

> If they should go to Brest would it not be our best plan, after taking [possession of] Voorn and securing Brille and Helvoetsluys, to attack Brest with our whole force British and Russian? I think an army of twenty thousand men would do the business. Sir Charles Grey has often pledged himself at any time to do it with 30,000.[1]

By August 30, when Dundas next wrote to Spencer on the subject, his recollection of General Sir Charles Grey's opinion had changed; he now recalled that he had said that 10,000 men would be enough, and 'if double or treble that number would [do], it should be done, and we have the means'. He went on to reflect on the curious situation that might arise; the British government was committed to the restoration of the French monarchy, 'but I am sure that country always will be the natural enemy of this, and if it is in our power we ought to use our best exertions to annihilate their naval power'.[2]

At this time the principal military concern of the British government was the expedition to the Netherlands, which had sailed on 13 August. After being delayed by bad weather, the landing began on 27 August four miles south of the Helder under supporting fire from the guns of the covering squadron. The advanced guard, under Sir Ralph Abercromby, advanced successfully and on 30 August Vice

1   Corbett (ed.), *Spencer*, Vol.III, p.109.
2   Corbett (ed.), *Spencer*, Vol.III, p.109.

Admiral Mitchell pushed his squadron up the channel between the Helder and Texel and captured the whole of the Dutch fleet there, consisting of seven ships of the line and eighteen smaller craft. However, Abercromby failed to continue his advance and although in the second week of September a substantial Anglo-Russian Army arrived, and the command was taken over by the Duke of York, the operation ground to a halt. By then there were 40,000 troops in Holland, so it was immediately tempting for the British government to assume that part of this force might be used against Brest.

Pitt had asked Spencer to review a paper from Sir Charles Grey on the prospects for a successful operation, and on 2 September Spencer sent him a detailed review of the considerations to be borne in mind. He summarised the conclusions of the officers with whom he had talked, including Bridport, Warren and Pellew, under three heads:

1   That as large a force as possible should be landed in as short a time as possible.
2   That the landing should be as near as possible to the town of Brest.
3   That it should be made at a place where constant communication can be kept open with the fleet as well for the purpose of support and assistance in carrying on their operations, as for ensuring and protecting the retreat of the troops whenever it shall become necessary.[3]

These were obviously sensible principles on which to proceed. Applying them to the possible landing places, Spencer found defects in most of them. Much the best option was, he concluded, Douarnenez Bay, but this had the defect that it was the furthest from Brest itself, which could only be reached by a march of at least 35 to 40 miles, with two or three rivers to cross, over difficult roads.

Spencer was concerned that Grey now had in mind a much larger force, augmented by seamen from the fleet: the demands on the ships involved however, meant that this would not be practicable. Overall, Spencer thought that a landing in Douarnenez Bay would be best; once the landing force had got far enough towards Brest, an attack should be made by sea on the Conquet Peninsula and by land on the Camaret Peninsula. If the batteries on both sides of the Goulet could be seized, an enemy fleet in Brest Water could be destroyed without difficulty.

Meanwhile the British Cabinet, led by the Foreign Secretary Lord Grenville, who was now a convert to the idea of an attack on Brest, had been hoping for a speedy victory in the Netherlands, which would release troops for the Brest operation. On 19 September, however, the Anglo-Russian attempt to break out of the Zijpe position had been soundly defeated at the battle of Bergen. Bad weather delayed a fresh attempt until 3 October, when the Duke of York launched an attack at Egmond aan Zee which was to some extent successful, but which, due to the exhausted state

3   Corbett (ed.), *Spencer*, Vol.III, p.118.

of the troops, was not exploited. Although Alkmaar, the principal objective, was taken, the Franco-Batavian army of General Brune was still more or less intact, and an indecisive battle at Castricum on 6 October inflicted heavy casualties on both sides. As a result, the Anglo Russian army was obliged to retreat to the line of the Zijpe, with nothing to show for its efforts. When the British Cabinet heard this news, it was at once recognised that the campaign had failed, and the troops must be withdrawn. After armistice negotiations had been successful, the troops were safely re-embarked, to the great relief of the Cabinet, which feared that the army might have been lost.

The project for an attack on Brest remained alive during October, but it gradually ceased to be seen as readily attainable. It lingered on until 11 January, when it was finally put aside as a result of Grey's further and very unfavourable opinion. Pitt, however, had not entirely abandoned hope that the project might be revived, writing to Dundas: 'I see no prospect of our having at present any such report as would justify encouraging the scheme, and I shall endeavour to keep the whole subject in suspense till your return'.[4]

In September Nepean wrote to Bridport to tell him that he had commissioned the marine painter John Thomas Serres to join one of the ships of the Channel Fleet in order to make a number of illustrations of views of the French coastline at and around Brest. Nepean suggested that he be put on board the frigates that were close in shore. He was, he told Bridport, going to give Serres a large sum for this service.[5] By the time Nepean wrote to Bridport, Serres had already embarked in the *Royal George*, and as soon as she arrived off Ushant he got down to work, producing a number of views. At the end of October he transferred to the frigate *Clyde*, although severe gales soon drove the whole fleet back to the English coast, and he went on shore. He returned to the fleet in May of the following year, in due course re-joining the captain of the *Clyde*, Charles Cunningham, with whom he had a close working relationship.

In the autumn of 1799 Bridport had got into trouble with the Admiralty over an order he had given to his frigate captains to take under their command all frigates belonging to other squadrons not under the direct command of the Admiralty. One such was the *Alcmene* from St Vincent's Mediterranean Fleet. Nepean wrote sternly to Bridport on 5 October:

> I have it in command to acquaint you that their Lordships do not approve of Captain Pierrepont's having taken the *Alcmene* under his orders (as you will have perceived by my letter to you of yesterday's date) and to signify their direction to your Lordship, except in situations where the urgency

4   Corbett (ed.), *Spencer*, Vol.III, p.130.
5   M.K. Barritt, *Eyes of the Admiralty – J.T. Serres An Artist in the Channel Fleet 1799-1800* (London: National Maritime Museum, 2008), p.17.

of the public service shall require it, not to take under your command any ship or vessel not put under your orders by them.[6]

Bridport was not, the letter went on, to 'interfere with the ships under the orders of any other officer'.

It was incidents of this kind, and the policy which Bridport wished to pursue in respect of his frigates, that increased the desire of the Admiralty to manage more closely the conduct of the blockade of Brest. The detail into which their instructions to Bridport went is shown by the letter which he wrote from Torbay on 8 November:

> I have received your letter of the 6th instant signifying their Lordships' direction for me not to send the *Dragon* again off the Penmarks nor any ship of the line in her stead. Also to order the captains of the respective ships in this bay to complete their provisions to at least four months with all possible expedition.[7]

With the wind coming easterly, Bridport was ordered to return to his station off Brest, taking with him thirty ships of the line. This was judged to be sufficient for the present, the Spanish Commander-in-Chief having gone to Paris, and there being evidently an unsettled situation following Napoleon's seizure of power.

What concerned the Admiralty in particular was the freedom with which the French could come and go, particularly in the Iroise, despite the presence of the Channel Fleet. French frigate squadrons were able to sail much as they wished, and convoys could be escorted into the port. D'Auvergne reported in November on French shipping movements which not only involved frigates but also ships of the line, in taking up stations to cover the incoming convoys: when necessary, going as far as Lorient. In December Bridport went on shore leave, instructing Gardner to carry out the Admiralty's instructions to interdict the French convoy routes and the movement of warships to cover them. In this, Gardner was unsuccessful; his report to the Admiralty of 28 December illustrated all too clearly the problems faced in attempting an effective close blockade:

> We have had continual gales of wind from the ENE to the ESE with very little variation and the fleet have therefore been unable to maintain their station off Brest and have been driven upwards of sixty leagues to the westward of Ushant, frequently obliged to lay to under a close reefed

6   Morriss (ed.), *Channel Fleet*, p.417.
7   Morriss (ed.), *Channel Fleet*, p.430.

maintop sail only. I have the satisfaction to add that the squadron have not hitherto suffered any material injuries in their masts, yards or sails.[8]

Nonetheless, the wear and tear on the ships of the Channel Fleet was progressively wearing them out, notwithstanding the frequent opportunities to return home for a refit.

The Admiralty continued to manage closely the arrangements for the blockade; Gardner, who had returned to Torbay, was on 12 January ordered to return to his station off Brest. Reports had been received that an enemy fleet had sailed from there, consisting of fifteen ships of the line. The orders now sent to Gardner were intended to address all the alternative eventualities with which he might have to deal. He was to sail at once; if the enemy was still in port, he was to cruise off it until the wind settled in the west, and then return to Torbay. If part of the Combined Fleet had put to sea, he was to send Cotton after it with a suitable force (being twelve ships of the line if the enemy strength was unknown). If Cotton could not ascertain where the enemy had gone, he was to cruise off Cadiz. If he then found the French had entered the Mediterranean, he was to follow through the straits and proceed to Port Mahon; if he did not meet Keith there, he was to go to Malta, and await orders.

Bridport, meanwhile, was in London, from where he made an abortive attempt, once again, to deploy frigates to cruise from Belleisle to the Garonne; once again the Admiralty forbade it, at least at first, but later relented when the *Amethyst* and *Nymphe* at Plymouth were ready for sea. In February, still concerned that part at any rate of the Brest fleet might put to sea, the Admiralty ordered Bridport, still in London, to send three frigates at once to cruise off Ferrol to look for the enemy; in what was now the fashion of Admiralty orders to the Channel Fleet, the orders went into considerable detail to set out the alternative situations that might arise.[9]

Gardner was soon able, however, to confirm that the enemy still had about forty two ships of the line in Brest, of which thirty were ready for sea, apparently not including the fifteen Spanish ships; this prompted the Admiralty to cut short Bridport's leave, and to order him to go to Torbay as soon as he could. On 17 March he was ordered to put to sea with all the ships there, and to join Gardner off Brest. As with previous instructions, his orders were extremely lengthy, and addressed in detail all the various alternative circumstances which he might encounter. As Roger Morriss has written: 'This growing body of instructions formed a legacy inherited hereafter by all the fleet and squadron commanders blockading Brest during the remainder of the wars against Napoleonic France'.[10]

8   Morriss (ed.), *Channel Fleet*, p.426.
9   Morriss (ed.), *Channel Fleet*, pp.430-431.
10 Morriss (ed.), *Channel Fleet*, p.405.

Bridport was ordered to remain off Brest, keeping with him twenty eight ships of the line and all the frigates he found there, sending Gardner into port with all the rest, of which six plus the *Royal Sovereign* were to go to Cawsand Bay for repair and re-provisioning while the remainder went to Torbay. What the French intended was far from clear; a close watch must be kept on them, and every effort made to hinder the delivery of supplies of all descriptions to Brest. If it was only the French that came out, it was to Ferrol that he must send the pursuing squadron, with the usual instructions to follow into the Mediterranean if necessary. And so on and so forth; the orders went on:

> Your Lordship will direct the officer commanding the squadron you detach to follow that of the enemy to any part of the world to which it may go as long as he shall be able to obtain information on which he may with certainty depend of the route it has taken; and if it should go to the West Indies he is in that case to repair with all possible expedition to Martinique, and not hearing of them there to make the best of his way to Jamaica, and follow the orders of Admiral Sir Hyde Parker.[11]

The possibilities of a wild goose chase were enormous; the reference to the West Indies illustrates the Admiralty's continuing anxiety about that theatre. The strategy of covering it from the Bay of Biscay was, in itself, very hazardous, as the Admiralty well knew.

The month of March had already demonstrated the kind of risks which the constant blockade of Brest always ran, as James described:

> On the 9th March the 64-gun ship *Repulse*, Captain James Alms, having been detached by Sir Alan Gardner to cruise off the Penmarcks, for the purpose of intercepting some provision vessels expected at Brest, experienced a violent gale of wind; in the height of which Captain Alms, by the rolling of the ship, was thrown down the companion-ladder, and so seriously injured as to be incapable of doing any further duty on deck. For two or three days previous the weather had been so thick as to render it impracticable to take an observation; and on the 10th at about 10.00 pm, the *Repulse*, then going about six knots an hour, struck on a sunken rock, supposed to be the Mace, about twenty five leagues south west of Ushant. After beating on the rock for nearly three quarters of an hour, during which the water rushed in so fast that the lower deck was flooded, the *Repulse* got off, and, by great exertions, was kept afloat long enough to be able to approach and run aground upon the French coast, near Quimper.[12]

11   Morriss (ed.), *Channel Fleet*, pp.435-438.
12   James, *Naval History*, Vol.II, pp.426-427.

The obvious fragility of Bridport's health led to the Admiralty issuing, as a precaution, an order to Rear Admiral Pole empowering him to take command of the Channel Fleet in the event of Bridport's death while Pole was serving as Captain of the Fleet, an event which their Lordships sincerely trusted was not likely to happen. Even if it did not, however, the time was clearly fast approaching for a change in the command, as appears from a letter which Spencer wrote to St Vincent on 27 March:

> I was truly concerned at the receipt of your note of the 24th by which I learnt that you were so much indisposed as to prevent your giving me the pleasure of your company on this day sennight. I hope you are getting well fast as it is not improbable that I may have to call on you soon for your services.[13]

Intelligence reports from d'Auvergne suggested that the French were preparing an expedition involving up to 14,000 troops under the command of General Brune, supported by a fleet of 14 French ships of the line with 7 frigates and 4 avisos; the general belief was that their destination was Ireland, although no such operation materialised. Bridport kept some 30 ships of the line on station off Brest until early April, when he returned to Torbay. It was not long before he was again ordered to take the Channel Fleet to sea with all the ships of the line available as soon as the wind changed to allow the enemy to get out of Brest. These orders provided for the steps he should take if, on arriving off Brest, he should find that part of the Combined Fleet had sailed. Ireland remained his first responsibility. As it was, however, Bridport had reached the conclusion that he had had enough, and he availed himself of the permission to send out the fleet under Gardner, and to come on shore, as he reported to Spencer on 10 April.

Spencer lost little time in reporting to the King Bridport's readiness to retire, suggesting that the pill might be sugared with the award of a viscountcy. George received the news 'with infinite satisfaction,' and raised no objection to Bridport's advancement in the peerage. He hoped that no time would be lost in appointing St Vincent to the Channel Fleet in his stead; and displayed his grasp of the personalities involved by suggesting a civil letter from the Board of Admiralty to Gardner 'whose meritorious services deserve every attention'.[14] The formal order to Bridport to strike his flag went to him on 22 April, and he duly did so, handing over command to Gardner two days later.

Thus Bridport's long and arduous tenure of office came to an end. Throughout, he had had a difficult relationship with Spencer, and with the Board of Admiralty, as well as some of his subordinates, notably Warren and Pellew. The latter was

13   Morris (ed.), *Channel Fleet*, p.442.
14   Corbett (ed.), *Spencer*, Vol.III, pp.325-326.

especially malevolent on the subject of Bridport, writing to his friend Alexander Broughton:

> You will have heard that we are to have a New Commander in Chief, heaven be praised. The old one is scarcely worth drowning; a more contemptible or more miserable animal does not exist. I believe there never was a man so universally despised by the whole Service. A mixture of Ignorance, avarice and spleen.[15]

The extreme violence of Pellew's opinion was not typical of his professional colleagues. Bridport may not have been especially popular, but he had earned considerable respect over a long period of time. An example of his relationship with his officers can be seen in a letter in which he replied to one from Captain Byam Martin not long after his retirement from command:

> It will always give me the most pleasing satisfaction in knowing from you, as well as from all who served under my command in the Channel fleet, that the King's service was carried on with activity and correct discipline, on their part as well as on mine, for the advantage of the public and interest of the nation, and I trust that your future services will be attended with success, and all possible feelings of content.[16]

Cuthbert Collingwood, who served under Bridport for a considerable time, had ample opportunity to observe him and form an opinion, and he was never backward in expressing his opinion in a most candid manner. He did not pass adverse comments on Bridport; on hearing the news of his pending retirement, he mildly observed:

> I rather think Lord Bridport will retire from the command soon, but who to succeed him I cannot tell. Lord St Vincent and the D[uke] of Clarence have both been named. I hope it will be the first.[17]

Collingwood was, however, concerned that discipline in the Channel Fleet had grown slack, writing to Alexander Carlyle that he was 'afraid that there are a great many ships where the reins of discipline are held very loosely, the effect of a long war and an overgrown navy'.[18] He was also very much aware of the extent to which

---

15   Quoted Parkinson, *Edward Pellew*, p.228; capitalisation as original.
16   Hamilton (ed.), *Byam Martin*, Vol.I, p.285.
17   Hughes (ed.), *Admiral Lord Collingwood*, p.103.
18   Quoted Warner, *Lord Collingwood*, p.97.

Lord St Vincent's regime was of a very different nature, commenting in 1798 after returning home from the Mediterranean in the *Excellent*:

> The station I left was latterly rather disagreeable. The strange innovations which the Chief made in all the ordinary modes of discipline, and the high hand with which he carried himself to some officers, made it very unpleasant for all. For my part, I had the good fortune to keep clear of all disputes, nor do I know he ever said an unkind thing to me or of me, and that is a very singular case, for very few escaped the asperity of his temper.[19]

The prospect of coming under the command of St Vincent was not one to which the officers of the Channel Fleet much looked forward. In due course St Vincent was greatly annoyed by a story that in one wardroom, it was said, a toast had been proposed, allegedly in Bridport's presence, to the effect that 'May the Mediterranean discipline never be introduced into the Channel Fleet'.[20]

Perhaps the most serious of the charges laid by historians against Bridport's conduct of the blockade came from the pen of Admiral Mahan. After reviewing the course of the French expedition to Ireland in 1796, for which he relied heavily on the account given by James, he examined the strategic and tactical errors that were made. As to the former, he criticised Bridport's delay in getting away from St Helens, and the strength of his squadron:

> An inadequate force at the decisive point, inadequately maintained, and dependent on a reserve as large as itself, but unready and improperly stationed, – such were the glaring faults of the strategic disposition.[21]

He was equally censorious about the tactical dispositions of the Channel Fleet, noting that it was 'so far at sea as to derive no shelter from easterly storms'. At the critical moment Colpoys instead of being close in to Ushant was over forty miles to the west. The detachment in the Iroise was so small that the French could comfortably drive it off station; to watch Brest properly an inshore squadron of handy and weatherly ships of the line was required. Once the French had gone back to Brest, he noted that 'Bridport returned to Spithead and the old system was resumed'. He went on to pillory Bridport for the lack of discipline in his fleet:

19   Warner, *Lord Collingwood*, pp.87-88.
20   O.A. Sherrard, *A Life of Lord St Vincent* (London: George Allen and Unwin, 1933), p.159; Morriss (ed.), *Channel Fleet*, p.514.
21   Mahan, *Sea Power*, Vol.I, p.366.

It is no more than just to note, in this slack and shiftless conduct of the war, the same sluggish spirit that, after making all allowances for the undeniable grievances of the seamen, was also responsible for the demoralisation of discipline in the Channel fleet, which soon after showed itself openly – among the crews in the mutinies of 1797, and among the officers, at a later day, in the flagrant insubordination with which St Vincent's appointment was greeted. Both show a lax hand in the chief naval commander; for while a government is responsible for its choice of the latter, it must, especially in so technical a profession as the navy then was, depend upon him for the enforcement of discipline and for the choice of measures, at once practicable and adequate, to compass the ends of the war. Upon him more than upon any other, must fall the responsibility of failure; for he knows, or should know, better than the government, what the fleet can be made to do, what the state of discipline really is, and what his own capacity to carry out the one and support the other.[22]

As to the charge that Bridport was dilatory in getting the fleet to sea in December 1796, it should be pointed out that he was endeavouring to collect as many ships of the line as he could in order to meet the French; the state of readiness of those ships was not his responsibility but that of the Port Admiral; and the fleet was seriously delayed by the adverse weather, which Seymour reported to Spencer, as well as the accidents which took place as the ships came down to St Helens.

Mahan's allegation that Bridport contributed in some way to the Spithead mutiny of 1797 is more difficult to deal with, because it is never easy to prove a negative. It is a charge which has been repeated by later historians. Charles B. Arthur, for instance, in his study *The Remaking of the English Navy by Admiral St Vincent,* which deals with the period 1795-1805, is particularly emphatic, finding the principal cause of the mutiny, which did not occur in the Mediterranean, as being:

> The wretched state of discipline and the poor administration in the Channel and North Sea squadrons. The slack and shiftless conduct of the war by Howe, Bridport, and the admirals, captains and officers, who owed their status to political influence rather than ability, had destroyed all respect and confidence in the rank and file of the fleet.[23]

This conclusion Arthur borrows wholesale from Mahan; but neither has put forward any evidence to demonstrate that Bridport's command style contributed

---

22   Mahan, *Sea Power*, Vol.I, p.366.
23   Charles B, Arthur, *The Remaking of the English Navy by Admiral St Vincent* (Lanham MD: Rowman & Littlefield, 1986), p.72.

at all to the seamen's mutiny. Their grievances were very real. It is unclear whether it is being suggested that they were insufficiently submissive and cowed by the regime under which they served; or, indeed, that they went to their duty in battle in a less satisfactory manner than their opposite numbers in the Mediterranean Fleet. Nor is it explained how Admiral Duncan was responsible for the Nore Mutiny, since presumably it is being said that this was the case. It is unquestionably the case that harsh and despotic treatment by some officers constituted a most serious grievance on the part of the men, in addition to their demands about pay and conditions. In his concluding summary of the courses of the mutinies, Conrad Gill does not suggest that it was the leadership of the fleet that was to blame:

> The mutinies were brought about by the persuasion of an active minority working on a multitude of loyal but dissatisfied spirits. And although by far the greater number of the seamen were content with the simple redress of their grievances… it cannot be denied that there was in the minds even of the most loyal men in the fleet a sense of injustice, a belief in liberty and the rights of man, that was essentially political.[24]

The same view was taken by Dobrée and Manwaring; 'the two issues which particularly rasped the men's feelings were the arrangements for pay and the tyranny of the officers'.[25] As they also observed, it was 'remarkable that the men should have fought with such valour for a country which maltreated them so callously'.

So far as Bridport's personal approach was concerned, and in particular to the management of his officers, it was certainly true that he chose not to conduct a harsh or dictatorial regime. He expressly intimated to a member of the Board in 1798 that it was 'better not to irritate but smooth the execution of public measures'.[26] He was; in addition to his considerable responsibilities, subject to constant pressure from subordinates, both personal and professional.

The comparison between the effects of Bridport's regime and that of his successor is one that can properly be made. Whether St Vincent's disciplinary methods were as beneficial as his admirers have claimed is an open question. Collingwood was a shrewd and thoughtful observer of events in the fleet, and his opinion can be gauged by the letter he wrote to his father in law during the summer of 1800, some time after St Vincent had assumed command of the Channel Fleet:

> Every officer and man in the fleet is impatient for release from a situation which daily becomes more irksome to all. I see disgust growing round me very fast. Instead of softening the rigours of a service which must from its

---

24 Conrad Gill, *The Naval Mutinies of 1797* (Manchester: University Press, 1913), p.357.
25 Manwaring and Dobrée, *Floating Republic*, p.241.
26 Morriss (ed.), *Channel Fleet*, p.312.

nature, be attended with many anxieties, painful watchings and depriva-
tion of any thing like comfort a contrary system is pursued which has not
extended to me, but I see its effects on others and deplore them. What I
feel is a great misfortune is, that there is no exercise of the military part of
the duty, no practice of those movements, by a facility in which one fleet
is made superior to another.[27]

In their perfectly understandable enthusiasm to portray St Vincent as one of
Britain's great naval heroes, which of course he was, Mahan and other historians
have perhaps somewhat exaggerated his superiority over Bridport as an effective
commander of the Channel Fleet.

It is certainly correct to say that Bridport, like Howe before him, never favoured
a close blockade of Brest for the reasons which have been previously explored.
It is also true that while he was in command of the Channel Fleet the French
not infrequently came and went from their ports on the Biscay coast with relatively little difficulty. However, by whatever means the blockade was conducted
throughout the Revolutionary and Napoleonic Wars, it was never going to be easy
to prevent this. In fairness to Bridport, it must be said that during his long and
arduous period of command, though not one of Britain's very greatest admirals,
and in some respects a flawed character, he was a safe pair of hands. Like many of
his colleagues, he was from time to time not helped by confusing and contradic-
tory orders from the Admiralty. Whatever King George III, from one perspective,
or Sir Edward Pellew from another, may have thought of him, he was a good and
faithful servant to his countrymen.

---

27   Warner, *Lord Collingwood*, p.99.

17

St Vincent

At the start of 1800, the Royal Navy had 100 ships of the line in commission. 17 of these were three deckers, 4 being first rates of 100 guns or more and 13 being second rates of 90 guns or more. The remainder were two deckers, carrying up to 80 guns. 5 of these carried 80 guns, 57 were 74 gun ships, and the remaining 21 were 64s. There were a further 24 ships of the line in ordinary or undergoing repairs. There were 17 smaller two deckers, principally 50 gun ships, the usefulness of which was doubtful, and which were largely employed in escort duties. As for frigates, the want of which bedevilled practically all the fleet operations of the Navy, there were 102 in commission, with 8 more undergoing repair. In addition, there were 266 smaller vessels in commission.[1] It was a huge force, the administration of which was undertaken by an impossibly small number of bureaucrats; but it was astonishingly successful.

To man this enormous fleet there were 3,653 commissioned officers and masters. This total included 38 admirals, 41 vice admirals and 47 rear admirals, with a further 31 rear admirals on the superannuated list; and no less than 515 post captains on the active list. Funds had been voted by Parliament for 120,000 seaman (including 22,696 marines) at the start of the year, reduced after two months to 110,000. The wage bill was £5,437,500.

In 1800, as was the case for practically the whole of the period 1793-1815, the largest component of the Navy was the Channel Fleet, which was the most important command to which the seagoing admirals could aspire. Not many of them, however, were regarded by the Admiralty as suitable to command this fleet. It was no great surprise, therefore, that it should be to St Vincent that the Admiralty turned on the retirement of Lord Bridport. Among the senior admirals it was he who had gained the most striking victory at sea, when as Sir John Jervis he defeated the Spanish off Cape St Vincent, and he had become the Navy's most authoritative commander with a correspondingly high opinion of his own judgment. One of his biographers described him thus:

---

1   James, *Naval History*, Vol.II, p.480.

The signal victory which Jervis had gained had a marked effect upon his character, the more so as it had come upon the heels of great disappointment and depression. Jervis had always been a self-reliant, strong-willed man. He now became doubly assured. Long before this he had been accustomed to remonstrate with the Admiralty and to offer advice; but from this date onward his correspondence took on a firmer and more forthright tone. The remonstrances shed the last lingering air of diffidence; the advice became more vigorous and assured.[2]

To one man, however, St Vincent's appointment to the command of the Channel Fleet came as a very great surprise indeed. The 58 year old Vice Admiral Sir Alan Gardner had been, in his capacity as second-in-command of the fleet, deputising for Bridport on a number of occasions. He had become a post captain at the age of 24, and for five years from 1790 had served as a member of the Board of Admiralty. He had, it will be recalled, narrowly escaped serious bodily harm when he lost his temper with the Spithead mutineers in 1797. It was that volatile temperament which led him to explode with rage and disappointment that he should not have been seen as Bridport's natural successor. When he received Spencer's letter of 21 April telling him of St Vincent's appointment his response was immediate and furious:

> This communication so very unexpected, from the situation I have so long had the honour of holding in the Channel Fleet under the command of the late Lord Howe and Lord Bridport, has mortified me exceedingly, and I have no doubt will completely humble and disgrace me in the eyes of the fleet, in which I have been serving (I was vain enough to think) with some degree of credit to myself, and service to my country for the last seven years – I leave your Lordship to suppose what my feelings must be on this occasion.[3]

The problem was that Spencer, among others, had gained the firm impression that Gardner did not want to take on the responsibility of Commander-in-Chief. The subject had cropped up in his discussions with St Vincent before the latter was appointed, and St Vincent, displaying uncharacteristic delicacy of feeling, had told him that he would be unwilling to accept if it was likely to hurt Gardner's feelings. Spencer told Gardner of his astonishment at his reaction, reminding him that in every conversation between them Gardner had left him with the impression that he did not want the command-in-chief. In the correspondence which followed, the outraged admiral did not really address the point, but he remained hurt and

2   Sherrard, *Lord St Vincent*, p.113.
3   Corbett (ed.), *Spencer*, Vol.III, p.304.

angry, and behaved extremely badly to St Vincent on first boarding the latter's
flagship *Namur* on 2 May. In spite of this, St Vincent turned the other cheek,
writing to Gardner next day an emollient letter to the effect that no man thought
higher of his pretensions than he did and that he was 'the last person to supplant
them'. It did little good; Gardner remained bitter and thoroughly bloody-minded
in dealing with St Vincent, to the point where the latter wrote on 8 June to Nepean:

> Either Sir Alan Gardner or I must retire from this squadron, or the King's
> service will suffer essentially; the uncivil return he makes for every atten-
> tion I show him beggars all description, and must produce party and fric-
> tion in the worst shape; for although I acquit him of any such design, the
> disgust he shows upon all occasions will necessarily bring it forth.[4]

To Spencer, St Vincent privately reported his belief in the cause of Gardner's
bitterness:

> Having always lived on friendly terms with this gentleman, I cannot
> account for his rudeness to me in any other way than his having been
> worked up by a party which considers my elevation as an obstacle to the
> further aggrandisement of them – I mean the Hoods, who have shown
> hostility to me ever since the court martial on Admiral Keppel.[5]

In the end the problem was resolved in August by the retirement of Kingsmill
from the Irish command in August; when offered the post, Gardner accepted it
with a good grace, and the incident was closed. This pleased the King, who told
Spencer that he was 'certain there are few Admirals that have more merit in the
profession, and as private men none can exceed him in the goodness of his heart'.[6]

Meanwhile St Vincent had continued with his charm offensive towards the
officers of the Channel Fleet. His first reaction was more favourable than his distant
observations from the Mediterranean would have suggested. He told Spencer: 'The
squadron as far as I have yet seen is in good order and temper, with a fair appearance of emulation'. Some of the ships were short of complement; The *Ville de Paris*,
to which he transferred his flag, was short of 40 or 50 men. He was disturbed to
find inconsistencies in the reports made by his frigates of the state of the enemy
fleet, as he told Spencer; but he was very sceptical of the reports from d'Auvergne:

> Little reliance seems to be placed on the intelligence conveyed by the
> persons who act under the orders of the Prince of Bouillon [d'Auvergne];

5   Corbett (ed.), *Spencer*, Vol.III, p.314.
6   Corbett (ed.), *Spencer*, Vol.III, p.321.

Admiral John Jervis, 1st Earl of St Vincent. (Anne S.K. Brown Collection)

yet it must be very defective indeed if the number of ships at Brest in readiness for sea is not ascertained daily as I understand that a number of persons are employed in it.[7]

St Vincent's doubts about the reliability of d'Auvergne's intelligence were shared by Berkeley, commanding the inshore squadron. After one such report had been proved false, Berkeley wrote that he had experienced 'the fallacy of intelligence from that quarter before,' and was not surprised at it.[8]

It was not long though before St Vincent was complaining about the conduct of wardroom officers, for which he was quick to blame Bridport; he wrote on 10 June to Vice Admiral Pasley, the Commander-in-Chief at Plymouth:

> The licentious conversation of the wardroom officers and in some instances at the tables of officers of high rank in the navy has occasioned infinite mischief, for it soon diffuses through the ship… Everybody appears tired of the war and the abominable drunkenness of the men both in port and at sea works up the passions and produces evils that were formerly unknown… From the little knowledge I have of the conduct of my immediate predecessor it appears he took no kind of responsibility upon himself in cases of the greatest exigency, which renders my situation the more critical.[9]

It appears to be soon after this that St Vincent heard the story of the toast being drunk that concerned the Mediterranean discipline, for he wrote to Spencer on 21 June to tell him of it. Spencer's response, giving his understanding of what had been said, cannot have improved St Vincent's opinion of Bridport:

> The sentiment was expressed by the Admiral on their breaking up but it was not given by anyone as a toast. The subject of discussion had been on the topic and on going out of the cabin, I am told that Lord B said, 'God forbid that the discipline of the Mediterranean should be established in the Channel'.[10]

It certainly annoyed St Vincent sufficiently to pass this account on to his friend John Lloyd later in the year. He was, however, soon boasting that his new disciplinary measures were taking effect, writing on 3 July to Captain Robert Fanshawe, the Plymouth Dockyard Commissioner:

7   Morriss (ed.), *Channel Fleet*, p.464.
8   Morriss (ed.), *Channel Fleet*, p.513.
9   Morriss (ed.), *Channel Fleet*, p.485.
10 Morriss (ed.), *Channel Fleet*, p.517.

I have the satisfaction to acquaint you that the Mediterranean discipline so much deprecated is introducing into this squadron by slow degrees and no open resistance made to it. The improvement in our movements and general economy is hardly to be credited considering the short time we have been at it and the repugnance felt by some to change old and bad habits.[11]

By 1 August he was boasting to General O'Hara, the Governor of Gibraltar of his continuing success:

I am sure it will give you pleasure to know that this fleet which, when I came to it was at the lowest ebb of wretched and miserable discipline, is now above mediocrity and will, in three months if we are not driven into Torbay by tempestuous weather, be to perfection.[12]

Perhaps more significantly in the same letter he described the methods by which he was tightening the blockade:

We keep the combined fleets completely in check by anchoring a small squadron of ships of the line in the Iroise, near the Parquet Rock, and by a squadron of frigates and cutters plying night and day when the weather will permit in the opening of the Goulet between Camaret and Bertheaume, two ships of the line with a cutter and lugger are placed off the Raz du Frontenac and are generally at an anchor in Hodierne Bay during an easterly wind.[13]

St Vincent, who had a good opinion of Warren, also rated Captains Thornborough and Saumarez highly, and pressed for their promotion to flag rank; otherwise, he told Spencer, the blockade would languish. He told Pellew that he had pressed for promotion for him also; the news can hardly have been especially welcome to the latter, since the issue of seniority meant that he was to wait for another four years before he reached the rank of rear admiral. Pellew was no doubt comforted by the fact that St Vincent's opinion of him was also extremely high, as he told Spencer; 'he greatly excels Sir J Warren in seamanship and arrangement, and is equal to him in enterprise'.[14]

11 Morriss (ed.), *Channel Fleet*, p.528.
12 Morriss (ed.), *Channel Fleet*, p.542.
13 Morriss (ed.), *Channel Fleet*, p.542.
14 Corbett (ed.), *Spencer*, Vol.III, p.363.

As between Pellew and St Vincent the feeling was mutual, as the former made clear in a number of florid letters to the Commander-in-Chief. Typical of these was a letter of 2 July:

> I must be divested of every common feeling if I did not express to your Lordship, and that too in the strongest terms, my thankfulness for all the kindness you have already shown me, and for these your intentions towards me your goodness leads you to express.[15]

Admiral Richmond, when editing volumes III & IV of the *Spencer Papers*, was very struck by the characteristically robust expressions by St Vincent of his opinions of his officers:

> St Vincent's judgement was not infallible – his view that Nelson was a partisan and no more is a well known example – but it is impossible to doubt that this wise, shrewd and observant old Commander's opinions are true pictures, with just that touch of exaggeration of some of the more prominent characteristics which an artist tends to employ in his portraiture.[16]

St Vincent recognised that perfection was not to be expected; but one quality he valued above all others was the power to take responsibility. This he found, for instance, in Warren, Troubridge, Thornborough, Saumarez and Pellew, but lacking in a large number of officers very much senior to them. The practice of promoting by seniority meant that a large number of indifferent post captains would have to be promoted for his favoured officers to reach admiral's rank. He was pleased to see that the process was at least ongoing, writing to Spencer in March 1799 that 'the promotion to the Flag has happily removed a number of officers from the command of ships of the line who at no period of their lives were capable of commanding them'.[17]

St Vincent had his differences with Collingwood, who stood up to him, but he recognised his merit; he commented on this by comparison with others when writing to Spencer on 27 June 1800:

> The admirable example my friend Collingwood has set, in getting the *Barfleur* filled up and paid in so short a time, will I hope produce some effect on the Captains of frigates whose dilatory conduct in port annoys me beyond expression. All the married have their wives there, which

15 Corbett (ed.), *Spencer*, Vol.III, p.359.
16 Corbett (ed.), *Spencer*, Vol.IV, p.3.
17 Corbett (ed.), *Spencer*, Vol.IV, p.5.

plays the devil with them, for although the measures I have taken imply a very strong disapprobation, hitherto no advantage has been derived from them.[18]

Of Colpoys, he wrote that he 'must command the fleet of England if we have another war while he is fit for service'. Sir Robert Calder was someone who he hoped would soon hoist his flag, but he could not give him command of the inshore squadron after the autumn equinox, for this 'would produce his annihilation'. He had a good opinion of Warren's fighting qualities, but was aware of his limitations:

> He is a good fellow in the presence of an enemy, but runs a little wild in other matters when detached; he cannot bear being confined to a fleet, no more than our friend Nelson, and will be miserable when he is obliged to serve *en masse*.[19]

His forthright comments were no doubt stimulated by his awareness that dissident captains would correspond with members of the Board of Admiralty behind his back. It made the government of the Channel Fleet almost impossible, he wrote, so much so that neither he, 'nor any other person who may be thought fitter for the purpose, can command it'. Spencer should, he suggested 'put an extinguisher upon the gossiping correspondence'.

Domett, who had been close to Bridport, rather surprisingly pleased St Vincent considerably. In writing to Spencer in September 1800 about him, however, he was unable to resist a side swipe at his predecessor in command of the fleet:

> Permit me to recommend Captain Domett to your special favour: his conduct towards me has been everything that could be expected from an able officer and worthy man. Between Lord Bridport and Vice Admiral Pole, equally an old woman, there was neither discipline nor subordination in the *Royal George* when I went into her.[20]

In the following month he repeated his views about the *Royal George*: 'If Captain Domett had not been overruled by those old women Admirals Bridport and Pole he would have set her to rights. His nerves are so shook he is not up to it now'.[21]

A constant theme of St Vincent's correspondence with Spencer was his praise for Troubridge, Saumarez, Thornborough and Pellew, all of whom deserved in his opinion an admiral's flag, but there was not much he could do about it. He groaned

18 Corbett (ed.), *Spencer*, Vol.IV, pp.5-6.
19 Corbett (ed.), *Spencer*, Vol.IV, p.14.
20 Corbett (ed.), *Spencer*, Vol.IV, pp.16-17.
21 Morriss (ed.), *Channel Fleet*, p.59.

to Spencer that 'the rust and vermin you would get rid of by this much wanted promotion, is a matter of more serious moment than you are aware of'.[22] And another of his hobby horses was his sweeping dismissal of the Scots as sea officers: 'You will never find an officer, native of that country, figure in supreme command, they are only fit for drudgery. Lord Keith is by far the best I ever met with by land or sea'. Remarks like this, of courses, showed that when working up a fine head of steam, St Vincent allowed his pen to run away with him. One particular Scotsman annoyed him above all others; he wrote to Nepean on 5 May 1797 with a violent denunciation of Sir Charles Middleton:

> He neither possesses a mind to direct great features, nor was ever in a situation as an officer to acquire knowledge or experience: the utmost extent of his abilities having gone no further than the forming a swaddling system of morality for his ship's company, and compiling with that dull dog, Patton, the most voluminous stupid code of signals that has been exhibited by the signalmongers of the present age. For God's sake get rid of every principle he gave you, except those in the way of Schedule.[23]

Extravagant and unjustified criticism of this kind shows St Vincent in an unattractive light, and not always as wise and shrewd as his admirers would claim.

One practice of the Channel Fleet which was especially prevalent and of which St Vincent particularly disapproved was that of senior officers sleeping ashore. It was his belief that this contributed substantially to ill-discipline, and he sternly forbade it. This naturally caused a good deal of indignation, which moved St Vincent not at all. He realised that edicts of this kind would be hugely unpopular; but he had a poor opinion of many of the officers of the Channel Fleet, describing them as 'old women, some of them in the shape of young men'.[24] To Isaac Coffin he wrote angrily on 15 November:

> Seven eighths of the captains who compose this fleet (subtracting from the number all who served long under me in the Mediterranean) are practising every subterfuge to get into harbour for the winter... I am at my wits' end to compose orders to meet every shift, evasion and neglect of duty'.[25]

As with his predecessors, St Vincent naturally had strong views on the way in which naval strategy should be conducted, and in his correspondence with Spencer

22   Corbett (ed.), *Spencer*, Vol.IV, p.19.
23   Sherrard, *Lord St Vincent*, p.113.
24   James D.G. Davidson, *Admiral Lord St Vincent: Saint or Tyrant?* (Barnsley: Pen & Sword, 2006), p.169.
25   Morriss (ed.), *Channel Fleet*, p.584.

he did not hesitate to express them. An early issue concerned the proposed attack on the Spanish port of Ferrol. On 6 July St Vincent told Spencer that in his decided opinion 'Ferrol is of all parts of Spain, the least vulnerable'. Furthermore, he thought that the troops which would be employed in such an attack were 'not up to a difficult enterprise'.[26] Nonetheless, the plan was pursued, Warren being put in charge of the naval side of the operation. The military side, however, did not go well; Warren, with evident disgust, described the feeble ending of the attack:

> I have since heard by the report of others, that a council was held upon the heights among the general officers, of the propriety of moving forward to attack the town of Ferrol, when there were three in favour of retirement and two in favour of advancing. In consequence an enterprise which had every advantage that could have been wished was abandoned, and the officers and men of both services, who were zealous and anxious to have opened the passage to the harbour, and to have done their country an important service, were prevented destroying the naval force of their enemies.[27]

Pellew, too, was mortified by the failure of the attack on Ferrol, writing to Spencer on 15 October that 'the means provided by his Majesty's Ministers were ample, and the surprise complete. The fair opportunity of striking the finest blow ever meditated on a country has been lost'.[28] Towards the end of the month St Vincent, never guilty of false modesty, was even more outspoken at the news that an assault on Cadiz had not been pursued due to the fear of plague in the town; he wrote to Spencer: 'Your Cadiz business is worse than Ferrol. Sir Charles Grey and I would have been masters of the first in three weeks and of the last in forty eight hours'.[29]

Although Spencer did not presume to offer as much in the way of advice and suggestion to St Vincent as he had to Bridport, he took a close interest in the way the blockade of Brest was being conducted. Fierce gales at the end of September obliged the Channel Fleet to seek shelter in Torbay, leaving Saumarez before the port with the inshore squadron. Spencer wrote on 27 September to St Vincent approving the decision to withdraw:

> It answers no good purpose to tear our ships to pieces by keeping them off Brest at such a time, when there is no possibility for the enemy to move. Would not this observation apply equally to the advanced squadron under Sir James Saumarez? His force is not equal to cope in any degree

26 Corbett (ed.), *Spencer*, Vol.III, p.361.
27 Quoted Corbett (ed.), *Spencer*, Vol.III, p.369.
28 Corbett (ed.), *Spencer*, Vol.III, p.371.
29 Corbett (ed.), *Spencer*, Vol.III, p.372.

with the French fleet, and frigates should be equally proper for watching their motions, and giving you information of them.[30]

Leaving so many ships of the line to face the hard westerly gales would, he thought, result ultimately in a reduction in the numbers available to St Vincent if he had the chance of meeting the French. St Vincent, though, would have none of it, telling Spencer that 'frigates are not worth a pin off Brest: the enemy outnumbers and drives them off at will. Sir James Saumarez is at anchor in Douarnenez Bay and in greater safety than we are here'.[31] Spencer was content with this, and was rather smugly pleased that his earlier advocacy of Douarnenez Bay as an anchorage was being borne out.

It was not, however, only the ships that were being worn out; St Vincent wrote to Spencer on 13 October for permission to take a break from seagoing duty: 'My cough increases and I am full of apprehension that I shall be compelled to retire from this command unless you give me the winter's sun in the region of Torbay'.[32] Permission was at once given to him, and Sir Henry Harvey was instructed to take command of the blockading fleet, while St Vincent took up his residence at Tor Abbey which overlooked the anchorage and was, he said, 'a well sheltered delightful situation in all respects'. He did not, however, intend to relax his grip on the conduct of the blockade, issuing stern orders to Harvey to report every infor- mation he received with regard to the French fleet, and everything concerning the ships under Harvey's command. St Vincent had no very high opinion of Harvey, whom he regarded as altogether too lax; commenting on the imminent arrival of Sir Hyde Parker to join the Channel Fleet, he told Nepean that he was glad he was coming, 'for Sir Henry is very nearly *kilt* with responsibility already'. And to Spencer he said that 'he is a worthy good and gallant man but sinks under responsibility'.[33]

When Hyde Parker arrived in November St Vincent sent him off to the Channel Fleet with a precise summary of the way in which the blockade was to be conducted:

> The principle on which the squadron acts with the wind easterly is to wear the sternmost and leewardmost first, which we are pretty expert in the practice of, once during the night so as to be within a couple of leagues of Ushant at daylight in the morning. This is the more necessary when the flood makes early and if it flows strong you will find much shelter between Ushant and the Black Rocks during the day and when at a greater distance the communication is well kept up by the inner advanced squadron at

30 Corbett (ed.), *Spencer*, Vol.III, p.372.
31 Corbett (ed.), *Spencer*, Vol.III, p.375.
32 Morriss (ed.), *Channel Fleet*, p.567.
33 Corbett (ed.), *Spencer*, Vol.III, p.382.

anchor between the Black Rocks and the Parquette and the outer under
sail between them and Ushant.[34]

There were by now clear indications that the French were preparing an expedition. D'Auvergne had reported six ships of the line and three frigates preparing
for sea, and this was confirmed by a reconnaissance conducted by Saumarez on
20 November. A further report from d'Auvergne announced the arrival at Brest of
Rear Admiral Ganteaume, expected to take command of the squadron. St Vincent
regarded the command of the inshore squadron as too important to be left to his
admirals, remarking to Keith that he employed Saumarez and Pellew because they
were more capable; this, he said, subjected him to 'some hatred and malice'. The
intelligence gathered by the inshore squadron was of the greatest value; it enabled
the Admiralty to conclude that there was no immediate likelihood of the whole of
the French fleet coming out, and as result to order St Vincent to keep only twenty
ships of the line off Brest. This, it was considered, would be more than enough to
deal with a squadron of the size being prepared.[35]

In spite of an awareness that Ganteaume might shortly make an attempt to
escape from Brest with part of the French fleet, he was nonetheless successful
on 7 January in doing so through the Passage du Raz. Harvey, who had in the
meantime been reinforced by a squadron under Collingwood, chased him, and
Ganteaume abandoned his sortie and returned to port. It was still unclear where
he was going when, in a strong gale, he sailed again through the Iroise, and was
not seen again for four days, when Captain Barton in the frigate *Concorde* sighted
him 75 miles off Finisterre. Barton at once sailed to Plymouth to report the news.
Nelson, having joined the Channel Fleet and hoisted his flag aboard the *San Josef*
on 17 January, had heard the news on 29 January, and wrote to Spencer to say
that he was 'ready and wishing to follow' with a good sailing squadron; it would,
he said be his 'pride and pleasure to fly to the relief of Lord Keith and to save the
squadron and the army' if Ganteaume was headed to Egypt.[36]

That was, indeed, Ganteaume's destination; as usual, however, the fear was for
the West Indies, and Sir Robert Calder was sent there with six ships of the line.
Ganteaume, en route to Egypt, with 5,000 troops aboard, captured the frigate
Success, from the crew of which he learned that it was likely by now that a British
army had landed there, and he accordingly aborted his mission and sailed for
Toulon.

St Vincent wrote to Spencer from Tor Abbey to comment on the escape of
Ganteaume's squadron on 3 February:

34 Morriss (ed.), *Channel Fleet*, p.584.
35 Morriss (ed.), *Channel Fleet*, p.591.
36 Corbett (ed.), *Spencer*, Vol.III, pp.379-380.

The escape of the French squadron is an unlucky, though unavoidable circumstance, and no measure, in future, can prevent the like happening but the departure of the squadron from this bay the instant the wind veers to NNWd, night or day.[37]

St Vincent's first news of Ganteaume's escape had come from d'Auvergne; in addition to reporting to Spencer, he also notified Keith, being already pretty sure that it was to the Mediterranean that the French were bound.

Meanwhile at Westminster a political crisis had developed which was to result in Spencer leaving the Admiralty. On 3 February William Pitt tendered his resignation and that of most of his government. Although the King accepted it, Pitt continued in office for another five weeks. Spencer's departure was considered particularly regrettable by the King, who wrote to him on 9 February:

The uniform conduct of Earl Spencer since I have had the pleasure of having [him] in my service, as well as the real good opinion I had of his character at all times, makes me particularly feel reluctant in consenting to his retiring from his present employment. He knows so well that it is a principle of the strongest nature, that of religious and political duty, that has alone guided the King through the present most unpleasant scene, that it is unnecessary to add more on the present occasion.[38]

It was a compliment which Spencer well deserved. He had been a remarkably effective First Lord, not least in the constant attention which he had paid to the conduct of the blockade of Brest. His departure from the Admiralty would mean a different approach to its management, as well as a significant change in the command of the Channel Fleet.

37 Corbett (ed.), *Spencer*, Vol.III, p.381.
38 Corbett (ed.), *Spencer*, Vol.III, p.304.

18

Cornwallis

It was Pitt who suggested that St Vincent should succeed Spencer as First Lord of the Admiralty. He was not an obvious choice, not least because on the issue of Catholic Emancipation, which had been a prime cause of Pitt's resignation, he agreed with the outgoing ministry. Summoned for an interview with the King, he candidly told him that it was his opinion that Catholics were entitled to be put on the same footing as Protestants; but that 'he held his life and his utmost services at His Majesty's disposal' and was ready to serve in any capacity the King desired. George's response was both handsome and realistic; he told St Vincent that he had behaved like an honest and honourable man:

> Upon the question of Catholic Emancipation my mind is made up, from which I will never depart. And therefore, as it is not likely that it will be a matter agitated and discussed between us, I can see no reason why you should not take the Admiralty, where I very much wish to see you, and to place the Navy entirely in your hands.[1]

St Vincent himself had hesitated before accepting the appointment. He expressed his doubts in a letter to Keith:

> What sort of figure I shall make will be seen. I have known many a good admiral make a wretched First Lord of the Admiralty. I will, however, support Commanders-in-Chief upon all occasions, and prohibit any intrigue against them in this office.[2]

It was no doubt the opportunity to tackle what he saw as much needed reforms which in particular prompted him to take up the challenge.

---

1   W.V. Anson, *The Life of John Jervis Admiral Lord St Vincent* (London: J. Murray, 1913), p.283.
2   Quoted Davidson, *Admiral Lord St Vincent*, p.174.

In March, in a letter to Dr Carlyle, Collingwood reflected on St Vincent's appointment as First Lord:

> The navy, I doubt not, will be ably directed by Lord St Vincent. His ambition, which has ever been his ruling passion, has kept him all his life in the continual exercise of his powers, and established in him habits of business which will enable him to keep the Admiralty as active as his predecessor, with more knowledge of the character and ability of all the officers. I do not know how the changes can affect me. Under the present circumstances I am satisfied with my station in the fleet, but I believe Lord St Vincent is very kindly disposed towards me, and if he thought some other situation might be more advantageous to me I do not think he wou'd ask me anything about it.[3]

A few days later Collingwood remarked in a letter to his cousin that St Vincent had 'more hours for business than most men, having little taste for pleasure, and seldom sleeps more than 4 or 5 hours in a night'.[4]

Spencer's departure from the Admiralty meant, of course, that there was now no obstacle to the appointment of Cornwallis to a sea command and St Vincent was in no doubt that he should be his successor in command of the Channel Fleet. The new First Lord wasted no time; he took up his post on 18 February 1801 and next day Cornwallis was appointed Commander-in-Chief, hoisting his flag in the *Ville de Paris* on 25 February. The *Times* wrote of his appointment to the Channel Fleet: 'Next to the noble Earl, who has resigned that command, there is no officer of whom the Navy has a higher opinion than of the noble admiral nominated as his successor'.[5]

The first request that Cornwallis made was that his old friend and former flag captain, John Whitby, who was at that time serving in the West Indies, should rejoin him in the same capacity; this was granted, and Whitby soon arrived to take up the post. In the meantime, Cornwallis had put to sea in the *Ville de Paris*, and the Channel Fleet took up its station off Ushant. Here he received intelligence from both Saumarez, who had succeeded Thornborough in command of the inshore squadron off Brest, and Pellew, who was blockading Lorient and the ports to the south, which suggested that the enemy was preparing a sortie. This information accorded with that received by the Admiralty; St Vincent thought that if the French put off attempting their escape they would find it difficult when the days were longer and the weather more moderate. On 28 March he wrote to Cornwallis:

> I never did give credit to the intention of the combined fleet to measure with ours until within these few days; but on combining the intelligence

3   Hughes (ed.), *Admiral Lord Collingwood*, p.126.
4   Warner, *Lord Collingwood*, p.107.
5   Cornwallis-West, *Admiral Cornwallis*, p.349.

from every quarter I do in my conscience believe you will have the honour and happiness of finishing the war by a glorious achievement.[6]

St Vincent was somewhat susceptible to flattery, and the prospect of a fleet action prompted Cornwallis to reply that if the enemy did come out, 'I believe the chief inducement with them is that they are pretty sure of not meeting your Lordship at the head of the English Fleet'. St Vincent was evidently pleased with this, and graciously replied that 'The French have seen, felt and understood so much of your character that theirs must be changed materially if they face you in preference to your very sincere and obedient servant'.[7]

In appointing Cornwallis as his successor, St Vincent was no doubt satisfied that he could count on him to follow his policy in relation to the blockade, and this in general was what Cornwallis did. Cornwallis was, however, rather more relaxed in his approach to disciplinary matters. He found himself in difficulty with the Admiralty, for instance, in July 1801, when he interfered with a court martial sentence. A seaman had been sentenced to the grotesque penalty of 300 lashes for desertion. Since to take the punishment as a whole might kill him, which would be unlawful, he had to take it by instalments. Notwithstanding this, he was not confined, but carried out his duties voluntarily, and his captain asked Cornwallis to intercede with the Admiralty to get the rest of the sentence remitted. Confronted with this appalling circumstance, Cornwallis at once remitted the sentence, only subsequently informing the Admiralty. For this he was seriously rebuked.[8]

Cornwallis was also rather more relaxed than St Vincent about the precise station to be kept by the ships undertaking the blockade, allowing the fleet to remain further off Ushant. Gambier, who maintained a correspondence with the former First Lord, told Spencer of this on 6 June:

Your Lordship knows pretty accurately the spot on which we usually cruise here – we are generally from five to ten leagues distant from Ushant – never so near as you may remember the fleet was accustomed to be when under the command of Lord St Vincent, though always near enough for the purpose for which we are here, as the two frigates stationed within Ushant keep a good watch upon the enemy and two or three decked ships between them and the fleet keep the communications to the Commander-in-Chief, who no doubt knows how matters go on as far as can be known – by sight in Brest.[9]

6   Cornwallis-West, *Admiral Cornwallis*, p.351.
7   Cornwallis-West, *Admiral Cornwallis*, p.351.
8   Cornwallis-West, *Admiral Cornwallis*, p.354.
9   Morriss (ed.), *Channel Fleet*, p.637.

Admiral Sir Edward Thornborough. (Anne S.K. Brown Collection)

The inshore squadron was commanded alternately in six week shifts by Thornborough and Saumarez, whose thoroughly competent handling of their ships ensured that Cornwallis had most of the time the detailed intelligence to which Gambier referred. Some reports as to the activity of the French and Spanish squadrons in Brest were however conflicting, although by mid-April it certainly appeared that their preparations for sea were more advanced than had been expected. D'Auvergne's information was that they were destined for Rochefort, although their ultimate objective could only be guessed at. On 16 April Cornwallis reported that it was probable that a larger force might sail from Brest than previously suggested. In addition, he went on:

> They have produced a force at L'Orient and Rochefort beyond what Sir Edward Pellew declared he had any conception of and he has spared no pains, I believe, to obtain information. He informed me that he had sent a boat on board the French admiral when he was in Basque Road to endeavour to learn what their intentions were.[10]

The practice of sending in a vessel under a flag of truce in an effort to gain information was not uncommon. What was remarkable was how much intelligence could be gained in this way. On the present occasion Lieutenant Pilfold was able to give a remarkably detailed report of the condition of the French ships lying in the Aix Roads, as well of the astonishingly frank conversation he was able to have with their commander, Admiral Bedout:

> The Admiral informed me that two thousand men were landed on Isle d'Aix on the first day we stood in to reconnoitre them, and that more troops were expected there every hour; that, about a week ago, 20,000 troops had passed within a few Leagues of Rochelle, on their Route to join the Spanish Troops on the Frontier of Portugal. The French Squadron under Admiral Ganteaume had also escaped from Toulon, but no accounts had been received of them since.[11]

The Admiralty's reaction to the news of the French preparations was to suggest to Cornwallis that he should divide the Channel Fleet, sending part to support Pellew while the remainder continued to support the inshore squadron off Brest. Cornwallis was extremely doubtful of the wisdom of this suggestion, pointing out in his letter of 16 April that Saumarez was already urging the reinforcement of the inshore squadron as a result of the enemy activity:

> I therefore submit to their Lordships whether it would be prudent to leave half the ships or, in fact, all of the ships of two decks separated from the rest of the squadron and without any certainty of their joining me should the enemy come out in force. I am perfectly ready, however, to execute their Lordship's commands if they think such a measure advisable. If the French squadron intended for Rochefort has not sailed within these few days, that intention is, at least for the present, given up as from the

10   Morriss (ed.), *Channel Fleet*, p.633-634.
11   Cornwallis-West, *Admiral Cornwallis*, p.352.

violence of the wind I have been driven ten or twelve leagues to the west-ward. They were all at anchor on the twelfth.[12]

The continual frustration of not being able to fight the French in a regular battle naturally gave rise to consideration of ways of getting at them in port. One of Cornwallis's captains, Captain Brisbane, put forward the suggestion of attacking the enemy fleet in Brest by the use of fire ships. Cornwallis was enthusiastic, and in June sent Brisbane home in a cutter to discuss the matter at the Admiralty. He took with him a letter from the Commander-in-Chief to St Vincent:

> His spirit of enterprise is certainly very honourable and truly commend-able. As no attempt of the kind has been made, if the utmost secrecy is observed and it meets with your Lordship's approbation, I should hope something may be done. If the enemy do not push out before this plot is ready to be put in execution, I fear they will have given up their intention.[13]

St Vincent was supportive, responding that whatever the outcome, he would 'suggest it and every other attempt you may judge fit to make on the Enemy's Fleet'. In the event, however, the project was not at this time proceeded with; it would, though, resurface in different circumstances in due course.

In spite of the lengthy periods of time in which his ships were at sea off Brest, Cornwallis was fortunate in their condition. In April severe squalls had resulted in a collision between the *Mars* and the *Centaur*. The former was Thornborough's flagship, and he reported to Cornwallis that she was taken aback and came about on the starboard tack, everything possible being done to avoid the *Centaur*:

> She ran across us and carried away our bowsprit and head and, before I could get the ship before the wind, our foremast fell and soon after our main topmast. I was not on deck until our bowsprit was gone. Captain Lloyd was on deck.[14]

Given the frequent storms suffered by the Channel Fleet, such accidents were inevitable, but during the year the condition of the fleet remained extremely good. Ships of the line went into port on a regular basis for refitting, three at a time.

The wear and tear on their commanders, however, was not inconsiderable. Collingwood, writing to Dr Carlyle in August to thank him for his enquiry about his health, spoke for a lot of his colleagues:

12   Morriss (ed.), *Channel Fleet*, p.634.
13   Cornwallis-West, *Admiral Cornwallis*, p.354.
14   Morriss (ed.), *Channel Fleet*, p.631.

Thank God I am now very well, but have been more out of health this cruise than I ever was, which I attribute very much to long confinement. This is the third summer that I have hardly seen the leaf of the trees, except through a glass at a distance of some leagues… nothing can be more insipid than the service of watching a port where I have now been seven months, with the exception of a fortnight that I was at Plymouth.[15]

While the condition of his ships remained surprisingly good, Cornwallis had an opportunity of seeing for himself the state of some of the units of the French fleet, as he reported to the Admiralty on 27 July:

The morning of the 22nd two line of battle ships with a large frigate stood out of Brest. A signal was made to me that they had anchored in one of the bays. I therefore stood early in the morning to the entrance of the harbour to see whether anything could be done with them, but they weighed as soon as the tide would serve and worked into the harbour. It, however, gave me an opportunity of seeing the state of these ships. They appeared to be very ill equipped, the topsails of one of them seemed out of proportion to the yards, the ropes were constantly giving way and the jib of the other was split across, which remained in the same state.[16]

As the year wore on, the negotiations between Britain and France to bring the war to an end seemed increasingly likely to succeed, and St Vincent had this in mind when he wrote to Cornwallis in August:

I am sorry that the state of the Enemy's preparations at Brest has rendered it a matter of absolute necessity to keep you so long at sea, the Board will however have it in its power to reinforce you immediately and enable you, if you judge fit, to send in some of your ships to refresh. You will have heard by the public Prints and by other communications that the negotiation with France draws to a conclusion.[17]

The prospect that the talks might result in peace was not one which pleased Admiral Lord Hood. Writing to Cornwallis on 31 August, he offered an opinion on the subject of the blockade:

My fears are we shall have no peace but such a one as I shall view as a very serious misfortune instead of a blessing until you have beaten the

15 Hughes (ed.), *Admiral Lord Collingwood*, p.129.
16 Morriss (ed.), *Channel Fleet*, p.638.
17 Cornwallis-West, *Admiral Cornwallis*, p.364.

combined fleet at Brest. Therefore cease blocking the port, and tempt it out. I have ever held that opinion, and am persuaded the war has been prolonged by the blockade. A temporary one, under particular circumstances, may not only be prudent but perfectly wise; but a perpetual one must bear us down, which the French know as well as we, and that I conceive will make against a good peace.[18]

That was the position in August; but by 2 October it was beginning to look to Cornwallis as if nothing was after all to come of the peace talks, in which case he was convinced that the French 'must attempt something,' as he remarked in a letter to young Captain Thomas Byam Martin, at that time commanding the frigates watching Brest. He was pleased with the reports he was getting from Martin, and the plans showing the position of the French ships. The news that French soldiers had been embarked on the Spanish ships 'looks like business should an opportunity offer, which they expect at this season'. Martin at this time had seriously annoyed St Vincent by pressing the Board of Admiralty to promote one Lieutenant Pipon, whose services did not seem to the First Lord to warrant it, and he expressed his 'surprise at the manner in which you have thought fit to address me upon the subject of it'. Martin, however was not so easily put down, responding frostily to St Vincent: 'Until I received your Lordship's letter of the 16th instant, I was not aware of the impropriety of addressing the First Lord of the Admiralty in behalf of a deserving officer'.[19] St Vincent appears not to have taken offence at this and to have relented, since Lieutenant Pipon was promoted in the following year.

Notwithstanding Cornwallis's pessimism, the peace talks were successful, and on 3 October news of the armistice reached him, both from St Vincent and from Villaret-Joyeuse, his old adversary, who had just reassumed command at Brest. The latter enclosed with his extremely courteous letter a copy of the telegraph which he had received announcing the armistice. St Vincent wrote to Cornwallis, who had taken the fleet back to Torbay, at the start of November to express his appreciation of his services:

I have derived the highest degree of satisfaction from your obliging letter of the 1st and shall always consider your having been placed at the head of the Channel Fleet as an event of the greatest importance to the country at large, and of the most solid comfort to me.[20]

Thus Cornwallis's first stint in command of the blockade of Brest came to an end; he cannot have guessed that he would again take up his duties there after a what

18 Cornwallis-West, *Admiral Cornwallis*, pp.368-369.
19 Hamilton (ed.), *Byam Martin*, Vol.I, p.295.
20 Cornwallis-West, *Admiral Cornwallis*, p.372.

proved to be a very short interval of time. The truth was that for different reasons both Napoleon and the British government of Henry Addington needed peace at that moment and were prepared to conclude it without looking too far ahead. The detailed peace terms were finally agreed on 27 March 1802. They were criticised as being excessively favourable to France, but St Vincent, as a member of the government, stridently supported them. In a letter to Lord Uxbridge he wrote that he considered the peace to be the very best the country had ever made, saying that it was the 'happiest event of my life to have contributed to so great a blessing'.[21] Once the peace treaty had been signed, Cornwallis could strike his flag and return to Newlands, his home in Hampshire. For St Vincent, however, the ensuing months were to be a time of enormous stress.

The blockade of Brest had, since the outbreak of war in 1793, been maintained with varying degrees of effectiveness. Its success did not lie merely in discouraging sorties from the port. In fact, the French had often been able to put to sea when they wanted to do so. The blockade had achieved much more than that, as Mahan pointed out:

> The result of this strict blockade and of the constant harrying of the French coasts from Dunkirk on the North Sea to the Spanish border, was to paralyse Brest as a port of naval equipment and construction, as well as to render very doubtful the success of any combination in which the Brest fleet was a factor.[22]

The success of the Royal Navy in interdicting the coastal trade necessary to bring in the necessary stores and equipment to Brest is convincingly demonstrated in the brilliantly edited collection of documents on the blockade from 1793-1801 produced by Roger Morriss for the Navy Records Society. The crucial effect of the constant presence of British warships off the port and along the French coastline has generally been readily accepted by historians; as the letter from Lord Hood referred to above would seem to indicate, it was perhaps not wholly realised at the time.[23]

21 Davidson, *Admiral Lord St Vincent*, p.182.
22 Mahan, *Sea Power*, Vol.I, p.376.
23 Morriss (ed.), *Channel Fleet*, p.622.

19

Peace

During the first part of his spell as First Lord of the Admiralty, St Vincent could look with satisfaction on three operations that had resulted in a considerable success. On 2 April 1801 at Copenhagen, Nelson had, in spite of Sir Hyde Parker, won a brilliant victory over the Danish fleet. St Vincent handsomely acknowledged it:

> Your Lordship's whole conduct from your first appointment to this hour is the subject of our constant admiration. It does not become one to make comparisons; all agree there is but one Nelson.[1]

Meanwhile in March, in the eastern Mediterranean, Lord Keith had successfully conveyed and then landed Abercromby's army at Aboukir Bay in a well managed combined operation, following which the French army was decisively defeated. On 2 September the French capitulated and surrendered Alexandria. Finally, in July, Saumarez reversed the outcome of a previously unsuccessful engagement with a French squadron when he engaged a combined Franco-Spanish force at the Battle of Algeciras, sinking two and taking a third ship of the line against the odds. The news prompted St Vincent to exclaim: 'I knew it, I knew it. I knew the man. I knew what he could do. It is the most daring thing that has been done this war. It is the first thing. I knew it would be so!'[2]

St Vincent, as has been seen, very much approved of the peace. It now left him to face the challenge that had brought him to the Admiralty: to overcome the corruption and inefficiency that tainted the administration of the Navy and in particular the dockyards. He was assisted by a Board of Admiralty of considerable ability. The sea officers were Rear Admiral Sir Thomas Troubridge, described by St Vincent as 'the ablest adviser and best executive officer in the British Navy,

---

1   Quoted Davidson, *Admiral Lord St Vincent*, p.176.
2   Davidson, *Admiral Lord St Vincent*, p.179.

with honour and courage bright as his sword,' and Captain John Markham.[3] The lay members were Sir Philip Stephens, a past First Secretary, and William Elliot, James Adams and William Garthshore. Evan Nepean continued as First Secretary and William Marsden as Second Secretary.[4] The new Board had met for the first time on 20 February 1801, in a confused political situation as a result of the illness of the King. Addington's new Cabinet had previously met, rather ineffectively, and St Vincent had, according to Lord Malmesbury, reacted testily to the ineffectual discussion of its members:

> Lord St Vincent, it is said, assisted a day or two ago at a sort of Cabinet; finding nothing like business going on, he got up, and said, if he was not wanted, he must go away, as really he had no time to throw away; and so left the Cabinet.[5]

His new colleagues would have to get used to St Vincent's robust manner of doing business.

St Vincent made no secret of what he intended to do, and was under no illusion as to the size of the task confronting him. On 15 March 1801, soon after taking office, he wrote to Collingwood:

> There is much to do, and a late attempt of my great Predecessor meets with every species of opposition and obloquy. I mean 'a partial reform in our Dock Yards,' and comparing small things with great (which must come or we are ruined) I shall have a very difficult task to perform, if I preside at this Board in times of Peace.[6]

One of St Vincent's problems was caused by the desire of the great and the good to exercise their patronage in favour of individuals seeking employment or preferment. He was resolved from the outset to stand up to this whenever appropriate, regardless of the power and influence he was confronting, and to do so in terms which left no doubt of his determination. An instance of this was in May 1801, when he rejected a request by the King's brother to appoint a Mr Whitehead:

> Although all the persons in the Transport Board agree with me that a more amiable or virtuous man does not exist, yet no one who is, or has been, a member of that Board, will say that he is by any means capable of

3   Anson, *Life of John Jervis*, p.288.
4   David Bonner-Smith (ed.), *Letters of Admiral of the Fleet Earl of St Vincent* (London: Navy Records Society, 1922), Vol.I, p.18.
5   Bonner-Smith, *Earl of St Vincent*, Vol.I, p.20.
6   Bonner-Smith, *Earl of St Vincent*, Vol.II, p.167.

fulfilling the duties of his present employment. This being unfortunately the case, I fear it will not be in my power to appoint him a Clerk of the Cheque of a Dock Yard, as under the new Regulations a person filling that office ought to possess a degree of precision and energy not to be found in Mr Whitehead, and without these endowments the corruptions and abuses, which are very much to be attributed to that department, never can be rooted out.[7]

There were very many such letters, and a lot of them must have given considerable offence; but St Vincent was unmoved by the extent to which he was thus arousing hostility. One of his biographers described in these terms the view of the corruption in the dockyards which he had formed while in the Mediterranean:

> While Parliament voted lavish sums for the naval service, the fleet was supplied but scantily, and that, while contactors grew rich and jobbery flourished, the store-houses were empty and the Navy crippled. But he had at that time no idea of the frauds and abuses and the idleness he now met with at every turn and in every yard.[8]

First and most significant of the targets which St Vincent was determined to attack was the Navy Board. Soon after taking office he delivered a thunderous broadside to Sir Andrew Hamond, the Comptroller, which amounted to a declaration of war:

> Every sentence I have read of the remonstrances of the Clerks in the Dock yards proves their Corruption and the total dereliction of duty in their principles, with the positive necessity of the reform planned by Lord Spencer. The representation of the Masters Attendant is made upon false principles and cannot be justified. Mr Nepean will write a strong letter to your Board upon these subjects soon; in the meanwhile, every discouragement should be given to those false assumptions, which appear to have a very mischievous tendency.[9]

In August 1802 the Board resolved to make a series of visits to all the dockyards and rope yards, 'having received reports from various quarters of flagrant abuses and mismanagement existing in the several departments, which there is reason to believe are but too well founded'. The Board's resolution added that it should be accompanied on its visitation by the Comptroller and three other members of the Navy Board. The members set off at once, starting their tour at Plymouth.

7   Bonner-Smith, *Earl of St Vincent*, Vol.I, p 304.
8   Anson, *Life of John Jervis*, p.297.
9   Bonner-Smith, *Earl of St Vincent*, Vol.II, p.167.

From there they visited Portsmouth, then Chatham and finally Sheerness, before returning to the Admiralty. They then completed their visitation by going to Woolwich and Deptford. In the course of this investigation they found much that was wrong; but it was at Sheerness that the most extravagant instances of fraud were revealed. These prompted a letter to the Navy Board strongly criticising the failure to do anything effective about it; it conveyed the Admiralty's 'high disapprobation' of the Navy Board's conduct, as a result of which the public purse had been 'suffered to be defrauded to a very considerable amount, and delinquencies passed unpunished'.[10]

During the Board's visitation, St Vincent had set in motion the process of introducing a Bill into Parliament to establish a Commission of Enquiry, writing to Addington:

> We find abuses to such an extent as would require many months to go thoroughly into, and the absolute necessity of a Commission of Enquiry to expose them appears to the Admiralty Board here in a much stronger light than ever.[11]

It was Markham who on 13 December 1802 moved in the Commons for leave to bring in the Bill. It encountered opposition, not least in Cabinet from the Lord Chancellor as well as from Canning and others in the Commons, but St Vincent was insistent, to the point of threatening resignation, and the Bill received royal assent on 29 December. The Chairman of the Commission was to be Vice Admiral Sir Charles Pole; it started work early in the New Year.

St Vincent had also been determined to reduce the annual expenditure on the Navy, and in the course of two years cut the total by two millions. It was a mater of dispute as to the effect of this on the Navy's readiness: his political enemies accused him of weakening it to a dangerous extent. After the formal signing of the Treaty of Amiens, he had disbanded the Sea Fencibles, paid off 40,000 seamen, reduced the number of active ships of the line by fifty per cent and dismissed thousands of dockyard workers. Captain Anson, in his biography of St Vincent, contends that he was 'careful not to reduce the number of ships and men below the strength that would be required in the event of England being compelled to resume hostilities'. James Davidson concedes that he may have weakened the Navy's fighting strength, but suggests that 'in the longer term his reforms were salutary and essential'.[12]

In St Vincent's defence may be quoted another very sharp letter he wrote in December 1803 to Hamond, the Comptroller, who was responsible for overseeing the building of new warships:

10   Bonner-Smith, *Earl of St Vincent*, Vol.II, p.14-15.
11   Bonner-Smith, *Earl of St Vincent*, Vol.II, p.17.
12   Anson, *Life of John Jervis*, p 301; Davidson, *Admiral Lord St Vincent*, p.390.

It must be fresh in your recollection that I have seldom conversed with you upon any subject without introducing the urgent necessity of entering into contracts for building as many 74 gun ships as you could find fit persons to undertake in every part of the Kingdom. I cannot therefore refrain from expressing a considerable degree of surprise at the tone of your letter of yesterday which requires that I should repeat, in the strongest terms, the opinion I have so frequently given.[13]

It was St Vincent's earnest hope that there should be no resumption of hostilities with France. Certainly the work of his Commission would be seriously hampered by the outbreak of war. In the event it produced a total of fourteen reports together with a further supplementary report, and conducted its inquiries with the greatest diligence, and it was clear to all save those it exposed that it had been a remarkably successful exercise: 'it shook corruption to its very foundations, and traced the sources of peculation to their most secret recesses'. In his introduction to the edited correspondence of Captain John Markham, Sir Clements Markham wrote:

It reflected the highest credit on the Commissioners, and also on the Board of Admiralty, which resolutely insisted on the investigations, and had supported the Commissioners regardless of clamour, above, misrepresentation, and the host of rancorous enemies their Lordships made for themselves.[14]

On May 2 1805 the House of Commons formally voted its thanks to the Commissioners.

The characteristic vigour and determination which St Vincent brought to his attack upon corruption and inefficiency had however had unfortunate effects upon the productivity of the shipbuilding and ship repairing functions of the dockyards. A comparison of the size of the Royal Navy during the second year of the war against Napoleon with that of the Revolutionary War shows that there were ten fewer ships of the line in commission than formerly, as James pointed out:

This arose chiefly out of the extensive plan of reform, projected by the First Lord of the Admiralty, and since put in practice with all the vigour and perseverance which characterised the proceedings of the gallant earl. Many old and useful officers, and a vast number of artificers, had been discharged from the King's dockyards; the customary supplies of timber, and other important articles of naval stores, had been omitted to be kept

13   Davidson, *Admiral Lord St Vincent*, pp.196-197.
14   Sir Clements Markham (ed.), *Selections from the Correspondence of Admiral John Markham* (London: Navy Record Society 1904), p.x.

up and some articles, including a large portion of hemp, had actually been sold out of the service. A deficiency of workmen and of materials produced, of course, a suspension in the routine of dockyard business. New ships could not be built; nor – and a very serious misfortune it was – could old ones be repaired. Many of the ships in commission, too, having been merely patched up, were scarcely in a state to keep the sea.[15]

Middleton, reviewing the state of the fleet in March 1805 in the light of the attacks upon the Admiralty, was in no doubt as to St Vincent's culpability, writing to Melville to outline the defence which he should make in Parliament:

The rigid measures that were pursued at this time would have produced much good to the service if they had been delayed till the peace was established; and I am persuaded Lord St Vincent must have thought it secure when he attempted this method of reformation. On any other ground it was madness and imbecility in the extreme… it may be safely asserted, that if a few months credit be given, there will be more improvements brought forward in both the civil and military parts of the service than have ever been thought of for a hundred years past.[16]

St Vincent may have hoped for a lasting period of peace, but the war clouds had soon begun again to gather. When Napoleon had negotiated the Treaty of Amiens, he had in mind only a temporary interruption in the hostilities between France and Britain; his intention was that the peace might last four or five years. However, his ambitions, and profound British mistrust of these, soon began to erode hopes that there might be a lasting peace. The signs of what lay ahead were there from the outset. On the day after the signature of the treaty, Napoleon sent an army of 30,000 men under Ney into Switzerland; his garrison in Holland was not withdrawn. British trade was excluded from all territories under French control; Napoleon began to prepare far reaching schemes of overseas expansion. It was the continued occupation of Holland that most threatened Britain in strategic terms, as Admiral Sir Herbert Richmond observed:

It was Napoleon's refusal to evacuate Holland that brought matters to a head, for the Britain of Addington could no more tolerate the presence of a powerful naval and military power at Antwerp and in the Scheldt than the England of Elizabeth.[17]

15   James, *Naval History*, Vol.III, p.217.
16   Laughton (ed.) *Lord Barham*, Vol.III, p. 69.
17   Sir Herbert Richmond, *Statesman and Sea Power* (London: Clarendon, 1946), p.216.

For her part, Britain continued to retain possession of Malta, notwithstanding the obligation under the Treaty of Amiens to return it in due course to the Order of the Knights of St John. It had become plain that only by holding the island could Britain hope to maintain an effective strategic presence in the Mediterranean, and of course of this Napoleon was well aware. On 13 March 1803 matters came to a head at a reception in the Tuileries in the course of an angry exchange between Napoleon and Lord Whitworth, the British ambassador. Referring to precautionary steps taken by the British government he burst out:

> 'Why these armaments? Whom are those precautions directed against? I have not a single vessel of war in the ports of France; but if you want to arm, I shall arm too; if you want to fight, I shall fight too. Perhaps you may destroy France, but you will never intimidate her'.

Whitworth made a placatory response, saying that Britain would like to live on terms of good understanding with France. This enraged Napoleon still further: 'Then respect must be paid to treaties. Woe to those who do not respect treaties! They should be made answerable to all Europe'.[18]

St Vincent was finding it all too much, and on 30 March wrote to the Prime Minister:

> I am so unstrung today I dare not venture out, otherwise I should have waited on you to say, what I really feel, that it is highly improper for me to continue longer at the head of a Department on which so much depends, in the very precarious state of my health and that the sooner my successor is appointed the more I shall be obliged.[19]

Nothing came of this, nor of a further letter to Addington on 19 May, when St Vincent wrote that his health was rapidly declining. 'Let me therefore entreat you to place this important office in other hands'.[20]

It was evident on both sides that war had become inevitable; and on both sides preparations began to renew the war that had formally ended only a year before. Whitworth was soon instructed to present an ultimatum, insisting not only on the British retention of Malta but on the immediate withdrawal of the French armies of occupation of Holland and Switzerland. If these demands were not accepted, he was to ask for his passports. Attempts by Talleyrand to postpone the breaking off of diplomatic relations failed, and on 18 May the British government formally declared war.

---

18   Quoted Marcus, *Age of Nelson*, p.217.
19   Bonner-Smith, *Earl of St Vincent*, Vol.III, p.209.
20   Bonner-Smith, *Earl of St Vincent*, Vol.II, p.212.

20

The Blockade Resumed

The Treaty of Amiens has often been described as rather more an armistice than a substantive or long lasting peace, and certainly Napoleon anticipated that the struggle between Britain and France would be resumed. As the diplomatic situation deteriorated, and Britain was clearly preparing for the possibility of war, Napoleon increasingly became convinced that it would be better to pre-empt these armaments and bring matters to a head. He had, during the early part of 1803, made plain to Whitworth that the real issue was the possession of Malta; the British failure to give it up was a quite sufficient *casus belli*. Bringing forward the outbreak of hostilities by provoking the British ultimatum, however, gave the French navy no chance of bringing itself to a state in which it could hope to challenge the Royal Navy on anything like equal terms. Napoleon was perfectly aware of this, sating that 'Peace is necessary to restore a navy, – peace to fill our arsenals empty of material, and peace because then only the one drill-ground for fleets, the sea, is open'.[1]

Napoleon was a realist; in the existing state of the naval imbalance, he accepted that he must write off French hopes in the Caribbean, abandoning Santo Domingo and selling off Louisiana to the United States. As early as January 1803 he issued stringent orders intended to prevent the activities of British agents in the area of Brest. But steps of this kind could not of themselves do much to put the port into a state of preparedness for war. It had been in a parlous state for several years, which was why the activities of the fleet moored there had been so circumscribed.

When Count Louis de Caffarelli was appointed Naval Prefect of Brest, he was soon mournfully reporting: 'Brest is no longer as I have known it; it lacks everything':[2]

---

1 Quoted Mahan, *Sea Power*, Vol.II, p.107.
2 John Leyland (ed.), *Despatches and Letters Relating to the Blockade of Brest 1803-1805* (London: Navy Records Society, 1899), Vol.I, p.xi.

Men were wanting for the forts, the ships, and the building yards. The batteries had not more than a quarter of their due complement. When the *Venteux* was taken [in June], according to the Prefect, they did not open fire, and their help could not be greatly counted on. At the Ile de Batz the gun-mountings were rotten; some guns were of calibre too small, and the men did not know how to handle them. At other points upon the coast the batteries were badly equipped and badly provided, and the men were few.[3]

On the other side of the Channel the situation was very different. The likelihood of war was now seen as so great that preparation of the ships at Portsmouth and Plymouth was put in hand, and the work of fitting out proceeded apace. The Channel Fleet was concentrated at Torbay, and steps were taken to man the ships as rapidly as possible. On 7 May alone some 700 men were impressed in the Portsmouth area, and in Plymouth the press was so hot that many men retired inland. Elsewhere the press was similarly active; serious disturbances were caused at Portland. Regular reports to Nepean from Rear Admiral George Campbell in Torbay described the progress being made towards manning the ships; at Plymouth a captain's picket of 50 men paraded the town to maintain order.[4]

Cornwallis had, as early as March, written to St Vincent to offer his services, and he was in due course reappointed to the command of the Channel Fleet, hoisting his flag on board the *Dreadnought* at Plymouth on 10 May. In spite of the vigorous activities of the press gangs, St Vincent was disappointed by the results obtained, as he wrote to Cornwallis:

I lament the ill success of the general Impress from Protections in the vicinity of Torbay. I hope however before this reaches you that Admiral Dawes has sent you some hundreds from Plymouth, the more so as you may expect to receive your orders early on Monday morning, and I know you will carry them into execution with promptitude.[5]

Collingwood, too, had answered the call of duty promptly, as he wrote to Dr Carlyle on 13 March:

We are again threatened with war, and all its miseries. I have little hope that it can be avoided and, in that case, I suppose I shall be employed immediately. I received a letter five days since from Sir Evan Nepean to know if I was ready (in the event of being wanted) to go on service at very short notice. I answered 'To be sure I was' and packed up my trunk and

3   Leyland (ed.), *Blockade of Brest*, Vol.I, p.xi.
4   Leyland (ed.), *Blockade of Brest*, Vol.I, p.8.
5   Cornwallis-West, *Admiral Cornwallis*, p.388.

my signal book and am now waiting for a summons to take my station wherever it may be.[6]

Collingwood went on to reflect on the abuse heaped on St Vincent as a result of his efforts at reform. He spoke for most of the Navy when he wrote:

> I have heard the complaints that are made against the First Lord of the Admiralty, and am not surprised at it, because I know how great a clamour a few rogues can make. The abuses and peculations in the navy were to an extent that were a burthen to the government, and reproachful to ministers to allow, yet they have allowed it, rather than contend against so numerous a band as were concerned in them. He has undertaken to correct them and accustomed to that promptitude which is the soul of military operations, would proceed in the same right lined ways against their knaveries, which would be perhaps more effectually suppressed and with less danger of giving annoyance to innocence, by making discovery of the crooked paths the reptiles work in.[7]

Orders came for Collingwood during May, and on 3 June he hoisted his flag in the frigate *Diamond*, and sailed to join Cornwallis and the Channel Fleet. His arrival was very welcome to the Commander-in-Chief, who remarked: 'Here comes my old friend Coll, the last that left and the first to join me'.[8] Collingwood had been appointed to the *Venerable*, 74, to command the inshore squadron, but he had to make do with the frigate for two months.

Thus the Royal Navy, far better prepared than its immediate adversary, entered once more into a global war, of which the most crucial focus was the blockade of Brest. In 1803 it possessed 111 ships of the line, of which 21 were first or second rates and the remaining 90 third rates. There were 11 fourth rates, 102 fifth rates and 22 sixth rates, together with a total of 142 sloops, bomb-vessels, fire ships, brigs and cutters. The total tonnage of these vessels was 356,400. In 1803, the total of the sums voted by Parliament for expenditure on the Navy amounted to £10,211,378.[9]

With the outbreak of war St Vincent had reiterated his request to be relieved from office on the grounds of his health; but he was regarded as being too valuable to be dispensed with. In a debate in the House of Commons on 3 June the Secretary at War, Charles Yorke, argued strongly that the country was in an adequate state of defence. Hansard reported that he went on to refer to St Vincent:

6   Hughes (ed.), *Admiral Lord Collingwood*, pp.146-147.
7   Hughes (ed.), *Admiral Lord Collingwood*, p.147.
8   Quoted Warner, *Lord Collingwood*, p.119.
9   Clowes, *Royal Navy*, Vol.IV, pp.9-10.

We never before commenced war under such favourable circumstances of strength, both in the Army and the Navy. He bestowed the highest encomiums upon the First Lord of the Admiralty, both on account of his extraordinary abilities as a Commander, and from his having rooted out those inveterate abuses which had produced such great expense and inconvenience. He drew a comparison between the superior force lately sent to sea, and the preparations last war in a much longer period, when the French possessed 85 sail of the line.[10]

On 17 May, the day before the formal declaration of war, Cornwallis, flying his flag in the 98-gun *Dreadnought*, sailed from Cawsand Bay with five ships of the line and several frigates, to take up the blockade of Brest. These were shortly followed by the *Ville de Paris*, to which he shifted his flag, and three other ships of the line. His departure was followed by the despatch of smaller squadrons, one to cruise in the Bay of Biscay, one in the Irish Channel and one in the North Sea. A further twenty ships of the line were being fitted out for sea at Plymouth and Portsmouth. Meanwhile Nelson had been appointed to command the Mediterranean Fleet and left Portsmouth in the *Victory*, accompanied by the frigate *Amphion*, on 20 May. If, when he met with Cornwallis, the latter required the *Victory*, Nelson was to proceed to the Mediterranean in the *Amphion*. Not being able to contact the Channel Fleet, which had been blown off station, Nelson shifted his flag to the *Amphion*, and left Captain Sutton in the *Victory* to join Cornwallis. When Sutton finally joined the Channel Fleet, Cornwallis at once sent him on in the *Victory* to re-join Nelson, who was profoundly grateful, writing to Cornwallis:

> The *Victory* joined me last night, having been, via Malta, seven weeks from Gibraltar. I can only say to you thanks for not taking the *Victory* from me; it was like yourself and very unlike many others which you and I know. She has been tolerably successful, and indeed except the *Amphion* the only ship under my command who have taken anything of any consideration. The Admiralty not allowing me to come out in the *Victory* direct from Portsmouth has lost the capture of two 74's and probably two frigates, and perhaps by this time much more.[11]

Cornwallis intended to conduct the blockade of Brest in a similar fashion to that adopted at the end of the previous war. He formed an inshore squadron under Campbell of three ships of the line and two frigates; the intention was that the vessels of the squadron should be frequently rotated to ensure that they were maintained in good condition. Cornwallis was also responsible for watching

---

10   Bonner-Smith, *Earl of St Vincent*, Vol.III, pp 36-37.
11   Cornwallis-West, *Admiral Cornwallis*, p.389.

Lorient and Rochefort; he assigned a squadron of three ships of the line and a frigate under Pellew (*Tonnant, Spartiate, Mars* and *Aigle*) to this task, but Pellew was distracted by also being required to intercept a number of Dutch warships, which were apparently about to sail from Ferrol. The Dutch got away, and for what seemed to Pellew to be excellent reasons: he was convinced that they had sailed to Madeira, and he set off after them. He had guessed wrong, however, and on July 12 was obliged to report to Cornwallis that he had lost them.[12]

In the meantime the Admiralty had news that Rear Admiral Jacques Bedout, commanding a French squadron in the West Indies, had been ordered home. It was assumed that he would sail for the Mediterranean, and detailed orders were sent to Cornwallis for Campbell to take the *Canopus, Malta* and *Sceptre* to pick up the *Conqueror* off Cape St Vincent, and to intercept Bedout. The latter's squadron was said to consist of the *Argonaute, Fougueux, Redoutable* and *Héros.* If Campbell did not meet with Bedout by 20 July he was to join Nelson in the Mediterranean. Collingwood, with three ships of the line (*Venerable, Minotaur* and *Culloden*) and the frigates *Aigle* and *Naiad*, was to take over the duties of the inshore squadron. Cornwallis continued to cruise off Ushant; he reported on 3 July to Nepean that the *Thunderer* and *Plantagenet* were watching Lorient and that Pellew was probably by then before Rochefort.[13]

Campbell's task was not made easier by the fact that the frigate *Doris* and the cutter *Fox*, intended to form part of his squadron, were both committed on detached duties near Gibraltar. As it turned out, Bedout heard of the outbreak of war as he approached Cape St Vincent, and he swung north, arriving safely at Corunna on 14 July without having been spotted. He subsequently moved his ships to Ferrol, where their continued presence required the maintenance of a constant blockade. This was conducted by Pellew after he returned from his abortive pursuit of the Dutch. It was a task that called not only for seamanship but also diplomacy; Pellew maintained a courteous relationship with the Governor of Ferrol which enabled him to be well informed of what was going on with the French squadron, Spain still being neutral at this time. John Leyland observed:

> In the blockade of Ferrol and Corunna Pellew showed himself both a fine seaman and a tactful diplomatist. As a seaman he accomplished the different task of maintaining his squadron off a dangerous and stormy Coast, with no base nearer than Plymouth or Berehaven. He was constantly buffeted by the gales, and suffered terribly in the tremendous weather of December 1803 and January 1804, when for twelve successive days, the seas were so great that his ships were reduced to the necessity of

12 Leyland (ed.), *Blockade of Brest*, Vol.I, p.71.
13 Leyland (ed.), *Blockade of Brest*, Vol.I, p.59.

setting sail or losing masts, and their people were worn out, with a sick list upon an average of above sixty.[14]

Pellew's arrival off Corunna, and his subsequent blockade of that port and Ferrol, put him precisely where St Vincent had intended he should be; the First Lord wrote to Cornwallis on 24 May:

> I hope you will soon be joined by some of the ships in Cawsand Bay and that you will be enabled thereby to make a detachment off Ferrol, the coast of which I believe Sir Edward Pellew is better acquainted with than most officers in the navy from his having been much employed there when in command of a frigate and on the expedition of Sir J B Warren and Sir J Pulteney, which has induced the Board to point him out in the character of Senior Captain.[15]

As the summer proceeded, Pellew had something of a setback when two more French ships made the crossing of the Atlantic from the West Indies. Visibility on 2 September was not good, when the *Duguay Trouin*, 74, and the frigate *Guerriere*, 40, suddenly appeared to windward of him and made for Corunna. Only the *Culloden* of Pellew's squadron was far enough to windward to exchange broadsides with them, and her captain handled her so badly that his cannonade was totally ineffectual, and the French ships were soon safely under the protection of the Spanish forts. Next day Pellew was temporarily relieved by Sir Robert Calder: returning home for a short period of leave, he reported to Cornwallis off Ushant on 16 September and was in Cawsand Bay by 20 September. He was back off Ferrol by 9 October to resume his blockade of the French squadron which, having nowhere to go, was unlikely to venture out, even though deteriorating weather conditions might give it the opportunity to do so.[16]

Cornwallis, like so many British fleet commanders, was being seriously hampered by the lack of frigates. It was this that had obliged him to station the ships of the line *Thunderer* and *Plantagenet* off Lorient. When the Admiralty heard that the *Thunderer* had taken a French vessel in a position which suggested that her captain might have been tempted out of station in pursuit of prizes, Nepean wrote to Cornwallis on 25 July that he should keep his squadron more collected off the ports of the enemy. Next day, having evidently discussed his suspicions at a meeting of the Board, Nepean wrote again:

14   Leyland (ed.), *Blockade of Brest*, Vol.I, p.xlvi.
15   Bonner-Smith, *Earl of St Vincent*, Vol.II, p.306.
16   Parkinson, *Edward Pellew*, p 296.

Their Lordships have commanded me to refer you to my letter of yesterday, and to acquaint you that it appears to them to be essentially necessary, from the accounts received of the state of the enemy's force, that you should not detach any of your line-of-battle ships on services of that nature, and that you should call on the captain of the *Thunderer* to account for his being so far off his station on the 6th, it appearing by your disposition that he had been stationed by you off Lorient.[17]

Nepean's criticism must have irritated Cornwallis, but he sent a placid enough reply:

I detached Captain Bedford off Lorient for a week once before, and he returned exactly to the time, which circumstance, added to the ship being thought the best sailer of the two-decker ships, induced me to detach him occasionally upon such service. The *Plantagenet*, being a very deceiving ship, without a poop, I thought, when a two deck ship could be spared for a few days, might, in the place of a smaller ship, have a chance of checking the depredations of the enemy's cruisers.[18]

On 7 August he sent the *Thunderer*'s Journal to the Admiralty, so that this ship's proceedings might be clearly understood. It demonstrated just how busy the ship had been during the month of July, stopping and examining a large number of vessels, and being obliged to chase many of them. In the course of these activities she took three prizes, two of them being recaptured French prizes, and the third being the privateer *Vénus*, of whom Captain Bedford wrote to Cornwallis that she was 'a fine vessel, quite new, sails remarkably fast, well found, coppered, and measures 358 tons'. He added that she was 'calculated for his Majesty's service'.[19]

Cornwallis could be entirely happy with the proceedings of the inshore squadron, of which Collingwood took over the command on 30 June. It consisted of three ships of the line and two frigates. Collingwood was soon able to report on the intelligence gained by the pilot Jerome Hamon, who had gone into Brest harbour from the inshore squadron. He reported that there were four ships of the line, with three frigates, four corvettes and two brigs in the outer road, with fifteen ships of the line, five frigates and a Dutch brig in the inner road. Hamon noted that there were five gunboats completed, with seven more fitting and four or five more building. These, he thought, were the principal focus of attention, and he found that the invasion of England was the main subject of conversation. Passing on Collingwood's report to the Admiralty, Cornwallis wrote of Hamon:

17   Leyland (ed.), *Blockade of Brest*, Vol.I, p.83.
18   Leyland (ed.), *Blockade of Brest*, Vol.II, p.108.
19   Leyland (ed.), *Blockade of Brest*, Vol.I, pp.85, 110-119.

'The merit of this daring man seems to be very great, and I have no doubt will be so considered by their Lordships'. The Admiralty ordered that Hamon be paid £50 for his services.[20] He certainly deserved it; he had experienced a good deal of difficulty in getting away from Brest, finally sculling on his own in a borrowed rowing boat towards the ships of the inshore squadron, where he was picked up by a cutter, having been spotted from the *Culloden*. In his report, he wrote:

> I verily believe but for this fortunate circumstance I should have died of thirst and fatigue, for the boat, being leaky, was occasionally to be baled with one of my boots, and what with that, my anxiety, and sculling upwards of fourteen hours without so much as a drop of water to refresh me, I dare say my being nearly exhausted will not surprise you.[21]

The priority being given to the gun boats by the ship builders of Brest was significant, and reflected Napoleon's determination to prepare an invasion fleet. With all the resources of France at his disposal, his determination was to strike a direct blow at Great Britain by launching an assault directly on the British Isles. Admiral Mahan mused on the extent to which a bold stroke of this kind was a reflection of Napoleon's personality:

> The very greatness of the peril in crossing the Channel, and in leaving it between him and his base, was not without a certain charm for his adventurous temper; but, while willing to take many a risk for so great an end, he left to chance nothing for which he himself could provide. The plan for the invasion was marked by the comprehensiveness of view and the minute attention to detail which distinguished his campaigns; and the preparations were on a scale of entire adequacy, which he never failed to observe when the power to do so was in his hands.[22]

What Napoleon did not grasp was the effect of concentrating all the shipbuilding capability of northern France on the construction of the invasion fleet, consuming all the available material and employing the whole of the workforce. In this way he seriously damaged the nation's ability to develop its real navy, ensuring that his squadrons were perpetually at risk of being outnumbered. This in turn meant that assembling an adequate covering force for the invasion flotilla would require the most skilful combination to unite a fleet strong enough to stand up to the forces that the Royal Navy could bring against it. When and if the time came, of course, the responsibility of the blockading squadrons would be very great. Meanwhile

---

20   Leyland (ed.), *Blockade of Brest*, Vol.I, pp.60-63.
21   Leyland (ed.), *Blockade of Brest*, Vol.I, p.66.
22   Mahan, *Sea Power*, Vol.II, p.109.

the task of locking the French fleets tight into their bases went on, evoking from Mahan one of the most famous and often quoted passages of his work:

> They were dull, weary, eventless months, those months of watching and waiting of the big ships before the French arsenals. Purposeless they surely seemed to many, but they saved England. The world has never seen a more impressive demonstration of the influence of sea power upon its history. Those far distant, storm beaten ships, upon which the Grand Army never looked, stood between it and the dominion of the world.[23]

Nowhere were the demands made on the ships of the Royal Navy greater than those faced by the inshore squadron off Brest. The difficulties of maintaining an effective blockade of the port were described by Collingwood to his father-in-law on 9 August:

> The Admiral sends all the ships to me, and cruises off Ushant by himself; but with a westerly wind, it is impossible with one squadron to prevent ships getting into Brest Harbour; for it has two entrances, very distant from each other, one to the south of the Saints, but which, off Ushant, where we are, is entirely out of view. I take the utmost pains to prevent all access, and an anxious time I have of it, what with tides and rocks, which have more of danger in them than a battle once a week.[24]

For the inshore squadron the arrival of the mail was an important event, usually brought by a packet or a cutter. Collingwood was amused in September when it was the ship of the line *Atlas*, commanded by his friend Captain John Purvis, that arrived with the despatches, as he wrote to express his thanks:

> Though I should have had great pleasure in seeing you, I am very glad you did not give yourself the trouble to come on a business which your Lieut. has performed admirably… I think when Bonaparte is informed that our packet boats carry ninety guns he will not look to the sea for his glory.[25]

The Admiralty's intelligence about French intentions led to the strengthening conviction that another descent on the Irish coast was planned, either as a substantive invasion or possibly as a feint intended to draw the Channel Fleet away to cover the embarkation of the army at Boulogne for an invasion of England. Nepean wrote to Cornwallis on 26 October to spell out the action he should take if the

---

23   Mahan, *Sea Power*, Vol.II, p.118.
24   Warner, *Lord Collingwood*, p.121.
25   Iain Gordon, *Admiral of the Blue* (Barnsley: Pen & Sword, 2006), p.114.

French fleet escaped from Brest; the terms of his letter suggest that the Admiralty was becoming decidedly jittery:

> Having taken your station off the Lizard, you will not quit it in pursuit of the Enemy until you shall receive such intelligence as may leave no doubt of his destination, and supposing it to be directed to the coast of Ireland, you will follow it to whatever point it may proceed, but as I have before observed, you will not quit your station off the Lizard without the most authentic information of the Enemy's movements, and this is the more necessary as, in the event of any favourable opportunity presenting itself, it is not impossible that the Enemy may attempt to run up Channel either for the purpose of landing the Troops which may be embarked in the Squadron, or for covering any body of troops destined to act against this country which may be ready on the Enemy's coast to be thrown across the Channel under cover of this squadron, which, during your absence, it might not be possible to prevent.[26]

St Vincent was by no means well, and spent a good deal of time at Rochetts, his home in Essex; much of the correspondence with Cornwallis was accordingly conducted by Nepean, who, nonetheless, copied it to the First Lord.

In Brest, meanwhile, Caffarelli was under constant pressure from Decrès, the Minister of Marine, to prepare an expedition. In August he was ordered to prepare for the embarkation of 32,000 men in the ships of the fleet at Brest; shortly afterwards that was changed to 20,000 men and 500 horses. Decrès was monitoring closely the state of readiness of the fleet, and noted on 3 November that four of the ships of the line intended to go to sea were not ready; the total available at that time was twenty. The fleet was to be completed by the four outstanding vessels no later than 11 January; no delay would be acceptable. Orders went at the same time to Lorient and Rochefort, where a number of ships were fitting out. The Prefect at Rochefort was told that the intention was that 10,000 men were to be embarked:

> While admitting that the ships at Corunna and Pasages, or Lorient and Nantes, may later on join those of Rochefort, I calculate approximately that you will have to supply the insufficiency of the warships by chartering transports, capable of carrying about 7,000 men.[27]

There seemed, however, to be some slackening of the preparation being made in Brest. On 16 September Collingwood reported to Cornwallis:

---

26   Cornwallis-West, *Admiral Cornwallis*, p.399.
27   Leyland (ed.), *Blockade of Brest*, Vol.I, p.131.

222 FAR DISTANT SHIPS

Since the last communication I had the honour to address to you on the 10th instant there has been no apparent change in the state of the enemy in Brest. The ships in the Road exercise less, their gun vessels do not come out as they were used to do, and they appear less active in forming their men to naval exercises than they were two months since.[28]

One matter that was greatly exercising Cornwallis's mind at this time was his urgent desire to have Captain John Whitby reappointed as his flag captain. The two men had become close friends after first meeting in the Far East in 1790; Cornwallis had a very high opinion of the young lieutenant, whom he appointed to the command of the *Despatch* schooner in 1792. Whitby had served as Cornwallis's flag captain until Cornwallis hauled down his flag on conclusion of the peace. At the beginning of 1803 Whitby married the talented and beautiful Theresa Symonds, and brought his young bride to live with Cornwallis at Newlands, the admiral's house near Lymington in Hampshire. However, when war broke out Whitby was posted to the *Belleisle* in the Mediterranean, where he was serving when in August 1803 his wife had a premature baby who shortly afterwards died. Deeply concerned for Theresa Whitby, Cornwallis had previously asked for Whitby to come home to serve as his flag captain; reckoning that this was perhaps the only way she could be comforted, he renewed his request, which St Vincent was not immediately able to gratify:

> I am very desirous to comply with your wishes respecting Captain Whitby, more especially since the afflicting loss Mrs Whitby has sustained. Unfortunately the squadron in the Mediterranean requires to be considerably reinforced and at this moment we have not the means, consequently cannot call anything from thence until it can be amply replaced.[29]

Later, however, St Vincent relented, in November telling Cornwallis that no time should be lost in sending out a captain to relieve Whitby, who would be appointed to Cornwallis's flagship, the *Ville de Paris*. Whitby was overjoyed, writing to Cornwallis:

> Everything you mention in your letter makes me know how truly I am indebted to your kindness and affection… In coming out here as a sense of duty I sacrificed every feeling in the world, and had I not had you to befriend my dear wife with your kind care perhaps I might not have

28   Leyland (ed.), *Blockade of Brest*, Vol.I, p.155.
29   Bonner-Smith, *Earl of St Vincent*, Vol.II, p.309.

summoned the strength of mind to have parted; in short, I owe every-thing to you.[30]

It was, however, to be some time before the move could be carried into effect.

30   Cornwallis-West, *Admiral Cornwallis*, p.397.

21

Napoleon and the Admirals

The *Naval Chronicle* for January-June 1804 published a brief account of Cornwallis as he appeared at that time:

> In respect to person, he is of the middle size, stout and portly, with a certain degree of prominence before, which may be disposed to add dignity to a Commander-in-Chief, and must be allowed not to be unbecoming in an officer now in the sixtieth year of his age. As to talents, his skill and bravery are undoubted, his seamanship is in particular in high repute; and a long apprenticeship, of more than forty years, during which he has had fewer intervals of relaxation on shore than perhaps any other officer of equal rank in the British navy, has enabled him to acquire a degree of professional capability, which renders no disaster unknown, and no situation unusual to him. In point of habits, he is a reserved man; and is so little desirous of bustle when on shore that on its being observed, during a temporary residence near Chichester, that 'he must be lonely,' he replied 'that the cabbage stocks in his garden were sufficient company for him'. At times he enjoys his glass freely; but is so abstemious while on duty that he has been known for six months together to drink no more than a couple of glasses of wine at dinner, after which he carefully abstained from any other refreshment during the succeeding part of the day.[1]

His immediate opponent, in command at Brest from 17 September, was 51 year old Vice Admiral Count Laurent Truguet. He enjoyed a high reputation in the navy before the French Revolution, after which he continued to be trusted by the new regime, visiting England in 1791 to report on the Royal Navy and its resources. In the following year he was promoted to rear admiral; he was then imprisoned, but after his release became Minister of Marine, before going to Madrid as ambassador. He was in trouble again in 1798 for refusing to return from Spain, and was

---

1   Cornwallis-West, *Admiral Cornwallis*, pp.407-408.

listed as an émigré before Talleyrand intervened. His immediate subordinates at Brest were Rear Admirals Missiessy and Dordelin.[2]

Unfortunately, Truguet's appointment proved to be a mistake. Not only did Decrés despise him for his vanity and weakness, but Truguet soon began a prolonged row with Caffarelli. The Prefect was working with all his strength to prepare the fleet for sea, as he had been doing since his own appointment in 1800, in spite of the many difficulties which he encountered. Truguet treated him extremely disrespectfully, and had the temerity to prepare a decree which would effectively have annulled Caffarelli's position; this caused Napoleon to intervene, to lay down precisely the extent of the duties and authority of each of them. It might be supposed that Truguet, who apparently prided himself on being a diplomat, might have learned something from this. However, when in 1804 Napoleon proclaimed himself Emperor, Truguet made one false step too many when he expressed the opinion that the title of First Consul was more honourable than that of Emperor. Napoleon was furious; he soon put paid to Truguet, writing to Decrés on 1 May that the admiral was to be removed for disobedience of his orders. In particular, he had not sufficiently trained his crews in seamanship by getting the fleet under way every day, nor had harassed the blocking squadron or covered the passage of the flotilla from Audierne. Truguet was succeeded by Ganteaume, hitherto the Naval Prefect at Toulon, of whom Napoleon had a high opinion.

In the autumn and winter of 1803 the weather was exceptionally bad. In November fierce storms drove many of the ships to seek shelter in Cawsand Bay; in December Rear Admiral Sir Thomas Graves, then commanding the inshore squadron, was blown off station and his ships became separated, and he made his way in the *Foudroyant* to Cawsand Bay, where he found ten other ships of the line had taken refuge. Cornwallis himself, with only the *San Josef* and the *Dreadnought,* remained off Ushant as long as he could, but 30 December found him sheltering from the gale in Torbay. The risk was that in the westerly gales he could have been driven further up Channel. Three days later he was on his station again; there could be no possibility that the French could have got out with the winds as they were.

Cornwallis's fixed determination whenever the fleet was obliged to take shelter was to get to sea again as soon as he could. His practice of keeping the Blue Peter flying to signal his imminent departure brought him the nickname of 'Billy Blue;'; previously he had been known as 'Billy Go-Tight' in reference his florid complexion. In spite of all his efforts, however, the strength of the blockading force was desperately low. During December there was an average of only eight ships of the line on station; at the end of December the number was down to four, and in the first three weeks of the new year the average was only six. His constant order to his captains was that they should rejoin him with all possible speed. Further

2   Leyland (ed.), *Blockade of Brest*, Vol.I, p.156.

violent gales on 19 January and again on 28 January, however, compelled him to run for Torbay. A large number of vessels had suffered serious damage in these storms, including the *San Josef, Impétueux, Foudroyant* and the frigates *Boadicea* and *Loire*. Nonetheless, Cornwallis was determined to get back to sea as soon as he could, and he ordered Captain Ryder, the Regulating Officer at Falmouth, to tell any of his ships that put in there that he expected to meet them off Ushant.[3]

There seemed a real risk that the French would have available a force stronger than could be seen and possibly stronger than the blockaders; Cornwallis issued orders to Graves to take account of this:

> From the information which has been received relative to the designs and force of the enemy's ships at Brest, there is reason to believe they are in greater force than can be observed from our ships. A very strict lookout is, therefore, necessary, and for you to be constantly on your guard. I should think, as the wind seems to set in from the eastward, you might occasionally anchor, which has been before practised. I shall place some ships to look out between you and the squadron for the purpose of communicating to me the motions of the enemy. Upon any appearance of their movement you will instantly detach a ship to make the same known to me.[4]

By the time that the Empire was proclaimed in May 1804, it had already become apparent to Napoleon that preparations for the invasion of England were well behind schedule and that it must be postponed. As many historians have observed, it is difficult to be entirely sure of Napoleon's intentions at any given time or even whether his projected invasion of England was no more than a gigantic bluff intended to distract attention from plans for military operations in mainland Europe. Given the scale, and the cost, of the preparations for a cross-Channel invasion, and the amount of time which he devoted to tours of the invasion harbours and the army's camps, it is quite inconceivable that this could all have been a huge charade. His willingness to postpone the launch of the invasion reflected not so much a doubt as to whether to launch it at all, but realistic awareness that to succeed everything must be in place.

The situation in May 1804 was that the Boulogne flotilla was far from ready. There had been a large build up of troops along the Channel coast. There were problems with the guns on the invasion vessels. Work on new warships and the fitting out of those existing had been seriously hampered by the focus on building the invasion vessels; the need for a sufficiently powerful covering force of warships was now accepted, and it was clear that a complex scheme of assembly of the

3   Leyland (ed.), *Blockade of Brest*, Vol.I, p.260.
4   Leyland (ed.), *Blockade of Brest*, Vol.I, pp.272-273.

French fleets would be necessary. Napoleon, of course, even if realising that this was so, still did not grasp how difficult would be the task of the covering force, famously writing to Decrés; 'Let us be masters of the Straits for six hours and we shall be masters of the world'.

Napoleon was not at all satisfied with the competence of his admirals. Bruix had been chosen to lead the invasion flotilla, but he was proving difficult to coerce into accepting Napoleon's views of what should be done. Against the advice of the admiral, Napoleon insisted on the carrying out of gunboat drill in adverse weather; Bruix refused to order it and was sacked: the drill took place and a number of gunboats, with their crews, were lost. Subsequently, Bruix was rein-stated, but the Emperor continued to be displeased with him. One admiral whom he did particularly admire was Louis de Latouche-Tréville, the commander of the Toulon fleet, and in June 1804 he was designated as the overall commander of the covering forces.

Napoleon was also dubious about the qualities of Decrés as Minister of Marine; he wrote to Cambacérès on the subject:

> Some functions of the naval ministry … are obviously neglected, and I am beginning to suspect that Decrés does not have the understanding of command and continuity, prime quality of an administrator. However he has other qualities … [so despite] his carelessness over most impor-tant matters I decided to wait another three months to come to a decision because in the end there is little to gain from a change.[5]

In spite of his continuing doubts, Decrés remained in office, the butt of repeated imperial gibes about the abilities of senior naval officers.

Meanwhile the blockade of the French fleet in its various ports went on, as its fitting out continued. In March, the Channel Fleet suffered a serious blow when the *Magnificent*, 74, was lost on an uncharted sunken rock off the Black Rocks, though her crew was saved by the boats of the inshore squadron. Such an acci-dent was almost inevitable, given the dangers faced by the fleet around Brest. The imminence of a French breakout continued to dominate Cornwallis's thinking; this was reflected in an order to Captain Thomas Byam Martin of the *Impétueux*, temporarily commanding the inshore squadron, on 31 March:

> The enemy having a very considerable force at Brest, said to be on the point of sailing, it is, therefore, of the utmost national importance that the port should be as closely watched as possible … Should the enemy put to sea you are to give me – off Ushant – the earliest notice by the frigates,

---

5   Quoted Robert Asprey, *The Rise and Fall of Napoleon Bonaparte* (London: Little, Brown & Co., 2000), Vol.I, p.461.

or smaller vessels stationed there, under your direction. In the meantime you are at a proper distance to observe their motions and the course they steer, keeping between the enemy and the squadron with me, and by spreading your ships, communicate to me the route they are taking, to enable me to pursue them without loss of time with the whole force.[6]

When Graves resumed command of the inshore squadron, the order was repeated to him.

Meanwhile, Pellew had been engaged in a struggle of a very different nature. Back in London, the government had been facing serious difficulties in the House of Commons when Pitt began a series of attacks upon the state of the Navy and its administration. In February he had declared that of his own knowledge the naval defence was very defective. Anticipating Pitt's next move, St Vincent wrote to Pellew, then in London in his capacity as an MP, on 10 March that it would be important for him and Lord Hobart to have a conversation before Pellew went back to sea.[7] As a result, when Pitt on 15 March put forward a motion for naval returns designed to show that the navy was unprepared, that ships were not being built and that the strategy was wrong, Pellew was able to intervene effectively in the debate. Newly arrived from the fleet, his words carried conviction:

I know and can assert with confidence, that our navy was never better found, that it was never better supplied, and that our men were never better fed nor better clothed. Have we not all the enemy's ports block-aded from Toulon to Flushing? Are we not able to cope, anywhere, with any force the enemy dare to send out against us? And do we not even outnumber them at every one of those ports we have blockaded? It would smack a little of egotism, I fear, were I to speak of myself (Hear! Hear!) – but as a person lately having been in command of six ships, I hope I may be allowed to state to the House how I have been supported in that command. Sir, during the time that I was stationed off Ferrol, I had ships passing from the fleet to me every three weeks or a month; and so much was the French Commander shut up on that port deceived by these appearances, that he was persuaded, and I believe is to this very hour, that I had twelve ships under my command; and that I had two squadrons to relieve each other, one of six inside, and another of six outside.[8]

Pellew was soon followed by Markham; when the question was put, Pitt's motion was defeated by 71 votes.

6   Leyland (ed.), *Blockade of Brest*, Vol.I, pp.299-300.
7   Bonner-Smith, *Earl of St Vincent*, Vol.II, p.312.
8   Tracy (ed.), *Naval Chronicle*, Vol.III, p.8.

Pellew returned to his station off Ferrol, reporting to Cornwallis on 11 April. He did so from his flagship the *Tonnant* lying at anchor in Betanzos Bay, which he had in February adopted as an anchorage for his squadron to shield it from the fierce gales that had been experienced. It was a bold move; the bay enjoyed an evil reputation for foul ground, and the French Admiral Gourdon, who had succeeded Bedout in command of the Ferrol squadron, was sure that Pellew would suffer for it. It was said that he frequently made his way overland from Ferrol to inspect the British squadron from the beach at Betanzos Bay, hoping to see it in difficulties. In this he was disappointed; the health of Pellew's men was much improved, and his ships suffered much less damage from the storms than otherwise would have been the case.[9] When the wind was in the west, Pellew would send a party on shore to watch the French squadron from a windmill on the neck of land separating Betanzos Bay from the harbour of Ferrol; with the wind in the east, he anchored just outside the harbour itself.

Pellew was careful to do nothing that would offend the Spanish authorities, even though they were giving support and help to the French squadron as it prepared for sea. He was convinced that, as soon as they were ready, they would make for Rochefort, Lorient or Brest to reinforce the squadron there. When, at the beginning of May, Pellew finally received his long awaited promotion to rear admiral, he handed over command of the blockading squadron to Rear Admiral Alexander Cochrane. In his final report to Cornwallis, Pellew suggested that Gourdon's preparations for sea were by no means as advanced as had been supposed. As for relations with the local authorities, he wrote: 'The utmost cordiality prevails between the Spaniards and the squadron, and upon every occasion their civilities are uniform'.[10] His successor did not however build on the spirit of cooperation which Pellew had established, soon reporting to Cornwallis that he had 'a hard battle to fight with the people here;' they had, he said, been 'so accustomed to dishonest practices that it is no easy matter to bring them again within bounds'.[11] Cochrane was also quick to write direct to the Admiralty seeking more small vessels with which to destroy enemy privateers and recapture their prizes.

Pellew's contribution to the House of Commons debate had certainly helped ensure the defeat of Pitt's motion, but this served to delay for only a short time the fall of the government. Addington did not see how it could continue in office while faced with Pitt's open hostility, and he resigned on 10 May. Pitt's return to power, of course, swept away St Vincent, who was outraged at the attacks which had been made on him and his conduct of the affairs of the Admiralty, and which he never forgave. He was succeeded as First Lord by Lord Melvillle. Pellew's biographer noted that he 'had damned himself for ever in the eyes of Pitt. And it was

9   Leyland (ed.), *Blockade of Brest*, Vol.I, pp.263-265; Parkinson, *Edward Pellew*, p.298.
10   Leyland (ed.), *Blockade of Brest*, Vol.I, p.315.
11   Leyland (ed.), *Blockade of Brest*, Vol.I, pp.334-335.

Pitt who was in office'. One of the last actions of the outgoing government had been to confer on Pellew the command of the East Indies station, and it might have been expected that this would have been revoked, in view of Pellew's speech in the house. In the event, however, it was not.[12]

In Brest, Ganteaume had arrived to take up his command in succession to Truguet on 8 June, and four days later he wrote a decidedly upbeat letter to Napoleon reporting on his initial impressions. He had hoisted his flag in 'the superb vessel, the *Vengeur*'. In the following days he had inspected all the vessels and in general found them in good order and in the beset condition possible. It was, he said, his intention to organise a squadron to operate in the Iroise, since it was impossible to exercise the ships in the restricted waters of Brest Roads without exposing the ships of the line to danger. On the other hand, this was not the case in the bays of Bertheaume, Camaret and St Mathieu.[13] By 21 June, however, some of the less satisfactory aspects of his command had become apparent to him, as he explained in a further letter to the Emperor. He was, he said, short of 2,800 seamen, and needed to replace another 1,069 who were sick, while 400-500 more were hopelessly unfit and quite useless. What were needed were at least 4,000 hardy conscripts that he would be able to train; with these he would answer for the organisation of his fleet.[14]

In February Nelson was at last authorised to release Whitby and send him home. He wrote to Cornwallis to say that he was keeping him a little longer as his successor had not arrived:

> I have recommended Whitby to remain a short time longer in order to reap the harvest of all his toils in the *Belleisle*; he has had an uphill work in her, and I should wish him to reap the fruit of his labours alongside a Frenchman. I expect them every hour to put to sea; they have ten sail ready or nearly so. What a dreadful winter you have had, my dear friend; we must not compare our Mediterranean weather with that of the Channel.[15]

Anxious to oblige Cornwallis, Nelson sent Whitby in a frigate to Gibraltar, in spite of his repeated complaints that he did not have enough of them.

Whitby got back to London on 10 June 10 next day he wrote to Cornwallis with some very trenchant comments on the way in which Nelson was conducting his blockade of Toulon:

---

12   Parkinson, *Edward Pellew*, pp.321-322.
13   Leyland (ed.), *Blockade of Brest*, Vol.I, pp.347-348.
14   Leyland (ed.), *Blockade of Brest*, Vol.I, p.364.
15   Cornwallis-West, *Admiral Cornwallis*, p.413.

Tho' Ld Nelson is indefatigable in keeping the Sea, there are so many Reasons that make it possible for the French to escape thro' the Mediterranean, which of course the Government are not told by him, and which perhaps he does not consider, (at least I think so) that I have been long determined to warn you of the circumstance upon my Arrival, not choosing to trust it from the Mediterranean. First, then, he does not cruise upon his Rendezvous; second, I have consequently repeatedly known him for a Week to Three Weeks and even a month unfound by ships sent to reconnoitre: the *Belleisle* herself was a week; thirdly, he is occasionally obliged to take the whole squadron in to water, a great distance from Toulon; fourthly, since I came away the French Squadron got out in his Absence, and cruised off Toulon several days, and at last when he came out, he only got sight of them at a great Distance to see them cruise at their own Harbour. From all this I draw one general Conclusion that it is very possible for them to escape him.[16]

He went on to say that if they had so chosen, the French could have got to the West Indies without discovery; if the Toulon fleet relieved Cadiz, Ferrol and Rochefort en route to Brest they would have forty one ships of the line, 'and if on their way to Brest you meet them some morning, when they are attempting a great junction, I shall not be surprised'. He added that he would not dare give his opinion on the Mediterranean blockade to anyone else, 'for doubtless my Ld Nelson is actuated by a thorough zeal to do right, for he is indeed a great and glorious Officer'. The contrast between the blockade of Toulon and that of Brest is obvious; above all things, Nelson wanted to lure the French out, while Cornwallis was doing all he could to keep them in.

Whitby's speculations about what the French might do were of course not far wide of the mark. Nelson's view, however, was firmly inclined to believe that if the French did get out of Toulon it would be Egypt that was their destination, and this was always to colour his thinking. Napoleon, meanwhile, had been writing to Latouche-Tréville at Toulon to keep him au fait with his ideas. In a letter of 2 July he showed that he had a comprehensive grasp of the force that might be available to be assembled, if his combinations came off, as well as the strength of the British opposing them. He gave the admiral an account of the invasion fleet itself, and of the army it was to carry. The letter ended by stressing the importance of carrying out the operation before the onset of winter, observing that even if Latouche-Tréville sailed before 30 July, it was probable that he would not arrive off Boulogne before September. By then the nights would be getting longer, but it was to be hoped that the weather would not be bad for lengthy periods. However, Latouche-Tréville did not put to sea; and he died on 19 August aboard his flagship,

16 Cornwallis-West, *Admiral Cornwallis*, pp.409-410.

the *Bucentaure*. On 28 August, writing to Decrés, Napoleon suggested that the choice of Latouche-Tréville's successor should lie between Bruix, Villeneuve and Rosily.[17]

Cornwallis and Melville knew each other quite well, the latter having been Treasurer of the Navy in a previous administration, and the new First Lord soon adopted Spencer's practice of writing many important letters to the Commander-in-Chief personally; he encouraged Cornwallis also to write privately to him whenever he wanted. By mid-July there seemed to be some indication that at Brest there was in preparation an expedition involving nine or ten ships of the line, and it seemed very unlikely to the First Lord that such a small force could be intended to try conclusions with the Channel Fleet. It appeared to him, as he wrote to Cornwallis on 14 July, that the force might be intended for an attack either in the West Indies or upon the Cape of Good Hope. Alternatively, perhaps it was planned to fall upon the blockading squadrons off Rochefort and Ferrol, overcoming them by strength of numbers, and then, after releasing the French ships held there, proceed to the Mediterranean, where their combined forces would then be substantially superior to Nelson. Or, perhaps, they would proceed directly to the Mediterranean. Melville added:

> I am aware that all these Speculations proceed on the supposition of their escaping your Blockade, which I believe to be very difficult; but there are so many Examples of their having on former occasions succeeded in so doing, that it would be indulging an over Confidence to calculate upon this chance as altogether impossible under various Contingencies.[18]

Cornwallis, whose flagship *Ville de Paris* needed to come in for a refit, was about to go on leave, and his instructions to Sir Charles Cotton, his second in command, reflected the possibilities that Melville had contemplated:

> Should any circumstance or accident occasion the French Squadron to escape without being observed by the squadron with you, or the ships cruising closer to the mouth of the harbour, you are not to follow them, unless you can be very sure of the route they have taken, or leave the mouth of the Channel unguarded, as the enemy might in that case take the opportunity to push up the Channel for the purpose of aiding the threatened invasion of His Majesty's dominions, the protecting of which at this particular time being the principal object of the force under my command.[19]

17   Leyland (ed.), *Blockade of Brest*, Vol.I, p.362.
18   Leyland (ed.), *Blockade of Brest*, Vol.I, p.367-368.
19   Leyland (ed.), *Blockade of Brest*, Vol.I, pp.368-369.

The scale of the responsibilities which Cotton temporarily inherited was enormous. As has been noted, Cornwallis pursued a rather more relaxed policy in the station he took up off Brest than St Vincent. It is, though, not really correct, as John Leyland observed, that his blockade of Brest 'did not differ essentially from that of Nelson at Toulon'. It was necessary to watch the port much more closely; this being the purpose, the French were certainly not being encouraged to come out and fight, which was the way Nelson approached the matter. Leyland reviewed the scope of Cornwallis's duties, remarking that in the collection of papers dealing with the blockade was the 'evidence of how close was the watch he held upon the French:'

> It will be seen, even in this selection, with what vigilance he was ready for every emergency and prepared for each contingency; how he kept to his rendezvous in the teeth of tremendous gales until endurance would have been danger, and he then bore up for the shelter of Torbay; how he varied and strengthened, as the need arose, the watch upon Lorient, Rochefort and Ferrol; how he arranged for the safety of the homeward bound trade; what was his system of sending in ships to refit and replenish; how generously he supported his officers and praised them for their exertions and achievements, and how little he said of himself.[20]

During his period of leave Cornwallis took the opportunity to discuss with the First Lord a scheme for the destruction of the French fleet in Brest which had been devised by Captain Peter Puget of the *Foudroyant*. Puget had discussed the plan with Captain Patrick Campbell, of the *Doris*, as well as a number of lieutenants, before presenting it to Cornwallis on 23 June. He proposed an attack by fireships – ten brigs of 100-130 tons and three sloops of 50-60 tons, the brigs to go into Brest and the sloops into Camaret Bay. The force would not require a great deal of manpower, all of whom would be volunteers. Led by two captains, it would comprise ten lieutenants, ten master's mates, ten midshipmen and one hundred seamen to man the brigs, with three lieutenants, three midshipmen and eighteen seamen in the brigs. Puget planned to attack at night, in the last quarter of the flood tide, covered by the frigates of the inshore squadron which would anchor off the mouth of the Goulet. In Brest Water, the brigs should be divided into two divisions, one to attack the northern part of the French fleet and one the southern. Puget was confident of success, writing:

> There certainly appears, at the first glance, something like desperation in the attempt, but, when it is considered that our plans have the advantage of arrangement, and the enemy off his guard, we may presume that the

---

20   Leyland (ed.), *Blockade of Brest*, Vol.I, p.xli.

boldness of the measure I propose, its sudden operation, and the certain confusion and consternation it would produce, will induce success to this enterprise.[21]

Puget proposed that he should lead the first division and Campbell the second, and that the lieutenants whom he had consulted should also take part. Secrecy was, he emphasised, of crucial importance if surprise was to be achieved; without that, the prospect of success would be hugely reduced. Melville was enthusiastic, telling Cornwallis that if successful 'it would certainly rebound much to the splendour of the British navy and its enterprising officers, and the means pointed out for the attempt are certainly on a moderate scale'. While disowning his technical ability to make a judgment on the scheme, it was his impression 'that very bold and daring enterprises' generally succeeded. In his discussions with Cornwallis, however, they concluded that the overall command of the operation should be entrusted to the very experienced Captain Charles Brisbane, which certainly was a great disappointment to Puget and his friends, who nevertheless continued to be enthusiastic about the scheme.[22]

Brisbane somewhat revised the scheme, providing for rather larger fireships, which were to attack in three divisions, approaching in line ahead before entering the Goulet, when they would approach the French fleet in line abreast. In the instructions which he prepared, he insisted that in the event of any fireship being disabled by enemy fire so that it could not close with the French fleet, it was not to be set on fire, but was to wait until some of the enemy ships were on fire. If the boats of the fireship squadron were unable to retreat through the Goulet, their crews would come ashore and cross the neck of land separating Brest Roads from Douarnenez Bay, where a frigate would be waiting. It was, he wrote, his positive order that the brigs should not be set on fire until absolutely grappled with their target.

Unfortunately, a series of delays meant that the operation had to be put off more than once. Melville was extremely angry about this, telling Young, the Port Admiral at Plymouth, that he was 'satisfied there were unnecessary delays in more quarters than one'.[23] He had also consulted his naval colleagues on the Board, led by Gambier, from whom he received an entirely negative opinion about the project, which he communicated to Cornwallis. This obliged the latter to convey the fact to Brisbane, to whom he wrote on 17 September:

Lord Melville, in his last letter, tells me he had mentioned the intended secret service to the sea officers at the Board, and from them he has received

21 Leyland (ed.), *Blockade of Brest*, Vol.II, pp.2-8.
22 Leyland (ed.), *Blockade of Brest*, Vol.II, p.xv.
23 Leyland (ed.), *Blockade of Brest*, Vol.II, pp.23-24.

no encouragement to persevere. They concur in thinking the enemy must be supine beyond example, and totally negligent of the common vigilance which the commander of a fleet etc etc, and that it gives the most remote chance of success.[24]

In the face of this timorous advice, Cornwallis was in grave doubt as to whether the operation should proceed; and by the end of the month he decided to abort it, sending the intended fireships to the Downs to join the forces there commanded by Lord Keith. One of his reasons for doing so was the vexed issue of who should command the fireships, since replacing the officers in command of them when they joined the Channel Fleet by those who had been involved in the project from the start would cause great offence. Melville, when he heard this suggestion, dismissed it out of hand, as 'a matter certainly not to be put in competition with the execution of so important and brilliant a service'. Nor did the First Lord think that the opinion of the naval members of the Board should have been decisive; it was a decision for Cornwallis and those involved in the operation.[25] Cornwallis reacted firmly, saying that removing from the command of the fireships officers who had all declared themselves ready to undertake the operation would have been disgusting to the service. In any case, the delays in carrying it out had materially affected the chance of success, as the French had changed their position.

Although at first he contemplated proceeding without revealing the views of the Board, it is hardly surprising that on further consideration Cornwallis, with Brisbane, Puget and Campbell, was no longer so willing to risk his men on so dangerous an enterprise.[26] It was a disappointing conclusion to a project that might have had a far reaching success, but it did not prevent Puget from subsequently putting forward a further scheme, for a closer blockade, with fireships always in readiness.

Apparently at the time unaware of the fireship scheme, Graves, commanding the inshore squadron, had put forward to Cotton just before Cornwallis returned from leave, another proposal for an attack on the French fleet in Brest, writing:

> I am so much convinced of the practicability of destroying the Arsenal of Brest; and of either Capturing or destroying the whole of their Ships at that port; that I cannot resist offering you my ideas on the subject of such great importance; which are, to land Five or Six Thousand Men to the Southward of Brest, and at the same time, to permit with Eight or Ten Sail of the Line to Enter the Harbour – by which means I am persuaded

24   Leyland (ed.), *Blockade of Brest*, Vol.II, p.25.
25   Leyland (ed.), *Blockade of Brest*, Vol.II, pp.27-28.
26   Cornwallis-West, *Admiral Cornwallis*, p.441.

we shall do the business effectually without much loss, as I do not think their Ships will be prepared for such an attack.[27]

It was not greatly different from schemes that had been considered during the previous war. Melville, when Cornwallis forwarded the suggestion to him, was doubtful, observing that it would be 'attended with many difficulties,' and did not accord with the intelligence presently available.

27   Cornwallis-West, *Admiral Cornwallis*, p.436.

22

Prelude to Trafalgar

During his period of leave Cornwallis also had the opportunity to review extensively the existing situation, not only in respect of the blockade of Brest itself but also on those other strategic considerations that must be taken into account. In the course of discussions with the First Lord, they identified the principles on which the blockade was to be conducted, and the action to be taken in various eventualities. In these discussions Melville was assisted by Sir Charles Middleton, who had become his confidential adviser when he assumed office and who, as Lord Barham, was in the following year to succeed him at the Admiralty.

These discussions culminated in the issue to Cornwallis of secret orders dated 24 August, which were a comprehensive statement of the way in which the blockade was to be conducted, and the action to be taken in the event of the escape from Brest of all or part of the French fleet. These orders were dated the day after he returned to the Channel Fleet from his leave, and upon these he based the instructions which he issued to Calder, off Rochefort, and Cochrane, off Ferrol, on 3 September; and on the following day to Captain Rathbone, who was to cruise off the Passage du Raz. So significant are they that it is useful to set out in full the abstract which Cornwallis made of the secret orders which he had received:

> Enemy supposed about to take advantage of some favourable opportunity, and if sail without considerable number of forces, probably meant to cover a descent on the coast of England.
>
> Watch motions of the enemy closely to collect intelligence to ascertain their real object in order to frustrate, and they probably attempt to mislead us.
>
> If, by stress of weather, or other cause, they escape – must act according to the best of judgement. If intelligence should lead to belief their course is for England or Ireland, go off the Lizard until you can learn if they have passed up Channel. If not, proceed off Cape Clear or other post according to information. If you cannot discover their route, continue upon your rendezvous, or return off Brest. Employ small vessels, etc., to look out. If a part only sail, with a considerable body of troops, then Ireland probably

the object: detach an adequate part instead of going with the whole. If they proceed out in detachments, without any considerable body of troops, to the southward – may have some other destination than [England] or Ireland – Mediterranean; if five or six of the line full of troops, probably Leeward Islands. Send a detachment, who are to endeavour to discover their destination and pursue; but if they cannot, they are to return to their station. If with whole, or part, object may be blockading squadrons. Calder and Cochrane to form a junction, N. part of coast of Spain or elsewhere, to inform them of the fleet or squadron having left port; not to quit their station but from appearance of superior force or stress of weather; to form a junction, if the enemy continue in those parts, then return. Inform Admiral and Lord Gardner.

Watch Passage du Raz; the frigates and sloops or cutters to the southward. Blow strongly from west, etc. Lastly [incomplete].

Two frigates and two sloops or cutters to the southward of the Passage du Raz, close to it, with instructions to commanders to give earliest intelligence to me, to Vice-Admiral Calder and Rear-Admiral Cochrane in case of the enemy's passing that way; a small vessel or two to be kept well up between Toulinguet Pass and Passage de Raz.

If it should blow hard from westward: reduced to topsail, not to risk damaging the ships by contending, and, but bear up – advanced squadron also, should the gale increase so as to make it necessary. Frigates and small vessels to resort to most western anchorages. The whole to return to their stations the moment the weather becomes favourable for that purpose.

To keep the squadron victualled to five months and stored the same: to send them in succession to Cawsand Bay for that purpose, and to inform Vice Admiral Young at Plymouth of such supplies as you may require, from time to time, that he may give directions to the agents for victualling. These to send them to you when the weather is favourable for receiving supplies at sea. If anything should occur to which these are not applicable, to act at discretion, informing the Commander-in-Chief for the information of their Lordships.[1]

Julian Corbett, in his study of the Trafalgar campaign, regarded these instructions to Cornwallis as being of the greatest importance, since they were the fruit of the crucial discussions between the admiral, the First Lord, and Middleton:

They therefore may be taken as the highest expression of the living strategical tradition as it existed after the great maritime wars of the eighteenth century, and as such they deserve the most deferential study. Over

---

1   Leyland (ed.), *Blockade of Brest*, Vol.II, pp.48-50.

and above the strategical exposition, it will be observed that they afford a characteristic example of the extent to which the Admiralty was accustomed to control the action of admirals in home waters, and that they also reveal how little the Board regarded the invasion as a serious danger.[2]

While Cornwallis was away on leave, Cotton had been having an anxious time of it. Graves, in command of the inshore squadron, was firmly convinced that the French would attempt to leave Brest at the first opportunity, while Calder was concerned that he had insufficient forces under his command to deal with any operation which involved French squadrons at both Brest and Rochefort. He wrote to Cotton on 10 August:

> It will be absolutely necessary for me to keep the squadron under my orders further out in the offing than I otherwise could wish to do for the watching the enemy here, otherwise I might be caught between this squadron from Brest and that at Rochefort; when, if the wind should be to the westward, it would be impossible for me to get out clear of the land. I shall therefore keep this squadron for the present plying between Baleines Lighthouse and the Isle Dieu. I must beg leave to repeat that it is now become absolutely necessary to have one or two line of battle ships added to this squadron, with two frigates and a cutter, besides the *Hawk*, who I should hope to be on her passage to rejoin me.[3]

He saw clear signs that the Rochefort squadron, now comprising six ships of the line, five frigates and two corvettes, was indeed planning a joint operation with a squadron from Brest. Cotton accepted the need for Calder's reinforcement and sent the *Warrior*, 74, and *Acasta*, 40, to join him.

As summer gave way to autumn, Melville and the Board became increasingly convinced that the French were planning a descent on the coast of Ireland. The First Lord wrote privately to Cornwallis on 17 October to set out his thinking on the subject. Recent agitation in Ireland had suggested that some assurances of support had been received from France:

> You probably will be likely to know sooner than any person when there are any appearances in Brest harbour indicative of any effort to get from thence. But, indeed, independent of any intelligence, I never had had a doubt that, if an attempt seriously to invade the King's dominions at home is meant to be made, the object must be Ireland... I have resolved to make a great exertion to afford them an additional naval protection. As

---

2   Julian S. Corbett, *The Campaign of Trafalgar* (London: Longmans, Green, 1910), p.15.
3   Leyland (ed.), *Blockade of Brest*, Vol.II, pp.41-42.

> Brest is the place to be chiefly watched, I remain in the opinion I formerly
> conveyed to you that, exclusive of the blockades of Rochefort and Ferrol,
> you must never have less than a blockading force of sixteen sail of the line
> under our immediate command for watching the movements of the Brest
> fleet.[4]

What he wanted was to have ten or twelve ships of the line under Gardner, based
on Cork; this might be achievable if the Spanish preparations for what was coming
to seem an inevitable declaration of war were not speeded up. With such a force in
place, in addition to the ships under Cornwallis's command, Melville thought 'an
attempt to invade Ireland must be a very desperate undertaking, and can only end,
if attempted, in the ruin and discomfiture of their fleet'.

A month later intelligence received by d'Auvergne suggested that the Irish operation might indeed be imminent, as he reported to the Admiralty:

> Information has reached me from Brest, of the 14th inst. that nine sail
> of the line, some frigates, and store ships, particularly destined for an
> early expedition, had received on board from 20,000 to 24,000 men (*de
> toutes armes*); the storeships, a large proportion of entrenching tools, and
> chests of spare army clothing, accoutrements, and money; which from
> all circumstances my correspondents, could collect, are destined for
> Ireland. The Irish Legion, commanded by a divisionary general (the rebel
> O'Connor) is among the troops embarked.[5]

A few days later d'Auvergne corrected the report to say that the troops embarked
were from 10,000 – 14,000, the error being due to 'our hasty reading of the cipher,
confused in the washing of the sympathetic ink'.

That the principal responsibility for the defence of Ireland was acknowledged to
fall to the Channel Fleet underlines the fact that its function extended well beyond
the mere blockade of Brest. Corbett pointed out Napoleon's misunderstanding of
its strategic functions, which were no different from those of the Western Squadron
over half a century earlier:

> Napoleon regarded it, as many do to this day, as a squadron blockading
> Brest, whereas it was in reality a squadron holding the approaches to the
> Channel for all purposes of home and trade defence. The blockade of
> Brest was incidental, as were the blockades of Rochefort and Ferrol, and in
> no circumstances of reasonable war risk could a serious hostile squadron
> enter or even approach the Channel until the Western Squadron had been

---

4   Leyland (ed.), *Blockade of Brest*, Vol.II, pp.95-96.
5   Leyland (ed.), *Blockade of Brest*, Vol.II, pp.131-132.

brought to action and defeated. The mere confronting of that squadron with superior force had been found useless over and over again.[6]

It was on this appreciation of the correct role of the Channel Fleet that the detailed instructions to Cornwallis were based.

Napoleon was finding it necessary to spend a lot of time keeping his admirals up to the mark. Not the least of his concerns was that, remaining in harbour, his fleets lacked the training and preparation necessary if they were to take on opponents who had the benefit of prolonged and demanding experience of ship handling. It was a subject he addressed in a letter to Ganteaume on 6 September, intended to encourage him to prepare for a sortie. He had, he wrote, given orders that the shortage of 1,273 men, of which Ganteaume complained, to be made good. With 21 ships of the line, he hoped that something could be achieved. Ganteaume's movement on 24 July had 'struck terror into the English. They know well that having all the oceans to defend, a squadron that escaped from Brest would be able to inflict incalculable damage'. He went on to discuss the effect of landing 16,000 men and 500 horses in Ireland, 'which would be fatal to our enemies'.[7] As for the training of the fleet, he observed:

> I perfectly understand that a sortie such as you made requires weather conditions that are not always present; but I do not understand why your ships do not come out every day into the roads. What sort of danger is there in that? The *mirliflores* of the squadron may laugh and mock these large movements; nonetheless, by these continual exercises you will give your squadron both confidence and a precious experience.[8]

He continued in this vein, showing a considerable understanding of naval matters – or sufficient, at any rate, to convince himself that, when he came to issue operational orders, he could unhesitatingly override the opinions of his naval advisers.

The Irish venture had been sidelined in the spring of 1804, but as his letter to Ganteaume, and another of the same date to Decrés showed, it was now back on the table as a live proposition. Ganteaume reported on 14 September to Decrés that the army would be ready in ten days, but there was difficulty organising the transports due to the lack of seamen available. Decrés asked Napoleon to make good this lack by demobilising part of the invasion flotilla, to which he got a favourable response. Napoleon's plans for the operation were outlined in a detailed letter to Decrés of 29 September. He had come to the conclusion that the best point for a landing would be in the north of Ireland, at Lough Swilly. Having landed the

6   Corbett, *Campaign of Trafalgar*, p.12.
7   Leyland (ed.), *Blockade of Brest*, Vol.II, p.60.
8   Leyland (ed.), *Blockade of Brest*, Vol.II, p.60.

troops, Ganteaume was to return; not to Brest, but to Cherbourg, where he would receive news of the preparedness of the invasion flotilla at Boulogne; if, arriving there, he encountered contrary winds, he was to go on to the Texel to pick up seven Dutch ships of the line and embark 25,000 men, and take them to Ireland. 'One of these operations must succeed; and then whether we have 30 – 40,000 men in Ireland, or whether I am in England and eighteen thousand in Ireland, victory is ours'.[9] Prior to this the Toulon fleet under Villeneuve would put to sea and, leaving the Mediterranean, head for the West Indies, while Missiessy with the Rochefort squadron sailed to Martinique, took St Lucia and Dominica and then joined Villeneuve for an operation against Surinam.

Meanwhile relations between Britain and Spain were rapidly deteriorating, as Napoleon increased the pressure on Madrid to enter the war. Cochrane, off Ferrol, reported the arrival of French troops there, with more on the way; he estimated that within a month the Spanish could have six ships of the line ready for war at Ferrol, which with the five French gave them eleven ships of the line:

> The finances of this country are low. They only wait the arrival of frigates with treasure to put on a different countenance. I cannot conceive that Spain, even if at war with America, could require so many line-of-battle ships, for similar orders are given at Cadiz and Cartagena.[10]

The preparation of the Spanish ships corresponding with that of the French squadron tended, he thought, to show that 'they have some united object in view'.

The imminent arrival from the New World of four frigates carrying treasure was well known. For the British government it posed a serious problem; war with Spain seemed likely, but it had not yet broken out, and a pre-emptive strike at the treasure fleet would be a clear breach of international law. The government did not hesitate for long; on 22 September Cornwallis gave sealed orders to Captain Moore of the *Indefatigable* to head to Cadiz to intercept the treasure ships, picking up such other vessels as he could find. Moore reached Cadiz a week later; next day he was joined by the *Medusa*, which he sent off to pick up the *Amphion*, in the Straits; on October 2 he was joined by the *Lively* and on 3 October by the *Medusa* and *Amphion*.

Moore did not have long to wait; on 5 October the treasure fleet was sighted; it consisted of four frigates. Moore sent an officer to Rear Admiral Bustamente, its commander, to tell him that he had orders to detain the fleet and that if bloodshed was to be avoided, Bustamente must make up his mind at once. This attempt at a peaceful resolution failed; after warning shots were fired, the second astern of the Spanish squadron opened fire on the *Amphion*, and a fierce battle was joined.

---

9   Leyland (ed.), *Blockade of Brest*, Vol.II, pp.82-84.
10 Leyland (ed.), *Blockade of Brest*, Vol.II, pp.64-65.

In the course of this the frigate *Mercedes* blew up, and the other three frigates were captured. On 18 October Melville wrote to Cornwallis to tell him that the proposed detachment of a squadron of five ships from the Channel Fleet to join Gardner at Berehaven would not now take place; although he did not think that the Spanish were yet ready to undertake any offensive operations, 'The safest side to err upon is to be on our guard, for the Spaniards will be angry, and will make every exertion'.[11]

Spain had, of course, every reason to be very angry indeed; Moore's action was wholly illegitimate. Mahan justified it thus:

> The seizure of the treasure ships is less easily excused, though the obloquy attending it has been unduly heightened by the tragic explosion. Its best palliation lies in Great Britain's previous experience that, in the commercial decadence and poverty of Spain, the treasures of the colonies were a determining factor in the negotiations. While they were on the sea, Spain temporised; when they arrived, she stiffened.[12]

The Board of Admiralty had been again reviewing the conduct of the blockade of Brest, and Melville wrote to Cornwallis on 10 October to convey their opinion on the practice of using ships of the line as part of the inshore squadron, of which they disapproved. Melville explained this to the Commander-in-Chief somewhat diffidently:

> The ground of their opinion is that when you are at Torbay, or when you are at a great distance from Brest with the great body of your fleet, the inshore squadron can only be of use to watch the enemy, and not to fight them, and therefore smaller ships are equally available for that purpose as large ones, and far preferable, insofar as they are not liable to receive the same damage as the large ships are. I did not pretend to have any opinion different from my naval colleagues on such a subject, but, before I give my concurrence to send it out as an official order, I wish to know what are your sentiments on the subject.[13]

The purpose of keeping some ships of the line with the inshore squadron was of course not merely to watch the enemy, which a couple of frigates could do perfectly well, but to have a force sufficient to deal with the attempted escape of a detachment of the Brest fleet.

---

11 Leyland (ed.), *Blockade of Brest*, Vol.II, p.97.
12 Mahan, *Sea Power*, Vol.II, pp.138-139.
13 Cornwallis-West, *Admiral Cornwallis*, p.455.

The suggestion was one which Cornwallis was prepared to accept, although his acquiescence related only to the winter months. Smaller ships would, without ships of the line to support them, be driven away. A more serious concern was the question of dividing the blockading fleet, which had been put forward as a reason for keeping the ships of the line concentrated. Cornwallis remarked that during the previous winter he had found the inshore ships operating further from Brest than the main fleet; he reckoned that the commander of the inshore squadron 'should have a particular turn for that kind of service'.[14]

Melville's letter of 18 October, telling him that the proposed detachment of five ships of the line to Gardner had been cancelled, had crossed with one from Cornwallis pointing out the extreme danger of weakening the blockade by the detachment of the five ships, and it brought from the First Lord an important statement of policy dated 2 November. He was careful to reassure the Commander-in-Chief that his views would be listened to but went on to explain that the difficulty of complying with his wishes arose simply from a lack of the means to do so. It was necessary, he said, to make the most of the ships available 'by a judicious arrangement and distribution of our force' until it was possible to bring forward additional ships. For this reason he could not hold out any hope of maintaining the Channel Fleet at a constant strength of more than sixteen ships of the line. To keep up that number required several more to cover for accidents and for ships refitting. He went on to deal with Cornwallis's concern about keeping up a close blockade:

> I observe what you state relative to the policy of relaxing the strictness of Blockade formerly resorted to. I admit the *Chances* of what you state, but, on the other hand, I cannot shut my eyes against the *Certainty* of what we must all experimentally know, that you have not the means of sustaining the necessary extent of Naval Force, if your ships are to be torn to pieces by an eternal conflict with the elements during the tempestuous months of winter, and allow me to remind you that the occasions when we have been able to bring our Enemy to Battle and our Fleets to Victory have generally been when we were at a distance from the Blockading Station. I am perfectly aware of the peculiar situation of Ireland, and how much it requires to be specially attended to, but I believe it cannot be better done than by helping your Fleet in a sound and effective Condition, appropriating (exclusive of the Fleet stationed off Brest) at the same time a separate force for the protection of Ireland, to guard against the chance of an invading force under a detachment from the fleet in Brest Harbour, making an abrupt departure from Brest during the time the Fleet under your command is obliged from weather to leave the Blockading Station.

---

14 Leyland (ed.), *Blockade of Brest*, Vol.II, pp.94-95.

As to the state of the French fleet in point of manning it is a point certainly incapable of being precisely ascertained, but I am led to believe it is inadequately manned from various circumstances. In the first place, although the French got back at the Peace a great number of their Seamen, they have since had very little commerce and without that source to feed it there will always be infinite difficulty to furnish the supply of Seamen to any Fleet. Secondly, it must be recollected that those immense flotillas to which they have turned so much of their attention must exhaust the great body of their Seamen. And, lastly, I understood, by the Reports which came from your own fleet, that when, in the course of the summer, ten or twelve of the French fleet came down Brest water, apparently with a view to sailing, they were obliged to man that detachment of their Fleet by taking a considerable portion of the Men from the remaining Ships.[15]

Concerns about the exposure of the fleet to damage from the autumn and winter gales led Melville to raise once again the old chestnut of the possible use of Douarnenez Bay. Captain Hurd had been commissioned to make a survey of the Bay of Brest, and Melville was sufficiently impressed with his conclusions to write to Cornwallis:

I have given the subject the most mature consideration, and have determined to send Captain Hurd to you with as little delay as possible, in order that you may send him, with such other officer or officers as you may think proper, into the Bay for the purpose of ascertaining, beyond all doubt, whether the opinion is correct which he entertains of that anchorage being sufficiently commodious and secure for the fleet under your command in every contingency.[16]

Melville thought Cornwallis should take the earliest opportunity of going into Douarnenez Bay to see for himself. He also urged him to consider Hurd's recommendation that the islands of Ushant and Moléne should be occupied; this, not least, would deny the French those vantage points from which to observe the movements of the Channel Fleet, as well as providing an anchorage for part at least of the fleet. In addition of course, they would provide lookout points which would improve the observation of the French fleet.

Hurd unequivocally recommended the use of Dounarnenez Bay as offering 'better anchorage and security against all winds and weather than either Cawsand Bay or Torbay,' while the ships could anchor out of range of the French artillery and could closely observe the Passage du Four. Cornwallis, however, as Bridport

---

15   Cornwallis-West, *Admiral Cornwallis*, pp.454-455.
16   Leyland (ed.), *Blockade of Brest*, Vol.II, pp.104-113.

had done a decade earlier, firmly rejected the proposal. In particular he was absolutely opposed to Hurd's conclusion that while the French fleet could not move with the wind blowing from the west, with a wind favourable to their leaving port it was perfectly practicable for the British fleet to keep a position close in with Brest, either by anchoring or keeping under way close in with the land. Cornwallis scornfully observed that some of the bravest captains in the previous war got into three deckers to avoid serving in the inshore squadron in such a position. Would Captain Hurd, he asked rhetorically, 'place the whole squadron, chiefly composed of three deckers, in such an alarming situation?'[17]

It was not long before Cornwallis had a drastic illustration of the dangers to which his ships were subject. On 25 November Captain Thomas Byam Martin, of the *Impétueux,* had to report the total loss of the *Venerable*, 74, off Paignton. She had gone aground and Martin had hopes to be able to get her off, but she became a total wreck. The first that Cornwallis knew about it was when on 25 November, after he had gone to sea, he was surprised to discover that four of his ships were missing. The *Britannia* turned up next day; but the *Impétueux* and *Goliath* had stayed to effect rescue operations around the stricken *Venerable*. Reporting to the Admiralty, Cornwallis explained that for all its virtues as a convenient anchorage for the Channel Fleet, Torbay was not without its problems, which were yet another instance of the risks of the blockade:

> It is well known when the wind comes to the eastward a great sea heaves into the bay, and it is difficult for the ships to get their anchor. On that account, as well as to get to our station, as soon as possible, which with all our expedition must be long after the enemy have an opportunity of getting to sea. If Torbay is to be considered as a harbour, and the ships are not constantly kept in a state for sea, upon a change of wind they are in greater danger, in that bay open to so many points of the compass, than if they were moored, and prepared to ride a gale out, by making a snug ship, which was the mode three years ago when we remained at that anchorage from 1st November 1801 to the end of April following. We were particularly fortunate during the time, for had it blown home from east southeast to south, I apprehend most of the ships would have been lost.[18]

Meanwhile Collingwood was watching Rochefort, where it was evident that preparations for getting a French squadron to sea were continuing. He was not very optimistic about his ability to prevent the French escaping, as he wrote to his father-in-law on 4 November:

17   Leyland (ed.), *Blockade of Brest*, Vol.II, pp.122-124.
18   Leyland (ed.), *Blockade of Brest*, Vol.II, pp.133-135.

I am here watching the French squadron in Rochefort, but feel that it is not practicable to prevent their sailing if it be their intention, and yet, if they should get past me, I should be exceedingly mortified. At this moment, and for two days past, it has blown a hard gale of easterly wind, and we are driven thirty leagues from the port. The only thing that can prevent their sailing is the apprehension that they may run amongst us, as they cannot exactly know where we are, to avoid us.[19]

Writing later in the mouth to Cornwallis to report that there had been no significant change in the situation of the French, Collingwood described another problem faced by the blockaders. Aboard his flagship *Dreadnought*, 98, there was very little serviceable gunpowder in the ship due to the damp state of her magazines; the damp 'dissolves the nitre of the powder to such an extent that every 3 or 4 days they have to remove the puddle it makes on the floor, and in the drawers under the racks'.[20]

Collingwood was succeeded by Graves in command of the squadron off Rochefort, and it was on the latter's watch that Missiessy attempted his escape from the port in accordance with Napoleon's urgent instructions. Early in January 1805 Graves took his squadron into Quiberon Bay to water, leaving Captain Patrick Campbell in the frigate *Doris* to keep watch. On 8 January Campbell went close inshore and found Missiessy engaged in embarking troops and taking on stores, evidently for an imminent expedition. Hurrying out, Campbell met the schooner *Felix*, from which he learned that the squadron was in Quiberon Bay, and he sailed north to report, leaving the *Felix* to keep an eye on Missiessy. The latter's preparations were completed by 11 January, and that afternoon the French admiral sailed in thick weather and snow, aiming to avoid the blockaders in the night. Next morning, however, the *Felix* spotted him, and followed as he headed north in an increasing south westerly wind, until as night fell, turning to report to Graves at Quiberon Bay.

Meanwhile Campbell had run into difficulty, suffering severe storm damage to the *Doris's* rigging. He, too, had sighted Missiessy; but when he got into Quiberon Bay he found that Graves had sailed and was southwest of Belleisle. As the gale increased, he became desperate to warn Graves, for if once he took shelter in the bay he would not get out again until the wind changed. The *Doris*, however, was in a very bad state; severe leaks had appeared, necessitating constant pumping, and after two days of struggle it was clear that she could not survive. The *Felix* took off her crew; on 16 January Graves reappeared, to be told that the French were out, but he was unable to turn back in the face of the furious gale, and could not weather Belleisle. Graves was obliged once again to seek sanctuary in Quiberon

19   Leyland (ed.), *Blockade of Brest*, Vol.II, p.120.
20   Leyland (ed.), *Blockade of Brest*, Vol.II, p.128.

Bay, from where he reported to Cornwallis. He thought that the French, if they had not appeared off Brest, must have returned to Rochefort.[21]

In this, Graves was wrong. Missiessy, in spite of his squadron also suffering severely in the dreadful weather, had got clean away. Once out of the Bay of Biscay he set course for the West Indies in accordance with his instructions, and thereby initiated the complex and long drawn out campaign that was to culminate off Cape Trafalgar in October. Much, though, was to happen before then.

21   Corbett, *Campaign of Trafalgar*, pp.27-29.

23

Barham

With a Spanish declaration of war obviously imminent, Pitt was concerned to strengthen the forces watching the principal bases of their fleet and he approved the creation of an additional command, operating off Cadiz but covering the sector from the straits of Gibraltar as far north as Finisterre. Beyond this, the responsibility remained with Cornwallis; the squadron off Ferrol would remain part of the Channel Fleet. What was surprising about this decision, however, was the choice of commander of this force. In 1799 Vice Admiral Sir John Orde had become involved in a violent quarrel with St Vincent over what he considered to be the unjust treatment of his officers. The dispute escalated; St Vincent relieved him of his command in the Mediterranean Fleet and Orde demanded a court martial. When this was refused he grotesquely attempted to restore his reputation by challenging St Vincent to a duel – a challenge which the King forbade St Vincent to accept – and he was never again employed at sea, either while Spencer was at the Admiralty or during St Vincent's term of office there. After Pitt returned to power, and Melville became First Lord, Orde wrote to the Admiralty in May 1803 offering his services, but the offer was not taken up. Now, however, having been promoted to vice admiral of the red on 19 October 1804, he was appointed to the command of the squadron off Cadiz.[1]

Melville had had his doubts about appointing Orde to the Channel Fleet, and took the precaution of writing to Cornwallis on the subject soon after Orde had applied for employment:

> You are no stranger to the terms on which Sir John Orde was with Lord St Vincent. He is naturally very anxious to get into employment now that Lord St Vincent is not in his way, and either by himself or his brother, Lord Boston, has made to me various propositions for that purpose. Among others he urges being put on service in the Channel Fleet, and states that

---

1   Kathrin Orth, 'Sir John Orde' in Peter Lefevre and Richard Harding (eds.), *British Admirals of the Napoleonic Wars: Contemporaries of Nelson* (London: Chatham, 2005), p.83.

Vice Admiral Sir John Orde. (Anne S.K. Brown Collection)

such an arrangement, from the habits you are upon, he is convinced, would be extremely agreeable to you. Under such circumstances people are apt to deceive themselves! I am not sure that at any rate it would be in my power to gratify him in this wish, but before I take his proposition even under consideration it is necessary as a preliminary with me to know how you feel about it.[2]

2   Cornwallis-West, *Admiral Cornwallis*, p.463.

Melville told him not to be uneasy about expressing his feelings candidly; but Cornwallis seems not to have raised any objection in principle to Orde joining the Channel Fleet.

News of Orde's appointment came as a nasty surprise to Nelson, commanding the Mediterranean Fleet. Hitherto that station had included the operational area now assigned to Orde's squadron. The latter's orders included the duty of taking possession of 'any ships laden with treasure coming from the Spanish colonies and bound to Spain'. He was then to 'send them forthwith to a British port for our further directions respecting them, taking every possible precaution to secure the treasure which may be on board them from plunder and embezzlement'.[3] Quite apart from his chagrin at the potentially huge loss of prize money which this rearrangement would cause him, Nelson was on bad terms with Orde. This derived from the latter's belief that he should have been appointed by St Vincent to command the fleet with which Nelson won the Battle of the Nile, about which he was very upset at the time. Ironically, by 1804, he had become an admirer of Nelson, and Corbett speculated that perhaps this was Melville's reason for making the appointment, which had been expressly approved by the King. He was not altogether persuaded by Nelson's frequent assertion that his discontent with Orde's command had nothing to do with prize money:

> Be that as it may, the fact that is of importance is clear – from first to last Nelson regarded Orde, with whom it was of the utmost importance that he should cooperate frankly, with a rooted suspicion that tended seriously to imperil the interests of the country.[4]

Nelson, when he learned of Orde's appointment, poured out his feelings in a letter to Marsden at the Admiralty which really leaves little reason to doubt that prize money was the key factor in his mind:

> We have an odd report that Sir John Orde has been near three weeks off Cadiz. I cannot believe it. It would be so very odd that the last Admiralty should have sent Admiral Campbell to take all my sugar from me, which he did completely, and that this Admiralty should send and take all my golden harvest from me. I begin to doubt if I have served well and rendered that state some service. Surely I must have dreamt, or the Admiralty could not have served me so. As it is, I am, I believe, a poorer man than when I left England …But nothing ever shall shake my faithful line of conduct to

3   Leyland (ed.), *Blockade of Brest*, Vol.II, p.115.
4   Corbett, *Campaign of Trafalgar*, p.31.

my king and country. If Sir John does not make haste I shall get hold of the French fleet and then he may hang himself in a golden cord.[5]

There was a touch of paranoia in Nelson's suspicions of Orde; fearful that the latter might intercept his despatches, he sent them via Captain William Parker of the *Amazon* to Lisbon, telling him to steer a course to avoid Orde's squadron.

Nelson was soon to have much more serious issues with which to concern himself. On 17 January Villeneuve, taking advantage of Nelson having left his station off Toulon a week before, put to sea with eleven ships of the line and nine frigates and brigs, with 6,300 troops under the command of General Lauriston. That evening the fleet was sighted by the frigates *Active* and *Seahorse*, which shadowed Villeneuve until 2.00 am on the following day. By that time Villeneuve was some eighty five miles south of Toulon. The two frigates hastened to locate Nelson, whom they found at 3.00 pm on 19 January anchored in Agincourt Sound in the Maddalena Islands. Taking on board the available water and stores, Nelson put to sea as soon as he could, steering eastwards, having concluded that Villeneuve's purpose was to threaten Sardinia, Sicily, the Morea or Egypt.

Nelson had, however, guessed wrong. Villeneuve had sailed with orders to proceed to the West Indies to join Missiessy there. In the event, however, his fleet suffered considerable storm damage, sufficient for him to consult Lauriston as to whether they should proceed. When the general conceded that it might be best to abort the mission Villeneuve, always excessively cautious, thankfully turned back, and was back in Toulon by 21 January, while Nelson, hoping to intercept a quarry that had got safely home, beat up and down in the waters between Sardinia, Sicily and Italy. Finding nothing, and although suspecting that Villeneuve might indeed have returned to Toulon, he felt obliged to head into the Eastern Mediterranean to assure himself that Egypt was in no danger. It was not until the end of February that Nelson finally had confirmation that the French fleet was back at its base; it was 13 March before he returned to his station off Toulon.

Napoleon received the news of Villeneuve's lacklustre performance with extreme rage; his contempt for his admirals knew no bounds, as he wrote in February:

> What is to be done with Admirals who allow their spirits to sink and determine to hasten home at the first damage they may receive?... A few topmasts carried away, some casualties in a gale of wind are everyday occurrences. Two days of fine weather ought to have cheered up the crews and put everything to rights. But the greatest evil of our Navy is that the men who command it are unused to all the risks of command.[6]

5   Quoted John Sugden, *Nelson: The Sword of Albion* (London: Bodley Head, 2012), p.723.
6   Quoted Frank McLynn, *Napoleon* (London: Jonathan Cape, 1997), p.327.

Even before Villeneuve's abortive escape, Napoleon's fertile imagination had produced another extravagant plan, this time for an attack on India, to be carried out by Ganteaume. The Brest fleet, having escaped the blockade, was to move south to pick up additional ships of the line from Lorient and Rochefort, together with 2,000 additional troops; there were to be 15,000 in all. It was then to move on to Ferrol, to pick up five French and five Spanish ships of the line, with a further 6,000 troops. From thence the whole force would sail to Mauritius, to collect another 3,000 troops. With this force Napoleon was confident that Ganteaume could 'make a terrible war on England which may bring about a final decision'.[7]

This plan went into the waste paper basket when news came that Villeneuve was back in port. Since Villeneuve, who had been intended to link up with Missiessy in the West Indies, would no longer be able to do so, the latter was ordered to operate independently and then return to France, probably to Rochefort. Villeneuve's squadron was to have 'another destination,' as yet unspecified. Napoleon accordingly turned his mind to a fresh scheme; orders went to Ganteaume on 2 March to take command of the whole of the next operation. The plan called for him to escape from Brest, attack the British squadron off Ferrol, and pick up Gourdon's Franco-Spanish fleet there. From there he was to sail to Martinique to meet Villeneuve and Missiessy. The latter's orders to return home were cancelled.

Once he had collected Villeneuve and Missiessy, which would bring his strength to 40 ships, Ganteaume was to return to Europe, to attack the Channel Fleet off Brest, and then enter the Channel. At Boulogne, he was told, he would meet Napoleon, who would give him his further instructions. Napoleon's order ended with an expression of confidence: 'In giving you the command of so important a fleet of which its operations would have so much influence on the destiny of the world, we count on your devotion, on your talents and your support for our person'.[8] Ganteaume travelled to Paris for a personal briefing with Napoleon and Decrés, which Napoleon followed up with a further letter to the admiral on 15 March, repeating his conviction of the great destinies which he held in his hands. If Ganteaume did not eschew boldness, he wrote, success was certain.

This scheme was coupled with a revival of the invasion plans. This required a lot of what had previously been done to be done all over again; the Channel ports from which the invasion flotilla was to emerge had largely been silted up, and huge dredging operations must be put in hand. Many of the vessels of the flotilla had rotted in idleness, and a large programme of refitting was necessary. For a while, as the French fleets began to embark on the strategy determined by Napoleon, the preparations continued, and by August there were no less than 2,300 vessels available to transport the Army of England.

---

7   Corbett, *Campaign of Trafalgar*, p.34.
8   Leyland (ed.), *Blockade of Brest*, Vol.II, pp.199-202.

It is usual for historians to ascribe the uninhibited audacity of Napoleon's naval schemes to a high degree of self delusion, as well as a massive ignorance of the realities of naval warfare. For some, indeed, his plans were simply crazy. Corbett, reviewing Napoleon's actual or pretended revival of his invasion strategy, wrote:

> Whether he still believed in his heart the invasion was possible we cannot tell. If he did, it can only have been by the well known trick of his gambler's mind, that every thing was possible on which he had set his desire. His star had once removed mountains; he had trusted it to make the desert flow with milk and honey, and now, perhaps, he believed it could bridge the sea. Nothing less will explain the madness of the resumed attempt.[9]

Ganteaume, at any rate, was ready to attempt the breakout from Brest by 24 March, and reported this by telegraph to Napoleon. However, he explained that there were fifteen British ships of the line in the Iroise, and it was impossible to leave without risking a battle. Napoleon replied at once: 'a naval victory in these circumstances would lead to nothing. You have only one object, and that is to carry out your mission. Leave without fighting'.[10] Cornwallis at this time had gone on leave; Gardner had been ordered to take over the command of the Channel Fleet in his absence, but since he had not put in an appearance, Cornwallis passed the temporary responsibility to Cotton, the second-in-command, sailing from Torbay to Spithead in the *Ville de Paris* on 18 March. Thus it was Cotton who was on station as Ganteaume prepared to leave, and he reported on 28 March that the Brest fleet was anchored in the Goulet.[11] By the time Gardner joined the fleet to take command on 3 April Ganteaume had withdrawn into Brest harbour, where he received news from Napoleon that Villeneuve had escaped from Toulon with eleven ships of the line, six frigates and two brigs. On 11 April Ganteaume was told that Gravina was to join Villeneuve from Cadiz with eight ships of the line and two frigates, so upon combining with these forces he would have more than 50 ships of the line. Napoleon ended his letter characteristically: 'You hold in your hands the destinies of the world'.[12]

Collingwood, now serving with the main body of the Channel Fleet, was concerned to find Gardner at a low ebb, as he wrote on 9 April:

> Lord Gardner joined us a week ago, to command the fleet in the absence of Admiral Cornwallis. I saw him yesterday for an hour or two, and was sorry to find him altered for the worse – old and out of spirits; yet, I think,

---

9   Corbett, *Campaign of Trafalgar*, p.37.
10 Leyland (ed.), *Blockade of Brest*, Vol.II, p.215.
11 Leyland (ed.), *Blockade of Brest*, Vol.II, p.217.
12 Leyland (ed.), *Blockade of Brest*, Vol.II, p.224.

if he were established he would recover again, and be as active as ever, for there is no officer a more perfect master of the discipline of the fleet than he is.[13]

Collingwood, an acute observer of all about him, had previously noted the effect of the blockade on the commanders responsible for it: 'This incessant cruising seems to me beyond the powers of human nature. Calder is worn to a shadow, quite broken down, and I am told Sir Thomas Graves is not much better'.[14]

Instructions to Missiessy, revoking the order for him to return home, reached him too late. After a partially successful cruise in the West Indies, he sailed back across the Atlantic to Rochefort, in pursuance of his previous orders, so that one part of the jigsaw was already missing when Villeneuve, having picked up Gravina's Spanish squadron from Cadiz, sailed westwards. Napoleon, aware that Ganteaume, paralysed by his orders to avoid risking a battle, was still in Brest, and that Missiessy was probably on his way back, on 11 April devised a fresh scenario. Assuming that Gravina did join Villeneuve, and that two more ships of the line under Magon at Rochefort could also escape, the Toulon fleet should, after reaching Martinique, return with 22 ships of the line and sail around Britain to the north of Scotland and proceed to the Texel to free Marmont's corps and the Dutch fleet before arriving at Boulogne. In this fanciful scheme he relied on Ganteaume's fleet detaining Cornwallis before Brest, and Missiessy's squadron holding up a further force off Rochefort. Two days later a fresh plan burgeoned in Napoleon's mind. This time Magon was to sail at once after Villeneuve with orders that if in 35 days Ganteaume had not appeared Villleneuve was to return to Ferrol, release the Franco-Spanish squadron there, and proceed to Brest to lift the blockade. He was then, in conjunction with Ganteaume, to force the Channel and proceed to Boulogne to cover the sailing of the invasion flotilla. All these plans, of course, were conceived while Napoleon remained in ignorance of what was actually happening at sea. The orders were sent to Magon on 17 April.

Before considering what had in fact occurred, it is necessary to record that the management of the Royal Navy was by then no longer in Melville's hands. On 9 April, following a vote of censure concerning Melville's actions many years before while serving as Treasurer of the Navy, and which arose from the Commissioners' Tenth Report, the First Lord resigned. For Pitt, it was a fearful setback; Melville had been the most effective and supportive member of his Cabinet, and the blow had fallen at a critical point in the naval war against France. At any time the replacement of a First Lord was a grave matter for a Prime Minister; now, Pitt knew that he must not make a mistake in his choice. He turned first to Lord Hawkesbury, his capable Home Secretary, who preferred to stay where he was. There was no other

13 Hughes (ed.), *Admiral Lord Collingwood*, p.130.
14 Hughes (ed.), *Admiral Lord Collingwood*, p.130.

obvious choice among the politicians. Appointing one of the active sea officers was also not a solution; Gardner was seen as lacking administrative ability, while Keith was junior both to him and to Cornwallis, and his appointment would offend the upper echelon of the Navy. Looking for a safe pair of hands, Pitt turned to the 79 year old Sir Charles Middleton, who was appointed on 30 April, becoming Baron Barham of Teston next day.

It was an inspired appointment. There were some – St Vincent among them – who did not rate Barham highly, but his tenure of office entirely justified the struggle which Pitt had to embark on to get him appointed. The King wanted Chatham back, or Castlereagh, or Charles Yorke, a former Secretary for War. Addington demanded the post for one of his supporters. But Pitt held firm, and Barham at once, on the day of his appointment, embarked on a thorough reorganisation of the Admiralty. He exhibited all the energy and determination of a much younger man, and earned the generous comment made by Yorke when he heard of Pitt's decision:

> The news today is, Sir Charles Middleton is to be First Lord. I was not aware that at his advanced age his health and faculties were equal to such a post. If they are he is indisputably the fittest man that could be chosen to occupy it at the time. His abilities were always considered great, his experience is consummate, and he has few equals in application and method of business.[15]

Professor John E. Talbott, Barham's biographer, draws attention to the change of heart of Sir John Laughton, who originally belittled Barham's stature and achievements but who, after editing his papers, soon came to a totally different conclusion, observing that as far as Trafalgar was concerned, Barham was 'the master mind and director of the whole campaign'.[16]

Melville's resignation had deprived Cornwallis of one of his stoutest supporters, and it was not long before those Tories who were agitating for the return to duty of St Vincent made their influence felt, although in Barham they encountered another admirer of the Commander-in-Chief. Cornwallis had always enjoyed an excellent relationship with the new First Lord, to whom he wrote on 28 April to say that he was very glad that he had accepted the office, explaining that he had come on shore to stretch his legs after almost two years on board, but that he hoped to return to duty in the middle of May. Cornwallis was, however, aware of the existence of intrigues to get St Vincent back into the command of the Channel Fleet, and he sought advice from Lord Hood, who was then enjoying his retirement in command at Greenwich Hospital. On 31 May Hood responded:

15   Corbett, *Campaign of Trafalgar*, p.72.
16   Laughton (ed.) *Lord Barham*, Vol.III, pp.xiv-xv.

Many thanks, my dear Admiral, for your very affectionate and confidential letter of Monday last, and from what you therein state it certainly appears more is intended than meets the eye. Be that as it may, the consciousness of your own mind in having discharged your duty with persevering zeal and fidelity must afford you much consolation and comfort, and enable you to bear up against that want of candour and attention your services must justly entitle you to expect.[17]

Given the extent of his command responsibilities, it is hardly surprising that Cornwallis should be sensitive to political conspiracies against him; but his position was certainly quite safe while Barham continued in office.

Villeneuve's orders were to make for the West Indies, although Napoleon had given him an inkling of more far-reaching operations when he told him that the Toulon fleet was 'destined for an operation of an importance quite above that for which I first intended it'. He sailed from Toulon on 30 March; at this point Nelson had taken refuge from stormy weather in Pula Roads. The first he knew of Villeneuve's escape was on 3 April when one of his frigates reported that on the morning of 31 March the French had been sighted 60 miles south-west by west from Toulon. A second frigate lost touch with Villeneuve on the night of 31 March: the latter had altered course to pass inside the Balearic Islands on hearing where Nelson was.

Ignorant, therefore, of Villeneuve's whereabouts or course, Nelson took up a position between Sardinia and the Tunisian coast, from where he could effectively cover Naples, Sicily and Egypt. When Villeneuve failed to appear, he moved north on 7 April to a point 50 miles north of Palermo, where he would still be well placed to intercept any French thrust at Naples or Sicily. Villeneuve by then was off Cartagena, where there were six Spanish ships of the line. Obsessed by the need for haste, he could not wait for them to get to sea, and he took advantage of a favourable wind to run through the Straits of Gibraltar. As he did so, he was observed by Captain Lord Mark Kerr of the frigate *Fisgard*, which was refitting there, and by Sir Richard Strachan in the *Renown*, which was returning there after seeing the homeward bound convoy past Cape Spartel.

Both Strachan and Kerr realised at once the importance of what they had seen. Kerr, leaving behind half his gear, put to sea as soon as he could, sailing on 10 April to take the news to Ireland and to the blockading fleet off Ushant. Strachan, meanwhile, had headed for Cadiz to warn Orde of Villeneuve's proximity. Ironically, this sudden crisis which Orde had to face arose only a couple of weeks after Orde had asked to be relieved: he was suffering severely from gout; he complained of the insufficiency of his squadron for the duties he was required to perform; and he was extremely put out that Nelson, though junior to him, had appointed a prize

---

17   Cornwallis-West, *Admiral Cornwallis*, pp.474-475.

agent at Gibraltar who would deal with prizes taken by Orde's squadron. His letter was addressed to Melville; by the time it arrived, Melville was gone, but the Board minuted on 6 May that Orde's request for permission to retire should be granted.[18]

When Strachan came in sight of Orde's squadron on 10 April, it was engaged in taking on board supplies from a number of store ships. Orde at once sent away his store ships and got his squadron into line of battle. His flagship was the *Glory*, 98; he also had the *Renown*, *Defence*, *Polyphemus*, *Agamemnon* and *Ruby*. It was not a large force with which to meet Villeneuve and Gravina, the commander of the Spanish squadron in Cadiz, to which Villeneuve was now heading. Orde moved away towards Lagos, to cover his store ships, while Villeneuve moved directly to Cadiz. Orde's retreat attracted no criticism from the Admiralty, but some later writers have been less charitable. Alan Schom, for instance, has written scathingly that Orde 'simply fled panic stricken in the opposite direction, not even leaving frigates behind to follow the enemy or to inform Nelson'.[19] Clowes wrote of Villeneuve's approach:

> At 4.00 pm he had stood into Cadiz Bay, after frightening away Sir John Orde, who, apparently oblivious of the fact that his command held a place in the general strategical scheme, even after its work in blockading Cadiz, made the best of his way towards the Channel.[20]

Corbett, on the other hand, made a careful review of Orde's situation, and the way in which he dealt with it, reaching the conclusion that the general contemptuous dismissal of Orde's actions was less than just. He described Orde's retirement as having been 'a narrow escape, but there had been no panic or hurry, no cutting or slipping, but a thoroughly seamanlike retreat'.[21] Orde had now to decide what to do. Strachan suggested that Villeneuve's escape meant that Nelson had sailed to Egypt; the news that Ganteaume's fleet was in Bertheaume Roads, and Villeneuve's obvious intention to link with Gravina, led Orde to conclude that the French were aiming at a major naval concentration. That being so he decided to take his ships of the line to reinforce Gardner.

In the messages Orde sent ahead of him, he told the Admiralty of the conclusions he had reached:

> I am persuaded the enemy will not remain long in Cadiz, and I think the chances are great in favour of their destination being westward where by a sudden concentration of several detachments, Bonaparte may hope to

---

18   Laughton (ed.) *Lord Barham*, Vol.II, pp.302-304.
19   Alan Schom, *Trafalgar: Countdown to Battle, 1803-1805* (London: Atheneum 1990), p.211.
20   Clowes, *Royal Navy*, Vol.V, p.99.
21   Corbett, *Campaign of Trafalgar*, p.63.

gain a temporary superiority in the Channel, and availing himself of it, to strike a mortal blow.[22]

If he could have believed that Villeneuve would return eastwards, he would not, he said, have hesitated to pass the Straits, even though he had no information from Nelson as to his movements. Corbett summarised Orde's movements as being 'in line with the British strategical tradition of concentration on the Western Squadron ... based on a sagacious penetration of Napoleon's war-plan'. At the time, Orde was criticised neither by the Admiralty nor his contemporaries, but only by City merchants, fearful for the French threat to their interests in the West Indies.

Off Ushant, Gardner, before he heard of Villeneuve's activities, was uneasy about the possibility that Ganteaume would escape and fall on Calder's squadron off Ferrol. On 12 April he suggested to the Admiralty that Calder should be recalled, and he followed it up a week later to repeat that 'his remaining off Ferrol, unless he is reinforced, will serve no good purpose'. If Ganteaume did get out, he thought, Calder would be 'very unpleasantly situated'.[23] Gardner learned of Villeneuve's movements on 22 April, reporting that he would watch Brest with his seventeen ships of the line; he hoped that he would soon be joined by both Orde and Calder. Orde duly did so on 30 April; in view of the uncertainty as to the Toulon fleet, Gardner withheld the squadron of five ships of the line under Collingwood which the Admiralty had ordered to Madeira.

Throughout this period Napoleon had sent a stream of messages to both Decrés and Ganteaume to express his bewilderment and dismay that the Brest fleet had not put to sea. Paralysed by Napoleon's order that he must not risk a battle, Ganteaume had no choice but to remain where he was, unless and until an opportunity to escape unseen presented itself. Napoleon was also annoyed to discover that the two ships of the line at Rochefort under Magon had not been ready to sail until 2 May which prompted him to be decidedly critical of Decrés's Ministry. He was also convinced that the lack of readiness to sail owed something to the fact that captains, and crews, were not always on board; he had beard from various sources that Ganteaume's last sortie had failed because he had been held up for twenty four hours for this reason.[24]

Cornwallis, after his two months' leave, had notified the Admiralty of his readiness to return to duty; this, however, the Board deferred for the moment, and it was not until 7 July that he finally reassumed command of the Channel Fleet. Gardner, therefore, had to continue to deal with the uncertainties of the situation. Collingwood had been ordered to Cawsand Bay with seven ships of the line, while on 15 May Gardner had taken up a position off the Lizard 'in the hope of getting

22   Corbett, *Campaign of Trafalgar*, p.64.
23   Leyland (ed.), *Blockade of Brest*, Vol.II, pp.233-234.
24   Leyland (ed.), *Blockade of Brest*, Vol.II, p.249.

into smoother water'. The Admiralty now had to consider how many ships could be spared from the Channel Fleet to deal with the situation at Cadiz, to which an erroneous report from the Ambassador at Lisbon suggested that Villeneuve had returned. Pitt and Barham resolved to send Collingwood with a sufficient force – fourteen ships of the line – to blockade Cadiz if that was where Villeneuve was with the Combined Fleet. If he was not, having gone to the West Indies, and if Nelson had followed him there, Collingwood was to reinforce the latter as necessary; and if Nelson had not he was himself to go with at least twelve of the line. He was also to take steps to protect a convoy that was sailing to India until it was safely past Madeira.[25]

This plan had to be changed, however, in the light of Missiessy's unexpected return. Discussing it with Collingwood on 22 May, Gardner concluded that Missiessy must have got back into Rochefort or Lorient, so that the enemy's strength in their immediate neighbourhood was materially increased. Gardner resolved to detain five of Collingwood's ships of the line, commanded by Graves, and send him off with the rest to Cadiz. He reported this to the Admiralty, hoping that this would meet with approval – which in the event he did not receive.

Meanwhile Rear Admiral Bickerton, who had been detached to take command in the Mediterranean by Nelson before the latter set off for the West Indies, had received orders to reinforce Calder off Ferrol, to which he proceeded on 17 May. On 27 May Bickerton met Collingwood as he came south to take up his position before Cadiz, and gave him a full report of all that had happened culminating in Nelson's departure for the West Indies on 12 May in pursuit of Villeneuve. Collingwood was due to detach two ships after Nelson, but in view of Missiessy's return, and the activity in Cadiz and Cartagena, he decided to keep his whole force for the moment and take it down to Cadiz, reporting to the Admiralty his intentions: 'I consider the spirit of my orders demanded that I should not leave so large a force at liberty to sail in execution of their plans'.[26] Effectively now commander of the Mediterranean station, he sent Bickerton, who had gone on to join Calder before returning to Collingwood, back into the Straits, while he remained off Cadiz. Bickerton was to have four ships of the line; but on reflection Collingwood concluded that he should after all send two to follow Nelson, which he did. This left him with only seven, so he kept four and gave three to Bickerton, with which the latter was able to cover an important convoy of troopships, about which great concern had been felt, to its destination in Malta

Off Ushant, Gardner remained anxious, not only for Calder with his six of the line off Ferrol, but also for himself, since after detaching Graves to watch Rochefort he had only fifteen himself, of which two were 64s. Since Graves had six ships of

25   Corbett, *Campaign of Trafalgar*, p.119.
26   Quoted Corbett, *Campaign of Trafalgar*, p.150.

the line facing a similar number in Rochefort, the Admiralty ordered him to send two of them south to reinforce Calder.[27]

On 8 June Ganteaume reported to Decrés that all his ships were ready for sea. Napoleon was unimpressed, again impressing on Decrés on 16 June that a battle would achieve nothing. His plan was to plant false intelligence in the papers in the hope of misleading the enemy; in the meantime Decrés was not to mention Brest or the Channel at all. On 22 June he wrote again, repeating that he could see no good that could come of a sortie by Ganteaume at present: 'My intention will be to lull the English to sleep as much as possible about the Brest squadron, in a natural manner though, and to direct their attention to the Texel'. Decrés was told to pass this on to Marmont, commanding the corps there that was held ready for an invasion attempt.[28] At this time Napoleon was unaware of Villeneuve's circumstances; in fact, the latter had left the West Indies on 19 June, heading for the Azores, vastly relieved that he had evaded Nelson.

Pondering Marmont's position further, Napoleon developed a scheme for him to make preparations which would give the impression that a distant expedition was planned, while in reality he was to embark all his forces on 20 July in readiness to sail north about and descend on Ireland. This, Napoleon thought, would make it look as if Marmont was only waiting for a gale to drive off the blockading forces, compelling the British to keep at least ten ships of the line off the Texel.

Having reached his station off Cadiz, duly sent off two ships of the line to reinforce the West Indies, and then divided his force between Cadiz and Cartagena, Collingwood wrote to his father-in-law on 2 July to describe all that had been happening to him, and his present situation:

> Such is my employment at present, without means of giving much annoyance to the Spaniards, while they keep snug, and little expectation of their coming out. But I think it is not improbable that I shall have all those fellows coming from the West Indies again, before the hurricane months, unless they sail from thence directly for Ireland, which I have always had an idea was their plan, for this Bonaparte has as many tricks as a monkey. I believe their object in the West Indies to be less conquest, than to draw our forces from home.[29]

Collingwood had little doubt of what Napoleon was up to. If the Toulon fleet operated successfully in the West Indies, and caused great alarm at home, drawing a great force from England, the French would 'have so much less to oppose them in their real attack, which will be at home in harvest time'.

---

27   Leyland (ed.), *Blockade of Brest*, Vol.II, p.288.
28   Leyland (ed.), *Blockade of Brest*, Vol.II, p.292.
29   Warner, *Lord Collingwood*, p.134.

24

Calder's Action

The scope of the responsibilities borne by the Commander-in-Chief of the Channel Fleet was enormous. It was illustrated by a letter which Gardner wrote to Barham a couple of weeks before Cornwallis returned to reassume command. The theatre in which the fleet operated extended from the coast of Ireland to the Straits of Gibraltar, and involved the blockade of four major enemy bases in Brest, Rochefort, Ferrol and Cadiz. It was especially difficult to discharge these responsibilities as a temporary commander, as Gardner made clear:

> I am sure you must be aware of the very unpleasant situation in which I have been placed, both with regard to Admiral Cornwallis and Vice Admiral Sir Charles Cotton, which I can assure your Lordship has occasioned a degree of anxiety and uneasiness in my mind not easily to be described, and which has affected my health and depressed my spirits so much that I find myself unequal to the discharge of my duty in the manner I could wish; nor have I any hope of my being able to do so, until my mind is more at ease.[1]

The effect on Gardner's health was such that he applied for two months leave to recover.

Cornwallis had been given to understand that the reason for the postponement of his return to the command had been the complex strategical situation then existing, but it appears that this may not have been the whole reason. St Vincent's supporters were continuously agitating for him to be put in command of the Channel Fleet, and he apparently had an interview with the King at Windsor on 21 June. St Vincent's position was at this time that he would not hold office under Pitt unless he received an apology for the attacks made upon him. In the event no such apology was forthcoming, and Cornwallis was duly ordered back to sea. His effort to have John Whitby appointed as Captain of the Fleet had not succeeded,

---

1   Laughton (ed.) *Lord Barham*, Vol.II, pp.253-254.

the Admiralty insisting on a more senior officer. As a result of this, Vice Admiral Nugent, serving at the time with Calder, was appointed, which in due course was to result in strained relations between the three men.

Cornwallis returned at a moment of imminent crisis, and was at once plunged into the critical decisions that must be taken. He was not, however, a happy man and in addition may not have been well. That, at any rate was Whitby's opinion, which he expressed in a letter to his wife shortly before Cornwallis's return:

> The Admiral's letter is written in a very odd style of humour altogether: he writes seemingly out of sorts with everybody – Admiralty, sea-people and every other person; and professedly says he means to come again to disappoint people who want to get him out. This would be all very well on common occasions, but consider his health! Is it for the cause of our country to have no other object than pique or displeasure. If he were well it would be otherwise, and no man would rejoice more than I to see him once more at the head of this fine fleet![2]

While Cornwallis was resuming his command, Barham was pondering the strategic situation. After reviewing the current disposition of the forces available to him, he concluded that he should send ten of the ships of the line off Brest to reinforce Collingwood off Cadiz. It was his intention that each of the blockading squadrons should manoeuvre to give themselves the best chance of intercepting Villeneuve's fleet as it returned home, regardless of his actual destination. Before, however, he could issue instructions to this effect, which were based on the best guess that could be made of Villeneuve's intentions, the situation was suddenly clarified. On 7 July the brig *Curieux* arrived at Plymouth. Sent by Nelson from the West Indies with the latest news of the French, the brig had on its way home sighted Villeneuve's fleet standing to the northward some 900 miles north-north-east of Antigua, which indicated that he was heading for the Bay rather than the Straits of Gibraltar. Captain Bettesworth hastened up to London, arriving late at night on 8 July, to find that Barham had retired to bed and no one dared wake him.

Next morning, early, Barham learned the news, and was furious to discover that a precious seven or eight hours had been lost. Without waiting to dress, be jotted down a note of what he considered should be done. His first inclination was to reinforce Calder, off Ferrol, by taking ships from Cornwallis to bring Calder's numbers up to fifteen of the line. On reflection, however, he concluded that this would endanger the fleet off Brest; as amended, his note read:

> My idea is to send the intelligence direct to Admiral Cornwallis who may be directed to strengthen Sir Robert Calder's squadron with the Rochefort

2   Cornwallis-West, *Admiral Cornwallis*, p 473.

squadron and as many ships of his own as will make them up to 15, to cruise off Cape Finisterre from 10 to 50 leagues to the west. To stand to the southward and westward with his own ships, at the same distance for 10 days. Cadiz to be left to Lord Nelson.[3]

Barham was in this way prepared to sacrifice the blockade of Rochefort to strengthen his forces at the decisive point.

When he got to the Admiralty later in the morning, the necessary orders were drawn up and signed; he also wrote a personal note to Cornwallis to say that, if they were not too late, he thought there was a chance of intercepting the Toulon fleet. Barham's dispositions were, in fact, what Napoleon had suggested to Decrés on 18 July would be the proper course for the British to follow if they got news of Villeneuve's approach.[4] Two days later Napoleon wrote direct to Gantaume to confirm the lifting of the Rochefort blockade, and to give him some affirmative instructions:

> We have already given you the order to sortie and to chase off the enemy frigates, and to reconnoitre where the enemy has gone. If you find off Brest a number of less than sixteen ships of the line, our firm intention is that you should engage them with your twenty one ships of the line.[5]

He added that if the British were not there, having gone to Ferrol to encounter Villeneuve, Ganteaume was to enter the Channel and proceed off Boulogne, where everything was ready and where, master of the sea for three days, he would be 'able to determine the destiny of England'.

Before he received the news that Stirling, with the blockading squadron from Rochefort, had been ordered to join him, Calder wrote to Bickerton with regard to the likelihood of his encountering the Toulon fleet:

> The Admiralty have cautioned me to be upon my guard as they may on their return to Europe pay me a visit, of this I have little or no doubt of, if things turn out as they have calculated.[6]

He added a hope that Nelson ' would put a stop[p]er over all their plans'. To Cornwallis he wrote four days later:

3   Laughton (ed.) *Lord Barham*, Vol.IV, p.257.
4   Leyland (ed.), *Blockade of Brest*, Vol.II, pp.306-307.
5   Leyland (ed.), *Blockade of Brest*, Vol.II, p.308.
6   Nicholas Tracey, 'Sir Robert Calder' in Lefevre and Harding (eds.) *British Admirals*, p.205.

I shall pay every attention in my power to prevent being surprised, or to be caught by them embayed, and, as far as the force placed under my directions will enable me, I shall endeavour to prevent the combined squadrons expected from the West Indies from making a junction with those now at Ferrol, which I have little doubt is their intention, and then to make the best of their way to Rochefort.[7]

Cornwallis had immediately complied with Barham's order as to Stirling's squadron, and the latter joined Calder on 15 July. When he arrived with his squadron, he brought with him no additional instructions that would have illustrated Barham's strategic intentions; nor did Cornwallis add anything of this kind himself. When Barham told Cornwallis that he believed that there was a chance of catching Villeneuve, it must be taken as read that this meant the destruction of the Combined Fleet, or at least inflicting so heavy a defeat as to remove it as a threat, but no such words were used to Calder.

At Rochefort, Missiessy's health having given way, the command of the squadron was entrusted to the able Captain Zacharie Allemand. His orders were to sail when the opportunity arose and head for the coast of Ireland to create a diversion. However, on returning to Fontainebleau from Turin, Napoleon had come up with fresh schemes for Allemand and for Villeneuve. The former was now to wait for word from Gourdon that the coast was clear, and then go straight to Ferrol. The order arrived at Rochefort too late; as soon as Stirling lifted the blockade, Allemand put to sea in pursuance of his previous orders, as the Naval Prefect there reported to Decrès on 17 July.

Napoleon's orders to Villeneuve reflected his uncertainty as to the current situation, and also the advice which he had received from Ganteaume as requested. The latter had emphatically given as his opinion that the Brest fleet should go to Ferrol rather than attempt to force an entry into the Channel. He went on to calculate that Cornwallis had a fleet of 21 ships of the line, of which twelve were three deckers, and could call in addition on five more from Ireland, with 15 in reserve. He had only 22:

> To attempt an expedition so important as that of Boulogne in a sea so stormy as the Channel, and one which is not always practicable for the boats employed in that expedition, I think we must be able to count on having the passage free for at least a fortnight. With only twenty one vessels we should be in constant fear of seeing thirty suddenly appear, whose force would be nearly double that of our fleet.[8]

7   Leyland (ed.), *Blockade of Brest*, Vol.II, pp.303-304.
8   Corbett, *Campaign of Trafalgar*, pp.188-189

To Villeneuve, Decrès had written on 16 July 16 to convey the Emperor's wishes:

> His Majesty desires that the fleet under your command shall carry through the great project of the invasion of England, conceived so long since by his genius, but so much time has gone by since the issue of your original orders, so many things may have happened, that in his wisdom the Emperor considers we should not give you an absolute order to that effect in spite of his persistence in this great design, but rather rely on your sagacity and boldness.[9]

Barham's promptness of action on 9 July was duly rewarded; he had told Cornwallis of his view that there was a chance of intercepting Villeneuve, and on 22 July he was proved right. Calder was that morning some 300 miles west by north of Ferrol, which was the limit of his cruising ground, and he turned back south-west, signalling his fleet to close up. At noon the *Defiance*, one of his two advanced ships, sighted the Combined Fleet, and Calder formed his fleet into two columns and cleared for action. At that point the two fleets were some sixteen miles apart, but for the next two hours the thick weather reduced visibility at times almost to zero. Villeneuve's 20 ships of the line were sailing in three columns, with Gravina's Spanish squadron to starboard. He was, at the moment of contact, sailing east towards Ferrol. When at 1.00 pm his advanced ships identified the course and strength of Calder's fleet, Villeneuve formed line on the Spanish squadron and cleared for action.

By 2.00 pm Calder's frigates, which had passed down the enemy line, were able to signal the exact strength of the Combined Fleet, which was somewhat greater than had been expected. Calder had 15 ships of the lime, but they included four three deckers, which narrowed the difference between the two fleets. Calder's plan was to concentrate on the enemy's rear and centre, which would effectively mean ignoring Gravina's squadron, at least for the time being. By 3.30 the fleets were about eight miles apart, with Calder approximately north-east of Villeneuve, and he signalled his fleet to prepare to engage, steering south-south-west. Shortly after this, the fog closed down again, and the fleets were for the next quarter of an hour out of sight of each other. When it lifted, each could see that they were now sailing in parallel, on opposite tacks, just out of range. Villeneuve saw this as meaning Calder's intention was to double on his rear, and made the preparatory signal for his fleet to wear in succession as soon as firing broke out.

Fortunately for him, Gravina began his turn as soon as he saw the preparatory signal and he led his squadron down the starboard side of the French fleet. As he did so, the *Hero*, leading the British line, had reached the French centre, and Calder ordered his fleet to attack in succession, intending to engage on what

---

9   Corbett, *Campaign of Trafalgar*, p.187.

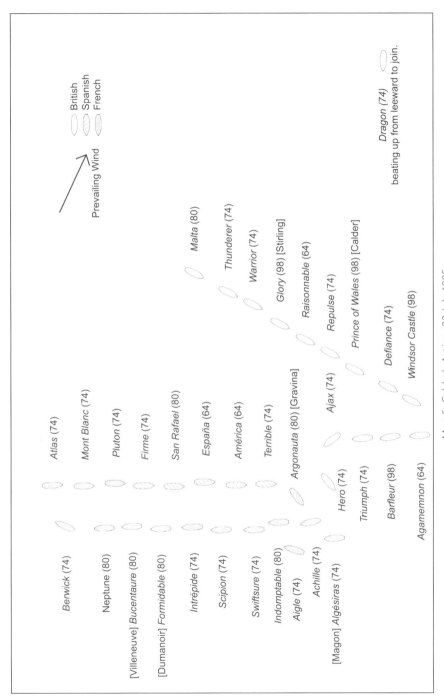

Berwick (74)

Neptune (80)

[Villeneuve] Bucentaure (80)

[Dumanoir] Formidable (80)

Atlas (74)

Mont Blanc (74)

Pluton (74)

Firme (74)

San Rafael (80)

Intrépide (74)

Scipion (74)

España (64)

América (64)

Swiftsure (74)

Terrible (74)

Indomptable (80)

Argonauta (80) [Gravina]

Aigle (74)

Achille (74)

Hero (74)

[Magon] Algésiras (74)

Triumph (74)

Ajax (74)

Barfleur (98)

Agamemnon (64)

Repulse (74)

Defiance (74)

Windsor Castle (98)

Malta (80)

Thunderer (74)

Warrior (74)

Glory (98) [Stirling]

Raisonnable (64)

Prince of Wales (98) [Calder]

Prevailing Wind

British
Spanish
French

Dragon (74)
beating up from leeward to join.

Map 5 Calder's Action, 22 July 1805.

appeared to be the same tack as the enemy, hoisting the signal 'Engage the enemy's centre'. This signal appears not to have been seen by Captain Gardner of the *Hero*, who now saw Gravina's flagship, the *Argonauta* bearing down on him; the Spanish execution of Villeneuve's order meant that as things stood, the fleets would engage on opposite tacks. This, due to the thickening of the weather, Calder could not see, and Gardner, on his own initiative, came about, to lead the fleet on to the same tack as the enemy.

While Gravina stood west-south-west to cover Villeneuve's rear, Calder remained in ignorance of the way the battle had developed for the next forty five minutes, at which time the *Ajax*, which had followed the *Hero*, hailed to warn him what was happening. As a result, he went about himself; as Corbett points out, 'his well meant attack was spoiled by circumstances beyond his control'. He must now fight an altogether different engagement:

> Calder was now committed to a concentration on the van and centre, an evil method of engaging which led inevitably to a counter concentration on his own rear as the enemy's rear came up. He had, moreover, only twelve ships in action. The *Hero* as well as the *Ajax* had been driven out of the line before he himself tacked, and the *Barfleur*, 98, the fourth ship, was now at grips with Gravina. And not only were the two weak leading ships gone, but the powerful *Dragon* was still beating up from to leeward, and indeed did not succeed in rejoining till the action was over.[10]

Immediately following the *Bucentaure*, Villeneuve's flagship, was Rear Admiral Dumanoir in the *Formidable*, which was engaged by the *Malta* at the end of Calder's line. Behind Dumanoir most of the French rear did not get into action at all. By 6.00 pm in the smoke of battle, and with the fog thickening again, no ship could see much further than her own length. The only targets at which they could fire were the flashes of each other's guns, and the confusion was more or less complete as the two fleets headed west-south-west. As night fell, Calder ordered his fleet to break off the action, and firing ceased at about 9.00 pm. In the course of the battle two Spanish ships had struck, the *Firme* and *San Rafael*, after suffering extensive damage. A third, the *Espana*, might also have been lost if the French *Pluton* had not borne up out of the line to cover her.

On the British side the worst of the damage was suffered by the *Windsor Castle*, which lost her foretopmast, and she and the *Malta* suffered the heaviest casualties, losing nearly half the 199 killed and wounded suffered by Calder's fleet; Villeneuve's total casualties amounted to 496 killed and wounded. Both admirals claimed that the outcome was a victory for their fleet. Calder described it to Cornwallis 'a very decisive action which lasted upwards of four hours, when I found it necessary to

---

10 Corbett, *Campaign of Trafalgar*, p.201.

bring-to the squadron to cover the captured ships'.[11] Villeneuve was no less affirmative: 'The enemy then made off. He had had several vessels crippled aloft and the field of battle remained ours. Cries of joy and victory were heard from all our ships'.[12]

Understandable though these claims were, neither was justified, but it was what happened next that gave the action its significance. As far as it went, the engagement was a tactical success for Calder's fleet. When dawn came next day, however, Calder found his fleet widely scattered, with the main bodies some seventeen miles apart; visibility in the continuing haze was still poor. The ships of each fleet were making little way in the light breeze, which was north-west by west. Calder's van was about five miles ahead of him to windward; six miles further off was Villeneuve's advance squadron with the rest of the Combined Fleet another five or six miles further off. The *Windsor Castle*, with the *Dragon* preparing to take her in tow, the *Thunderer* and the frigates and prizes were out of sight to leeward. Calder, concerned about the extensive damage to rigging, decided to call his van to rejoin the main fleet and then bear up to get in touch with his cripples.[13]

At this point Calder drafted a report to Cornwallis. After a brief description of the action, he went on:

> The enemy must have suffered greatly. They are now in sight to windward, and, when I have secured the captured ships, and put the squadron to rights, I shall endeavour to avail myself of every opportunity that may offer to give you some further account of these combined squadrons. At the same time it will behove me to be on my guard against the combined squadrons at Ferrol, as I am led to believe they have sent off one or two of their crippled ships last night for that port. Therefore, possibly I may find it necessary to make a junction with you immediately off Ushant with the whole squadron.[14]

He added that he was sending back the *Windsor Castle* as a result of the damage she had sustained.

During that day Villeneuve made a half-hearted effort to renew the action from the weather position; he claimed that Calder would not let him close, while Calder maintained that Villeneuve avoided coming within range. Calder regarded as his principal duty the prevention of a junction between Villeneuve's fleet and the combined squadron in Ferrol; he thought it best, he said, to keep his squadron

11   Leyland (ed.), *Blockade of Brest*, Vol.II, pp.311-312.
12   Corbett, *Campaign of Trafalgar*, p.202.
13   James, *Naval History*, Vol.III, p.363; Corbett, *Campaign of Trafalgar*, p.203.
14   Leyland (ed.), *Blockade of Brest*, Vol.II, pp.312-313.

together and not to force the enemy to a second engagement till a more favourable opportunity arose, while preventing Villeneuve from getting into Ferrol.

On July 24 the wind changed, enabling Calder to attempt to renew the action if he chose, but he did not do so, believing that to force an action would endanger the prizes and his damaged ships. He saw his principal duty to continue to deny Villeneuve undisputed access to Ferrol. Calder's correspondence makes clear, however, that another major consideration in his mind was a concern that the Ferrol squadron might come out, in which case he would be hopelessly outnumbered and between two fires. In fact, Villeneuve, abandoning his attempt to reach Ferrol as the weather began to deteriorate sharply, also gave up a projected run for Cadiz and made for Vigo.

History has not been kind to Calder. Quite soon after the news of the action was known, his failure to renew it or even attempt to do so, attracted strong criticism, both publicly and professionally. He was shocked and surprised by the outcry; so sure was he that his victory would be well regarded, that he put in a word with Barham about how he might be honoured for it, writing to the First Lord on 23 July:

> I hope your Lordship and my royal master will think I have done all that it was possible to have be done. If so, and you should think me deserving of any mark of his royal bounty, I beg leave to observe I have no children, but I have a nephew, the son of an old faithful servant of the crown, who died in the service as a general and Lieut. Governor of Gibraltar, – to whom I hope his Majesty's royal bounty may extend, if my services should be thought worthy of any mark from his Majesty.[15]

It is certainly an unappealing letter, indicative of a lack of insight, which was confirmed when Calder demanded a court martial to pronounce on his conduct. This took place after Trafalgar, by which time perhaps the atmosphere was such that a more vigorous conduct of the action would be taken for granted; the outcome was that he was reprimanded for an error of judgment. It should be recorded, however, that the first reaction of the Admiralty, once news was received of the encounter with Villeneuve, was to order Cornwallis to write to Calder to convey approval, which he reported as having done on 12 August:

> I have written to Vice Admiral Sir Robert Calder, communicating to him, as expressed, their Lordships' satisfaction and approbation of his conduct and that of Rear Admiral Stirling, the captains, officers, and men under the orders of the Vice Admiral, in the action with the combined fleets of France and Spain on the 22nd of last month, and expressing their

---

15   Laughton (ed.) *Lord Barham*, Vol.IV, p.26.

Lordships' hopes that the advantage obtained will be improved to the utmost of his power.[16]

Of course in adding the closing words, the Admiralty could have no idea what had transpired in the immediate aftermath of the battle.

Corbett reflected on the proper judgment of Calder's conduct:

It is probably one of the most difficult cases in history – a case of delicate choice between the primary object of destroying the enemy's fleet and the ulterior object of defending England against invasion. Most modern writers condemn him out of hand as a man of little heart, who did what was obviously the wrong thing out of sheer pusillanimity.

This, though, would be to look only at the question of whether Calder did do all he could to renew the action, rather than the reason for the course he adopted:

In his view it was his duty in the circumstances not to renew the action and not to try to destroy every ship of the enemy. His duty was to keep his fleet in being and prevent the enemy getting to Ferrol.[17]

Looking at what he understood correctly to be the position in the light of the intelligence available, it is hard not to feel that he has been too harshly judged.

16   Leyland (ed.), *Blockade of Brest*, Vol.II, p.336.
17   Corbett, *Campaign of Trafalgar*, pp.205-206.

25

Trafalgar

Cornwallis enjoyed the full confidence of Barham and the Admiralty, but even he at times came in for criticism which he regarded as unjustified. One such instance was in July 1805 when, as with many of his predecessors, he was rebuked for his employment of his frigates. This scarce commodity was frequently in the collective mind of the Admiralty, which suspected commanders-in-chief of rewarding frigate captains with distant and potentially lucrative cruises. On this particular occasion, the frigates in question had been sent out by Gardner while in temporary command, as Cornwallis pointed out. He also observed that when he took over from St Vincent he found many frigates cruising. For himself, he said that when he selected frigates 'for a distant and what I deemed a necessary service,' he chose vessels that deserved a relief from closely watching enemy ports, not for what they could make in prize money:

> But if their Lordships are pleased, notwithstanding the display of consequence in my appointment, to leave so little to my discretion, I request of you to assure them that I shall continue to execute their orders with all possible diligence and attention.[1]

Cornwallis was certainly entitled to feel that he could indulge himself in heavy irony on this occasion, though he was careful thereafter to report the missions on which he despatched his frigates.

Almost immediately after Barham had sent off the orders which led to Calder's action, the First Lord was confronted by another apparent threat. Napoleon's instructions to Marmont, which suggested that a squadron would sail from Rochefort and go north-about to the Texel to free his corps for a feint attack gave rise to alarming intelligence reports. Barham felt obliged to respond, and ordered Cornwallis to send three 74s to reinforce Keith in the North Sea; the latter was highly sceptical about the threat from this quarter, and was extremely reluctant to

---

1   Leyland (ed.), *Blockade of Brest*, Vol.II, p.310.

sail with his flagship as part of a close blockade of the Texel. Barham resorted to a threat to take away Keith's flagship: although he gave in and sailed off the Texel during the spring tides, the admiral was extremely annoyed.[2]

Meanwhile, having put to sea three days after Stirling's departure from Rochefort to join Calder, Allemand endeavoured to carry out the orders originally given to him, which involved cruising off Ireland. Although the dates for this exercise were long past, he attempted nonetheless to get to the north; the winds at first were fair, but soon turned against him, and by 23 July he was obliged to head for Finisterre for an intended rendezvous with Villeneuve. Julian Corbett was amazed at Allemand's remarkable good luck in avoiding contact with a British squadron:

> In all naval story there is probably no adventure so full of fantastic fortune as this incredible cruise of Allemand's. Pursuing a plan that was crossed at every point by Barham's finished disposition, he sped from danger to danger as his master's wilful blindness had doomed him. Wandering in the midst of well disposed squadrons hungering for his destruction, again and again he escaped by a hairsbreadth – appearing and disappearing like a phantom fleet – his every move forestalled, yet always sheltered by some bewildering turn of fortune or happy stroke of judgment. When we consider that the whole episode was born of that little interlineation in Barham's order, whereby he altered his mind at the last moment and sent Stirling to Calder, its mythical colour is complete. It is as though some unseen power were resolved to remind the veteran First Lord how helpless was his art against the Fortune of War.[3]

Villeneuve, of course, was in no state to keep the rendezvous off Finisterre. The port of Vigo, in which he had taken refuge, had no facilities to repair his ships damaged in the action with Calder. Gourdon, to whom Villeneuve wrote requiring the Ferrol squadron to join him, refused; he had not even been able to get out to Corunna. Villeneuve had no choice but to try and get to him; on 31 July he put to sea and sailed up the coast. The strong south-westerly breeze that carried him up to Corunna had forced Calder to leeward, and Villeneuve was able to reach his destination unmolested.

Away to the south, Nelson was revictualling at Gibraltar, from where he wrote to his friend Collingwood on 18 July:

> I am, as you may imagine, miserable at not having fallen in with the enemy's fleet; but for false information, the battle would have been fought

2   Kevin D. McCranie, *Admiral Lord Keith and the Naval War Against Napoleon* (Tallahasse FL: University of Florida Press, 2006), p.14.
3   Corbett, *Campaign of Trafalgar*, p.215.

where Rodney fought his, on June 6. […] The moment the fleet is watered, and has got some refreshments, of which we are in great want, I shall come out and make you a visit – not, my dear friend, to take your command from you, (for I may probably add mine to you) but to consult how we can best serve our country by detaching a part of this large force.[4]

As it turned out, the two friends were unable to meet on this occasion. Adverse winds kept Nelson in Gibraltar, and he then received the news that made it clear that Villeneuve had not headed for the Mediterranean. Accordingly, leaving eight ships of the line to strengthen Collingwood and Bickerton, he sailed for home, reaching the Channel Fleet off Ushant on 15 August. Cornwallis, as his senior officer, agreed to Nelson's request that, leaving the rest of his fleet off Ushant, he should go home to Spithead with the *Victory* and the *Superb*, the latter badly in need of a refit. Nelson was back in Spithead on 18 August.

Calder had in the meantime judged it best to re-join the Channel Fleet off Ushant, which he reached on 14 August. In his official report to Cornwallis of his action, he had foreshadowed the possibility that it might be necessary to do so; now, he found to his dismay, that the Admiralty when publishing his report omitted the final paragraph which explained this. He wrote to Barham to complain, saying that it had led the press 'to bestow on [him] many remarks, and to publish a great deal of nonsense'.[5] Calder's arrival, and that of Nelson, brought the Channel Fleet up to a total strength of 36 ships of the line, which would have been more than enough to deal with Villeneuve before Ganteaume could come to his assistance, even if the roving Allemand had been able to find the Combined Fleet.

Villeneuve, having finally united with the Ferrol squadron, notified Decrès that he planned to put to sea again on 10 August, and would sail either to Brest or Cadiz according to circumstances. Contrary winds delayed his getting out until 13 August; the Combined Fleet now numbered 29 ships of the line. By the evening of 15 August he had reached a point some 240 miles west-north-west of Cape Finisterre: it was time to make up his mind, and Villeneuve, lacking confidence in his fleet, and believing that so much had happened that Napoleon's orders no longer held good, opted to turn south for Cadiz, whence he reported to the Emperor.

Villeneuve's arrival off the port on 20 August was such as to give Collingwood a dreadful fright, as he explained in a letter next day to his wife:

> I have very little time to write to you, but must tell you what a squeeze we had like to have got yesterday. While we were cruising off the town,

---

4   Warner, *Lord Collingwood*, p.135. The action of Rodney's referred to here is the most famous of his victories, that of the Saintes, fought of Dominica on 12 April 1782.
5   Laughton (ed.) *Lord Barham*, Vol.III, p.95.

down came the combined fleet of thirty six men-of-war; we only three poor things, with a frigate and a bomb, and drew off towards the Straits, not very ambitious, as you may suppose, to try our strength against such odds. They followed us as we retired, with sixteen large ships; but on our approaching the Straits they left us, and joined their friends in Cadiz, where they are fitting and replenishing their provisions. We, in our turn followed them back, and today have been looking into Cadiz, where their fleet is now as thick as a wood. I hope I shall have somebody come to me soon, and in the meantime I must take the best care of myself I can.[6]

While he was retreating towards Gibraltar, Collingwood had put on a bold front, sending the *Colossus* back towards the oncoming French ships, to reconnoitre them. When they closed on her, he tacked with the rest of his vessels, and stood towards her in support. Writing a few days later, he speculated on the reasons for the French retirement:

Whether they suspected by these movements that we had discovered a reinforcement or were afraid of being drawn through the Straits and separated from the body of their fleet I do not know, but soon after, they all hauled off and made the best of their way to Cadiz. Two chased the *Thunderer*, and certainly they might have taken her in half an hour, but with great good management she ran so near the shoals that they did not like to follow, and they all seemed careful to secure a retreat to Cadiz.[7]

Barham's workload during this stressful time was enormous. One of his greatest anxieties was the want of sufficient seamen to man the ships which he worked night and day to get to sea. It was a problem which he left Pitt in no doubt was putting the country in great danger. When writing to the Prime Minister on 3 August to reiterate his concerns, he also described the burdens which he bore:

The charge I have taken upon me is, I own, a heavy one, and the service so increased in every point of view as to bear no comparison with former times. I seldom have the pen out of my hand from 8 in the morning till 6 at night; and although I see no person but on public business, yet I don't find my own finished at that time; and if I did not make a point of doing so, the current business must overpower us. This labour is very much increased from a want of men, and 'tis mortifying in the highest degree to

---

6   Warner, *Lord Collingwood*, pp.136-137.
7   Warner, *Lord Collingwood*, p.137-138.

have no prospect of success, notwithstanding we have removed the grand
obstacle in the forwarding ships.[8]

So far as his Board of Admiralty was concerned, Barham was very much the master
in his own house, but he was well supported there. The naval Lords were Vice
Admirals Gambier and Patton, and Captain Lord Garlies, while among the Civil
Lords were Sir Philip Stephens and Sir Evan Nepean, both past First Secretaries.
The current First Secretary was the capable and experienced William Marsden,
and the Second Secretary was John Barrow. As soon as he took office, Barham had
reorganised the Navy Board, bringing the Comptroller into the centre of naval
administration. He had always asserted the prime importance of this post, as he
put it to Melville: 'No price can purchase a man fit for this extensive office; he must
be in every part of it and know everything that is going on, in and out of it'.[9] He
made full use of his naval Lords, assigning to each the principal responsibility for
one section, while remaining himself the final authority, and solely responsible for
naval operations.

   In Cornwallis he had the great benefit of an operational commander who thoroughly understood the nature of the strategic issues facing Barham, and this was
nowhere better illustrated than the crucial decisions taken by Cornwallis during
August 1805. Corbett saw in the steps taken by the First Lord and the Commander-
in-Chief the essential difference in understanding of the true situation; Napoleon
thought he knew what was going on – indeed, he was sure of it, as his arrogant
and impatient letters to Decrès and the admirals make clear. Corbett found the
Emperor's 'failure to grasp the foundations of the game' almost incredible in so
great a genius:

> His confident egotism would not recognise that he was playing against
> past-masters of a game at which he was only an amateur. What he took
> for astute strategical inspirations were to his opponents the common
> places of their craft, and while he stood fuming between bewilderment
> and wounded self confidence, making confusion worse confounded, the
> men of the old tradition were playing in sure mastery high over his head.[10]

On 16 August, the day after Nelson's arrival off Brest, Cornwallis ordered Calder
to take eighteen ships of the line, together with the *Dragon* and *Goliath* which he
was to pick up en route, and sail south to Ferrol. His task was to prevent the enemy
putting to sea, or to fall upon them if they were rash enough to attempt it. Calder
had with him five three deckers, and although outnumbered by Villeneuve he had

---

8   Laughton (ed.) *Lord Barham*, Vol.III, p.95.
9   Leslie Gardiner, *The British Admiralty* (London: Blackwood, 1968), p.206.
10   Corbett, *Campaign of Trafalgar*, p.246.

a fleet that, having regard to the relative condition of the ships and morale of the men, was probably equal to the French. This was the move which, for Corbett, was the masterstroke of the Trafalgar campaign. Although it was a decision taken by Cornwallis, it was entirely consistent with Barham's intentions. Although it was to be some days before the admiral knew it, Barham wrote on 15 August to give a broadly similar instruction, although naming Cotton rather than Calder, in whom confidence had been lost, to command the fleet off Ferrol.

Villeneuve's move was denounced by Napoleon, when he heard of it, as an '*insigne betise*' – remarkable stupidity. He wrote despairingly to Decrès on 29 August of the opportunity that had been lost:

> What a chance Villeneuve has missed! By coming upon Brest from the open he might have played hide and seek with Calder's squadron and fallen upon Cornwallis; or with his thirty of the line have beaten the English twenty, and obtained a decisive superiority.[11]

Napoleon's view has been shared by a number of historians. Mahan considered that Cornwallis's 'division of his fleet, which is condemned by the simplest and most generally admitted principles of warfare, transferred to Villeneuve all the advantage of central position and superior force'.[12] Clowes followed Mahan, considering 'it certainly was a strategical blunder, such as one would not have expected an officer of Cornwallis's great ability to make'.[13]

Another powerful critic of Cornwallis's action was John Leyland, who addressed the issue in his introduction to Volume II of *The Blockade of Brest*:

> It was undoubtedly a bold move, and in the presence of a stronger man than Villeneuve might have had unfortunate results. It left Cornwallis with a force that would have been inadequate to deal with the squadron of Villeneuve if he had been able to outmanoeuvre Calder and appear off Ushant, and at the same time there was Ganteaume's fleet of twenty one ships to take account of. It seems possible that in such circumstances Cornwallis would have had no course but to fly, and that the great concentration of fifty ships in the Channel, which Napoleon had hoped for, might have been brought about.[14]

It is a view which Corbett firmly rejected. Cornwallis had ten three deckers and the rest were seasoned ships of eighty and seventy four guns to face Villeneuve,

---

11   Corbett, *Campaign of Trafalgar*, p.248.
12   Mahan, *Sea Power*, Vol.II, p.176.
13   Clowes, *Royal Navy*, Vol.V, p.119.
14   Leyland (ed.), *Blockade of Brest*, Vol.II, p.xxxix.

with his 'motley' Franco-Spanish fleet, of which ten were 'mere floating barracks'. Cornwallis could either fight, in which case Villeneuve would be fit for little afterwards; or he could move to the west, until Calder rejoined him. In the unlikely event of Ganteaume and Villeneuve together having the nerve to enter the Channel without having dealt with him, Cornwallis would have hung to windward of the enemy; 'he might have refused action except on his own terms, but it was against all tradition and practice that he should have run away'.[15] It might have been added that it would be directly contrary to Cornwallis's character to do so.

Cornwallis, however, knew perfectly well what he was doing, and correctly assessed the real extent of the risks involved. He reported his move to the Admiralty on the same day, observing the immediate consequences:

> I have left for the service here at present but a few ships. I trust, however, to some joining me soon, and the remainder of those sent to the Downs. I have thought the step I have now taken might meet with their Lordships approbation, as a means of keeping the enemy's squadrons in check, if that from Rochefort is still at sea; and should their Lordships be pleased to order the ships in any other direction, it may be easily effected.[16]

Both Cornwallis and Barham were very much aware that it was the time of year for the return to England of the great convoys, and in particular those from India and from the West Indies. The concentration at Ferrol amounted to a powerful threat to their safe return, and the detachment of Calder gave the added bonus of thereby protecting the convoys, an objective of very great importance.

Corbett, therefore, was able to conclude 'that if the movement be considered in the light of whole situation, it was one which has ample justification in the universal principles of strategy'. Furthermore, it was 'for a naval power to command the sea for all purposes if it has the power, which required a proper consideration of the balance of advantage against risk'.[17] Given the circumstances faced by Cornwallis and the Admiralty, Corbett's view is surely right. It has been supported by more recent historians, such as Ruddock Mackay and Michael Duffy, who regard Cornwallis as having shown a well developed grasp of strategy, and moral courage allied to his excellent judgement, in taking 'an unselfish and courageous decision.[18]

Before all these developments were known, however, Napoleon had been an active correspondent. His arrival at Boulogne on 3 August was of course a defiant

15 Corbett, *Campaign of Trafalgar*, p.253.
16 Leyland (ed.), *Blockade of Brest*, Vol.II, p.243.
17 Corbett, *Campaign of Trafalgar*, pp.252-252.
18 Ruddock Mackay and Michael Duffy, *Hawke, Nelson and British Naval Leadership 1747-1805* (Woodbridge: Boydell & Brewer, 2009), p.183.

statement of his intention to lead an invasion of England, and this was the moment when he expected his fleets to be in action. On 20 August he explained to Decrès that it was for Ganteaume, awaiting Villeneuve's arrival, to collect his fleet, anchor in Bertheaume Bay, and be ready to fight if not on the first day, at least the second. And he telegraphed Ganteaume to ask if he was now anchored there, and whether he had received any news from Ferrol: 'I hope that you realise the importance of this moment and that you know what I have a right to expect'. Two days later he wrote to Ganteaume, who, when Villeneuve arrived, was not to allow him to enter the port, but to sail with him into the Channel with fifty ships of the line, and make for Boulogne with all his forces:

> I count on your ability, your strength and your character at a moment of such importance. Leave port and come here. We shall have avenged six centuries of insults and of shame. Never for a greater object have my seamen and soldiers risked their lives.[19]

Ganteaume had already prepared to take action. On August 21 he had brought his fleet out to a point between Bertheaume and Toulinguet. Cornwallis, when informed of this, stood with his whole fleet towards the entrance to Brest and took the *Ville de Paris* above St Matthew's Point to see for himself what the French were up to. He described their position in a report to the Admiralty:

> They were at anchor across the Channel in no particular order, twenty one of the line, four frigates, one corvette, one brig. I thought at that time there was a prospect of being able to get at them. I therefore anchored the whole of the squadron, seventeen sail of the line, for the night off the Black Rocks, intending to attempt the attack in the morning, although I had heard of the numerous batteries lately erected along the shore.[20]

Cornwallis was very hopeful of getting to grips with the French, and at dawn weighed anchor in order to get in line of battle. Before he could complete this, the French, led by Rear Admiral Willaumez in the *Alexandre*, themselves got under way, and appeared about to launch an attack. However, when Willaumez had reached St Matthew's Point, and was almost within gunshot of Cornwallis's rear, he fired a broadside and then tacked, followed by the rest of the French fleet. Cornwallis ordered his fleet to wear, sending the *Caesar* and *Montague* to try to cut off the French rear. This attempt failed, due to the very heavy fire of shot and shells from the French batteries. Ganteaume led his fleet in, and anchored at the entrance to Brest Roads. In the action only the *Caesar* suffered fatal casualties,

19 Leyland (ed.), *Blockade of Brest*, Vol.II, p.349.
20 Leyland (ed.), *Blockade of Brest*, Vol.II, p.350.

losing 3 killed and 6 wounded. Aboard the *Ville de Paris*, Cornwallis was himself slightly wounded when he was struck by spent fragment of shot.

The day was thus a disappointment to the admiral. Captain Whitby wrote to his wife to describe the action:

> I think the sight of the little rencontre we had the other day was the most beautiful I have ever beheld, and as I have often said, the admiral, when he sees the enemy, rises up like the sun from behind the clouds – all dull and inky vapours vanish. This was, in my opinion, the most officer-like manoeuvre possible. The endeavour he made to coax the enemy to battle when he found them leaving their anchorage; his pushing the matter to exactly the right point, neither too far, shewed excellent judgment and knowledge. But fancy the British 17 sail to the French 21, within 3 miles of Brest waters, the hills covered with Frenchmen to stimulate their countrymen; their ships entirely covered by tremendous batteries on shore, and ourselves giving them a kick as it were by way of a challenge. The colours flying in the British line, and the *Ville de Paris* with the admiral's white flag leading, was beautiful beyond description.[21]

The incident raises again the issue of whether a close blockade, as St Vincent and Cornwallis applied it, was the most desirable way to deal with a French fleet in Brest. Unlike the much looser blockade adopted by Nelson (and as well by Howe and Bridport when on the Channel station), it seriously discouraged any enterprise on the part of the French. It was not, as Mackay and Duffy point out, the moment to try to lure the French out, with the immensely valuable East India convoy due shortly to arrive, but the incident sufficiently unsettled Ganteaume to the extent that when Cornwallis relaxed the blockade for a week at the end of September to cover incoming convoys, the French admiral remained in port.[22]

At Boulogne Napoleon had already found that however much he hoped to launch an immediate invasion, the Army of England was by no means ready. Instead of the 150,000 men poised to embark at a moment's notice, only 90,000 were available, while only 3,000 of the 9,000 cavalry horses were at hand. The naval preparations, on the other hand, had gone well. Some 1,200 vessels were ready at Boulogne, with another 1,100 available in adjoining ports, sufficient to embark all the army with space to spare. However, the problem of getting the whole enormous flotilla to sea had still not been satisfactorily resolved. It would still take three tides to get it into the open Channel, during which time it would be desperately vulnerable to British attacks. Napoleon, though, remained confident that he could pull off an improbable triumph.

---

21   Cornwallis-West, *Admiral Cornwallis*, pp.485-486.
22   Mackay and Duffy, *British Naval Leadership*, p.189.

That is, until 23 August, when the shattering news arrived that Villeneuve, after leaving Ferrol, had turned south for Cadiz. The shock which Napoleon felt caused him to lose control completely, foaming at the mouth and raving like a madman. He gave way to such a violent and sustained rage that those around him feared apoplexy. That night, as he calmed down, the Emperor wrote: 'What a Navy! What sacrifices all for nothing! All hope is gone! Villeneuve, instead of entering the Channel, has taken refuge in Cadiz. It is all over'.[23] As indeed, it was. The invasion project was in ruins and could never realistically be revived. Within days Napoleon committed himself to using the army that stood on the Channel at Boulogne in an assault on Austria, and was soon, unconvincingly, promoting the view that the invasion of England was a feint to deceive his enemies.

For Cornwallis and the Channel Fleet, however, the threat posed by Ganteaume remained. The French remained anchored outside the Goulet, and as Cornwallis explained to the Admiralty on 27 August, 'in this situation they can go to sea with almost any moderate wind, and require to be very closely watched'.[24] By September 5 he was still expecting trouble:

> The Brest fleet were reported to me yesterday to continue in the road. Their late movement would make me suppose they intended going to sea, as I never heard of a number of ships anchoring without the Points in the way they at first did, except previous to their immediately putting to sea.[25]

At this time he was acutely conscious of the potential threat to the valuable East and West India convoys posed by Allemand, whose whereabouts remained a mystery. He had detached Stirling on 28 August with six ships of the line, to pursue what was believed to be the Rochefort squadron which had chased the frigate *Melampus* on the day before. Further news of the squadron came from the sloop *Wasp*, which had narrowly escaped from a ship of the line and a frigate when with *Melampus* and which had another such encounter on 31 August.

Cornwallis's handling of Stirling has been criticised; he originally ordered him to check whether Allemand had returned to either Lorient or Rochefort, in which case he was to blockade him there. If not, he was to proceed northward to cover the incoming convoys and see them into the Channel.[26] Stirling remained off the entrance to the Channel, watching for Allemand. He thought he had found him on 19 September, when he sighted five ships of the line, but these turned out to be the force with which Nelson was sailing to take up his command off Cadiz. By now the West Indies convoy was safely home, and Nelson was able to tell Stirling

23 McLynn, *Napoleon*, p.332.
24 Leyland (ed.), *Blockade of Brest*, Vol.II, p.351.
25 Leyland (ed.), *Blockade of Brest*, Vol.II, p.355.
26 Leyland (ed.), *Blockade of Brest*, Vol.II, p.352.

that the East India convoy was also safe. With this in mind, Stirling sailed to rejoin Cornwallis.

As it happened, Allemand was at that moment less than 150 miles to the west. Cornwallis, however, kept Stirling with him rather than sending him back to the entrance to the Channel to cover any further incoming convoys. Corbett finds this an error of judgment – 'the only one that can be laid at Cornwallis's door during his admirable conduct of the station'. The situation was, though, by no means easy, and it was possible that Ganteaume might make a desperate attempt to break out to join Villeneuve.[27]

Villeneuve, meanwhile, had remained in Cadiz; Calder reported to Cornwallis on 21 September that the French fleet, of 35 ships of the line, was apparently ready for sea. The ships that had been damaged in the action of 22 July had apparently been repaired. One, the *Scipion*, appeared to be unserviceable. Three ships damaged in that action had apparently remained in Vigo, and two more at Ferrol. Calder added the news that the enemy were transferring seamen overland from these two ports to reinforce Villeneuve's fleet.

Ganteaume's continued quiescence allowed Cornwallis to leave his station off Brest, putting five ships of the line under Sir Richard Strachan to watch the port, and to protect the frigates and smaller vessels stationed close in, while he sailed to Falmouth, to cover the approaches to the Channel. It was a step taken with the approval of the Admiralty, which was mindful of the threat still posed by Allemand, as well as of the condition of the ships of the Channel Fleet that would be posed by the autumn and winter gales. On 9 October Marsden passed on to Cornwallis a recommendation which reflected this:

> The fleet under your command being now rendered, by the addition of the ships which have lately been put under your command, superior to that of the enemy, I have it in command from my Lords Commissioners of the Admiralty to recommend it to you to keep no more ships at present off the port of Brest than you may judge sufficient for preventing the enemy from putting to sea, but to station the excess either at Falmouth or Cawsand Bay as in your opinion may be most advisable.[28]

The ships brought back in this way were to be kept in constant readiness to put to sea if enemy action required it. If any French ships should escape, they were to be pursued by Cornwallis's best-sailing ships of the line.

Off Cadiz, Nelson arrived on 29 September to assume command. As he made his way southwards he had had very much in his mind the possibility that Ganteaume might escape from Brest during the equinoctial weather, and he left directions

27 Corbett, *Campaign of Trafalgar*, p.307.
28 Leyland (ed.), *Blockade of Brest*, Vol.II, p.365.

with the frigates watching the coast that if this occurred they were to report to him at once.

One of Nelson's first actions on taking up the command illustrated the very different view of close blockade that he held. For him, it served only to remove the chance of a fleet action by intimidating the enemy to remain in port. When he arrived, Rear Admiral Louis was commanding the inshore squadron close in to Cadiz, which consisted of the *Queen*, 98, and *Canopus*, 80, with three seventy fours. Nelson immediately recalled Louis to rejoin the main fleet. Apart from his general disapproval of such a close blockade, there was the danger to an inshore squadron of a sudden westerly squall. Corbett summarised Nelson's thinking:

> The inherent advantage of the blockader is his power of concealing from the enemy his actual strength, position and movements, and in Nelson's eyes full use should be made of this advantage. He had therefore decided to remove the whole of his battle fleet out of sight and to watch the port with a cruiser squadron only, which Blackwood was to command. The new disposition is significant, for it emphasises the growing expectation that the exigencies of the situation would force the enemy to sea if only they were given an apparent chance of escape.[29]

Nelson's arrival brought the shocking news to Calder of the public disapproval of his failure to engage Villeneuve again after the action of 22 July, and Calder was prompt in his letter of 30 September to demand an inquiry into his conduct. Granting him permission to return home for the purpose, the Admiralty ordered him to return in the *Dreadnought*, in which Collingwood was flying his flag, and which was due for a refit. Nelson, however, allowed Calder to return in the *Prince of Wales*, his own flagship. Both Nelson and Collingwood felt some sympathy for Calder's position; the latter wrote to Nelson: 'I am grieved whenever I think of Sir Robert Calder's case. I think he must be aware of his situation, and feels more about it than he chooses should appear. I wish he was in England, because I think he wants a calm adviser'.[30] Calder left for England on 13 October; next day, inviting Collingwood over to the *Victory* for a discussion, Nelson wrote:

> I am glad Sir Robert Calder is gone; and from my heart I hope he will get home safe, and end his enquiry well. I endeavoured to give him all the caution in my power respecting the cry against him; but he seemed <u>too wise</u>.[31]

29   Corbett, *Campaign of Trafalgar*, p.326.
30   Warner, *Lord Collingwood*, p.146.
31   Warner, *Lord Collingwood*, p.147.

Nelson and Collingwood were exercised about the failure of Villeneuve to put to sea. Collingwood wrote to Nelson on 18 October: 'It is very extraordinary the people in Cadiz do not make some movement; if they allow the war to begin in Italy, they cannot hereafter make up for the want of assistance they might give in the first instance'.[32] That unfortunate admiral had received orders to proceed to Naples; it was only a few days later that he heard that it was Nelson who had arrived to take command of the blockading fleet, and the news further depressed his spirits. Gravina, the Spanish commander, insisted on a Council of War to decide whether to execute an order which he regarded as thoroughly unwise. On 7 October a rancorous council was held, and a majority voted to remain at anchor, and receive an attack there should it come. Meanwhile Napoleon had ordered Villeneuve's supersession by the elderly Admiral Rosily, who reached Madrid on 12 October. It would take him a further ten days to reach Cadiz, but news of his coming reached Villeneuve by 18 October. It coincided with information that Rear Admiral Louis had been detached by Nelson to enter the Straits; to Villeneuve the news that Nelson had parted with six of his ships of the line meant that an unlooked for opportunity had arisen. He hesitated no longer, but it was with despair in his heart that he gave the general signal to prepare to weigh anchor. Next day the Combined Fleet put to sea; by nightfall on October 21 it had been smashed as an effective fighting force. The story of the battle of Trafalgar has been told so often, and in such detail, that an account of it has no place here; but it was the events off Brest, in the English Channel and the Bay of Biscay, and the strategic insight of Lord Barham at his desk in Whitehall, that led inexorably to one of the most decisive battles in naval history.

32   Warner, *Lord Collingwood*, p.147.

26

The Return of St Vincent

In the immediate aftermath of Trafalgar it was Strachan, who was at sea looking for Allemand's squadron, who encountered Rear Admiral Dumanoir making for Rochefort with four stragglers from the Combined Fleet. This was on 3 November, and he succeeded in taking all four with very little loss. Strachan and Cornwallis exchanged letters on the subject; Strachan thought himself profoundly fortunate to have fallen in with Dumanoir, and was extremely grateful to Cornwallis for having provided him with the opportunity. Cornwallis was of the opinion that after Trafalgar there would not be much in the way of French naval activity; Strachan was of a different view:

> I do not think with you that there will be nothing more to do. On the contrary, I think Bonaparte will be tempted to force his fleet out, or send them in detachments to annoy our trade or distant possessions. I have great hopes the Brest fleet may come out, that you may have the pleasure of giving an account of them … I dread the thought of our navy having nothing to do. Idleness will gain a greater victory over us than all our enemies combined; and, if the fleet is once allowed to lay in port any time, we shall lose all that excellent order which is now so well established. I hope always to be under your command, and that you never will leave us while the war continues. I am sure we shall have something to do; it generally happens when least expected.[1]

Strachan's opinion that the French might come out in detached squadrons was shared by Barham. There had been an intelligence report in late November from a British agent that the French were planning a sortie. Cornwallis was sceptical, observing that it was an expedition that must have been planned before Trafalgar; if they were coming out, the temptation to fall upon the damaged ships and

1 Cornwallis-West, *Admiral Cornwallis*, p.491.

prizes coming home from the battle would surely have motivated them. Barham responded in early December:

> I agree with you that the intended expedition must have been planned before the defeat of the Fleet, but I am very, very fearful of their breaking their ships into small squadrons, such as one or two line of battle ships and a frigate or two to accompany them for attacking our frigate convoys. In this case it will be necessary that all your supernumerary ships should be employed in the same way to counteract them, and I would hope to get possession of them.[2]

Barham and Cornwallis were still much concerned about the whereabouts of Allemand's squadron. There had been a report, which in fact was incorrect, of a sighting off Cape Finisterre on 3 November. By then, however, Allemand was in the Canary Islands, which he did not leave until 18 November, reaching the coast of Portugal in the following month. He was perfectly aware, from British prizes that he took, that there was a British squadron out searching for him, and decided to make for home. With the advantage of thick weather, and favourable winds, he returned to Rochefort on 24 December, although it was some time before this was reported to Cornwallis.

Following his visit to Falmouth, after which he had moved to Torbay, Cornwallis returned to his station off Ushant. However, as he was on his way there, the predicted escape from Brest took place. Two separate squadrons sailed from there on 13 December. The first was led by Vice Admiral Leissègues, with the *Imperial* (120 guns) *Alexandre, Jupiter, Brave* and *Diomède*, together with two frigates. He sailed to the West Indies, only for his squadron to be destroyed by Admiral Sir John Duckworth off San Domingo on 6 February 1806. The second, led by Rear Admiral Willaumez, consisted of the *Foudroyant, Vétéran, Cassard, Impétueux, Patriote* and *Eole*, and two frigates, sailed with orders to carry out a commerce raiding operation, first in the South Atlantic, then in the West Indies; finally, he was to sail north to Newfoundland to destroy the fisheries there. Willaumez found that the British had reoccupied the Cape of Good Hope, but had no luck with his commerce raiding there, so headed for the West Indies where, following extensive storm damage, his squadron was scattered and effectively disintegrated. He brought the *Foudroyant* back to Brest early in 1807; the *Cassard* had got back before him. The *Vétéran* got back into Concarneau; it was three years before she could be extricated from the tiny port. The *Patriote* finally returned home in 1808. The *Impétueux* was chased into the Chesapeake, ran aground, and was burned by her pursuers, while *Eole* and a frigate had been so damaged that they were sold

---

2   Cornwallis-West, *Admiral Cornwallis*, p.497.

in America. A total of seventeen prizes was all that this lengthy operation had produced.[3]

Cornwallis had always realised that the post of Commander-in-Chief of the Channel Fleet was very much in the public eye, and was often the subject of political manoeuvres. This led him from time to time to feel uneasy about his position. When he resumed his command in the summer of 1805 he did so feeling decidedly unsettled; and in the autumn he seems to have felt that Barham was not entirely supportive. He took the step of writing to the First Lord on 31 October to express his feelings:

> If the intercourse with which I have been honoured formerly by your lordship could be forgotten, I should from recent events be induced to believe that I am in your way here, and that you would prefer some other arrangement ... The directing me to confide nearly the whole of the ships and vessels under my ordered to the blockade, and supplying an admiral in port with cruisers to be sent upon what has always been considered belonging to this station, must of course, lower my consequence; and I should fear this and other restraints put upon me of late, will frustrate my chief object – that of serving the country in the best manner I am able, which prompted my offer of service to any part of the world at the commencement of the war.[4]

He was quite mistaken in his suspicions, and Barham was quick to reassure him, writing on 7 November:

> I can with truth declare to you that my confidence and regard for you is in no way diminished; but you must be aware of the difficulties I am under, from the habits that have been established and commands fixed before my return to the board; and although many of them do, in no shape, meet with my approbation, yet it is out of my power to make a direct attack on them.[5]

In particular, the First Lord explained, he totally disapproved of giving port admirals cruisers to send on distant cruises, and he was drawing off the King's ships to put them under the cruising admirals. He ended his letter by reiterating his support for Cornwallis: 'you have my unreserved confidence and good wishes'. The major influence in the Admiralty hostile to Cornwallis was probably Gambier;

3   Jenkins, *French Navy*, pp.267-268.
4   Laughton (ed.) *Lord Barham*, Vol.III, pp.281-282.
5   Laughton (ed.) *Lord Barham*, Vol.III, pp.283-284.

and there is little doubt that he was aware of this, and that it contributed to his sense of unease.

A few days later Barham was able to write to Cornwallis to congratulate him on his promotion to Admiral of the Red. Acknowledging this, the admiral wrote: 'I certainly consider the flag which you mention to have come down to me as an attention and civility. Some people value such things more than others; if I was a dozen years younger, I would rather be a senior captain than have a flag of any kind'.[6] He was still evidently feeling very grumpy.

The escape of Leissègues and Willaumez had meant, of course, a considerable reduction in the strength of the French fleet in Brest. By the end of January Cornwallis was reporting that there were now there ten ships of the line, of which two were three deckers, with four frigates and a corvette. Early in the following month Cornwallis returned home, first to Cawsand Bay and then to Torbay. It was in fact the end of his service with the Channel Fleet; the death of William Pitt on 23 January resulted in a complete reconstruction of the government, and it was soon being suggested that St Vincent would return as First Lord of the Admiralty. In fact he did not; the 'Ministry of all the Talents,' led by Lord Grenville with Charles James Fox as Foreign Secretary, included Charles Grey, who became Lord Howick in April, as First Lord. St Vincent's supporters, however, pushed hard for their man to take over command of the Channel Fleet, and the King invited him to accept the post. He hesitated, but only briefly; evidently determined to preserve the decencies, he wrote to Cornwallis on 6 February:

> I am now called upon again to serve and, in the state the empire is reduced to, I feel it an imperative duty to obey the call, with only one repugnance, which arises out of the esteem and respect I have for you; and I beg you will rest assured that every possible delicacy will be paid to your zealous services, for no man regards you more sincerely than, yours etc.[7]

Cornwallis, outwardly at any rate, seems to have borne no ill will towards St Vincent in respect of his supersession, writing to him in such terms that St Vincent responded by saying that his letter had set his heart 'quite at ease'.

Cornwallis was not, however, at all content with the way he had been treated; this, in all the circumstances, was hardly surprising. The terms in which he wrote to the new First Lord appear from the latter's reply on 27 February:

> I am very sorry that you should have found either in the conduct of the late Board or in the appointment of Lord St Vincent to the command of the Channel Fleet any cause of complaint. I can only say that I intended

---

6   Cornwallis-West, *Admiral Cornwallis*, pp.496-497.
7   Davidson, *Admiral Lord St Vincent*, p.212.

fully to acknowledge the merit of your past services, and, in carrying into effect an arrangement which it appeared to His Majesty's ministers expedient to adopt, to show you every personal attention in my power.[8]

These weasel words may have referred to the possible offer of a peerage, which George Canning, speaking for the opposition in the House of Commons, had called for. It is entirely possible, as Cornwallis's biographer observed, that the terms of his letter to Grey had made such an offer impossible; but even if offered, it is entirely likely that Cornwallis would have refused it. That he was prepared to write generously to St Vincent reflects considerable credit on him; the latter's willingness to supplant Cornwallis is perhaps not quite so creditable.

John Whitby, who had had a brief falling out with the admiral that was speedily resolved by the tact and good sense of his wife, wrote to her after Cornwallis struck his flag:

> It isn't given to every great sailor to win a victory at sea any more than it is to every military commander to win one on shore; there are other equally important achievements to be attained, and no one can deny the Admiral his share of having attained them.[9]

Sadly, Whitby died suddenly on 6 April, to Cornwallis's great distress. His widow, after leaving the admiral's home for a year, then returned to Newlands to live with him, and stayed there for the rest of his life. They were devoted to each other, in spite of the difference of nearly forty years in their age, and he was dependent on her not only for the comfort of their relationship but for her immensely efficient management of his affairs until his death in 1819.

John Leyland, looking back at Cornwallis's conduct of the blockade of Brest, wrote a powerful tribute to him:

> For the courage, endurance, resource, and generally for the great strategic and tactical ability of Cornwallis himself, these pages are testimony enough. They will entitle him to even a higher place among our great seamen than has hitherto even been assigned to him, and we can only regret, with Nelson, that some great opportunity of encountering the fleet, which he had watched so vigilantly and so long, was not vouchsafed to him. His work in the blockade was a masterpiece of the administrative and seamanlike handling of a great naval force in operations, of supreme importance to the country.[10]

8   Cornwallis-West, *Admiral Cornwallis*, p.507.
9   Cornwallis-West, *Admiral Cornwallis*, pp.507-508.
10 Leyland (ed.), *Blockade of Brest*, Vol.II, pp.xliii-xliv.

St Vincent hoisted his flag in the *Hibernia* on 22 February. In resuming the command of the Channel Fleet, he soon had a good deal to say about its general condition, its officers and the manner of conducting the blockade of Brest. He was in regular correspondence with Rear Admiral John Markham, appointed by the new First Lord to be the First Naval Lord on the Board, the other two being Sir Charles Pole and Sir Harry Neale. The weather in the Channel had been poor, and it was not until 12 March that St Vincent was first able to put to sea. When he reached Cawsand Bay he sent a furious letter to Markham to tell him what he had found at Plymouth, as well as his view of the blockade:

> The picture I sent you of the total want of vigour, discipline and subordination at Portsmouth is much heightened at this port, where nothing is thought of but contrivance to delay equipment and to frustrate the orders issued by superiors. The moment a ship arrives she is stripped, and her pretended defects coloured in a way that makes me sick … Without a squadron of good two-deck ships constantly kept off the Black Rocks, the French may go in and out of Brest with impunity.[11]

Later in the month St Vincent wrote to Markham from off the Black Rocks to denounce Cawsand Bay as an anchorage:

> In the winter months Cawsand Bay is a very unsafe place for large ships to resort to – dangerous in the extreme, and such a swell that five days out of seven nothing can lay alongside of them. Several have been put to the utmost hazard of knocking their bottoms out.[12]

In a familiar jibe at the captains, he thought that they were ashore and their lieutenants would not turn out in the night to strike yards and topmasts in time.

St Vincent soon convinced himself that standards in the blockading fleet had became extremely lax and he took steps to enforce a much tighter blockade. He wrote in March to Tucker, who had become Second Secretary to the Board, to say that he could 'perceive no principle of laudable ambition or patriotic spirit anywhere'. He went on:

> Prize money, or looking forward to retirement, with a good provision of some sort from the country, appear to be the governing actions of all the officers' minds I have seen. We go on quietly but steadily here, setting

---

11   Markham (ed.), *Admiral John Markham*, pp.37-38.
12   Markham (ed.), *Admiral John Markham*, p.43.

those right who are wrong, by signal, thereby shutting out discussion; and I think our conduct has already made some impression.[13]

St Vincent relied very heavily on Sir Charles Cotton, his second-in-command; his arrival had meant Cotton's fourth change of senior commander while serving with the Channel Fleet. St Vincent appears to have given Cotton some credit for improving the situation, writing to Markham in May:

> Although the example I set six years ago in the best mode of cruising upon Brest has not been followed by any of my successors, and the inshore squadron has most shamefully abandoned the station assigned to it, as I will explain when we meet, I think the system is now established on such principles as cannot be departed from; the more especially as Sir Charles Cotton has been witness to the certainty of keeping hold of Ushant in any wind or weather, by taking shelter under that island in an easterly gale, and profiting by the tides (which are as advantageous as about Scilly) in other circumstances.[14]

Since Cornwallis had been, except when on leave, St Vincent's' only successor as commander in chief, these observations were highly critical, and unjustified; but St Vincent was never troubled by the need to avoid exaggeration.

In August St Vincent was sent with a squadron to Lisbon, leaving Cotton in command of the rest of the fleet before Brest. The diminished size of the French fleet there did not, of course mean that the blockade could be relaxed; the escapes of Leissègues and Willaumez might well be emulated. The reason for the mission to Lisbon was the belief that the French were planning to invade Portugal with an army that was assembling at Bayonne. St Vincent's task was to support the Portuguese government, take possession of the Portuguese fleet and if necessary facilitate the escape of the royal family and court to Brazil. Before St Vincent's return, the invasion not having materialised, the blockading squadron off Rochefort fought a brisk action with a French squadron that emerged from the port with Martinique as its destination; four out of the five French frigates were taken.

Meanwhile in London the death of Charles James Fox necessitated a reshuffle of the government. Howick succeeded him as Foreign Secretary, and Thomas Grenville went to the Admiralty as First Lord. St Vincent was dismayed, and warned Tucker that if Howick left the Admiralty, he should 'prepare his Lordship for my retreat from the command of the fleet, for I will not submit to the quaint

13 Sir William James, *Old Oak. The Life of John Jervis Earl of St Vincent* (London: Longman, Green, & Co., 1950), p.199.
14 James, *Old Oak*, p.201.

Admiral Sir Charles Cotton. (Anne S.K. Brown Collection)

comments of a petulant and ignorant Admiralty'.[15] In the end, St Vincent was persuaded to remain in command. For a while Thomas Grenville contemplated replacing Markham, apparently due to the latter's tendency to make enemies. St Vincent, for whom this would have been a serious loss, wrote to him: 'You will find in Markham firmness and integrity to the backbone, happily combined with ability, diligence, and zeal'. Markham remained in post.

In March 1807 the government fell, and St Vincent at once resigned from his command, writing to Markham that the sooner both of them were out of harness the better. He had worked well with Grenville, whom he described as 'the truest patriot, the most upright man, the most faithful straightforward servant of the public' that he had ever met with; but he had no intention of continuing under his successor. He told Grenville that the support he had received from the Board while he was First Lord 'has enabled me to restore the Channel Fleet to the vigour in which I left it, seven years ago'. St Vincent's unwavering confidence in his own abilities had never left him; this conviction that he knew best accounts for his mistaken belief in the inefficiency of the Channel Fleet when he came to resume that command.[16]

15 James, *Old Oak*, p.206.
16 James, *Old Oak*, p.209.

27

Gambier

The new Board of Admiralty under Mulgrave, in choosing a successor to St Vincent, evidently felt it necessary to go for seniority and experience, and settled on the 65 year old Lord Gardner. Thus it come about that seven years after his outspoken disappointment in not being appointed to succeed Bridport, and his extreme discomfort at serving as a locum while Cornwallis went on leave, Gardner at last achieved in April 1807 his long-standing ambition to command the Channel Fleet. His tenure of office was to prove extremely uneventful. The departure of half of the Brest fleet's ships of the line with Leissègues and Willaumez at the end of 1805 meant that it represented a greatly reduced threat. Although the blockade continued, the Brest fleet remained largely quiescent, and the Channel Fleet was not called on to undertake any significant operation.

Gardner hauled down his flag after a year in post, and the Admiralty had to consider the question of who should succeed him. The lot fell on Admiral Lord Gambier, an understandable choice following his successful command of the naval forces sent to Denmark in 1807. After a three day bombardment of the city of Copenhagen, and the landing of troops under General Lord Cathcart, the Danes capitulated and Gambier took possession of the Danish fleet, which included eighteen ships of the line, twenty one frigates and brigs and twenty five gunboats. For this he was rewarded with a peerage. Still a relatively young man, being only 52 when appointed to the Channel Fleet, James Gambier had enjoyed a successful career at sea, culminating in his command of the *Defence* at the battle of the Glorious First of June in1794, when his was the first ship to break the French line. In the following year he was promoted to rear admiral, and became a member of the Board of Admiralty. Becoming a vice admiral in 1799, he returned to the Channel Fleet as third-in-command under Cornwallis. Following this, he served for two years as Governor of Newfoundland, before returning to the Admiralty, where his cautious approach to operational questions caused Cornwallis a good deal of heartache. He was not popular in the Navy; Cornwallis, for instance, received a letter from the wife of his former captain of the fleet in which she wrote:

Admiral Alan Gardner, 1st Baron Gardner.

> I understand that Lord Barham and Admiral Gambier are the movers and execute all and everything at the Board. My surprise is great at Admiral Gambier having so much consideration; I used to know him well formerly and always considered him a very weak man.[1]

Gambier was, however, extremely well connected. His aunt Margaret had married the 35 year old Captain Charles Middleton in 1761, one day to become Lord Barham and First Lord of the Admiralty, and all his life an influential figure in naval affairs not least through his close association with William Pitt. Middleton was, like his wife's family, a life long Evangelical, holding that 'there could be no reason to doubt that the world was ruled by a divine Providence, mysterious though its working

1   Cornwallis-West, *Admiral Cornwallis*, p.501.

Admiral James Gambier, 1st Baron Gambier. (Anne S.K. Brown Collection)

might be to many at any given moment'.[2] His biographer has observed that 'confi-dent of his own righteousness, he was quick to pass judgment on sinners', and Gambier shared this characteristic. Very much unlike the majority of seagoing officers, Gambier's religious convictions were manifest throughout his career, and he was known in the navy as 'Dismal Jimmy'. He distributed fundamentalist pamphlets to his men, was firmly opposed to alcohol, and refused to allow women on board his ship while in port. His conscience had been seriously troubled by the heavy bombardment of civilian areas of Copenhagen in 1807. While at the Admiralty Gambier was seen in the Navy as having 'led the direction and all the patronage of the Navy since Lord Mulgrave was at the board', as Collingwood wrote to his sister in June 1808.[3]

2   Talbott, *Pen and Ink Sailor*, p.14.
3   Hughes (ed.), *Admiral Lord Collingwood*, pp.248-249.

The French navy had been steadily strengthened by the building of new ships to replace many of those which at had lost at Trafalgar, but not much had been done with them. Now in early 1809 it appeared to Napoleon that the French possessions at Guadeloupe and Martinique were in danger of falling to the British, and he determined to do something to prevent this. He ordered Decrès to prepare for a sortie from Brest under Rear Admiral Jean-Baptiste Willaumez, who was to sail to the West Indies as soon as an opportunity was presented. At the end of January and during February continued westerly gales drove the Channel Fleet under Gambier off its station, and Willaumez seized his chance, putting to sea on 21 February. He flew his flag in the 120 gun three decker *Océan* (ex-*Peuple*, ex-*Montagne*), with the 80 gun ships *Foudroyant* and *Varsovie*, five 74s, *Tourville*, *Jean Bart*, *Tonnerre*, *Aquilon* and *Regulus*, and the frigates *Indienne* and *Elbe*.

Decrès ordered Willaumez to proceed to Lorient, and chase away the block-ading squadron in order to release the three ships of the line and five frigates of Commodore Troude; if when he got there the tide did not serve, he was to proceed to the Basque Roads, driving away the blockading squadron of Rear Admiral Stopford. There he was to release the three ships of the line, the *Calcutta*, flute, and the frigates there, and sail at once to Martinique to prevent the capture of that island. Willaumez, taking advantage of a north-north-easterly wind, had cleared the Passage du Raz when his fleet was sighted by the *Revenge*, one of the ships of the line of the inshore squadron under Commodore Beresford. The *Revenge* lost sight of the French fleet about 12.30pm, but regained touch at 3.15.

By 4.30 Beresford had come up with the rest of his squadron; seeing the way clear to Lorient Willaumez hauled his wind, and contact between the two squadrons was lost before the French arrived at the Ile de Groix. From there Willaumez sent a schooner to Troude to sail for the Pertuis d'Antioche, the entrance to the Basque Roads. Rear Admiral Stopford was anchored off the Chasseron lighthouse with a squadron consisting of the *Caesar*, 80, and two 74s (*Defiance* and *Donegal*) when news reached him on 23 February that Willaumez was heading for the Basque Roads. He weighed anchor and at dawn sighted Willaumez entering the Pertuis d'Antioche. He at once sent the frigate *Naiad* to report the news to Gambier. Before the frigate had got far, she signalled to Stopford that three strange sail were coming down from the northward, so Stopford left the frigates *Amethyst* and *Emerald* to watch Willaumez while he sailed towards the strangers.[4]

The new arrivals were three French frigates under Commodore Jurien, the *Italienne*, *Calypso* and *Cybele*. The tide had not permitted Troude to get his ships of the line out of Lorient, so Jurien went on alone. He was, however, followed by the British frigate *Aurelia* and a brig-sloop, the *Dotterel*; when Stopford came in sight, Jurien realised that he was cut off, and took refuge under the batteries of

---

4   James, *Naval History*, Vol.IV, pp.392-393.

Sable d'Olonne, anchoring close in with springs. Stopford's squadron, led by the *Defiance*, opened fire at 11.00 am; within the hour it was all over, as Jurien's frigates cut their cables and ran on shore. It was high water, and they could not be got off; this operation completed, Stopford returned to his station off the Chasseron lighthouse from where he could see Willaumez's squadron in Basque Roads. Next day he was joined by Beresford with his squadron.

On February 26 Willaumez led his squadron into the Aix Roads; unluckily the *Jean Bart* ran aground on the Palles shoal near Ile Madame: efforts to refloat her failed, and she became wrecked. The rest of the fleet, joined by the ships from the Rochefort squadron, anchored between the southern end of the Ile d'Aix and the Boyart shoal. There followed an incident not unknown to either navy, when a captain protested about the proceedings of his admiral. On this occasion it was Captain Bergeret of the *Varsovie*, who was discontented with Willaumez's conduct of the encounter with Beresford on 21-23 February and wrote to Decrès to complain. As a result, both were called to Paris, following which both were superseded. In place of Willaumez the redoubtable Vice Admiral Zacharie Allemand was sent to take command.

Gambier had first learned of the escape of the French from Brest on 26 February when on his way, with nine ships of the line, to resume his blockade of the port. He at once detached Vice Admiral John Duckworth with eight ships to locate and follow Willaumez, while he returned to Cawsand Bay in his flagship, the *Caledonia*. On the way there he met the *Naiad*, and learned that the French were in Basque Roads; he sailed with five of the line on 3 March to join Stopford in blockading them. When the *Defiance* and the *Triumph* left the fleet, Gambier had a total of eleven ships of the line, three of them three deckers, with which to deal with the French squadron. On 17 March he anchored his fleet in Basque Roads, with his frigates a mile closer to the land than his main force.[5]

Before he took up his position in the Basque Roads, Gambier had written to Mulgrave on 11 March to tell him that the works on shore presented no obstacle to a bombardment of the enemy's fleet, although noting this had been attempted unsuccessfully in 1803. He went on:

> The enemy's ships lie much exposed to the operation of fireships, it is a horrible mode of warfare, and the attempt hazardous if not desperate; but we should have plenty of volunteers for the service. If you mean to do anything of the kind, it should be with secrecy and quickly, and the ships used should not be less than those built for the purpose – at least a dozen, and some smaller ones.[6]

5   Clowes, *Royal Navy*, Vol.V, p.255.
6   Lord Cochrane, *The Autobiography of a Seaman* (London: Maclaren & Co., 1860), p.205.

For the moment Gambier was more concerned with the threat of a possible fire-ship attack by the French on his own fleet. He gave orders that all ships should be ready to slip their cables at a moment's notice, while boats were prepared with grapnels to tow away any attacking fireships.

The idea of using fireships had already occurred to the Admiralty, which issued orders for the preparation of a dozen of these as early as 7 March. On 19 March Gambier was notified of this and of the despatch of five bomb vessels, together with William Congreve who was also to join the fleet with a supply of the rockets of his invention. These, Gambier was told, would enable him to attack the French fleet at its anchorage if he found it practicable. The order continued:

> I am further commanded to signify their Lordships' directions to you to take into your consideration the possibility of making an attack upon the enemy, either conjointly, with your line of battle ships, frigates and small craft, fireships, bombs, and rockets, or separately, by any of the above means.[7]

On the same day that this order was sent, their Lordships received Gambier's letter with his suggestion; and on that day also, fatefully, the frigate *Impérieuse*, commanded by Lord Cochrane, arrived at Plymouth from the Mediterranean.

Born in 1775, the eldest son of the eccentric and impoverished Earl of Dundonald, Thomas Cochrane was the nephew of Alexander Cochrane, a combative naval officer who had by 1809 risen to the rank of Vice Admiral. This connection gave Cochrane an invaluable start to his career, which prospered from the moment when he was appointed at the age of 25 to the command of the 14 gun brig *Speedy*. In her he made his name when he fought and captured the Spanish frigate *Gamo* of 32 guns. Thereafter he had faced the hostility of St Vincent, who was responsible for a sustained vendetta against Cochrane, possibly because he had heard of some outspoken criticism by the young lieutenant of his handling of the Mediterranean Fleet in 1799. In the *Speedy*, Cochrane amassed a great deal of prize money before she was taken by a French squadron under Linois in the summer of 1801. In 1805 he succeeded in being appointed to the frigate *Pallas*, in which he enjoyed great success. Elected to Parliament in 1806, he took command of the *Impérieuse* later that year, and enjoyed further success in the Mediterranean when under the command of Collingwood, who was greatly impressed.

When news of his arrival at Plymouth reached the Admiralty, he was at once ordered to London to confer with the First Lord, and the two men met on 21 February. With Cochrane's successful operations off the French and Spanish coasts in mind, Mulgrave wanted to hear from him whether a fireship attack on the French fleet in the Aix Roads would be successful Cochrane was in no doubt that it could

7   Clowes, *Royal Navy*, Vol.V, p.256.

be, and outlined the plan which he would propose for the attack. Mulgrave was impressed, and asked him to put it in writing. After Cochrane had done so, the First Lord saw him again, and told him that the Board entirely approved the scheme, and asked him if he would carry it out. At first Cochrane demurred, on the grounds that it would cause serious problems with officers senior to him already on the spot, and Mulgrave had to think again. However, next day he sent once more for Cochrane, and said to him: 'My lord, you must go. The Board cannot listen to further refusal or delay. Rejoin your frigate at once. I will make you all right with Lord Gambier'. The First Lord added that Cochrane should be easy in his mind about jealous feelings on the part of senior officers; he would 'so manage it with Lord Gambier that the *amour propre* of the fleet shall be satisfied'.[8] After a further attempt to decline the command, Cochrane finally assented, and set off for Plymouth.

He joined the fleet in the *Impérieuse* on 3 April, to find that Gambier was beginning to doubt whether a fireship attack was practicable, observing in a letter to the Admiralty that 'the tide and wind that are favourable to this kind of annoyance to the enemy serve equally to carry them up the river'. He did, however, confirm that if their Lordships considered an attack practicable, he was ready to obey their orders 'however great the risk may be of the loss of men and ships'.[9] When Cochrane arrived, the twelve fireships ordered by the Admiralty had not arrived, detained in the Downs by contrary winds, and Gambier ordered that eight of the transports with the fleet be prepared as fireships together with the *Mediator*, flute. Three explosion vessels were also equipped. On 6 April the *Aetna*, with Congreve and his rockets, arrived, followed on 10 April by the missing fireships.

All was therefore practically ready; but in the meantime the nomination of Cochrane to lead the assault had brought forth the predicted reaction. The fiery Rear Admiral Eliab Harvey, the heroic captain of the *Téméraire* at Trafalgar, was outraged by the news, and stormed aboard Gambier's flagship to demand that he be put in charge of the operation. When Gambier explained that it was the Admiralty's order that Cochrane lead it, Harvey said he did not care: 'If I am passed by, and Lord Cochrane or any junior officer is appointed in preference, I will immediately strike my flag, and resign my commission'. When Gambier expressed his regret (almost certainly insincerely), Harvey burst out again, asserting that Gambier was unfit to command the fleet: 'If Lord Nelson had been here, he would not have anchored in Basque Roads at all, but would have dashed at the enemy at once'. Later, in the cabin of Sir Harry Neale, the Captain of the Fleet, he told Cochrane that he had no personal quarrel with him, but went on:

> This is not the first time I have been lightly treated and that my services have not been attended to in the way they deserved, because I am no

8   Cochrane, *Autobiography*, p.209.
9   Clowes, *Royal Navy*, Vol.V, p.258.

canting Methodist, no hypocrite, no psalm-singer and do not cheat old
women out of their estates by hypocrisy and canting.[10]

Cochrane mildly remarked that Harvey was using 'very strong expressions relative to the Commander-in-Chief,' to which Harvey replied that he had spoken to
Gambier with the same degree of prudence as he had to Cochrane and Neale. It
was, thought Cochrane, a strange notion of prudence. Even now Harvey was not
finished; on the quarterdeck he delivered a fresh outburst of his grievances against
Gambier to Captain Bedford, the flag captain, before leaving the ship. He subsequently returned to England, was court martialled and dismissed the service:
although reinstated in the following year, he was never again employed at sea.

One of Harvey's complaints, which Cochrane soon found to be entirely justified, was that Gambier had failed to take soundings of the channel leading to the
French fleet. All that had been done was some soundings of the Boyart Shoal,
furthest from the enemy. But for Cochrane's familiarity with these waters from
his time in the *Pallas*, 'this neglect would in all probability have been fatal' to the
carrying out of his plan. While preparations for the assault continued, Gambier
further annoyed Cochrane by sending over a number of tracts for distribution to
the crew of the *Impérieuse*; these he declined to distribute, finding some of them
'of a most silly and injudicious character'.[11] It was not a good start.

As soon as he arrived, Cochrane had gone close inshore to reconnoitre, and at
once wrote to the First Lord to propose an enlargement of the operation:

> Having been very close to the Isle d'Aix, I find that the western sea wall
> has been pulled down to build a better. At present the fort is quite open,
> and may be taken as soon as the French fleet is driven on shore or burned,
> which will be as soon as the fireships arrive. The wind continues favour-
> able for the attack. If your lordship can prevail on the ministry to send a
> military force here, you will do great and lasting good to our country.[12]

It was not a view which he felt able to express directly to Gambier, since the latter,
retracting his earlier view, was already on record as suggesting that the French
works must be regarded as a serious threat.

Part of Cochrane's plan involved in using 'explosion vessels,' carrying 1,500
barrels of gunpowder, several hundred shells and nearly three thousand hand
grenades. These would be used to shatter the boom laid by the French for their
protection. In addition, Cochrane hoped that once they had exploded, the French

10 Donald Thomas, *Cochrane: Britannia's Last Sea-King* (London: Andre Deutsch, 1978) pp.152-153;
     Cochrane, *Autobiography*, p.217.
11 Cochrane, *Autobiography*, p.219.
12 Cochrane, *Autobiography*, p.221.

would suppose that all the fireships had been similarly prepared, and that instead of their ships offering opposition to the attack, 'they would, in all probability, be driven ashore in their attempt to escape from such diabolical engines of warfare, and thus became an easy prey'.

Aboard his flagship *Océan*, Allemand, although having no intention himself of launching a fireship attack, was very much aware of the likelihood that the British would do so, and did his best to prepare for it. His orders from Decrés had been heavily influenced by Napoleon, who had always believed that a fleet moored under the guns of batteries on shore would be safe from attack, and who was especially confident about the position in Aix Roads. In June 1805 he had written to Decrés to pour scorn on the suggestion that a fleet there might be at risk:

> You may quiet your apprehensions that the enemy will attempt something against Ile d'Aix … nothing can be more insane than the idea of attacking a French squadron at Ile d'Aix. I am annoyed to see you with such notions … What on earth do you imagine is to be feared by a squadron of five ships of the line, with plenty of powder and supplies, well protected and ready to fight, lying at Aix?[13]

Allemand moored his fleet, with his ships' heads pointing north, in three lines bearing more or less north and south, in the passage between the south end of the Ile d'Aix and the western end of the Palles shoal, which runs out northwest from the Ile Madame. The innermost line, in six fathoms of water, consisted of the frigate *Elbe* and five 74s, the *Tourville, Aquilon, Jemappes, Patriote* and *Tonnerre*, moored at intervals of about 200 yards. The middle line, some 250 yards to the west, consisted of the *Calcutta*, flute, the *Cassard*, 74, *Regulus*, 74, *Océan*, 120, *Varsovie*, 80 and *Foudroyant*, 80. These were moored opposite the gaps in the eastern line. The outer line, a further 750 yards to the west, was composed of three 40 gun frigates, *Pallas, Hortense* and *Indienne*. Just inside this line was a strong and well anchored boom. The position was covered by batteries of a total of about thirty guns, mainly 36 pounders, located principally on the Ile d'Aix, which was garrisoned by 2, 000 troops.[14]

The arrival of the fireships, and the obvious British preparations, left Allemand in no doubt on 10 April that an attack was imminent. Indeed, Cochrane had been all for launching the attack at once, but Gambier forbade this. Allemand issued detailed instruction to his fleet and to the large number of boats which were to row guard during the night and be ready to board and tow away any fireships which approached. The frigates were ordered to be ready to get under way at a moment's notice. The ships of the line were ordered to strip down everything to their lower masts, to reduce the risk of fire.

13   Clowes, *Royal Navy*, Vol.V, p.259.
14   Clowes, *Royal Navy*, Vol.V, pp.259-260.

On the afternoon of 11 April Cochrane, in the *Impérieuse*, came in to towards the French fleet, anchoring north east of the Boyart Shoal, about a mile and three quarters from the nearest French frigate, supported by three more frigates to receive the crews who escaped from the fireships Three brigs equipped with rockets took up a position at the tail of the shoal, while the bomb vessel *Aetna* anchored to the northwest of the Ile d'Aix. Cochrane had briefed all the captains involved in the attack in the course of a meeting aboard the *Caledonia*; he told them that he would lead the assault in one of the three explosion vessels; the fireships were led by the *Mediator*, a large East Indiamen that had been hired and armed to serve as a warship, but which was now serving as a storeship. Two of the frigates served as a beacon to direct the fireships, displaying lights to guide them towards the enemy. The night was very dark, and a strong breeze favoured the approach of the attack, blowing directly towards the French fleet.[15]

Cochrane fired his explosion vessel about three quarters of a mile from the enemy line. The fuse should have ignited the explosion after fifteen minutes; as it was, it went off in half that time. In his *Autobiography*, Cochrane described the effect:

> The explosion vessel did her work well, the effect constituting one of the grandest artificial spectacles imaginable. For a moment, the sky was red with the lurid glare arising form the simultaneous ignition of 1,500 barrels of powder. On this gigantic flash subsiding, the air seemed alive with shells, grenades, rockets, and masses of timber, the wreck of the shattered vessel; whilst the water was strewn with spars, shaken out of the enormous boom, on which, according to the subsequent testimony of Captain Proteau, whose frigate lay just within the boom, the vessel had brought up, before she exploded.[16]

In fact, according to James and Clowes, it was the *Mediator* that broke the boom. Her commander remained on board until the very last moment, leaving it so late that some of his crew were killed and injured before they could take to the boats. On the basis of French accounts, Clowes asserts that one of the explosion vessels blew up about 120 yards from the *Indienne* and another, ten minutes later, nearby. The third was fouled by a drifting fireship, and when fired the fuse failed. About half a dozen of the fireships were well handled, and bore down on the French lines, although none actually ignited any of the enemy vessels. The rest, abandoned before they had got within two miles of the French, achieved little.

15   Peter Kirsch, *Fireship: The Terror Weapon of the Age of Sail* (Annapolis: Naval Institute Press, 2009, pp.224-225
16   Cochrane, *Autobiography*, p.229.

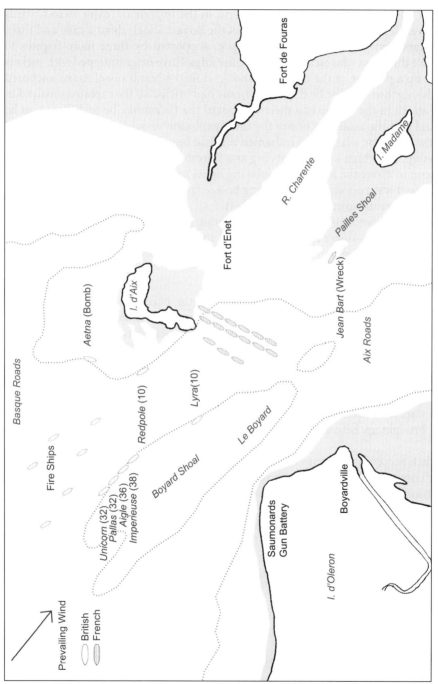

Fort de Fouras

I. Madame

R. Charente

Pailles Shoal

Fort d'Enet

Jean Bart (Wreck)

Aix Roads

I. d'Aix

Aetna (Bomb)

Basque Roads

Redpole (10)

Lyra(10)

Le Boyard

Boyard Shoal

Fire Ships

Unicorn (32)
Pallas (32)
Aigle (36)
Imperieuse (38)

Saumonards
Gun Battery

Boyardville

I. d'Oleron

Prevailing Wind

British
French

Map 6 Basque Roads: The Fireship Attack, 11 April 1809.

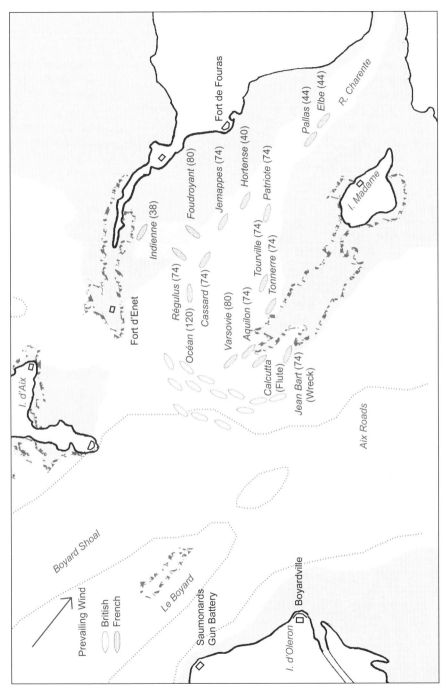

Map 7 Basque Roads: The Aftermath, 12 April 1809.

Fort de Fouras

R. Charente

Pallas (44)

Elbe (44)

Hortense (40)

Jemappes (74)

Patriote (74)

Foudroyant (80)

I. Madame

Indienne (38)

Tourville (74)

Tonnerre (74)

Fort d'Enet

Régulus (74)

Aquilon (74)

Océan (120)

Cassard (74)

Varsovie (80)

Calcutta (Flute)

Jean Bart (74) (Wreck)

I. d'Aix

Aix Roads

Boyard Shoal

Le Boyard

Saumonards Gun Battery

Boyardville

I. d'Oléron

Prevailing Wind

British

French

The attack had, however, achieved the result at which Cochrane was aiming, throwing the French into total confusion. Apart from the *Cassard* and the *Foudroyant,* whose captains kept their heads when all around were losing theirs, the French ships cut their cables and, lacking steerage way, began to foul each other before drifting, in the strong westerly wind, on shore. The *Océan*, deep laden with supplies for Martinique, grounded not on the Palles Shoal but while still in the Aix Roads. 500 yards south west of her, upon the Charenton rocks, lay the *Varsovie* and *Aquilon*, and nearby, on better ground, the *Regulus* and *Jemappes*. The *Tonnerrre* was north-west of the Ile Madame, while the *Calcutta* lay close to the wreck of the *Jean Bart*, on the edge of the Palles Shoal. The *Patriote* and the *Tourville* lay on the mud off the Ile Madame, close to the entrance to the Charente. The frigates were all aground on the mud, the *Indienne* about three quarters of a mile east of the *Océan*. Only the *Cassard* and the *Foudroyant* were still afloat.[17]

As dawn broke on 12 April it could be seen that although no French vessel had been destroyed, they were at the mercy of a further attack carried out by the British fleet. At that time the *Caledonia* was some twelve miles from the French fleet, and Gambier was dependent on Cochrane for information as to the situation. The latter was desperate to see a response from the Commander-in-Chief, to whom he made a series of signals, beginning at 5.48 am: 'half the fleet can destroy the enemy. Seven on shore'. He followed this at 6.40: 'Eleven on shore', and an hour later with: 'only two afloat'. It was only after his signal at 9.30 to the effect that the enemy were preparing to heave off that Gambier ordered the fleet to get under way, although he postponed this until about 10.45 to enable him to brief his captains on board the *Caledonia*.

Cochrane was beside himself, signalling at one point that the frigates alone could destroy the enemy, but this brought no response. The opportunity was, at that point, ideal, as he subsequently explained:

> The tide was fast rising, so that any ships sent to the attack of the stranded vessels would have had the flood tide to go in and the ebb to return, after having accomplished their destruction; whilst it was evident that if not attacked, the same flood tide would enable the French ships aground to float and escape, with which view some were heaving their guns and stores overboard.[18]

Gambier's caution was prompted by the fact that the restricted waters of the Aix Roads made manoeuvre difficult, and he feared for the safety of his ships of the line not only because of the shoals, but also the French batteries. This latter anxiety was probably illusory, as Cochrane later pointed out: the French, firing on his

---

17   James, *Naval History*, Vol.IV, pp.408-409.
18   Cochrane, *Autobiography*, p.233.

anchored ships from a fort on the Ile d'Oleron, failed to reach them. Gambier's fleet, having weighed at 10.45 am and stood towards Aix Roads, approached to within three and a half miles of the Ile d'Aix when, to Cochrane's baffled fury, it again anchored, out of range of the enemy. At this, Cochrane decided to try to force Gambier's hand, taking the *Impérieuse* in towards the French. At 1.30 pm he signalled: 'The enemy's ships are getting under sail'. Ten minutes later, he made the signal: 'The enemy is superior to the chasing ship', and five minutes later signalled: 'The ship is in distress, and requires to be assisted immediately'. These, given the limitations of the signal book, were the best he could do.

At 2.00 pm Cochrane anchored the *Impérieuse* in a position from which her starboard broadside could fire at the *Calcutta*, while her starboard forecastle guns and bow chasers could fire at the *Varsovie* and *Aquilon*. At about this time Gambier sent in the frigate *Indefatigable* followed by the rest of the frigates and the small craft, to Cochrane's support, and at 2.30 ordered his lightest ships of the line, the *Valiant* and *Revenge*, also to proceed towards him. One by one the British ships came to anchor in a semicircle around the grounded French ships. By 5.30 the *Varsovie* and *Aquilon* had struck, while the *Calcutta* was abandoned by Captain Lafon and his crew. At 6.00 the crew of the *Tonnerre* abandoned ship, setting fire to her as they left; she blew up at 7.30, and the *Calcutta* followed suit an hour later.[19]

The British movements had indicated to the French that another attack was imminent, and the *Foudroyant* and *Cassard* cut their cables, and headed for the safety of the Charente; both, however, grounded on the shoal at the mouth of the river. In the meantime the rising tide had been sufficient for several of the stranded ships to get afloat; the *Patriote*, *Regulus* and *Jemappes*, having done so, grounded again at the mouth of the Charente, while the *Océan* moved some 700 yards towards the river before grounding again. All these grounded vessels were vulnerable to a fireship attack, but all these had been expended. Stopford hastily prepared three transports as fireships, and at 5.30 pm with the *Caesar* stood in with these, and a number of launches carrying Congreve rockets. At 7.40, though, the *Caesar* took the ground at the south-eastern end of the Boyart shoal and it was nearly three hours before she was afloat again. The *Theseus* and *Revenge* got in to a decent anchorage between the Boyart and Palles, but the *Valiant* grounded on the edge of the latter. It was midnight before the three fireships were ready to be launched, but the wind then changed, and all that could be done was to burn the abandoned *Aquilon* and *Varsovie*. The sight of these in flames caused a further alarm among the French, thinking them to be fireships, and the *Tourville* was for a couple of hours abandoned by her crew before they returned. During this time she might have been taken by a British launch which approached, but which was chased off by a resourceful quartermaster, Eugène-Joseph Bourgeois, who had

19   Clowes, *Royal Navy*, Vol.V, p.265; Thomas, *Cochrane*, p.169.

returned, alone, on board: snatching up an armful of muskets, he fired twenty of these in quick succession.[20]

Next morning, at 8.00 am, Cochrane sent the brigs and the bomb vessel to attack the grounded French ships, and these opened fire on the *Océan*, *Regulus* and *Indienne*. The engagement went on for five hours, during which the tide rose, enabling the French to move further towards the Charente. Anticipating a signal recalling him, Cochrane signalled to Gambier that if permitted to remain, he could destroy the French ships. Soon after this, however, a boat arrived alongside the *Impérieuse* with two letters for Cochrane. In the public letter, Gambier wrote:

> You have done your part so admirably that I will not suffer you to tarnish it by attempting impossibilities, which I think, as well as those captains who have come from you, any further effort to destroy these ships would be. You must, therefore, join as soon as you can with the bombs, etc, as I wish for some information, which you allude to, before I close my despatches.[21]

Gambier added that he was sending three brigs and two rocket vessels to join Cochrane, with which he could 'make an attempt on the ship that is aground on the Palles, or toward Ile Madame, but I do not think you will succeed'.

Cochrane sent back a letter reiterating that he could destroy all the ships on shore; but it was to no avail, and next morning at 9.00 am Gambier hoisted the signal for his recall, and at 4.30 pm the *Impérieuse* weighed anchor to return to the fleet. The bomb vessel *Aetna* continued to fire on the French, with the brigs, but to little effect before ceasing the bombardment at about 7.00 pm. By then the *Aetna* had used all her 10-inch shells and her 13-inch mortar had split.

During the following days the remaining French vessels got free of the mud, and made their way into the Charente, where they anchored in safety. One, the *Regulus*, remained behind, and preparations were made to attack her. A French officer aboard the *Océan* wrote on 19 April:

> We begin to despair of getting off the *Regulus,* which ship is still in the same situation. The enemy continue in the Ile d'Aix road, to the number of 20 sail. They have not made any movement whatever for these three days: which is a thing not at all to be understood, for they might with ease attack the *Regulus*, and oblige her crew to abandon her.[22]

20   James, *Naval History*, Vol.IV, pp.417-418.
21   Thomas, *Cochrane*, p.170.
22   James, *Naval History*, Vol.IV, p.422.

In fact, between 20 and 24 April, the bomb vessel *Thunder* with four gun-brigs attempted to drive her crew out of the *Regulus,* but without success. On 29 April the French ship finally got afloat, and that day Gambier sailed for home.

Cochrane, in the *Impérieuse*, had been sent by Gambier to take Sir Harry Neale with the despatches to England. This followed an interview aboard the *Caledonia*, in which Cochrane told Gambier that 'the extraordinary hesitation which had been displayed in attacking ships helplessly on shore' must have been due to his being in command rather than more senior officers:

> I begged his lordship, by way of preventing the ill feeling of the fleet from becoming detrimental to the honour of the service, to set me altogether aside, and send in Admiral Stopford, with the frigates or other vessels, as with regard to him there could be no ill feeling; further declaring my confidence that from Admiral Stopford's zeal for the service, he would, being backed by his officers, accomplish results more creditable than anything that had yet been done. I apologised for the freedom I used, stating that I took the liberty as a friend, for it would be impossible, as matters stood, to prevent a noise being made in England.[23]

Gambier was not at all pleased, observing that if Cochrane threw blame on what had been done, it would appear that he was arrogantly claiming all the merit for himself. Cutting short Cochrane's protests, he ordered him peremptorily to take Neale and the despatches to England, and they sailed for Plymouth next day, 15 April, arriving on 21 April.

Cochrane was received everywhere as a triumphant hero, and on 26 April received news that the King had made him a Knight Companion of the Bath. He was very much less pleased, however, to read Gambier's despatches, which he considered, with some justification, minimised his achievements during the battle. When, after Gambier's return in early May, the First Lord told him that, as was usual, a vote of thanks would be proposed to Gambier in the House of Commons, Cochrane was outraged:

> Whereupon I told Lord Mulgrave that it was my duty to apprise him that in my capacity as one of the members for Westminster, I would oppose the motion, on the ground that the Commander in Chief had not only done nothing to merit a vote of thanks, but had neglected to destroy the French fleet in Aix Roads, when it was clearly in his power to do so.[24]

23   Cochrane, *Autobiography*, pp.243-244.
24   Cochrane, *Autobiography*, p.244.

Mulgrave was shocked, and attempted to dissuade Cochrane, promising him that he too would be included in the vote of thanks, but Cochrane would have none of it. A little later the First Lord tried again, telling the irate captain that the government was highly displeased, and offering him a commission to take three frigates to go to the Mediterranean to operate against the French coast. This bribe was equally ineffective; Cochrane felt that 'no man with the slighter pretensions to personal honesty or political consistency' could act otherwise than he did, regardless of the consequences.[25] The first of these was that on being told by the First Lord of Cochrane's intentions, Gambier on 30 May demanded a court martial.

Somewhat surprisingly the process began with a request from the Admiralty that Gambier rewrite his official despatch. He willingly embraced this opportunity effectively to write Cochrane out of the story of the battle of the Basque Roads, omitting the reference in his first despatch to 'the vigorous and gallant attack made by Lord Cochrane upon the French line of battle ships which were on shore; a well as of his judicious manner of approaching them'. Gambier had added that Cochrane's conduct 'could not be exceeded by any feat of valour hitherto achieved by the British navy'.[26]

The problem that Gambier's request for a court martial had caused Cochrane was one which the latter had perhaps not foreseen. Although of course seen publicly as Gambier's accuser, he was not permitted to cross examine witnesses; and being himself a witness was obliged to withdraw after giving his evidence. Furthermore, the composition of the court offered Cochrane little hope that it would come with au open-minded approach to the enquiry into Gambier's conduct. The president, Admiral Sir Roger Curtis, was a close friend of the Commander-in-Chief, as was Admiral Sir William Young, with whom Cochrane had had a serious clash when the latter ordered the *Impérieuse* to sea in 1806 from Plymouth when in a dangerous condition. Frederick Marryat, the novelist, was serving aboard as a midshipman, and later wrote: 'How nearly were the lives of a fine ship's company, and of Lord Cochrane and his officers, sacrificed in this instance to the despotism'.[27] They were not the only members of the court who might be expected to sympathise with Gambier: Vice Admiral Sir John Duckworth was the latter's second in command, while Sir John Sutton had also been party to a controversial dispute with Cochrane.

William James, in his account of the court martial, observed that several of the members of the court, and particularly Curtis and Young 'evinced a strong bias in favour of the accused'. He went on:

> On two or three occasions Admiral Young attempted to browbeat Lord Cochrane; and the cross examination of some of the witnesses, whose

25   Cochrane, *Autobiography*, p.246.
26   Cochrane, *Autobiography*, p.247.
27   Florence Marryat (ed.), *Life and Letters of Frederick Marryat* (London: R. Bentley, 1872), Vol.I, p.18.

Captain Lord Cochrane, from a contemporary caricature meant to highlight his dual roles as naval hero and radical politician. (Anne S.K. Brown Collection)

evidence went in support of the charge, would have done credit to a prac-
titioner of Westminster Hall. Nor must we omit to notice, that Captain
Maitland, of the *Emerald*, who had made no secret of his opinion on the
character of the proceedings in Aix Road, should happen, when the court
martial was about to take place, to be on the Irish station.[28]

The inference that his absence was not accidental is readily drawn; the Admiralty
were determined that Cochrane's allegations should not succeed.

James pointed to a number of serious flaws in the defence which Gambier put
forward, such as the erroneous claim that the most distant French ship was within
point blank range of the batteries on the Ile d Aix; that three of the seven ships
grounded on the Palles shoal were out of reach of the guns of any British ship that
could have been sent in; and that the other four were never so placed to be attacked
after the fireships had failed. In the opinion of James, since Gambier had been
doubtful of the success of the planned attack, another admiral should have been
sent to relieve him.

Another opinion hostile to Gambier was that of Napoleon, who on St Helena
was recorded as saying that if Cochrane had been properly supported he could not
only have destroyed them but could have taken them and brought them out. The
French ships had become panic-stricken:

> The terror of the fireships was so great that they actually threw their
> powder overboard, so that they could have offered very little resistance,
> The French admiral was an imbecile, but yours was just as bad. I assure
> you that, if Cochrane had been supported, he would have taken every one
> of the ships. They ought not to have been alarmed by your fireships, but
> fear deprived them of their senses, and they no longer knew how to act in
> their own defence.[29]

It was however, an opinion that was perhaps not entirely in accordance with his
bullish opinions of the safety of the Aix Roads as expressed in June 1805.

As the trial proceeded, a number of issues of fact emerged. One of these
concerned the boom. The report of Captain Woolridge, of the *Mediator*, was to
the effect that it was his vessel that broke through the boom; Cochrane argued
that it was the blowing up of his explosion vessel which shattered it. Another was
the extent of the soundings taken of the area in which the attack was to be made;
Cochrane relied on the French charts, which were deemed inadmissible as he
could not prove their accuracy. Instead, the court accepted the charts produced for
the Admiralty by Thomas Stokes, master of the *Caledonia*, and by Edward Fairfax,

28   James, *Naval History*, Vol.IV, p.325.
29   James, *Naval History*, Vol.IV, p.427.

master of the fleet. According to the latter, the navigable passage was no more than a mile wide, half the width contended for by Cochrane.

Cochrane gave evidence for the best part of two days, but certainly appears not to have made a good witness, easily provoked into intemperance and frequently denied the opportunity to make the case which he so passionately wished to put forward. On one occasion Young and he had a violent passage of arms, when the admiral interrupted Cochrane's answer to a question: 'This is really very improper. This has no sort of connection whatever with the question which is asked, and is only a series of observations to the disadvantage of the prisoner'. To this, Cochrane replied angrily that he wished to speak the truth, the whole truth, and nothing but the truth. 'This really has nothing at all to do with the question which is asked you', said Young. This observation provoked a further outburst from Cochrane: 'If the question is put by a person ignorant of the whole proceedings, and which does not lead to get the truth and the whole truth, I hold that I am to give the whole truth'. Over Cochrane's protests, the President cleared the court; his use of the word 'ignorant' as well as his manner, was not unreasonably seen as extremely disrespectful. When the court reconvened Curtis said that 'it was, in no small degree, indecorous to the court, to make use of such an expression,' and directed Cochrane to give 'a short and decisive answer' to the questions put.[30]

Georgina, Lady Chatterton, edited the *Personal and Historical Memorials of Lord Gambier*, published in 1861, and devoted a large part of the second volume to a detailed attack on the contentions put forward by Cochrane during the trial and on the views of William James; she also analysed with some care but little objectivity the passages in Cochrane's *Autobiography* relating to the court martial proceedings. Unsurprisingly she concluded that the outcome, which was Gambier's acquittal, was unmistakably in accordance with the evidence.

> Thus ended this memorable Court Martial, wherein we find a British officer tried, for having, with a loss almost nominal, broken up a very important hostile fleet in one of its own harbours, previously deemed impregnable.[31]

The verdict of the court martial was precisely what the Admiralty had wanted from the outset:

> The charge, 'That the said Admiral the Right Honourable Lord Gambier, on the 12th day of the said month of April, the enemy's ships being then on shore and the signal having been made that they could be destroyed,

30   Thomas, *Cochrane*, p.182.
31   Lady Georgina Chatterton, *Memorials Personal and Historical of Admiral Lord Gambier* (London: Hurst and Blackett, 1861), Vol.I, p.296.

did, for a considerable time, neglect or delay taking effectual measures for destroying them' has not been proved against the said Admiral the Right Honourable Lord Gambier; but that his Lordship's conduct on that occasion, as well as his general conduct and proceedings as Commander in Chief of the Channel Fleet employed in Basque Road, between the 17th day of March and the 29th day of April 1809, was marked by zeal, judgment, ability and an anxious attention to the welfare of His Majesty's service; and doth adjudge him to be most honourably acquitted.[32]

Out in the Mediterranean Collingwood received the news with relief, writing to Rear Admiral Paris:

> On the subject of Adml. Gamb.s court martial, I am sorry it ever happened, it was very injurious to the service, and is an instance that however zealous and correct an officer's conduct may be, it will yet be subject to the animadversion of wrong headed people. I hope such will never be in the squadron that I am.[33]

Cochrane must have seen it coming, but it did not stop him attempting to reopen the question in the House of Commons, by moving in January 1810 that the minutes of the court martial be produced before the House. This assault was comfortably overcome; the government had a majority in favour of an amendment, substituting 'sentence' for 'minutes' thus avoiding any discussion of the subject matter. When the motion for the vote of thanks was put, 161 approved it, with 39 against. For Cochrane it was a defeat that effectively ended his active career as a captain in the Royal Navy. Four years later, he was dismissed in disgrace following his conviction for a stock exchange fraud. He was not fortunate in his encounters with the law.

---

32 Chatterton, *Lord Gambier*, Vol.II, pp.293-294.
33 Hughes (ed.), *Admiral Lord Collingwood*, p.295.

28

Keith

Gambier completed his three years as Commander-in-Chief of the Channel Fleet in April 1811, and the Admiralty chose as his successor Admiral Sir Charles Cotton, at the time serving as Commander-in-Chief of the Mediterranean Fleet after succeeding to that post in 1810 following the death of Collingwood. Now aged 58, he had commanded the *Mars* during Cornwallis's retreat, and had more recently spent four years as second-in-command of the Channel Fleet, experience which made him an obvious choice for the command. The French fleet at Brest, Lorient and Rochefort now offered a very much reduced threat than it had formerly posed. When Cotton hoisted his flag in August, the principal activity of the French naval forces along the Biscay coast consisted of attacks on British trade, and they enjoyed a number of minor successes. His second in command was Rear Admiral Sir Harry Neale, who led the larger part of the Channel Fleet, usually off Lorient or Quiberon Bay. Other detachments covered Brest and Rochefort.

The lesser threat from the French fleet meant that the Admiralty could give the commander of the Channel Fleet greater discretion as to how he disposed his forces, although rather less than Cotton had enjoyed in the Mediterranean. In October 1811, therefore, as Cotton was preparing to put to sea in his flagship at Plymouth, he received the following orders.

> So soon as the *San Josef* shall be ready for sail, you are to proceed in her and join the blockading squadron either off Rochefort, Lorient or Brest as you may judge most advisable, or make such a distribution of your force as shall enable you to visit all those stations for such time as you may deem necessary.[1]

Cotton had inherited from his predecessor standard procedures for the operations of the fleet off Brest, and when he arrived there he confirmed these to the

---

1 Paul C. Krajewski, *In the Shadow of Nelson. The Naval Leadership of Admiral Sir Charles Cotton, 1753-1812* (Westport CONN: Greenwood Press, 2000), p.188.

commander of this squadron, Lord Colville. The only changes, based on the latest intelligence, were that if the French squadron in Brest got away undetected, Colville was to proceed to Corunna, Cape St Vincent and Madeira before returning to his station off Brest.[2] Cotton next joined Neale at Quiberon Bay, where he remained until early December. Neale's remit extended from Ushant to the mouth of the Garonne. Cotton then visited the squadrons off Rochefort and the north coast of Spain, commanded by Captains Fahie and Tobin respectively, before returning to Plymouth. He had the Admiralty's permission to exercise his command of the Channel Fleet from on shore, and this he now opted to do. On 23 February 1812, however, he died suddenly at Stoke House, Plymouth where he had been living with his family.

The choice of his successor fell on Admiral Lord Keith, who had been on half pay since the dissolution of his last command in the North Sea some five years earlier, at which point he had found himself out of favour with the new government that succeeded the 'Ministry of All the Talents'. He had had a close relationship with Thomas Grenville, which may not have endeared him to the latter's successor as First Lord. Keith himself wrote: 'No sooner was I removed from the command than that the House [of Commons] failed to reply to any letters when my secretary had occasion to address to it, thus it appears politicians are not confined to the higher circles'.[3] Importantly, however, he had remained good friends with the Prince of Wales and the Duke of Clarence; when the former became Regent with full powers in February 1812 he was able to influence senior naval appointments and Keith was at once appointed to command the Channel Fleet. Noting that this happened the day after Cotton's death, Keith's biographer speculates that Keith had in any case been earmarked to supersede him.

For a while, after the Nore Mutiny, he had been out of favour at the Admiralty until he received a subordinate command under St Vincent in the Mediterranean. He later succeeded to the command there, where he enjoyed a fractious relationship with Nelson. After a not very successful period during the siege of Cadiz, he led the naval forces that took Egypt in 1801. The operation firmly established him as one of the leading admirals of the Royal Navy and when war broke out again in 1803 he became Port Admiral at Plymouth before St Vincent appointed him to the North Sea command, which he held until 1807.

Keith hoisted his flag in the *San Josef*, but was to spend much of his time as Commander in Chief on shore at Plymouth on account of his health. He relied on the precedent set by a number of his predecessors, including in particular St Vincent. The command of the Channel Fleet was, not surprisingly since it was the most prestigious in the Navy, exercised by a number of admirals who were comparatively old when appointed. Keith himself frequently cruised off Brest, but

2   Krajewski, *In the Shadow of Nelson*, p.188.
3   Quoted McCranie, *Lord Keith*, p.150.

Admiral George Keith Elphinstone, 1st Viscount Keith. (Anne S.K. Brown Collection)

when he was not himself on station Sir Harry Neale, who continued as second-in-command, was usually in charge. In Basque Roads the commander of the blockading squadron was Rear Admiral Philip Durham. At Plymouth, Keith's second-in-command was, from October 1812, Rear Admiral Sir Thomas Byam Martin.[4]

At the time that Keith took command the Channel Fleet consisted of 15 ships of the line, 14 frigates and ten smaller vessels. It was estimated that the total of

4   Lloyd (ed.), *Keith Papers* Vol.III, p.222.

the French vessels in Brest and the other ports on the Biscay coast amounted to 11 ships of the line, with 12 frigates; 10 ships of the line and 2 frigates were said to be building. The largest concentration was to be found in the harbour of Lorient, where there were four ships of the line, together with two frigates or corvettes. It was this latter squadron that caused the first crisis of Keith's command, when Admiral Allemand succeeded on 9 March 1812 in escaping for a cruise against British commerce. Captain Ferris, of the frigate *Diana*, hastened to report to Keith:

> As I consider it of the greatest importance that the Lords Commissioners of the Admiralty should have the earliest information of the escape of the enemy's ships from L'Orient on the 9th inst, amounting to four sail of the line, and two frigates, I have directed the *Nimrod* cutter to proceed to the first port for the conveyance of this information, and I beg to signify at the same time that I kept watching them in the ship I command the 9th and 10th.[5]

Allemand's cruise was not very successful. His objective was a large East India convoy, but he captured only one escorting frigate before, in foul weather, returning to Brest undetected. This, perhaps is some indication of the extent to which the blockade was only partially effective.

This was the only sortie of any consequence with which the Channel Fleet had to deal throughout Keith's command. Its significance lies in the fact that it was the last such sortie from a Biscay port during the war. The feebleness of the French navy during this period of the war may be judged by the fact that as a result of Napoleon's shipbuilding programme there were no less than 56 ships of the line in commission at the start of 1812, yet no operations of any magnitude were undertaken.[6] The blockade of Brest therefore continued against an opponent from which for the time being not much was to be feared, although the British could not take that for granted.

Keith had remained in London throughout March 1812 and although well enough to travel to Plymouth early in the following month, a relapse kept him on shore, to the frustration of the Admiralty, which wanted to see him join the blockading squadron off Brest. By the end of April he was fit to do so, though obliged to wait for his flagship to be ready for sea. In the meantime he asked that the Admiralty's standing instructions for the operation of the blockade should be updated; they had not been revised since August 1809.

The new orders were issued on 24 April. They were based on an assessment that the French now had ready for sea five ships of the line and six frigates in Brest, with three of the line in Rochefort, with one frigate, and three frigates in Bordeaux. The

5   Lloyd (ed.), *Keith Papers* Vol.III, p.227.
6   Jenkins, *French Navy*, p.278.

strength of the Channel Fleet was established as ten ships of the line and twelve frigates. The instructions were in essence much as they had always been, with the familiar concern with the protection of Ireland:

> Objects to be provided for in the disposition. (1) To blockade the enemy. (2) To pursue them if they escape. (3) To protect the trade against their excursions. (4) To assist the Spaniards. (5) To annoy the enemy's trade. Blockade of Brest to be personally directed by the Commander in Chief. In case the enemy escape from Brest discretion to be exercised how to act if informed of the enemy's destination. If no certain intelligence is received, or if the ships have troops on board and are supposed to be bound for Ireland, to proceed off Cape Clear to receive information from the Admiral at Cork. If the ships have troops on board and are supposed to be bound for the West Indies, Canada, Lisbon, Cadiz, not to decide forthwith in pursuing them except on receiving positive information but to protect Ireland. Under certain circumstances to run to the westward in the track of the trade to obtain vital information of the enemy's course and to protect convoys.[7]

Rochefort was identified as next in importance to Brest, while Lorient was to be frequently reconnoitred.

In the following month Keith issued his own General Orders to the ships under his command, finding it necessary to adapt the Admiralty's instructions to some extent by reason of the insufficient number of frigates available to cover all the assigned tasks. The most important of these was to watch the enemy ports for as long as they could if bad weather drove the heavy ships back to Cawsand Bay or Torbay; but the frigate commanders were also, if they sighted an enemy squadron, to track it to its destination, and report this to the relevant local commanders.

After the assassination of Spencer Perceval, the Prime Minister, in April, the new ministry was headed by Lord Liverpool. Importantly, from Keith's point of view, the new First Lord was the second Viscount Melville, with whose father Keith had had an equivocal relationship. He soon struck up a good rapport with Melville, whose support he could almost invariably count on.

The new First Lord certainly did not take British naval superiority for granted. In February 1813 he produced for the Cabinet a paper reviewing the strength of the Royal Navy, and that of the enemy, and the factors that must be taken into account. Melville noted:

> Since the decisive battle of Trafalgar, the enemy has not been able, or has not ventured to push out to sea a single squadron of his ships with any

---

7   Lloyd (ed.), *Keith Papers* Vol.III, pp.227-229.

hostile purpose. He has not however been inactive in naval preparations. The possession of the ports of Holland and of Italy has more than doubled his former means of naval equipment and naval resources … The extent to which he has availed himself of these important resources, since the year 1805, compared with our own means of keeping up an efficient fleet, will afford a tolerably correct idea as to the period of time, when we may expect him to have advanced to a state of readiness to oppose to us an equal naval force, at least as to the number and magnitude of ships. That period is not very far distant.[8]

By his calculations, at the current rate of building, France could actually achieve superiority by 1816, when she could have 108 ships of the line to the British 99. One of the key reasons for the British vulnerability was the shortened life of ships due to the demands of the blockade: 'The present war has totally changed the character and system of naval warfare. It is blockade on our part, and a state of rest and preparation on that of the enemy'.[9]

Keith was obliged to devote a great deal of time and attention, as well as scarce resources, to the problem of cooperating with Wellington's army, along the north coast of Spain and, later, the Biscay coast of France. Wellington's demands were considerable, and he made a series of strident, though frequently unjust criticisms of the support which he was getting from the Navy. Keith did his best to defend the local commanders – first Popham, and then Collier – from the attacks made upon them, as did Croker, the First Secretary at the Admiralty. The latter, indeed, was so aggressive his correspondence that Lord Bathurst, the Secretary of State at War, was obliged to pacify Wellington:

> You must not read Croker's compositions as you would those of any other official person. He has the talent of writing sharply and with great facility – a great misfortune in an official person. His style is not what it should be to the other departments, but I take no notice for I know he means nothing, and you are the god of his idolatry.[10]

Like so many of his predecessors, Keith was obliged repeatedly to complain to the Admiralty that he had entirely insufficient forces to discharge all the tasks required of him. On 23 June 1813, for instance, he wrote to Croker:

> The enemy has twelve sail of the line besides the *Jemappes* in perfect read-iness for sea and fifteen frigates, besides smaller vessels, either ready or in

8   Michael Fry, *The Dundas Despotism* (Edinburgh: Edinburgh University Press, 2004), pp.320-321.
9   Fry, *Dundas Despotism*, p.321.
10 Lloyd (ed.), *Keith Papers* Vol.III, p.262.

great forwardness in the different ports and rivers above mentioned, and the force at present employed under my orders for watching that of the enemy, for cooperating with Lord Wellington and the Spanish authorities on the north Coast of Spain, for annoying the enemy's trade, and for keeping up the different reliefs, after allowing each ship and vessel a reasonable time in port to replenish, consists only of fourteen sail of the line, eight frigates, six sloops, two gun brigs, one schooner, and two hired cutters – in all thirty three sail, of which at the present moment eleven are either in port or on their way to refit, and the reminder at sea on the different stations assigned to them.[11]

In addition to the continuous concern that the French might launch a sortie, Keith's frigates had to be constantly on the alert for the presence of American frigates, once war had broken out with the United States in 1812. It had soon become clear that the large American frigates, well built and well manned, were usually more than a match for the British frigates which they encountered, as had been painfully demonstrated by a number of single ship actions which had caused utter dismay in the Royal Navy. As a result, discretion being the better part of valour, the Admiralty took steps to avoid further disasters. Keith, on 15 July 1813, issued the following order to all his frigate captains:

> The Lords Commissioners of the Admiralty having informed me that all American frigates are at sea, and that they do not conceive that any of HM frigates should engage single-handed the larger class of American ships, which though they may be called frigates, are of a size, complement and weight of metal much beyond that class, and more resembling line of battleships; and their Lordships having been pleased to direct that in the event of one of HM frigates under my orders falling in with one of these ships her Captain should endeavour in the first instance to secure the retreat of HM ship; but if he finds that he has an advantage in sailing he should endeavour to manoeuvre and keep company with them without coming to action, in the hope of falling in with some other of HM ships with whose assistance the enemy might be attacked with a reasonable prospect of success.[12]

It was not a very glorious prescription, but in the circumstances it was realistic.

Relations with Wellington were sufficiently strained for the Admiralty to send Thomas Byam Martin on a mission to him in September 1813. This followed a

---

11   Hamilton (ed.), *Byam Martin*, Vol.II, p.336.
12   Lloyd (ed.), *Keith Papers* Vol.III, p.241.

rising tide of complaints, such as a letter written by Wellington on 9 July, soon after he had commenced the siege of San Sebastian:

> I wrote to Sir G Collier the other day to make a particular disposition of one ship with the battering train, he being on the flank of the army at Passages, to blockade St Sebastian by sea; and he was obliged to quit his station himself for the purpose, having no vessel to send. This is not the way the service can be carried on.[13]

Melville believed that Wellington had failed to understand the problems of the Navy. In his briefing to Martin he wrote:

> There have been some unpleasant and most ill-founded complaints of the want of naval assistance at St Sebastian which I am thoroughly satis-fied Lord Wellington would not have made, or have been the channel of transmitting, if he had himself superintended the siege and been enabled personally frequently to communicate with Sir George Collier, and to see instead of learning from others how the service was conducted … Neither Lord Wellington nor those who are employed on the coast appear to have the least conception of what is physically practicable by ships and boats and seamen, and to be strongly impressed with the usual and complimen-tary notion that they can do anything.[14]

Martin's mission was to explain to Wellington what was practicable, and what was impossible, and 'to learn at first hand the extent of his wants and expectations as to naval cooperation'.

Keith sent Martin off with high hopes that he might sort out the difficulties, telling him that it gave him 'great satisfaction that an officer so distinguished and of such comprehensive knowledge is to be employed on a service which I consider of high importance'.[15]

Martin entirely justified Keith's confidence; he was able to report on 21 September that Wellington had received him with great cordiality. In the course of discussions, Wellington conceded that some of his comments had been based on conjecture. Martin was able to point out that Collier had been reinforced to an even greater extent than Wellington had asked. Before he left, Martin had the satisfaction of hearing Wellington make what he described to Keith as 'a very remarkable observation', which certainly indicated a much greater understanding of the Navy's contribution. He reported Wellington as saying: 'If anyone wishes

13   Hamilton (ed.), *Byam Martin*, Vol.II, p.xiii.
14   Lloyd (ed.), *Keith Papers* Vol.III, pp.262-263.
15   Lloyd (ed.), *Keith Papers* Vol.III, p.303.

to know the history of this war, I will tell them that it is our maritime superiority gives me the power of maintaining my army while the enemy are unable to do so'.[16] Keith, Croker and Melville all wrote to Martin in the warmest terms to express their appreciation of his success in defusing what could have become a damaging breakdown in inter-service cooperation.

The consequence of the resources of the Channel Fleet being so overstretched became apparent at the end of 1813 and the start of the following year. On 24 November two French frigates were able to evade the blockade when sailing from the Loire; a week later, two more got away from the Gironde; and in January 1814 three frigates were able to put to sea from Lorient. Taken together, these forces represented a powerful threat to British trade. Even more seriously, however, four of the French frigates at Brest succeeded in avoiding the blockading squadron during November and December.[17] These sorties were a further demonstration that the blockade was frequently ineffective, and that if the French navy had been required by Napoleon to undertake a more adventurous policy, the Channel Fleet might have found it hard indeed to maintain an effective mastery of the sea in the Bay of Biscay.

By the end of March 1814 it was becoming clear that the war was drawing to a close, and the principal demands on the Channel Fleet would be the need to support the advancing armies by undertaking operations on the coast of France. Melville, however, was still cautious as to how far to go, as he warned Keith in a letter of 31 March:

> I think it right to state for your Lordship's confidential information that though measures are taking for having arms etc. in readiness to land on the French coast, yet that no directions will be given to carry into effect any operations of that nature, nor for taking up the cause of the Bourbons, till we receive further advices from Lord Castlereagh, and shall thereby be assured that we are at liberty to pursue that system of hostility against Bonaparte.[18]

As it turned out, by then the end had been reached, and Napoleon abdicated on 16 April. With the ending of hostilities, however, the Channel Fleet remained on a war footing until Napoleon was safely on his way to Elba. Although some ships' companies were paid off, there remained the problem of the American War, and Keith had to supervise the huge task of moving British troops variously to England, Ireland, Canada and the United States.

16   Hamilton (ed.), *Byam Martin*, Vol.II, p.409.
17   McCranie, *Admiral Lord Keith*, pp.162-163.
18   Lloyd (ed.), *Keith Papers* Vol.III, p.351.

In May, Keith received his reward for his lengthy naval career in the service of his country, when Melville wrote to him that the Prince Regent had directed that the dignity of a viscount should be conferred on him.[19] It was not, however until 29 July that his various duties had been so far completed that Keith was able to return to Spithead to strike his flag and enjoy the beginning of a well earned retirement.

It did not last long; when it became known that Napoleon had escaped from Elba Keith was recalled to duty and ordered to take up again the command of the Channel Fleet. He hoisted his flag aboard the *Ville de Paris* at Plymouth on 29 May. On 22 June he heard the news of Waterloo; six days later he was warned of the possibility that Napoleon might seek to escape from France from a western port. Napoleon reached Rochefort on 3 July, hoping that a passport for the United States might be granted him; on 8 July he left France for the last time, embarking aboard the frigate *Saale* in Aix Roads. On 10 July Captain Maitland, in the *Bellerophon*, with the sixth rates *Slaney* and *Myrmidon*, moved close in to watch the *Saale* and another frigate, the *Meduse*.

On 1 July the Admiralty had issued orders to Keith as to how to deal with Napoleon in the event of his attempting to escape:

> Your Lordship will therefore repeat to all your cruisers the orders already given with further directions to them to make the strictest search of any vessel they may fall in with; and if they should be so fortunate as to intercept Bonaparte, the Captain of HM ship should transfer him and his family to HM ship and there keeping him in careful custody should return to the nearest port of England with all possible expedition. He should not permit any communication whatsoever with the shore, and he will be held responsible for keeping the whole transaction a profound secret until their Lordships' further orders shall be received.[20]

The Admiralty were taking no chances.

Napoleon's request to be allowed to proceed to America having been refused, he went aboard the *Bellerophon*, saying to Maitland: 'I am come on board your ship to place myself under the protection of England'. The *Bellerophon* reached Torbay on 24 July, and it was Keith who was obliged to undertake the discussions with Napoleon that were to culminate in his departure for exile in St Helena. It was a stressful time for Keith, obliged as he was to enforce the firm decision that Napoleon should sail as soon as possible, in the face of Napoleon's repeated protests. Off Berry Head on 7 August the Emperor was transferred from the *Bellerophon* to

---

19 Lloyd (ed.), *Keith Papers* Vol.III, p.257.
20 Lloyd (ed.), *Keith Papers* Vol.III, p.347.

the *Northumberland*, in which he was to sail to St Helena, and it was aboard that ship that Keith took his leave of him. That evening the admiral wrote to his wife from his flagship, the *Tonnant*: 'I am this moment returned and the Gentleman is off in good spirits'.[21] With these few words from its Commander-in-Chief the long vigil of the Channel Fleet came finally to an end.

21   Lloyd (ed.), *Keith Papers* Vol.III, p.403.

29

Health and Welfare

Professor N.A.M. Rodger has drawn attention to the grossly exaggerated effect of scurvy on the Royal Navy, pointing out that the disease on its own was normally a killer only on very long voyages, and that its practical effect on normal operations was merely to limit the time that a squadron could remain at sea. Nevertheless, it was a profoundly unpleasant and disabling disease. Its symptoms begin with progressive weakness, followed by swollen gums; teeth became loose, the breath foul and the tongue swollen. Blotches like bruises appear first on the legs and then over the rest of the body. Joints become stiff, and the heart is affected. Prevention was very much better than cure, and this was best achieved by diet. In 1759 Hawke, blockading Brest, was regularly supplied with fresh provisions, and as a result could remain at sea for longer that would formerly have been the case.[1]

For a squadron or fleet operating in home waters for any length of time, typhus was the most serious threat. Known also as jail fever, camp fever and ship fever, it occurred, as its various names suggest, under conditions of overcrowding, bad ventilation and insanitary surroundings. The fever begins suddenly, with headache, sickness, shivering and vomiting, and develops rapidly. After about five days a rash appears, spreading in the form of dark red or purple spots. The crisis usually occurs after about two weeks. In the conditions aboard ships of course, it could spread very rapidly indeed. Outbreaks of typhus were not uncommon, for instance wrecking the mobilisation of the fleet in the hard winters of 1739-1741, and again in 1755-1756. The cause of typhus, actually carried by lice in dirty clothes, was not appreciated, but the idea that 'corrupted air' as the transmitter of disease led to a growing emphasis on cleanliness.[2]

By the time of the Revolutionary and Napoleonic Wars, there had been further improvement in the health of seamen. A good deal of valuable scientific work had been undertaken by a number of doctors whose contribution to the operational

---

1   N.A.M. Rodger, *The Command of the Ocean: A Naval History of Britain 1649-1815* (London: Allen Lane, 2004), p.308.
2   Rodger, *Command of the Ocean*, p.308.

success of the Royal Navy was considerable. The first of these was Dr James Lind, later described as 'the father of nautical medicine'. Born in 1716, he joined the Navy in 1739, and by 1747 was surgeon of the 60 gun ship *Salisbury*, which was part of the Channel Fleet. While in his post he began to experiment with the effect of oranges and lemons on sufferers from scurvy, and in 1753 published his *Treatise of the Scurvy*. He was prompted to publish his findings by the staggering mortality rate caused by scurvy in Anson's voyage round the world, in the course of which 1,051 out of the total of 1,955 personnel died of the disease. In 1758 he was appointed senior physician to the newly opened naval hospital at Haslar, having the previous year published his influential *Essay on the Most Effectual Means of Preserving the Health of Seamen*. Second and third editions appeared in 1762 and 1779. The huge importance of the issue was emphasised by Lind in the introduction to the *Essay*:

> The number of seamen in time of war, who died by shipwreck, capture, famine, fire, or sword, are but inconsiderable, in respect of such as are destroyed by ship diseases, and by the usual maladies of intemperate climates.[3]

In fact, the disparity in the losses of men during the Seven Years War was astonishing; 133,708 were lost by disease or desertion compared with 1,512 killed in action.

Astoundingly, in spite of Lind's research, it was not until 1795 that the Admiralty laid down that lemon juice be issued after six weeks on salt provisions. Explaining this, Christopher Lloyd suggests that Lind was seen as an undistinguished physician by his contemporaries, naval medical service being lowly regarded, while his suggested cure for scurvy was only one among many.[4] The delay in introducing the remedy resulted in thousands of unnecessary deaths during the intervening period. An example of this in 1780 was that there were 2,600 sufferers from scurvy in the Channel Fleet after a six week cruise.

It was, therefore, of crucial importance to the maintenance of the blockade of Brest that Lind's recommendation was finally adopted; without it, it would have been scarcely possible to keep sufficient ships at sea. Roger Morriss has identified 1800 as the year that was the real turning point in overcoming scurvy; until then, the Admiralty's instruction of 1795 was only carried out by the issue to fleets of lemon juice on request, due to a shortage of supplies and the priority given to ships sailing to distant stations. In addition, at that time it was prescribed only as a cure

---

3   Christopher Lloyd (ed.), *The Health of Seamen Selections from the Works of Dr James Lind, Sir Gilbert Blane and Dr Thomas Trotter* (London: Navy Records Society, 1965), p.308

4   Lloyd (ed.) *Health of Seamen*, p.2.

for scurvy, rather than used as a preventive; Dr Thomas Trotter, the Physician to the Channel Fleet, was insistent that it not be used to prevent the disease appearing.[5]

Gilbert Blane, born in 1749, entered the naval service in an unusual way; he had been personal physician to Rodney, who suffered extremely from gout, and he sailed with him when he took command in the West Indies in 1780. Rodney appointed him to be Physician of the Fleet; this has been described by Christopher Lloyd as 'a piece of jobbery, which had the most beneficial consequences'.[6] His first published work on naval hygiene was *A Short Account of the Most Effectual Means of Preserving the Health of Seamen*, which he had distributed to all the captains of the fleet. His work in the West Indies, both on shipboard and in relation to hospitals on shore, brought about a considerable improvement in the health of the fleet.

After the end of the war, Blane took up a post at St Thomas's Hospital in London. While there, he published in 1785 the first edition of his *Observations on the Diseases of Seamen*; later editions appeared in 1789 and 1799. It has been pointed out that he was principally interested in preventive medicine and in administration, since at that time only in respect of a few diseases had cures been identified.[7]

In 1795, in one of the admirable appointments which Spencer made as First Lord, Blane was appointed to the Sick and Hurt Board. It was as a Commissioner that he introduced a number of crucial reforms. Beginning with the issue of lemon juice in 1795, he went on to provide soap on board the ships of the fleet and to recommend the issue of free drugs to surgeons. Lloyd suggests that he was also probably consulted over the reorganisation of medical services in 1805, when the pay and status of naval surgeons was greatly improved.[8] Blane was knighted in 1812, apparently partly due to his work in the enquiry into the Walcheren disaster. The extent of the improvement which he wrought can be seen in the casualty figures for the Navy between 1793 and 1815; this period of hostilities was far longer, and far more bitterly contested, than in any preceding war, but the proportion of the losses had greatly changed. 84,440 were lost to disease and individual accident, 12,680 from foundering, wreck, fire and explosion, and 6,540 from enemy action, producing a total of 103,660.

In 1815 Blane published a dissertation on the comparative health of seaman from 1779 to 1814. He was by then able to write of scurvy that it had been nearly eradicated by the use of lemon juice and other anti-scorbutic fruits containing citric acid. He gave credit to Lind for having promoted the benefits of lemon juice which had brought about this remarkable result. He also noted, however, the enormously beneficial effect of the liberal supply of fresh provisions and vegetables.

He went on to record the extent to which the threat of typhus had been overcome:

5   Morriss (ed.), *Channel Fleet*, p.14.
6   Lloyd (ed.) *Health of Seamen*, p.132.
7   Lloyd (ed.) *Health of Seamen*, p.133.
8   Lloyd (ed.) *Health of Seamen*, p.133.

This is to be ascribed to the improvements in the method of promoting ventilation and cleanliness, and particularly to the strict discipline adopted and enforced in the Channel Fleet. Air contaminated by foul and stagnant exhalations, particularly those from the living human body, is the ascertained cause of typhus fever … The infection of fever is generated by the breath and perspiration of men, crowded for a length of time in confined air, and without the means of personal cleanliness, particularly from the want of shifts of linen.[9]

Thomas Trotter, born in 1760, joined the Navy as a surgeon's mate in 1779. After the end of the War of American Independence he was obliged to serve aboard a slave ship, an experience which made him an ardent abolitionist. In 1788 he obtained his medical degree, and became Second Physician at Haslar hospital in 1793. Shortly after this Howe appointed him as Physician of the Fleet. He served afloat until 1795, when he was injured when climbing aboard the *Irresistible* after the engagement at the Ile de Groix, and thereafter served mainly ashore. Between 1796 and 1803 he published a three volume work, *Medicina Nautica*. He was an early advocate of inoculation against smallpox. He had a passionate concern for the welfare of seamen, and was in the forefront of reform.[10]

Unfortunately the fact of Trotter serving largely on shore prevented him from forming a satisfactory understanding with St Vincent, when the latter took command of the Channel Fleet. This was the more regrettable since they shared a determination to improve the facilities for the treatment of seamen at Plymouth Hospital. The relationship, however, soon broke down completely, and Trotter was excluded from the correspondence between St Vincent and the shore boards. He was opposed to the use of lemon juice as a preventive against scurvy, believing that it would weaken the constitution of seamen. In July 1800 matters came to a head; while praising Trotter on 9 July for his efforts to procure fresh vegetables for the fleet, St Vincent was critical of him for encouraging ships to remain in port on account of sickness. Four days later St Vincent repeated his criticism in harsher terms:

I very much disapprove your officious interference to prevent His Majesty's ships under my command from putting to sea the moment their beer, water and provisions are completed, which is ordered to be done with the utmost possible dispatch, and I desire that you will discontinue this practice.[11]

9 Lloyd (ed.) *Health of Seamen*, p.181.
10 Lloyd (ed.) *Health of Seamen*, pp.241-215.
11 Morriss (ed.), *Channel Fleet*, p.523.

For Trotter this letter was a crushing blow; although advised by friends to reply to the letter, which, as he wrote, had wounded him 'grievously,' he declined to do so, observing:

> It will not be wondered at, if after this transaction I resolved to trouble his Lordship no further with my correspondence: in this I was the more sorry, as I had cherished the hope, from his known discernment, to have perused those plans of improvement in the medical department, which were left unfinished through the indisposition and retirement of Admiral Earl Howe.[12]

The inevitable result of this was Trotter's dismissal by St Vincent, and his replacement as Physician of the Fleet by Dr Andrew Baird. Although not initially welcomed by all the commanders of the Channel Fleet, Baird undertook a number of reforms, including the enlargement of sick bays and the space in the cockpit, the improvement in the cleanliness of store rooms, the removal of pig-sties and the provision of a dispensary. He claimed that in September 1800, after the fleet had been at sea for four months, it was necessary to transfer only sixteen men to hospital. Blane, as Commissioner for Sick and Wounded, concluded that Baird's arrangements had made a major contribution to the morale of the sick.[13]

Reference has already been made to the problem of overcrowding. Given the size of a ship and its typical complement, it is hard to see that the problem could have been avoided. A typical 74 gun ship of the line would have been about 165 feet long and 45 feet in the beam; she would have a ship's company of between six and seven hundred men, most of whom were berthed on the lower deck, or gun deck. The hammocks were slung fore and aft from the beams of the deck head, each fourteen inches in width. Since the crew was organised in two watches, they were slung alternately, since one watch would always be on deck; this meant that the available space was twenty eight inches. The seamen ate their meals on the gun deck, and indeed spent most of the time there when not on duty. At sea the gun ports, six feet about the waterline, were kept closed, so the only light and air came from the main hatch. The limited facilities for washing, and the continuous close proximity of the men to each other, and the lack of ventilation, must have ensured that the smell was frightful. In addition, any amount of severe weather caused clothing to become damp, with no means of drying it.[14]

The professional quality of the surgeons, and their assistants, who were responsible for the health of the crew was extremely variable. Their skills, although subject to examinations by the Surgeons' Company, were far less than the skills of

---

12   Lloyd (ed.) *Health of Seamen*, p.246.
13   Morriss (ed.), *Channel Fleet*, p.523.
14   N.A.M. Rodger, *The Wooden World: Anatomy of the Georgian Navy* (London: Collins, 1986), pp.61-62.

physicians. In 1799 there were only three naval physicians on the Navy List; there were 634 surgeons. At that time there were 646 ships in commission, of which only about 400 carried a naval surgeon; the remainder had to make do with assistant surgeons, formerly known as surgeons' mates. It has been suggested that the Commissioners of the Sick and Hurt Board were, due to a perennial shortage of surgeons, not very fussy about those that were appointed.[15] At all events it was upon these men that fell the considerable responsibility for the medical care of the crew, both as to disease, accidents and injuries in battle.

Hawke's success in maintaining his blockade in the Seven Years War owed a lot to his ability to obtain regular provisions of beef, pork, beer and other essential supplies. It was a constant struggle; his correspondence contains frequent examples of the effort he had to make to get regular deliveries. Dr Lind, reviewing the campaign of 1759, observed that Hawke's fleet 'enjoyed a most perfect and unparalleled state of health'. He went on:

> It was hardly ever known before those ships could cruise in the Bay of Biscay, much above three or four months at a time, without having their men afflicted with scurvy. An exemption from which was entirely owing to this fleet having been well supplied with fresh meat and greens.[16]

Ensuring a regular supply of all the necessary items required to maintain the seamen in a good state of health raised immensely demanding logistical problems, particularly after the blockade was tightened up in 1800. It was essential to set up a reliable and punctual system for feeding and watering the Channel Fleet when it was on station off Brest. Roger Morriss has noted that by 1800 regular convoys of victuallers, escorted by sloops and cutters, made their way to the fleet off Ushant. In December 1800, it was ordered that the inshore squadron should receive fresh vegetables at least once a month. In addition, private trading vessels serviced the fleet, though these were disapproved of because they brought with them spirits. Morriss has concluded, rightly, that 'it was in the establishment of the administrative infrastructure that the real achievements of the blockade lay'.[17] The bureaucrats that oversaw the regular dispatch o those victualling convoys, and the merchant seamen that manned them, were entitled to much of the credit for the maintenance of the blockade.

15   Dudley Pope, *Life in Nelson's Navy* (London: Chatham, 1981), p.131-132.
16   Quoted G.J. Marcus, *Heart of Oak: Survey of British Sea Power in the Georgian Era* (Oxford: Oxford University Press, 1975), p.139.
17   Morriss (ed.), *Channel Fleet*, p.15.

Conclusion

The maintenance of the blockade of Brest between 1793 and 1815 made colossal demands on the resources of the Royal Navy, its ships and its men. It imposed on these a continuous period of stress, danger and hardship that was quite unlike that experienced by squadrons at sea, en route to a distant destination, even when these missions ultimately led to combat. Apart from the wear and tear to the ships conducting the blockade, the problems of supply were huge, and tested the administrative skills of the Admiralty, and especially the Victualling Board, to the limit. In addition, of course, the lengthy periods at sea which the blockade entailed exposed the crews to the dangers of scurvy, typhus and the physical injuries associated with the sailing of the ships.

Brest had been seen as the focal point of British naval activity since the War of the Austrian Succession. In 1745 the Admiralty had created a Western Squadron, the principal purpose of which was to cover British convoys as they passed through the Western Approaches. The other principal command in the Channel itself was further to the eastward, where Vernon commanded a fleet designed to prevent a French cross-Channel invasion. As has been seen, Vernon had expressed strong views about the way in which the Western Squadron should operate, writing in 1745 to the Duke of Bedford, the First Lord, that a strong squadron should be kept in the Soundings.[1]

When Anson took command of the Western Squadron in 1746, he undertook a long cruise well into the winter months in the hope of catching a substantial French expedition returning home from Canada. He did not, however, attempt a close blockade of Brest, and unlike Vernon was far more inclined to advocate keeping the fleet in port until the receipt of intelligence indicating that the French were preparing to sail, as he wrote to Bedford on August 1747:

> The French can never be so much annoyed, nor this kingdom so well
> secured, as by keeping a strong squadron at home, sufficient to make

---

1   Rodger, *Command of the Ocean*, p.250.

detachments, whenever we have good intelligence that the French are sending ships either to the East or West Indies.[2]

The genesis of the policy for a continuous close blockade of Brest may be said to have appeared with Hawke in the Seven Years War. In the spring of 1759 he ignored the Admiralty's order to limit his cruise off Brest during the month of May to fourteen days. He wrote to the Admiralty on 27 May to explain the reason for his action. After reporting that at least nine enemy ships of the line had been observed riding at anchor in Brest Roads, he went on:

> Upon the whole I do not think it prudent, as they may be joined by more from Brest Harbour, to leave them at liberty to come out by returning to Torbay till I shall receive further instructions from their Lordships or the wind shall appear to be set in strong westerly. When I do leave the station, I shall leave orders for Mr Keppel to follow me immediately with the ships under his command.[3]

Prior to this, in the early years of the Seven Years War, the Royal Navy had not sufficient ships available to maintain an effective blockade of the French ports. A number of sorties saw substantial French squadrons put to sea, especially for Louisbourg but also for the West Indies and the East Indies. In 1758 Hawke, in command of a squadron in the Bay of Biscay, was able to keep watch on Brest and Rochefort. However, he was unable to prevent several French sorties from Brest. It was evident to him that the system of watching Brest from the western ports of the English coast was by no means tight enough.

In June 1759 the Admiralty formally approved Hawke's decision to stay at sea off Brest, while reminding him of the need to send squadrons regularly into Plymouth or Torbay for replenishment. As it happened, Hawke was soon back in Torbay, as he reported to the Admiralty: 'For several days … we had had very fresh gales with a great sea. Yesterday it increased so much at southwest, with a thick fog, as to make several of the ships complain, more particularly the new ships'.[4] On this occasion it was of no great consequence, as the French fleet was pinned to Brest by the adverse winds. Later that month Hawke established the principle of maintaining a small inshore squadron to watch the enemy, appointing Augustus Hervey to command it.

That year Hawke remained on station off Ushant through the hot summer months, causing a serious problem of supply. Notwithstanding this difficulty he continued there through August and September until the middle of October, when

2   Rodger, *Command of the Ocean*, p.251.
3   Mackay (ed.), *Hawke Papers*, pp.220-221.
4   Mackay (ed.), *Hawke Papers*, p.225.

a fierce gale obliged him to return to Plymouth. The maintenance of an increasingly tight blockade of Brest was not, however, seen by the Admiralty as inevitable, as Ruddock Mackay and Michael Duffy point out. It was Hawke's determination to keep the sea as long as he could which kept the British fleet on station off Brest. Returning for a further short spell on blockade duty, Hawke was soon in the pursuit of the French under Conflans which was to lead to his stunning victory at Quiberon Bay.

Thus the precedent for a continuous, and close, blockade of Brest had been firmly set. There were, of course, those who doubted whether the policy was altogether wise. In his introduction to the *Hawke Papers*, Ruddock Mackay raises the question of whether a more open blockade would have been just as effective in preventing invasion, while avoiding the wear and tear on the ships conducting a close blockade. The alternative view, as he observes, is that the stationing of the main British fleet so close to the French ports on the Biscay coast achieved a more complete elimination of French trade and seaborne supply.[5] It was a debate that was to be continued in the Revolutionary and Napoleonic Wars.

It did not, however, arise during the War of American Independence. When France entered the war in 1779, the Royal Navy did not, for a variety of reasons, have the resources to embark on a close blockade of Brest or the other French ports. The Channel Fleet, under a succession of different leaders, found itself perpetually on the defensive. In any case, a number of key British admirals, such as Howe and Kempenfelt, were not much in favour of committing to a blockade the limited number of ships that were available for the defence of the English and Irish coasts. There were therefore no blockading operations of any consequence throughout the war.

An entirely different situation obtained at the outset of the war against Revolutionary France in 1793, when the Royal Navy faced an opponent that had fallen substantially into disrepair. No longer was the Channel Fleet faced by a French numerical superiority, and it was thus able to employ its relative increase in strength to undertake a more offensive policy. This meant the establishment of a powerful Channel Fleet, and the strategy which the Admiralty proposed to employ harked back to the precedent of the Sever Years War. However, neither Howe, its first commander, nor Bridport who succeeded him, were enthusiastic about the concept of a close blockade of Brest.

Howe in particular would not at all have agreed with Vernon, being inclined to keep the fleet in port, emerging only when required to cover the passage of important convoys; the effect of this was seen in November 1794 and January 1795 when the French fleet was able to make successful sorties from Brest. Bridport was in favour of a somewhat more active approach, preferring to cruise rather than

---

5   Mackay (ed.), *Hawke Papers*, p.xvii.

remain in port, but he did not usually attempt anything in the nature of a close blockade.

To the extent that the blockade was tightened up at all, it was as a result of pressure from the Admiralty, but it was not until after Bridport's departure that a very different approach was seen. His successors, St Vincent and Cornwallis, did believe in the value of the closest possible blockade, and conducted their operations off Brest accordingly. Even during their periods of command, though, it was not possible to prevent French sorties or completely to interdict the passage into Brest of both warships and merchant vessels. Nevertheless, it was soon the case that the public, political and professional belief in blockade as a strategy would have made it virtually impossible to abandon it. Upon the ships facing the hazards of the seas around Ushant was bestowed the responsibility for protecting the homeland from invasion.

On the other hand, there were voices raised at the time in alarm about the cost of a close blockade in terms of the damage to ships, which must be taken into account when the military, economic and political value of the blockading policy is considered. Anxiety about the attrition of the Channel Fleet prompted an editorial in the *Naval Chronicle* on 9 November 1804:

> We do not profess ourselves to be competent to pronounce a correct judgment of the merits of the blockading system. The late frequent accidents that have arisen to our ships from stress of weather, however, ought to lead to an examination of the question in all its bearings. It is evident that even ordinary wear and tear without the destruction of battles, must hurry our Navy to decay, and will demand some activity and attention to keep up the stock. It is the opinion of many naval men that the Ships are dreadfully shattered by the exposure to winds and tempests, and must be much sooner worn out than the usual calculation of their durability allows. If a severe storm were to attack our Fleet blockading Brest, after they have been stretched by so many hard gales, they might be so disabled (perhaps many of them lost) as not to be able to put to sea for some time, so that the enemy, availing themselves of such an unfortunate occurrence, might sail, and perhaps make their way to Ireland.[6]

So the question that must be addressed is whether the policy of blockade was justified and was successful in its objects. So far as the Revolutionary War is concerned, the clearest contemporary statement of the rationale for a blockade of Brest and other ports comes from Sir Charles Middleton, as he then was, in a letter to Captain Philip Patton of 27 June 1794; and separately in a draft memorandum as to the

---

6   Tracy (ed.), *Naval Chronicle*, Vol.III, p.70.

Western Squadron of the same month.[7] The blockade of Brest itself, and Lorient, was not actually instituted until July 1795, when it was seen as necessary to cover the operations being undertaken in Quiberon Bay. On 14 July Spencer, the First Lord, wrote to Bridport that it was now the plan of the government to maintain command of the seas in the Biscay area 'to keep by successive reliefs and squadron constantly cruising off the ports of Brest Lorient and occasionally communication with the officer commanding in Quiberon Bay.[8]

In his letter to Patton of the previous year Middleton took it for granted that the strategic priority was the blocking up of the enemy's ports, a measure which he argued could be made 'more clearly essential by reverting to what was actually done from the year 1757 to the year 1762'. It was a policy that was now no less necessary and practicable:

> Although several expeditions were undertaken during that period, they were subservient to blocking up and opposing the enemy at home, which were the first considerations, and which were truly the foundation of our successes through the whole war, when the fleet were kept off Brest and in Quiberon Bay. It consists with my own knowledge, that the ships were relieved alternately, and were supplied with fresh provisions, corned beef, potatoes, onions, greens and beer, during the summer; and Sir Edward Hawke and Admiral Boscawen relieved each other.[9]

Middleton's prescription for a blocking up of the port of Brest was of course very different to what Nelson would have advised. It was never his aim to intimidate the French into not leaving port at all; what he wanted was to tempt them out so that he might be on hand to annihilate them. His conduct of the blockade of Toulon illustrates the risky nature of his strategy which could, and famously did, allow the French fleet more than once to escape undetected, leaving him bewildered as to the course it had taken. John Whitby, Cornwallis's flag captain, was outspoken in his criticism of Nelson's strategy, and it was almost certainly just as well that St Vincent and Cornwallis conducted their blockades in the manner in which they did, rather than adopting Nelson's policy.

The maintenance of a policy of blockade was sanctioned by the Cabinet; and the fact that it was able to be put into effect was thanks to the efforts of the Victualling Board, which succeeded in setting up systems of feeding and watering the fleet when stationed off Brest, and to the decision to tackle the problem of scurvy by the issue of lemon juice. This last was due to the decision of St Vincent to adopt in 1800 the practice which had already been in effect in the Mediterranean since

7   Morriss (ed.), *Channel Fleet*, pp.45-47.
8   Morriss (ed.), *Channel Fleet*, p.95.
9   Morriss (ed.), *Channel Fleet*, p.46.

1795. The delay in applying it to the Channel Fleet had been due to the opposition of the Physician of the Fleet, Thomas Trotter.

Blockade having been adopted as the central strategy for dealing with Brest and the other Biscay ports, it is necessary to review the objectives it was intended to achieve. The blocking up of the port of Brest had as its first aim the prevention of any sortie aimed at landing troops on the coast of England or Ireland. The possibility of such an operation was usually picked up by the considerable flow of intelligence reaching the Admiralty; but this could not be absolutely relied on, and a continuous rather than occasional blockade was required to provide the necessary security.

Secondly, the blockading fleet must prevent the escape of French squadrons destined to operate elsewhere than in the Channel, such as, in particular, the West Indies and the East Indies. Next, it must by its presence guarantee effective cover to both inbound and outbound British convoys, which were large enough, and valuable enough, to be a very considerable attraction for major operations by the French fleet. The effectiveness of these foxes in the hen coop, when they could get out, shows how importantly this threat must be measured. In addition, the blockading squadrons must inhibit the escape of individual raiders that could prey on British trade. It was never going to be possible to prevent this entirely. On the other hand, the blockading squadrons could and did have a major impact on French seaborne trade, on which Brest in particular was heavily dependent for supplies of all kinds.

It cannot be said that the blockade was completely effective in blocking up the port of Brest. Indeed, so many were the occasions on which French squadrons were able to put to sea unmolested, and sometimes completely undetected, that it could be argued that they could generally come and go as they pleased. Furthermore, it was never going to be possible to interdict the movements of individual raiders. In any case, many of the privateers operated from smaller ports along the Channel and Biscay coasts, and could slip in and out more or less at will.

But there was one effect of the blockade that was very considerable but quite incalculable, and that was the effect on French morale. The constant presence of hostile squadrons off the entrance to their harbours exercised a profound effect, not only on the French seamen and their captains, but also the admirals that must lead them. This collective sapping of French naval confidence extended upwards, not only to the Minister of Marine, but also to the Emperor himself, who later in life bitterly acknowledged the extent to which the Royal Navy frustrated his combinations.

Taken together therefore, the operations of the fleets blockading Brest may he said to have been at least a qualified success; although often imperfect in its execution, the policy was probably worthwhile in its overall effect, and more effective than any other strategy would have been.

Writing of the achievement of Cornwallis and his captains, for instance, John Leyland observed that 'their work as blockaders was more important and more successful than that of Nelson at the same period. The tenacity of Cornwallis prepared the way for Trafalgar'.[10] When the difficulties for the blockading fleets presented by the weather, poor visibility and long winter nights are taken into account, it was remarkable that they achieved what they actually did. The success of the blockade endorsed the reputation earned by the Royal Navy in the much more spectacular fleet actions, a reputation that ensured that its near invincibility was accepted for a hundred years.

10 Leyland (ed.), *Blockade of Brest*, Vol.I, p.vii.

Bibliography

Adams, Max, *Admiral Collingwood: Nelson's Own Hero* (London: Head of Zeus 2005)

Anson, W.V., *The Life of John Jervis Admiral Lord St Vincent* (London: J. Murray, 1913)

Archibald, E.H.H., *The Wooden Fighting Ship in the Royal Navy AD 897*-1860 (Poole: Arco, 1968)

Arthur, Charles B., *The Remaking of the English Navy by Admiral St Vincent* (Lanham MD: Rowman & Littlefield, 1986)

Asprey, Robert, *The Rise and Fall of Napoleon Bonaparte* (London: Little, Brown & Co., 2000)

Balleine, Robert (ed.), *The Tragedy of Philippe d'Auvergne* (London: Phillimore, 1973)

Barnett, Len, 'Valentine Joyce – Naval Mutineer of 1797' at www.tribejoyce.com/valentine-joyce-naval-mutineer-of-1797/

Barritt, M.K., *Eyes of the Admiralty – J.T. Serres An Artist in the Channel Fleet 1799-1800* (London: National Maritime Museum, 2008)

Barrow, Sir John, *The Life of Richard Earl Howe* (London: J. Murray, 1838)

Berckman, Evelyn, *Nelson's Dear Lord: A Portrait of St.Vincent* (London: Macmillan 1962)

Bonner-Smith, David (ed.), *Letters of Admiral of the Fleet Earl of St Vincent* (London: Navy Records Society, 1922)

Chatterton, Lady Georgina, *Memorials Personal and Historical of Admiral Lord Gambier* (London: Hurst and Blackett, 1861)

Clowes, William, *The Royal Navy: A History from the Earliest Times to 1900* (London: Sampson Low, Marston and Co., 1899)

Cochrane, Lord, *The Autobiography of a Seaman* (London: Maclaren & Co., 1860)

Corbett, Julian S. (ed.), *Fighting Instructions 1530-1816* (London: Navy Records Society, 1905),

Corbett, Julian S. (ed.), *Private Papers of George, Second Earl Spencer* (London: Navy Records Society, 1913)

Corbett, Julian S., *The Campaign of Trafalgar* (London: Longmans, Green, 1910)

Cordingley, David, *Billy Ruffian* (London: Bloomsbury, 2008)

Cornwallis-West, G, *The Life and Letters of Admiral Cornwallis* (London: Robert Holden, 1927)

Custance, Sir Reginald, *The Ship of the Line in Battle* (London: William Blackwood, 1912)

Davidson, James D.G., *Admiral Lord St Vincent: Saint or Tyrant?* (Barnsley: Pen & Sword, 2006)

Davies, David, *Fighting Ships: Ships of the Line 1793-1815* (London: Constable, 1996)

Duffy, Michael and Roger Morriss (eds.), *The Glorious First of June* (Exeter: Exeter Maritime Studies, 2001)

Fry, Michael, *The Dundas Despotism* (Edinburgh: Edinburgh University Press, 2004)

Gardiner, Leslie, *The British Admiralty* (London: Blackwood, 1968)

Gardiner, Robert (ed.), *Fleet Battle and Blockade* (London: Chatham, 1996)

Gardiner, Robert (ed.), *The Line of Battle* (Annapolis: Naval Institute Press, 1992)

Gill, Conrad, *The Naval Mutinies of 1797* (Manchester: University Press, 1913)

Gordon, Iain, *Admiral of the Blue* (Barnsley: Pen & Sword, 2006)

Hamilton, C.I., *The Making of the Modern Admiralty: British Naval Policy-Making, 1805–1927* (Cambridge: Cambridge University Press, 2011)

Hamilton, Sir Richard Vesey (ed.), *Letters and Papers of Admiral of the Fleet Sir Thos. Byam Martin* (London: Navy Record Society, 1898-1903)

Henderson, James, *The Frigates* (New York: Dodd Mead, 1971)

Hill, Richard, *The Prizes of War: The Naval Prize System in the Napoleonic Wars 1793-1815.* (Stroud: Sutton, 1998)

Hood, Dorothy, *The Admirals Hood* (London: Hutchinson, 1941)

Hughes, Edward (ed.), *The Private Correspondence of Admiral Lord Collingwood* (London: Navy Record Society, 1957)

James, Sir William, *Old Oak. The Life of John Jervis Earl of St Vincent* (London: Longman, Green, & Co., 1950)

James, William, *The Naval History of Great Britain* (London: Richard Bentley, 1859)

Jenkins, E.H., *A History of the French Navy* (London: Macdonald and Jane's, 1973)

Kirsch, Peter, *Fireship: The Terror Weapon of the Age of Sail* (Annapolis: Naval Institute Press, 2009)

Konstam, Angus, *The British Napoleonic Ship-of-the-Line* (Oxford: Osprey, 2001)

Krajeski, Paul C, *In the Shadow of Nelson. The Naval Leadership of Admiral Sir Charles Cotton, 1753-1812* (Westport CONN: Greenwood Press, 2000)

Laughton, Sir John Knox (ed.), *Letters and Papers of Charles, Lord Barham* (London: Navy Records Society, 1910)

Lefevre, Peter and Richard Harding (eds.), *British Admirals of the Napoleonic Wars: Contemporaries of Nelson* (London: Chatham, 2005)

Lewis, Michael (ed.), *A Narrative of My Professional Adventures by Vice Admiral Sir William Dillon* (London: Navy Records Society, 1958)

Leyland, John (ed.), *Despatches and Letters Relating to the Blockade of Brest 1803-1805* (London: Navy Records Society, 1899)

Lloyd, Christopher (ed.), *The Keith Papers* (London: Navy Records Society, 1950)

Lloyd, Christopher (ed.), *The Health of Seamen: Selections from the Works of Dr James Lind, Sir Gilbert Blane and Dr Thomas Trotter* (London: Navy Records Society, 1965)

Lloyd, Christopher, *Mr Barrow of the Admiralty: A Life of Sir John Barrow 1764-1848* (London: Collins, 1970)

Mackay, Ruddock (ed.), *The Hawke Papers* (Aldershot: Navy Records Society, 1990)

Mackay, Ruddock, and Michael Duffy, *Hawke, Nelson and British Naval Leadership 1747-1805* (Woodbridge: Boydell & Brewer, 2009)

Mackesey, Piers, *The Strategy of Overthrow 1798-1799* (London: Longman, 1974)

Maffeo, Steven E, *Most Secret and Confidential: Intelligence in the Age of Nelson* (London: Chatham, 2003)

Mahan, Alfred T., *The Influence of Sea Power upon the French Revolution and Empire* (London: Sampson Low, Marston and Co., 1893)

Manwaring, G.E., and Bonamy Dobrée, *The Floating Republic* (London: Harcourt Brace, 1937)

Marcus, G.J., *Heart of Oak: Survey of British Sea Power in the Georgian Era* (Oxford, Oxford University Press, 1975)

Marcus, G.J., *The Age of Nelson. The Royal Navy in the Age of Its Greatest Power and Glory, 1793-1815.* (New York: Viking, 1971)

Markham, Sir Clements (ed.), *Selections from the Correspondence of Admiral John Markham* (London: Navy Record Society 1904)

Marryat, Florence (ed.), *Life and Letters of Frederick Marryat* (London: R. Bentley, 1872)

McCranie, Kevin D., *Admiral Lord Keith and the Naval War Against Napoleon* (Tallahasse FL: University of Florida Press, 2006)

McLynn, Frank, *Napoleon* (London: Jonathan Cape, 1997)

Morriss, Roger (ed.), *The Channel Fleet and the Blockade of Brest 1793-1801* (Aldershot: Navy Records Society, 2001)

Orde, Denis, *In the Shadow of Nelson: The Life of Admiral Lord Collingwood* (Barnsley: Pen & Sword, 2008)

Parkinson, C. Northcote, *Edward Pellew, Viscount Exmouth* (London: Methuen, 1934)

Pope, Dudley, *Life in Nelson's Navy* (London: Chatham, 1981)

Ranft, Bryan McL. (ed.), *The Vernon Papers* (London: Navy Records Society, 1958)

Richmond, Sir Herbert, *Statesman and Sea Power* (London: Clarendon, 1946)

Rodger, N.A.M., *The Command of the Ocean: A Naval History of Britain 1649-1815* (London: Allen Lane, 2004)

Rodger, N.A.M., *The Wooden World: Anatomy of the Georgian Navy* (London: Collins, 1986)

Schom, Alan, *Trafalgar: Countdown to Battle, 1803-1805* (London: Atheneum 1990)

Sherrard, O.A., *A Life of Lord St Vincent* (London: George Allen and Unwin, 1933)

Sugden, John, *Nelson: The Sword of Albion* (London: Bodley Head, 2012)

Syrett, David, *Admiral Lord Howe* (Staplehurst: Spellmount, 2006)

Talbott, John E, *The Pen and Ink Sailor: Charles Middleton and the King's Navy, 1778-1813* (London: Routledge, 1998)

Taylor, Stephen, *Commander: The Life and Exploits of Britain's Greatest Frigate Captain* (London: Faber & Faber, 2012)

Thomas, Donald, *Cochrane: Britannia's Last Sea-King* (London: Andre Deutsch, 1978)

Tracy, Nicholas (ed.), *The Naval Chronicle: The Contemporary Record of the Royal Navy at War* (London: Chatham, 1998)

Warner, Oliver, *The Glorious First of June* (London: Batsford, 1961)

Warner, Oliver, *The Life and Letters of Vice Admiral Lord Collingwood* (Oxford: Oxford University Press, 1968)

Willis, Sam, *The Glorious First of June: Fleet Battle in the Reign of Terror* (London: Quercus, 2011)

Winfield, Rif, *The 50-Gun Ship* (London: Chatham, 1997)

General Index

Index of Ships

From Reason to Revolution series – Warfare c 1721-1815

http://www.helion.co.uk/published-by-helion/reason-to-revolution-1721-1815.html

The 'From Reason to Revolution' series covers the period of military history c. 1721–1815, an era in which fortress-based strategy and linear battles gave way to the nation-in-arms and the beginnings of total war.

This era saw the evolution and growth of light troops of all arms, and of increasingly flexible command systems to cope with the growing armies fielded by nations able to mobilise far greater proportions of their manpower than ever before. Many of these developments were fired by the great political upheavals of the era, with revolutions in America and France bringing about social change which in turn fed back into the military sphere as whole nations readied themselves for war. Only in the closing years of the period, as the reactionary powers began to regain the upper hand, did a military synthesis of the best of the old and the new become possible.

The series will examine the military and naval history of the period in a greater degree of detail than has hitherto been attempted, and has a very wide brief, with the intention of covering all aspects from the battles, campaigns, logistics, and tactics, to the personalities, armies, uniforms, and equipment.

Submissions

The publishers would be pleased to receive submissions for this series. Please contact us via email (andrewbamford18@gmail.com), or in writing to Helion & Company Limited, 26 Willow Road, Solihull, West Midlands, B91 1UE.

Titles

No 1   *Lobositz to Leuthen. Horace St Paul and the Campaigns of the Austrian Army in the Seven Years War 1756-57* Translated with additional materials by Neil Cogswell (ISBN 978-1-911096-67-2)

No 2   *Glories to Useless Heroism. The Seven Years War in North America from the French journals of Comte Maurès de Malartic, 1755-1760* William Raffle (ISBN 978-1-911512-19-6) (paperback)

No 3   *Reminiscences 1808-1815 under Wellington. The Peninsular and Waterloo Memoirs of William Hay* William Hay, with notes and commentary by Andrew Bamford (ISBN 978-1-911512-32-5)

No 4   *Far Distant Ships. The Blockade of Brest 1793-1815* Quintin Barry (ISBN 978-1-911512-14-1)

Books within the series are published in two formats: 'Falconets' are paperbacks, page size 248mm × 180mm, with high visual content including colour plates; 'Culverins' are hardback monographs, page size 234mm × 156mm. Books marked with * in the list above are Falconets, all others are Culverins unless otherwise noted.